Layne Simpson's
SHOOTER'S
HANDBOOK

LAYNE SIMPSON

©2005 Layne Simpson
Published by

 **Gun Digest Books**
An imprint of F+W Publications

**700 East State Street • Iola, WI 54990-0001
715-445-2214 • 888-457-2873**

Our toll-free number to place an order or obtain
a free catalog is (800) 258-0929.

All photos in this book are courtesy of the author.

Library of Congress Catalog Number: 2004098421

ISBN: 0-87349-939-5

Designed by Paul Birling
Edited by Dan Shideler

Printed in United States of America

Dedication

This one, too, is for Phyllis.
And all those readers who took the time to write.

TABLE OF
Contents

Introduction

Through the years my work has been published in a number of hunting and shooting publications. They include, in no special order, *Shooting Times, American Hunter, American Rifleman, Wing & Shot, Rifle, Handloader, Gun World, Deer Unlimited, Petersen's Hunting, Shooting Sportsman, Field & Stream, Gun Digest, Guns Illustrated, Wildfowl, Guns & Ammo* and smaller publications too numerous to mention here. It is impossible to be in the business for so long without receiving thousands of letters from readers. Name a subject and if it has to do with hunting or shooting, I have probably been asked more than one question about it. Here, then, are some of the more interesting queries I have received on the subjects of rifles, shotguns, handguns, cartridges, reloading and optics.

Layne Simpson
Simpsonville, South Carolina

SECTION ONE

Rifles

A Gun That Shoots Around Corners?

My grandfather recently told me that during World War II, German soldiers had submachine guns that allowed them to shoot around the corner of a building without exposing themselves to return fire. How did such a firearm work?

During the war the German army adopted a curved barrel extension called a *Krummlauf* (curved path). Designed for attachment to the barrels of submachine guns and assault rifles, it was said to be effective out to 200 meters. The *Versuchs* model changed the direction of a bullet by 40 degrees while the *Panzer* model redirected the bullet a full 90 degrees. On some units a series of vent holes in the outer curved surface of the tube allowed escaping propellant gas to partially compensate for the gun's tendency to string shots away from the direction in which the muzzle of the device was pointed during firing. A special prismatic sight mounted at the muzzle served to refract the line of sight at the same angle as bullets were deflected by the *Krummlauf* device. A submachine gun with the attachment installed allowed a soldier to direct aimed fire from behind cover of a building or from inside a tank or foxhole without exposing himself to return fire.

Maximum Range of Inline Muzzleloaders?

What is the effective range of 45- and 50-caliber muzzleloaders on deer? At what distance do you zero this type of rifle? What is the longest shot you have ever made with one?

Everything considered, including accuracy, trajectory and downrange energy delivery, the effective range of a modern inline muzzleloader equipped with a telescopic sight is around 200 yards. When shooting three Pyrodex or Triple-7 pellets (150 gr. total), I prefer to zero a rifle three inches high at 100 yards. That puts the bullet about five inches below my line of sight at 200 yards. The longest shot I have made with an inline was on a mule deer in New Mexico while hunting with Steve Puppe and Steve Jones. The rifle I used was a 45-cal. Knight Disc Extreme loaded with Triple-7 and the Knight 175-gr. Red Hot saboted bullet. According to my Bushnell rangefinder, the buck was standing 216 yards away when I fired. The buck took one step backward and fell dead. I took my best whitetail buck to date while hunting with a T/C Encore 209x50 Magnum wearing a Nikon 3-9X scope. My rifle was loaded with 150 gr. of Triple-7 and the Hornady 250-gr. SST saboted bullet. The buck was standing about 65 yards away when I squeezed the trigger.

How Far Will Centerfire Cartridges Shoot?

Most .22 rimfire ammunition has "Danger: Range One Mile" or a similar warning printed on the box. Will such a tiny cartridge actually propel its bullet 1760 yards? What about centerfire cartridges? How far will they shoot?

The maximum range or danger zone of various cartridges varies considerably, depending on factors such as wind velocity and direction, bullet form and initial

velocity and elevation above sea level. With the muzzle of a firearm elevated at the optimum angle of 33 to 35 degrees, the maximum ranges of a few cartridges I chose at random are generally assumed to be approximately as follows in miles or fractions thereof:

22 Short high-velocity (0.5 mile)

22 Long Rifle high-velocity (0.9 mile)

22 Hornet (1.2 miles)

44 Remington Magnum (1.3 miles)

30-30 Winchester (1.7 miles)

45-70 Government (1.8 miles)

222 Remington (2.1 miles)

458 Winchester Magnum (2.3 miles)

25-06 Remington and 30-06 Springfield (2.6 miles)

7mm Remington Magnum (2.9 miles)

300 Winchester Magnum (3.0 miles)

How Do I Calculate Recoil?

Is there a way to calculate the recoil of various cartridges in rifles of different weights that does not require the use of a computer?

If the necessary information is known, calculating recoil is easily done by following these eight steps.

A: Multiply bullet weight X velocity.

B: Multiply powder charge weight (in grains) X 4000.

C: Add answer from A and B.

D: Divide answer from C by 225,400.

E: Multiply answer from D by 32.2

F: Divide answer from D by gun weight in pounds

G: Square answer from F and multiply by gun weight in pounds

H: Divide answer from G by 64.4 to get recoil in foot-pounds

As an example, I will calculate the level of recoil generated by the 30-06 cartridge loaded with 55.0 gr. of powder for a muzzle velocity of 2800 fps with a 180-gr. bullet. Rifle weight is 8.5 pounds.

A: 180 X 2800 = 504,000

B: 55 X 4000 = 220,000

C: 504,000 + 220,000 = 724,000

D: 724,000 divided by 225, 400 = 3.21

E: 3.21 X 32.2 = 103.36

F: 103.36 divided by 8.5 pounds = 12.16

G: 12.16 X 12.16 X 8.5 = 1256.81

F: 1256.81 divided by 64.4 = 19.51 foot pounds of recoil energy

Measuring group size is easy.

How Do I Measure the Size of Groups Fired with My Rifle?

I realize a group shot in a paper target is measured from the centers of the two holes farthest apart, but even when using a caliper to do so I find attempting to locate the exact centers of the two holes extremely difficult. At the very best, it is a slow and frustrating chore. Is there an easier way to measure groups?

Rather than attempting to measure from center to center of the two bullet holes of a group that are the farthest apart, measure from the outside edge of one hole to the inside edge of the other. This is a much easier and more accurate way to measure the extreme spread of a group. When measuring the size of a group fired with an extremely accurate rifle, where all the bullet holes are too tightly clustered to allow the method I have just described to be used, measuring from outside edge to outside edge across the widest part of the group and subtracting one bullet diameter will give you the center-to-center measurement you are looking for. Let us say, for example, that we have five shots from a varmint rifle in 223 Remington clustered in a group measuring .500 inch across at its broadest point. Subtracting .224 inch (bullet diameter for the 223) gives us a center to center measurement of .276 inch.

What Are Advantages of Titanium in the Manufacture of Firearms?

I noticed that Remington is offering a centerfire hunting rifle with a titanium receiver. Other than weight reduction, does that metal offer any advantage over steel?

The primary advantage to using titanium in the manufacture of a sporting arm is its light weight. And the difference can be substantial since titanium weighs only about 60 percent as much as steel. Respective weights for the Remington Model 700 Titanium in its short- and long-action versions are only 5-1/4 and 5-1/2 pounds. After either rifle is equipped with a scope and lightweight sling, it will still weigh less than seven pounds.

A rifle action made of titanium weighs only about 60 percent as much as one made of steel.

Why Did Daisy Build an Air Gun with No Sights?

A Daisy air gun I recently purchased at a very good price is much like the Daisy Red Ryder I owned when I was a kid. It differs from my old favorite by having a Monte Carlo style buttstock and no sights. When first looking at the rifle I thought the sights had been removed but closer examination proved they had never been installed. Why would Daisy build a rifle with no sights?

During the 1960s the U.S. Army began a program in which new recruits were taught instinctive shooting on aerial targets at close range without the use of the sights on their rifles. The training program was called Quick-Kill and air rifles with no sights such as the one you just bought were used. They were made for the Army by Daisy of Rogers, Ark. The rifle you have might be one of those used by the Army but since Daisy also sold the same rifle to the civilian market it could also be one of those. The civilian version came as part of a "Quick-Skill" kit in a cardboard box that also contained a supply of BBs, aerial targets, two pairs of safety glasses and a training manual.

Which Cartridge for First Rifle?

I am 16 years old and my father has agreed to buy for me a Remington Model 700 or if my grades are really good, a Weatherby Mark V. The deer in my area are quite small, but shots are often at long range. I am leaning toward the 30-06 but the 300 Weatherby Magnum might be even better. What cartridge should I choose for my first deer rifle?

Either cartridge you mentioned will certainly get the job done, but unless you are an experienced shooter, both may generate more recoil than you can comfortably handle. For shooting whitetail deer in open country, the 25-06 in a Remington Model 700 is tough to beat. It shoots as flat as the 300 Weatherby Magnum, delivers plenty of punch on deer at long range and it would be easier on your shoulder than a rifle in 30-06. If your grades in school earn you the Weatherby rifle instead, the 240 Weatherby Magnum would be just about ideal for you. I have taken enough deer with the 240 and the 25-06 to know both are excellent choices.

Which Rifle for Black Bear?

This year I'll be hunting black bear over bait in Quebec and can't for the life of me decide which of three rifles to use. One, a Remington 700 in 30-06, has done an excellent job on whitetail deer. Another candidate is a Browning Model 81 lever action in 358 Winchester. Then we have my most handsome rifle, a custom 1898 Krag in 30-40 caliber. A real beauty, it seldom fails to draw admirers anytime I take it to the range and I'd like nothing better than to hunt with it. The Remington and Browning rifles wear scopes while the Krag has a Williams receiver sight. I handload the 30-40 Krag with 180-gr. bullets and while that rifle is the one I'd really like to use on the bear hunt, I am not sure it is powerful enough. I know you've done a lot of bear hunting so which of those rifles would you use?

Hunting black bear over bait usually presents close to medium range shots at a stationary target so you should have plenty of time to place a good bullet where it does the most damage. I wouldn't hesitate to hunt under those conditions with either of your rifles as all are capable of delivering plenty of punch for the job. From a practical point of view, the two rifles with scopes would have the edge during late afternoon hunting when light is fast disappearing but if it were my hunt I'd take the rifle I most enjoy being in the woods with. The older I get and the more game I bag the more I feel that way. So enjoy harvesting a bear rug with that wonderful old Krag.

How Hot Must Barrel Be to Cook Off a Round in Chamber?

I shoot prairie dogs at every opportunity and often allow the barrel of my rifle to become extremely hot. Although I have never experienced a round cooking off in the chamber, how hot must the barrel become in order for that to happen?

How hot a barrel must become before a cartridge will pre-ignite in the chamber will vary somewhat due to slight variations in the ignition temperatures of primer compounds. But regardless of what that temperature might be, the average varmint shooter is not likely to fire enough rounds in his rifle between cool-down periods for pre-ignition to take place. During testing of the Army's new 30-caliber M14 rifle at Ft. Benning, Ga., during the late 1950s, one rifle was fired at a rate of one round per second and it went 3080 rounds before cartridges began to cook off in its chamber. Even then the rifle continued to function perfectly, although its wooden stock and handguard did burst into flames.

A Rifle with No Recoil?

In an old World War II movie I recently watched, one of the soldiers referred to a 75mm recoilless rifle. And sure enough, when he and his assistant knocked out a Jap tank, the gun seemed to generate practically zero recoil even though it was mounted on what appeared to be a rather light tripod. Could that happen only in the movies or is there really such a thing as a rifle with no recoil? If so, how does it work?

The idea of a recoilless rifle is thought to have originated in the U.S. around 1914 but the concept did not evolve to its final form until during the 1940s. The rifle you saw in action in that movie fired a 14-lb. projectile. It was commonly fired from a tripod and required a two-man crew, one who loaded the gun and another who aimed and fired it. There was also a lighter shoulder-fired, 57mm version that fired a 2.7-pound projectile. The weights of larger recoilless rifles capable of firing projectiles up to 155mm in caliber required that they be mounted on a jeep or other type of carriage.

In a nutshell, here's how the system works. The steel casing of the cartridge is perforated to allow propellant gas to escape into the enlarged breech section of the rifle barrel during firing. Gas escaping rearward through specially shaped nozzles at the rear of the breech compensates for and counteracts the recoil generated by those

Does Composite Barrel Heat Up More Slowly than an All-Steel Barrel?

While I was recently visiting a gun shop, a salesman showed me a Remington Model 700 rifle with a composite barrel. According to him, that type of barrel heats up more slowly and cools down more rapidly than an all-steel barrel. Have you found this to be true?

I performed heat-up and cool-down tests on a Remington Model 700 Composite and a Model 700 BDL Varmint with a heavy, all-steel barrel. Both rifles were in 223 Remington. Five-shot groups were fired with Black Hills ammunition loaded with a 52-gr. hollowpoint bullet. While there was very little difference in the amount of time it took the two barrels to cool down, the composite barrel heated up more slowly. During the tests, I attached the remote thermocouples of digital thermometers to the exterior surfaces of the two barrels. Here are the results of those tests. Note that the firing of 11 five-shot groups (55 rounds) with the rifle with an all-steel barrel heated its barrel to 153 degrees F while it took the firing of 19 groups (95 rounds) to heat up the composite barrel to about the same temperature.

Group Number	M700 Composite Barrel Temp (Degrees F)	Group Size (Inches)	Model 700 BDL Barrel Temp (Degrees F)	Group Size (Inches)
1	73.7	1.235	75.2	0.762
2	85.0	1.192	86.0	0.868
3	93.0	0.683	96.3	0.802
4	98.8	0.897	103.6	0.848
5	105.7	1.133	115.4	1.028
6	110.8	0.936	120.7	0.918
7	115.7	0.802	125.1	1.118
8	112.0	0.574	133.6	1.207
9	123.2	0.648	139.3	1.011
10	126.6	1.341	146.8	1.108
11	130.0	0.834	153.1	1.133
12	137.2	1.024	n/a	n/a
13	137.2	1.639	n/a	n/a
14	139.3	1.388	n/a	n/a
15	141.3	0.518	n/a	n/a
16	144.4	1.294	n/a	n/a
17	147.2	1.253	n/a	n/a
18	150.6	1.184	n/a	n/a
19	154.2	1.070	n/a	n/a
AVERAGE ACCURACY:		**1.070**		**0.982**

A composite barrel heats up more slowly than an all-steel barrel.

same gases as they push the projectile in the opposite direction and out the muzzle. Pre-engraved driving bands on the projectile allow the propellant gas to push it to an acceptable velocity at a relatively low chamber pressure. An extremely successful concept, it is still in use not only by the U.S. military forces but by the armies of other countries as well.

Difference between Clip and Magazine?

Some refer to them as clips while others call them magazines. One company even calls it a magazine clip. That's darned confusing. Is there a difference between a magazine and a clip or are they one and the same?

A magazine contains a spring and follower while a clip does not. There are two basic types of magazines. A good example of a magazine contained by the firearm can be seen in bolt-action centerfire rifles built by Remington, Weatherby, Winchester and other companies. The other type of magazine is detachable, like the one seen on the Remington Model 7400 and 710 rifles and on 22 rimfire rifles made by various companies. Clips are usually used for holding a supply of ammunition outside the rifle and for inserting those cartridges into the magazine of a rifle. There are many styles of clips. One of the more common is the en bloc clip used to load the internal magazine of the M1 Garand rifle. Another is the stripper clip used to load the magazines of various bolt-action rifles.

The detachable magazine of the Remington Model 710 differs from a clip by its spring and follower.

Can I Handload for My Remington Model 700 Etron-X?

I recently purchased a Remington Model 700 Etron-X in 22-250 and would like to handload for it. Are there any potential problems that I should be aware of?

The only thing different about reloading for the Etron-X rifle in 22-250 and any other Model 700 in the same caliber is the special primers that must be used. Available from dealers who sell Remington reloading components, the electronically-fired primer is easily seated into the case with any conventional priming tools designed to work with standard Large Rifle primers. Cartridge cases made by Remington as well as other companies such as Winchester, Federal and PMC can be used. The same powders that work in the regular 22-250 work equally well in the 22-250 Etron-X and load data published in various manuals can be used interchangeably in either cartridge

How Accurate Is the Weatherby Super VarmintMaster?

I am thinking about buying a Weatherby Super VarmintMaster to use for long-range varminting. How accurate can I expect that rifle to be?

The Super VarmintMaster in 220 Swift I tested was quite accurate. My best handload, 39.0 gr. of Reloder 15 behind the Shilen 52-gr. hollowpoint, averaged 0.49 inch for five, five-shot groups at 100 yards. That load was maximum in my rifle and the powder charge should be reduced by 10 percent for a starting load in any other rifle. Accuracy of the seven factory loads I tried in the rifle ranged from .57 to .97 inch for an overall average of .72 inch.

Why No 8mm-08?

While reading your article on the 308 Winchester family of cartridges, it dawned on me that we have never had a 8mm-08. I hunt whitetail deer a lot, and even though I find the 308 to be a fine performer, I believe it would be fun to work with a wildcat on that case. What is your opinion of the 8mm-08? How about the 308 case necked up for a 375- or 44-caliber bullet? Would it work?

Although I have never tried the 8mm-08, I am sure someone somewhere has, simply because all the new ideas in wildcats were used up many years ago. The reason it has never received a lot of attention is due to the lack of interest among American hunters in 8mm caliber cartridges in general. The quick rise and fall of the 8mm Remington Magnum is a good example of what I mean. This is not to say 8mm is not a good caliber. I have been shooting a custom T/C Contender in 8mm JDJ (on the 444 Marlin Case) for years and its performance is outstanding. I will have to admit, though, cartridges of 30 caliber will handle all jobs as well as those of 8mm caliber, another reason why it is not more popular in the United States.

Like all nonbelted, rimless cases, the 308 headspaces on its shoulder. Since its maximum shoulder diameter is .454 inch, .375 is about the largest its neck can be expanded to and still have enough shoulder area left for positive headspacing. Even that

Was Winchester Model 71 Available in 33 Winchester?

My father tells me that he once owned a Winchester Model 71 lever action rifle in 33 Winchester caliber. I have two Model 71s and everything I have read about this rifle stated that it was manufactured only in one caliber, the 348 Winchester. I suspect Dad was having a senior moment when making that statement and his rifle was actually a Model 1886 since it was commonly available in 33 caliber. The Model 71 differs very little from the Model 86, so I'm betting he is a bit confused about the model of his old deer rifle. Right?

If you and your father had a wager riding on the correct answer to your question and one of your Model 71s is at stake, the two of you now own one each. During the first few years of Model 71 production, it was available on special order in 33 Winchester. I doubt if many were built in that caliber, since the 348 was brand new and considerably more powerful.

Early in its production the Winchester Model 71 was available in 33 Winchester.

large a caliber would probably be pushing your luck a bit. Considering this, I believe 9.6mm (.366-inch bullet) is the largest caliber you should try on the 308 case.

Other Calibers Smaller than .22?

I have been shooting a Remington Model 700 in 17 Remington and think it is just grand. Recoil is almost nonexistent and its bullet flies across the land as flat as a moonbeam. I may also buy a rifle in 204 Ruger. Do you think we will ever see other calibers smaller than .22 introduced?

As you may know, we had a .20-caliber cartridge in the 5mm Remington Rimfire Magnum, and through the years various wildcatters have worked with centerfire cartridges of the same caliber. Back in the 1950s, the U.S. Army experimented with the 7.62 NATO (or 308 Winchester) case necked down to .18, but very little is known about that particular cartridge. The 14-caliber once made a tiny splash among varmint shooters, but barrels and bullets of that caliber were and still are difficult to find. Dies for reloading and case forming are available from RCBS for the 14 Carbine (30 Carbine case), 14 Hornet (22 Hornet case), 14-221 (221 Fire Ball Case), and 14-222 (222 Remington case). A few rifles chambered for several 12-caliber wildcat cartridges have also been built, but I have never seen one. All of this is fun and games for wildcatters, but I doubt if we will ever see a commercial cartridge with its neck squeezed down smaller than 17-caliber.

Another 220 Swift Fan?

After reading your "Hotshot 22 Centerfires," I find your experiences with the 220 Swift to parallel mine. I am 69 years old and grew up on a mountain farm in North Carolina. I recall starting out with a 22 rimfire rifle for shooting groundhogs, and at the time I knew no one who shot them with a 22-caliber centerfire. In 1949, I bought a Winchester Model 70 in 220 Swift and installed a Weaver K10 that T.K. Lee down in Birmingham, Ala., had installed one of his dot reticles in. As far as I know, I was first in my area to start using such a rifle for shooting groundhogs at long range. I was absolutely amazed at how far away I could tumble a varmint. Years later I bought a Remington 40-X in 6mm Remington and while it was extremely accurate, I couldn't kill a whistle pig any farther away with it than with the 220 Swift. I foolishly sold the Model 70 to a hunting partner, but I still have a longing for another rifle in 220 Swift. Now that Remington is offering it in the 40-X rifle, there's no doubt about what I intend to buy. I have seen the 220 Swift put down by gun writers over the years, and you are one of the few who speaks kind words about it. Contrary to misleading remarks that have been made by others, I find the 220 Swift to be the finest long-range varmint cartridge available.

Throughout history, some firearms writers have specialized in praising their favorite cartridges at the expense of other cartridges, some they have absolutely no experience with. Unfortunately, the 220 Swift has long been a victim of some of those barbs.

What Rifling Twist Rates for Rifles in 35 Whelen and 358 Win?

I plan to build two rifles, a 358 Winchester on a Remington Model Seven action and a 35 Whelen on a Winchester Model 70 action. In the 358 I will use handloads with bullet weights up to 250 gr. For the 35 Whelen I will go with 250- and 275-gr. bullets. When I order the two 35-caliber barrels from Shilen, what rifling twist rates should I specify?

Few of the manufacturers who have offered rifles in 358 Winchester have agreed on the correct rifling pitch rate for barrels. Winchester, Savage and Browning rifles have 1:12 inch twists; the Mannlicher-Schoenauer, 1:10; and the Ruger Model 77, 1:16 inches. My Winchester Model 88 in 358 has a twist rate of 1:12 inches and it shoots 250-gr. spitzers as accurately as those of lighter weights. On the other hand, my custom '98 Mauser in 35 Whelen has a slower 1:16 twist and it prefers roundnose bullets in the heavier weights. This leads me to believe a twist rate of 1:12 or 1:14 inches is best for stabilizing the longer spitzer bullets in this caliber.

Where Do I Find 38-55 Ammo and Reloading Components?

I have a Winchester Model 94 in 38-55 caliber. When was this caliber introduced in the Model 94? My rifle is in excellent condition, and I would like to hunt deer and black bear with it. Where can I find factory ammunition, reloading dies, jacketed bullets, bullet moulds, and load data?

The 38-55 and the 32-40 were the first two chamberings available in the Model 94 when Winchester introduced it in November, 1894. In those days both were loaded with black powder. The Model 94's first two smokeless chamberings, the 25-35 and 30-30, did not come along until sometime in 1895. Winchester still manufactures 38-55 ammunition but how long the company will continue to do so is anybody's guess. If I owned a rifle in that caliber I would most definitely stock up on ammo for it. In a pinch, the slightly shorter 375 Winchester case can be used for handloading, although due to its higher operating pressures, 375 Winchester factory ammo should never be fired in a rifle originally chambered for the 38-55.

For reloading dies, go see your RCBS or Redding dealer. As for jacketed bullets, the Sierra 200-gr. and Hornady 375-caliber, both of flatnose form, can be used in 38-55 handloads although cast bullets are often more accurate due to variations in bore and groove diameters of Winchester barrels in that caliber. The Lyman No. 375248 mold throws an excellent cast bullet for the 38-55. Weight will vary slightly depending on the alloy used, but it should pop from the mold at around 250 gr.

Convert 6mm Remington to 7mm-08 Remington?

I have a Remington Model Seven in 6mm Remington and would like to have it converted to a heavier caliber. Can the barrel be rebored and rechambered for the 7mm-08 Remington cartridge?

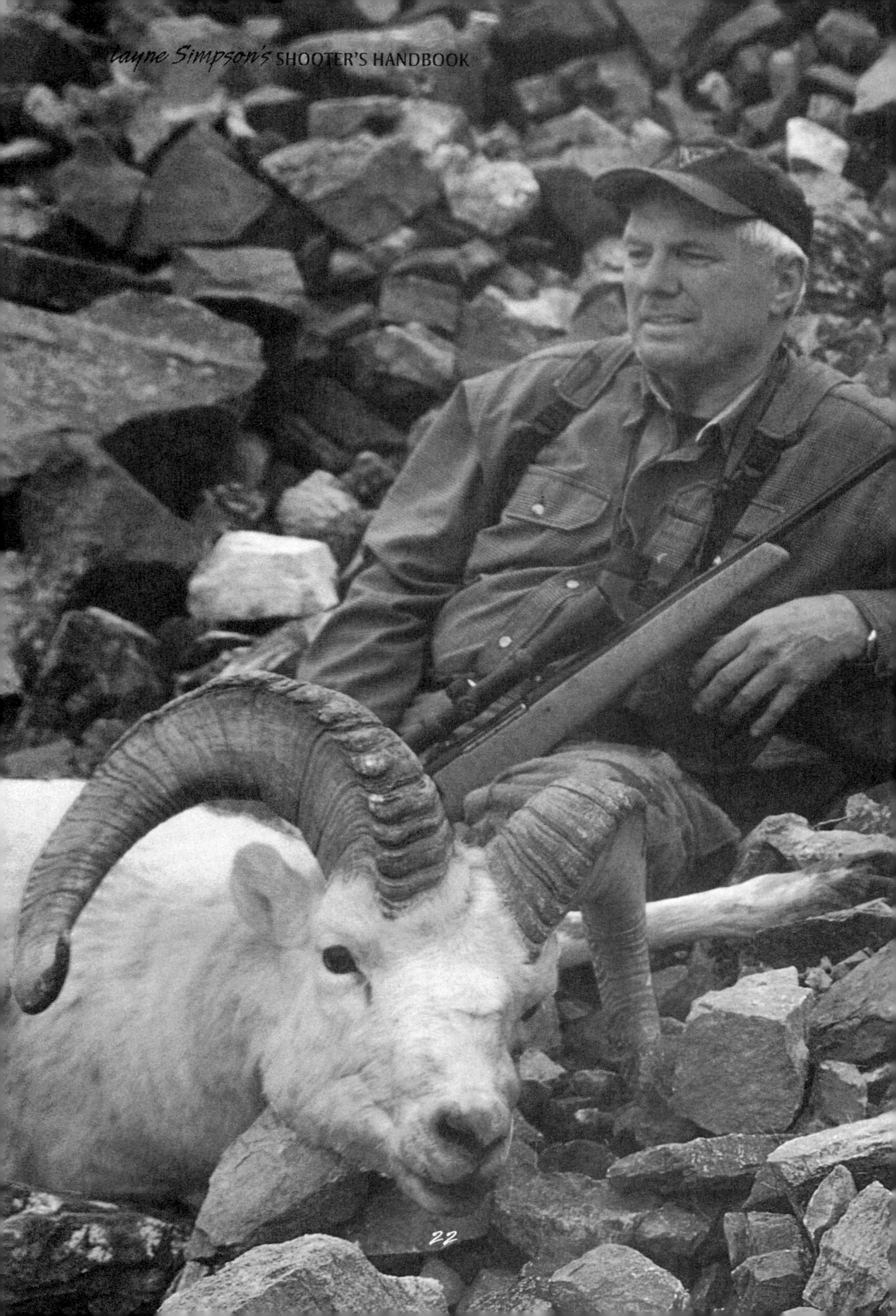

Why Is the Weatherby Ultra Lightweight So Light?

I plan to buy a lightweight rifle in 30-06 and since I have long wanted to own a Weatherby, I am taking a serious look at the Mark V Ultra Lightweight. According to the catalog, it weighs only 5-3/4 pounds. How is it that Weatherby can make it so much lighter than other Mark V variations?

Actually, two Weatherby Mark V rifles are rated at 5-3/4 pounds. One is the Ultra Lightweight you have your eye on and the other is called Super Big GameMaster. During the 2003 season I took a nice Dall sheep in the Wrangell mountains of Alaska while hunting with outfitter Terry Overly. The Mark V Super Big GameMaster in 280 Remington I used on that hunt weighed 7-1/2 pounds with Zeiss 3-9X scope, Conetrol mount, lightweight Weatherby nylon sling and four cartridges in its magazine. Weatherby makes those two rifles light by using a trigger guard/floorplate assembly, trigger housing, magazine follower and bolt shroud made of a lightweight alloy rather than steel. The bolt handle and shroud also have lightening cuts. A light synthetic stock is used and the lightweight 24-inch barrel is fluted over much of its length.

Weatherby Mark V Ultra Light is light for several reasons.

Since the 6mm Remington case has less body taper and is longer than the 7mm-08 case, the barrel of your rifle will have to be faced off at its breech end and set deeper into the receiver. This would enable a 7mm-08 reamer to clean out all of the original chamber. When this is done the contour of the barrel will not match its channel in the stock as nicely as it originally did.

357 Herrett in Winchester Model 94?

I am a fan of the 357 Herrett and believe it would be a fine cartridge for use in the Winchester Model 94, perhaps with a barrel measuring 18 inches or so. I realize we already have the 35 Remington in the Marlin Model 336 but I prefer the Winchester rifle. And besides, I want something every other deer hunter does not have. Since the 357 Herrett is formed from the 30-30 Winchester case, it seems to me that rebarreling a Winchester Model 94 for it would be a simple operation. Am I correct?

A Winchester Model 94 in 30-30 caliber could be rebarreled to 357 Herrett but I am not so sure the shorter cartridge would feed smoothly without some modification being made to the action of the rifle. Have you considered the old 35-30 wildcat? It is certainly different enough and has been around for many years. It is formed by necking up the 30-30 case to 35 caliber and reloading dies for it are available from Redding and RCBS. I believe that cartridge would feed more smoothly in the Winchester 94 than the 357 Herrett.

Why Did 7mm Magnum Not Drop Whitetail in Its Tracks?

During the past hunting season I used a rifle in 7mm Remington Magnum on deer for the first time. The handload I used consisted of 59.5 gr. of IMR-4831 behind a 140-gr. bullet. When I fired, the buck was standing broadside, about 20 yards away, and even though its heart had been totally destroyed, it managed to run about 25 yards before dropping. Was that reaction typical of a deer shot at close range with such a powerful cartridge? I intentionally used a light bullet, figuring it would expand quickly, but I am now wondering if I should move up to more bullet weight. Why didn't my 7mm Magnum drop that deer in its tracks?

Unless a bullet strikes the brain or spinal column, it is not at all unusual for a deer to run several yards before expiring, even if the hit proves to be fatal. Hunters disagree on this, but I find that an animal shot low in the heart area will run a bit further before dropping than one shot higher in the lung area. The longer I hunt, the more convinced I become that the way an animal will react to a shot placed anywhere except into the brain or spine cannot be predicted. I have had lung-shot deer drop in their tracks, and I have had them run off apiece before dropping, even when the same rifle and load are used and the ranges are about the same. Switching to a heavier bullet won't make any difference, although it will be capable of deeper penetration on quartering shots.

Is Winchester 94 in 32 Special, Special?

I have a Winchester Model 94 in 32 Special with a serial number of 2132879. Stamped on its barrel is the inscription, "Winchester Proof Steel." Is my rifle old enough to be a collector's item or is it just a good old gun?

Your Winchester was built during the late 1950s. Rifles of that vintage are often referred to as old-style or Pre-64 Model 94s since they were made before milled steel parts and screws were replaced by stamped parts and pins. The 32 Special chambering was introduced in 1902 and while it was never as popular as the 30-30, quite a large number were made. I remember sitting in deer camps as a youngster, listening in wide-eyed wonderment as old-timers argued about the merits of various deer cartridges. Back them I didn't know there is less than two cents worth of difference between the performance of the 30-30 and 32 Special and that both are nothing more or less than good old cartridges. Just like your rifle.

How Do I Weatherproof Mag-na-ported Barrel?

I have a Browning BAR in 300 Winchester Magnum and I am thinking about having Mag-na-port carve a muzzle brake into its barrel. I hunt a lot in snow and freezing rain and am concerned about water entering the bore through the ports of the brake and freezing. How do I prevent this from happening?

The muzzle brake on a rifle is easily weatherproofed by covering its ports with a strip of plastic electrical tape. You can find it at most hardware and electrical supply stores. When the rifle is fired, propellant gas blows the tape away and it has no affect on the efficiency of the muzzle brake. Place another strip of tape over the muzzle of the barrel and it is totally weatherproof. Incidentally, I also use the same trick anytime I hunt in dusty conditions. Just remember, the tape goes over the outside of the muzzle, not in it.

How Many Weatherby Cartridges?

My two favorite rifles are Weatherby Mark Vs in 240 Magnum and 300 Magnun. How many Weatherby cartridges have been available through the years?

I count 15. Beginning back in 1945 when Roy Weatherby opened his first shop and not in the order of their introduction:

220 Weatherby Rocket	30-378 Weatherby Magnum
228 Weatherby Magnum	340 Weatherby Magnum
224 Weatherby Magnum	338-378 Weatherby Magnum
240 Weatherby Magnum	375 Weatherby Magnum
257 Weatherby Magnum	378 Weatherby Magnum
270 Weatherby Magnum	416 Weatherby Magnum
7mm Weatherby Magnum	460 Weatherby Magnum
300 Weatherby Magnum	

How Difficult to Rebarrel Remington Model 504?

My Remington Model 504 in 22 Long Rifle is quite accurate but I want to come up with a real tackdriver by outfitting it with a heavy match-grade barrel. How difficult a job would that be? What would be involved in converting the rifle to 17 Mach 2?

Any good gunsmith who has a special wrench that fits the barrel retention bolt on the Model 504 can easily switch its barrels. Nothing more than rebarreling is required to convert a Model 504 in 22 Long Rifle to 17 Mach 2. Or you could simply trade your rifle for a Model 504 that came from the factory in 17 Mach 2.

Convert 1903 Springfield to 300 Winchester Magnum?

I have a high serial number 1903 Springfield in its original 30-06 chambering and would like to have it rebarreled and converted to 300 Winchester Magnum. Several people have told me this is a common conversion but I want your opinion on just how safe it actually is. If I decide to leave the rifle in 30-06, can I handload that cartridge faster than factory loads?

During its heyday, the 1903 Springfield action was considered one of the best and many fine custom rifles were built on it. I have one in 7x57mm Mauser built by Sedgley during the 1930s and I enjoy hunting with it even today. After World War II, many 1903s were converted to magnum cartridges, the 308 Norma Magnum being one of the more popular. Even so, the old soldier has celebrated its 100th birthday and it has to be getting pretty tired by now. I believe the best approach is to leave your rifle in its original chambering and never exceed maximum loads listed for it in various handloading manuals. By the time you have the rifle rebarreled and have its bolt face and feed rails modified for the 300 Winchester Magnum cartridge, your total investment will just about equal the purchase of a modern rifle in the caliber you want.

Is My Rifle a Mauser?

I have a very accurate bolt-action carbine in 6.5x55mm Swedish with the following markings on its receiver: a crown over a "G" (in script) above "CARL GUSTAFS STADS" (in all upper-case letters), followed by "GERVARSFAKTORY, 1916." Is my rifle a Mauser? Who made it?

Sweden adopted a slight variation of the Mauser Model 93 rifle in 1894. The markings on the receiver of your rifle translate to, "Carl Gustaf City Rifle Factory." Your carbine was built in 1916 in Eskilstuna, Sweden. Many Model 94 Swedish carbines were imported into the United States during the 1950s and sold on the military surplus market but they are a bit scarce today. During the 1950s and 1960s the Swedish carbine and the British Enfield jungle carbine, with no modifications, just as they came from the battlefields, were considered by those of us on tight budgets to be great bargains in deer rifles.

One Rifle, Two Cartridges?

I am partial to the 358 Winchester cartridge for hunting black bear, but I prefer the 308 Winchester when hunting deer. When hunting deer in upper Michigan, I often bump into bear. The deer loads I use in the 308 are a bit too light for use on bear, and my 358 bear loads are too heavy for deer. Rather than carry two different loads for the 308, I would like to have a double-barrel rifle with one barrel in 308 and the other in 358. Do you know of anyone who could build such a rifle?

I can't imagine a black bear that cannot be cleanly taken with the 308 Winchester, or a deer too small to shoot with the 358 Winchester. Neither can I think of a big-game rifle that would be more confusing to reload under pressure than a double with its barrels chambered for two different cartridges. Your best bet is to stick with one cartridge loaded with two bullets the same or similar in weight but of different construction. A good combination for the 308 would be to handload it with the Nosler 150-gr. Ballistic Tip for deer and the Nosler 150-gr. Partition for bear. An excellent combo for the 358 Winchester is the Speer 220-gr. softnose and Nosler 225-gr. Partition.

Why Doesn't Weatherby's 340 Magnum Get Any Respect?

I see a great deal written about the 338 Winchester Magnum and 338 Remington Ultra Mag, but the 340 Weatherby Magnum seldom gets the attention it deserves. The Weatherby cartridge is more powerful than the Winchester cartridge and so close in performance to the Remington cartridge they are ballistic twins. As the late Rodney Dangerfield might say, why don't the 340 Weatherby Magnum get no respect?

Your comparison of the 340 Weatherby Magnum with two other cartridges of the same caliber is absolutely correct. It is faster than the 338 Winchester Magnum and about as fast as the 338 Remington Ultra Mag. The main reason the 338 Winchester Magnum gets more attention from firearms writers is because most rifle manufacturers chamber for it while the Weatherby cartridge is seldom seen in anything but Weatherby rifles. The 338 Remington Ultra Mag has received a lot of attention lately because it is new and folks like you who buy firearms magazines like to read about new things.

Why Is The 17 Mark 2 Proving To Be So Accurate?

In every report I have read on the 17 Mach 2, it is more accurate than the 22 Long Rifle. Why is this?

The 17 Mach 2 is proving to be more accurate than the 22 Long Rifle because it is easier for a manufacturer to mass-produce an accurate jacketed bullet than a lead bullet. I can see this little cartridge eventually dominating world-class competition, assuming that the ruling bodies of various competitive shooting organizations approve it for such use.

The Remington Rolling-Block rifle can be quite accurate.

How Accurate Is the Remington Rolling Block?

I am interested in placing an order with the Remington custom shop for a single-shot, rolling-block rifle in 45-70 Government. Can you tell me what level of accuracy I can expect from that rifle?

Several years ago I hunted caribou in Canada with a Remington rolling-block in 45-70 Government. That rifle wore a globe-style sight up front and an adjustable aperture sight on the tang and it averaged less than two inches for five shots at 100 yards with the Remington 300-gr. factory load. I did not get around to trying the rifle with cast bullets but am sure it would have delivered even better accuracy with carefully prepared handloads.

29

Does Remington Model 700 Carbine Have Collector Value?

I have a Remington Model 700 with a 20-inch barrel in 222 Remington. Does a Model 700 with that barrel length have any collector value? I have tried several factory loads in my rifle, and its best accuracy to date is 2-1/2 inches for five shots at 100 yards. Do you think its barrel is worn out?

During 1962 and 1963, the first years of its production, the Remington Model 700 in all chamberings except the belted magnums was available only with a 20-inch barrel. I still have one with "6mm Remington Magnum" roll-marked on its barrel from the days when Remington almost changed the name of the 244 Remington to that. Considering the great number of Model 700s made during the first two years of production, your rifle has virtually no collector value unless it is new and in its original box. Even then it would not be worth a great deal of money.

Have you tried thoroughly cleaning the bore of your rifle? It takes a whale of a lot of shooting to wear out a barrel in 222 Remington and unless your rifle was previously owned by a very devoted prairie dog shooter, I doubt if the rifling in its barrel is washed out. I have restored the accuracy of many rifles by removing all powder fouling and bullet jacket residue from their bores with a brass brush, a good solvent and plenty of elbow grease. You should try that before making the decision to have your rifle rebarreled.

Bolt-Action Rifle in 300 Savage?

I consider the 300 Savage to be one of the most versatile big-game cartridges ever developed. I own a Savage Model 99 lever action and a Remington Model 81 autoloader in this caliber and I want to add a bolt action to my battery. Where can I buy a new bolt gun in 300 Savage?

I am afraid you are several decades too late to buy a new Remington Model 722 in 300 Savage as it was discontinued in 1962 but you should be able to buy one on the used gun market. Remington chambered the limited-production Model 700 Classic rifle in 300 Savage during 2003 and it is your best possibility for finding a new bolt-action in that caliber. Any rifle in 308 Winchester, 243 Winchester, 7mm-08 Remington or 260 Remington would be quite suitable for rebarreling to 300 Savage.

Do I Choose 308 or 30-06?

I plan to buy a Ruger Model 77 International. I will mostly use it for hunting deer in thickly wooded areas but may also take it along on an elk hunt or two. Does the 30-06 offer any performance advantage over the 308 Winchester in an 18-1/2 inch barrel, or does it simply kick harder and make more noise?

All else including barrel length being equal, the 30-06 Springfield will push most bullet weights from 100 to 200 fps faster than the 308 Winchester. Looking at it from a hunter's perspective, a rifle in 30-06 with an 18-1/2 inch barrel offers about the same performance as a rifle in 308 with a 22-inch barrel. The difference becomes more important when hunting elk simply because the 30-06 will send a 180-gr.

bullet on its way about as fast as a 150-gr. bullet leaves the muzzle of a rifle in 308. For hunting deer in wooded country, either cartridge will get the job done; for use on larger game, the 30-06 gets my vote.

Should I Drill a Hole in My Ruger 10/22?

My Ruger 10/22 will shoot five shots inside two inches at 50 yards. I like to keep its bore clean but am concerned about damaging the rifling when cleaning it from the muzzle. A friend has suggested that I drill a hole through the rear of its receiver so a cleaning rod can be inserted from that end, after the receiver has been stripped for cleaning. Should I do it?

You have good reason to be concerned about cleaning the barrel of your 10/22 from the muzzle end because the accuracy of many rifles has been ruined by careless people who do just that. Still, I wouldn't drill a hole in the receiver. If you know someone who owns a lathe, have him make a steel cleaning rod guide that fits tightly over the muzzle of your rifle. A hole slightly larger than the diameter of your cleaning rod should be drilled dead center of the guide. When used with care, it will prevent the cleaning rod from rubbing against the rifling when cleaning from the muzzle. Cleaning rod guides of this type are available for use with firearms of larger calibers but I know of no source for one designed to be used in cleaning a 22-caliber rifle.

Is Krag as Strong as Mauser?

Comments made by you in an article about the Norwegian Krag-Jorgensen rifle didn't tell its entire story. While it is true that the Krag has only one locking lug at the front of its bolt as you mentioned, you failed to mention a second lug located at the rear of the bolt that bears against the receiver bridge. In addition, when the bolt is closed and locked, the root of the bolt handle fits inside a mortise in the receiver. With all of this in mind, it appears to me that any strength advantage inherent in rifles such as the 1898 Mauser and 1903 Springfield with their dual front locking lugs is purely theoretical.

Take a closer look at the Krag action. The second lug you refer to is actually a safety lug and not a locking lug. Unless a Krag has developed excessive headspace from wear, permanent locking lug compression, or fracture of its single front locking lug, the safety lug does not bear against the receiver bridge. Its purpose is to prevent the bolt from flying from the receiver in the event of locking lug failure, hence the name safety lug. The root of the bolt handle also serves as a safety lug.

During days of yesteryear, American firms like Neidner and Griffin & Howe built custom rifles around Krag actions. I have one built by Neidner in 22 Hornet Improved and it is a very handsome little rifle. One of the important modifications offered by those shops was lapping in the bearing surface of the locking lug until the safety lug rested against the receiver bridge when the bolt was locked. This made the action a bit stronger but it is still inferior in strength to the '98 Mauser and '03 Springfield actions. The best that can be said of the Krag is it was far superior in performance to the trapdoor Springfield it replaced for U.S. military use; it has one of the smoothest and slickest actions of any turnbolt rifle, and its once-cheap war-surplus price allowed many working men to own their first deer rifle.

What Are Brown Stains in Rifle Barrel?

I used a Browning BLR in 308 Winchester for hunting deer this past season. I always clean my firearms thoroughly after each use. While cleaning the BLR, I noticed brown stains in its rifling at the muzzle. At first I thought it was rust, but after cleaning the bore with several different solvents, I believe the stain is something else. One thing is certain: the stuff won't budge. Can you tell me what the brown stain is and how it can be removed?

It sounds to me like the bore of your barrel is fouled with bullet jacket residue. This is a common occurrence in all rifles in which jacketed bullets are used. Mild streaks of copper fouling will not harm the bore, but if allowed to build up excessively, accuracy will begin to deteriorate – at which time the deposits will be more difficult to remove. Most bore-cleaning solvents available today do a good job of dissolving powder fouling but it takes one with more muscle to dissolve bullet jacket fouling.

A solvent such as Sweet's 7.62 with its high ammonia content will dissolve the bullet jacket fouling but if the fouling is quite bad it will take numerous applications to do it. Also, if that solvent is left in the barrel for more than five minutes or so it can actually etch the metal. Another way to remove the copper is to plug the chamber with a special chamber plug available from Sinclair International, stand the rifle on its butt, fill the bore with Shooter's Choice bore solvent, cap off the muzzle with tape, and let the rifle soak overnight. Doing so will not harm the barrel.

An electrical device called the Foul-Out from Outers does a great job of removing copper fouling, as well as leading left behind when lead bullets are fired, but it is quite slow. The quickest way to remover copper fouling is to scrub the bore with a cotton patch covered with paste called J.B. Nonimbedding Bore Cleaner which is available from Brownells. The extremely fine abrasive it contains is hard enough to wear away the copper but is too soft to harm the barrel. I have used it for decades with complete satisfaction.

What Scope for 378 Weatherby Magnum?

I plan to use my new Weatherby Mark V in 378 Magnum on a hunt for Cape buffalo in Zambia and want to mount a scope on it. What scope do you recommend?

Due the high level of recoil generated by the 378 Magnum cartridge, you should choose a scope with plenty of eye relief. Add to this the fact that most African professional hunters won't allow their clients to shoot at dangerous game beyond 100 yards and it becomes easy for me to prescribe several perfect scopes. One is the Schmidt & Bender 1.25-4X with its 3.75 inches of eye relief and 100-yard field of view of 96 feet. Another is the Leupold 1-4X Var-X-II with its four inches of eye relief and 70-foot field. Then there is the Burris 1.5-6X Signature Safari which has the same eye relief length and field of view as the Leupold.

Where Do I Get Rifles in 6mm-06 and 280 Remington?

Some years back several firearms were stolen from my home. One was a custom '98 Mauser in 6mm-06; the other was Remington Model 742 autoloader in 280 Remington. How do I go about replacing those two old favorites? Another question. Can a rifle in 243 Winchester I presently own be rechambered to 6mm Remington?

The Thompson/Center custom shop offers the 6mm-06 chambering in its barrels for the Encore single-shot rifle. I have one and used it to take a very nice pronghorn antelope in New Mexico. Any good gunsmith who specializes in installing barrels can build you a rifle in 6mm-06. Another possibility is to buy a Weatherby Mark V rifle in 240 Weatherby Magnum. The 240 Magnum and the 6mm-06 wildcat are ballistic twins. In the 240's favor, Weatherby offers factory ammo with a variety of bullet weights suitable for use on varmints and deer-size game. A Mark V Deluxe in 240 Magnum just happens to be one of my favorite deer rifles.

Availability of the 280 Remington chambering in the Remington autoloading rifle has long been an on-again off-again thing, but even if you are unable to find a new one they are available on the used gun market. Several variations of the Remington autoloader, including the Model 742, Model 7400 and Model Four have been manufactured in 280 caliber. Your rifle in 243 can be rechambered to 6mm Remington, but the barrel will have to be faced off a bit and set deeper into the receiver before the rechamber job. This is due to the fact that the 243 Winchester case has less body taper and is shorter than the 6mm Remington case. When modified in that manner, the contour of the barrel will no longer match its channel in the stock, and that can be rather unsightly. Considering the insignificant amount of velocity increase you would realize from such a conversion, your best bet (from a practical point of view) is to leave it as-is. Of course, you could kill two birds with one stone by having the rifle rechambered to 6mm-06 or 240 Weatherby Magnum.

Is Ruger .44 Carbine Extinct?

I am an American soldier stationed in West Germany. I recently visited our local rod and gun shop to see if my Winchester Model 94 Big Bore in 375 Winchester had appreciated in price. I had also planned to buy a Ruger autoloading carbine in 44 Magnum like the one my father owned when I was a kid, but neither it nor the 375-caliber Model 94 was available. Have both been discontinued? Will I be able to buy factory ammo for my Winchester when I return to the United States? I would also like to reload my fired cases. Where can I find bullets and load data?

If you are talking about the original Ruger 44 caliber carbine, you are quite a few years too late since it was discontinued during the early 1980s due to poor sales.

Ruger offers a similar rifle today but it is heavier and more expensive than the original. The 375 Winchester is still alive but just barely. The ammunition is available from Winchester and probably will be for years to come. Jacketed bullets of flatnose style that are suitable for handloading in the 375 Winchester are available from Barnes, Sierra and Hornady. Load data are also available from those companies. I have one of the first Model 94s built in 375 Winchester and its favorite powders are Reloder 7 and H322.

Two Rifles for Elk?

I am thinking about settling on two rifles for all of my elk hunting: one for open-country shooting where shots can be at long range, another for still hunting in wooded terrain during wet weather. Since I am accustomed to hunting with a heavy rifle, what do you think about the Remington 40X repeater in 300 Winchester Magnum for picking off a bull at long range? For woods hunting, I will stick with open sights and have narrowed my choices down to the Browning BLR in 308 Winchester; the Browning BAR in 300 Winchester Magnum; the Browning Model 1886 in 45-70; or the Remington Model 700 in 375 H&H Magnum.

While the Remington 40X is a marvelously accurate rifle, I would prefer to sacrifice a little accuracy for less weight in an elk rifle. When fed good ammunition, a well-tuned sporter-weight rifle will keep its bullets inside the vital area of an elk much farther away than many hunters are capable of shooting accurately. While the two-rifle concept you describe might sound appealing, it has never proven to be practical for me in the field. Seems like every time I go after elk with a woods rifle I end up hunting in open country where shots can be rather long. By the same token, of the few times I have hunted with a heavy rifle built specifically for long-range shooting, I have spent part of the time in thick woods where a lighter, quicker-handling rifle would have been a better choice. I believe it is best to choose one rifle suitable for both jobs.

Since you seem to be fond of Remington bolt-action rifles, I suggest that you take a look at the Model 700 BDL/SS in either of a variety of chamberings, including the 7mm Remington Magnum, 300 Ultra Mag and 300 Winchester Magnum. I would equip the rifle with a variable-power scope with no more than 9X at the high end of its magnification range. Such an outfit would shoot flat, hit hard, and be plenty accurate for shooting at long range. It would also be light enough to tote up steep elk mountains and quick-handling enough for woods hunting. The synthetic stock and stainless steel barreled action of the Model 700 BDL/SS would also have you covered for the wet-weather hunting you do. I know all of this to be true since I have used that exact rifle in 300 Ultra Mag (but with a 2.5-8X scope) to take a variety of game, including Alaska brown bear, moose and black bear.

How Do I Fix Mauser Extraction Problems?

I have a problem with one of my custom rifles, a '98 Mauser rebarreled to 308 Winchester. Cartridges feed fine when they are loaded in the magazine but when I try to load one directly into the chamber the bolt refuses to close. How do I fix the problem?

Most military versions of the '98 Mauser action are designed to feed cartridges only from the magazine. If a cartridge is single-loaded directly into the chamber, the bolt cannot be closed because the shape of the extractor claw prevents it from riding over the rim of the cartridge. Most gunsmiths who rebarrel the Mauser for sporting use grind a small bevel on the claw of the extractor and that allows it to slip over the rim of a chambered round and into its extractor groove.

Ruger Model 77 in 35-284?

I would like to have a Ruger Model 77 International with an 18-1/2 inch barrel chambered for a cartridge that will equal the performance of the 358 Winchester in a 22 inch barrel. What do you think about having my 308-caliber rifle rebarreled for the 35-284 wildcat? It would seem that the greater powder capacity of the larger case would be capable of compensating for velocity loss in the short barrel. If you agree that this project makes sense, what rifling twist rate would be best for bullet weights up to 250 grains? What would be the best all-around bullet to use?

The 35-284 (or the 284 Winchester case necked up for 35-caliber bullets) is capable of producing about the same velocities as the 35 Whelen. I have never worked with the 35-284 but I do have plenty of experience with the 350 Remington Magnum, which has about the same powder capacity. My Remington Model 600 in 350

Mauser rifles seldom have extractor problems.

Magnum will push all available bullet weights from its 18-1/2-inch barrel at about the same speeds as I can attain with my Winchester Model 88 in 358 Winchester with its 22-inch barrel. When converting the Model 77 RSI in 308 to feed the fatter 284 Winchester case from its magazine, you will likely have to open up the guide rails in its receiver just a bit. Choose a gunsmith who has experience in that modification because if too much metal is taken away the rifle is ruined. A 1:16 inch rifling twist rate in your new barrel will handle bullets as long as a 250-gr. spitzer. Bullets I have settled on for all-around use of my Remington Model 600 in 350 Magnum are the Nosler 225-gr. Partition and the Swift A-Frame of the same weight. Those bullets would work equally well in the 35-284 wildcat.

Rifle in 44 Magnum Good for 200-Yard Shooting?

I hunt whitetails in thick, brushy country where shots are at close range, but the wooded areas are intermixed with small clearings that can offer shots out to 200 yards. Ruger's autoloader in 44 Magnum looks like just the ticket for woods hunting but will it reach out and tag a buck across one of those clearings?

While the 44 caliber Ruger is an excellent choice for woods hunting, many gunshops have racks full of rifles far better suited for clean kills on deer at the longer ranges. For all-around use, the Ruger and its chambering have several strikes against them. When zeroed three inches high at 100 yards, the 240-gr. bullet from any 44 Magnum load will strike about a foot below the line of sight at 200 yards. Retained energy at that range is down to about 600 foot-pounds. Wind deflection at 200 yards in a mere 10 miles-per-hour crosswind is 19 inches. On top of all that, the Ruger autoloader I shot averaged around four inches at 100 yards which converts to roughly eight inches at twice that distance. Like I said, it is an excellent woods rifle for the deer hunter but no great shakes in any department once the distance to the target greatly exceeds 125 yards.

Needs Rimless Extractor for Martini Cadet

I want to build a varmint rifle in 17 Remington, 204 Ruger or 223 Remington around the Martini Cadet single-shot action. Where can I find an extractor that works with rimless cartridges?

I have a custom varmint rifle on the small Martini action but since it is in 222 Rimmed I did not have to change out its extractor. I did, however, buy a rimless extractor for it in case I someday decide to rebarrel for a rimless cartridge. That extractor came from Snapp's Gunshop, 6911 East Washington Rd., Clare, MI 48617.

Which 280 Improved?

I'd like to squeeze maximum performance from a 7mm caliber cartridge in my Winchester Model 70 without going to a magnum-size case. When having my rifle rebarreled, should I go with the standard 280 Improved, the 280 RCBS or perhaps another version?

The only difference between the standard and RCBS versions of the 280 Improved is their shoulder angles. Since their powder capacities are almost identical, they are ballistic twins. Maximum performance from the 280 Remington case can be achieved by decreasing body taper to .005 inch, increasing shoulder angle to 40 degrees, and relocating the shoulder forward for a neck length of .260 inch (same neck length as for the 7mm Remington Magnum). What you would have by doing this is a slightly modified version of the old 280 Gibbs. RCBS and Redding offer reloading dies for the Gibbs cartridge.

Where Do l Find Load Data for Pointed Bullets in the 30-30?

My son wishes to start hunting blacktail deer with me this year so l bought him a Harrington & Richardson Topper single-shot rifle in 30-30 Winchester. l would like to extend the range of his rifle by handloading pointed bullets in the 30-30. Where do l find load data for pointed bullets in the 30-30?

The effective range of several firearms available in 30-30 can be extended a bit by simply substituting a spitzer bullet in load data calling for a roundnose or flatnose bullet of the same weight. Besides your son's H&R single shot, there are the T/C Contender in both handgun and carbine form and the Remington Model 788. My Winchester Model 54, one of few bolt actions ever offered in 30-30, shoots more accurately with 125- and 150-gr. spitzers than with bluntnose bullets of the same weight. Regardless of the bullet you decide on, it is extremely important that you begin with starting loads published in various handloading manuals. And, of course, cartridges with pointed bullets should never be loaded in the tubular magazines of rifles such as the Marlin 336 and Winchester 94. Pointed bullets can be used in those rifles but only when cartridges are manually loaded directly into the chamber.

Rechamber Model 700 in 7mm-08 to 7mm SGLC?

l have a Remington Model 700 in 7mm-08 and would like to have it rechambered for your 7mm SGLC wildcat. Will it work? Where do l get the cases?

Your rifle in 7mm-08 can be rechambered to 7mm SGLC. Cases will be easy to form by firing 7mm-08 factory ammo in your rifle after the conversion.

Do l Choose 300 or 338 Magnum?

l am considering the addition of an all-around rifle to my hunting battery and have boiled its caliber down to the 300 Weatherby Magnum or the 340 Weatherby Magnum. Which do you consider the most versatile for use on all big game, including deer at long range and moose and grizzly bear at closer ranges? l am interested in a bolt-action rifle with a barrel no longer than 20 inches but a gunsmith says a 24-inch barrel is better for magnum cartridges. Do you agree?

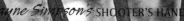

Rifling twist rate of Savage M99 and M1920 rifles is too slow to stabilize heavy bullets.

I am afraid there is no such animal as an all-around rifle. Either of the cartridges you are interested in will work, but each is better suited for certain applications. The 300 Weatherby Magnum shoots a bit flatter so that makes it a bit better for shooting deer at long range, while the greater power of the 340 Weatherby Magnum makes it better suited for shooting a grizzly bear at close range. If it came down to the last minute of the last day of a deer hunt and the only shot I had at a trophy buck was at 400 yards, I would prefer to have the 300 Magnum. If I had the crosshairs in my scope plastered on the shoulder of a 1000-pound brown bear some 20 paces away in an Alaska alder thicket, I would rather the rifle in my hands be chambered for the 340 Magnum. I agree with your gunsmith; a rifle chambered for either cartridge should have a barrel no shorter than 24 inches. Actually, 26 inches is none too long for the 300 Weatherby Magnum.

Why Are Bullets Fired from Savage 99 Unstable?

A Savage Model 99 I own was bought by my father during the 1930s. The rifle is in excellent condition and its bore is like new. Most of my hunting for whitetail deer is in wooded country so I have been trying to develop a handload for my rifle with the Hornady 117-gr. roundnose bullet. I like that bullet because when it is fired from one of my other rifles in 257 Roberts, it does a great job of penetrating a whitetail buck from any angle. On the other hand, when that same bullet is fired from my Savage 99 it either misses the paper target completely or lands sideways. A friend says the barrel of my rifle has the wrong rifling twist rate but I find it hard to believe that a reputable company like Savage would make a rifle that won't handle all bullets. Should I have my rifle rebarreled?

When Savage introduced the 250-3000 cartridge in 1915, it was first loaded with a 87-gr. bullet. Years later, in 1932, a 100-gr. loading was added. Early Model 99 rifles as well as Savage Model 20 bolt-action rifles have a rifling twist rate of 1:14 inches, which is plenty fast for stabilizing those two bullet weights. But it is too slow for a heavier (longer) bullet such as the 117-grain Hornady. I am not sure when Savage switched to a 1:10 rifling pitch rate for rifles in 250-3000, probably very soon after World War II. A Model 99 with the quicker twist rate will stabilize bullets weighing up to 120 grains.

I wouldn't dream of rebarreling a 1930s vintage Savage 99 in excellent condition like the one you have. Instead, you should try the Nosler 100-gr. Partition. Due to its higher velocity and tougher construction, that bullet will penetrate deeper on game than the 117-gr. Hornady and it is short enough to be stabilized by the 1:14 inch rifling twist in your barrel.

Can You Solve Our 244 Remington Mystery?

Several months ago I bought a like-new Remington Model 722 in 244 Remington. The dealer who sold me the rifle informed me that the 244 Remington and 6mm Remington are the same cartridge with two different names so he included in the deal four boxes of 6mm Remington factory ammo loaded with the 100-gr. Pointed Core-Lokt bullet. Before I had a chance to shoot the rifle at the range, a friend who also owns a Model 722 in 244 caliber informed me that due to the slow rifling twist rate of its barrel, accuracy with the 100-gr. factory load would range from terrible to nonexistent. Imagine our surprise when my rifle averaged less than 1-1/4 inches for five shots at 100 yards and several groups measured less than an inch. My friend tried 10 rounds of my ammo in his rifle and it averaged seven to eight-inch groups. He also brought along a box of old Remington 244 ammo loaded with the 90-gr. Bronze Point bullet. It averaged close to an inch when fired in both rifles! Can you solve our mystery?

A little-know fact about the Model 722 rifle in 244 Remington is that it was produced with two different rifling twist rates. From 1955, the year the 244 cartridge was introduced, until 1959, the twist rate was 1:12 inches. In response to shooters who complained that 244-caliber rifles would not stabilize the long 100- and 105-gr. spitzers, Remington quietly increased the rifling pitch rate to 1:9 inches in 1960. When Remington changed the name of the 244 Remington to 6mm Remington in 1963, the 1:9 twist was used in Model 700 rifles of that caliber. Your rifle was likely built during 1960 or 1961, the last two years of Model 722 production. Your friend's Model 722 is likely an earlier-production rifle. One way to find out for sure is the measure the twist rates of the two barrels.

Can 38-40 Be Rebored to 44-40?

I have a Marlin Model 1889 lever action rifle with a worn-out barrel. Can I bring the rifle back to life by having its barrel rechambered and rebored to 44-40 or is a totally new barrel the only solution?

A pitted 38-40 barrel can be rebored to 44-40, but only if the pits are not too deep. There is only .019 of an inch difference between the groove diameter of the 38-40 and the bore diameter of the 44-40, so if the pitting exceeds .019 in depth (as severe pitting sometimes will), reboring the 38-40 isn't an attractive option.

Where Do I Get Lever-Action Rifle in 35 Whelen?

I am left-handed, and would like to have a lever-action rifle in 35 Whelen for hunting bear. Where can I get such a firearm?

The easiest way to come up with a lever-action rifle in 35 Whelen is to buy one of Browning's Japanese-built reproductions of the Model 1895 Winchester in 270 or 30-06 caliber and have it rebarreled.

Is Remington's 5mm Rimfire Magnum Back?

I keep hearing rumors that a Canadian company will soon begin manufacturing 5mm Rimfire Magnum ammunition. I think it is a better cartridge than the 17 HMR. Are the rumors of a 5mm Magnum comeback true?

Remington Model 722 and Model 725 rifles were made with two different rifling twist rates.

I have not heard the rumor you mentioned, but if it turns out to be true, a lot of Remington rifles in that caliber will be dusted off and used in the field again. There was a time when I expected Remington to produce a run of 5mm Magnum ammo, but that hope was dashed when I learned the company had sold all case-forming and bullet-forming dies to a scrap metal dealer. You will just have to be satisfied with the 17 HMR.

Should I Have Savage Model 99 Rechambered?

I have a Savage Model 99R in 300 Savage and I am concerned about the future availability of ammunition for it. Should I have the rifle converted to 308 Winchester? What can you tell me about the Model 99R?

With the thousands of rifles in 300 Savage still in use, I expect factory ammunition to be available far into the 21st century. Given that plus the fact that the 300 Savage will do about anything the 308 Winchester can do, I believe you would be foolish to convert your fine old Savage rifle. Even if 300 Savage ammo should ever become scarce, the case is easily formed by running a 308 case through a 300 Savage full-length resizing die and trimming it to a length of 1.865 inches.

The Savage Model 99R was introduced in 1932 in 250-3000, 303 Savage and 300 Savage calibers. The 308 Winchester option was added in 1955, followed by the 243 Winchester and 358 Winchester in 1956. In 1957 the Model 99R was modified in several ways to cut production costs, only to be dropped from production three years later. During its heyday the Savage Model 99 was considered the Rolls-Royce of lever actions by many hunters and those built prior to the beginning of World War II are the cream of the crop.

Do I Choose 348 Winchester or 356 Winchester?

I am torn between the purchase of two used rifles. One is a Winchester Model 71 in 348 Winchester. The other is a Winchester Model 94 in 356 Winchester. I will use the rifle when hunting deer, wild hogs, black bear, and possibly moose and elk in thick timber. Since I don't handload, the availability of good factory loads is important. Between the two cartridges, which is available in bullets best suited for use on deer? How about elk and moose? Which rifle do you like best?

While either the 348 Winchester or the 356 Winchester would serve your needs as a deer cartridge, neither is factory-loaded with a bullet that I consider entirely suitable for use on elk and moose. This did not always hold true since Winchester once loaded both with 250-gr. bullets. The two cartridges are now available only with 200-gr. bullets and unless you decide to start handloading, that drops them from contention as elk and moose medicine. I own and have hunted with the Winchester Model 94 in 356 and the Winchester Model 71 in 348. The Model 94 is nice but it does not hold a candle to the Model 71.

How Clean is Squeaky Clean?

In your recent update on the 7mm STW you mentioned that you made it a point to keep the barrels of rifles in that caliber "squeaky clean and free of copper fouling." Please explain in detail how you got about doing that.

Immediately after shooting a centerfire rifle of any caliber I push a cotton patch saturated with solvent through its bore to remove the loose powder fouling. Various solvents available from Shooter's Choice, Birchwood Casey, Outers and Penguin Industries work quite well for this purpose. I then wet a bronze brush of the proper size with solvent and push it to and fro through the bore one time for each shot fired since the last cleaning and then push a clean dry patch through. Next I wrap a patch around a bore brush, saturate it with J.B. Nonimbedding Bore Cleaner and scrub the bore with 20 strokes to remove the copper. The cleaner is removed from the bore by pushing through four clean patches soaked with solvent. I finish up the job by pushing through two dry patches. Various bore cleaning solvents should be available at your local gun shop. If you don't see the J.B. copper remover sitting on a shelf, it is available from Sinclair International.

Convert Remington 760 to 358 Win?

My wife hunts with a Browning BLR in 358 Winchester and I would like to have my Remington Model 760 pump gun in 35 Remington rechambered for the same cartridge. I've discussed the project with several gunsmiths and they indicated that the conversion will entail nothing more than rechambering the barrel and opening up the bolt face counterbore slightly for the larger rim diameter of the 358 case. Since the Model 760 is also available from the factory in 270 Winchester and 30-06, they consider its action plenty strong for the 358 Winchester. I do, however, wonder if the rifling twist rate of the 35 Remington barrel (which I believe to be about 1:16 inches) is suitable for the 358 Winchester. Can you shed any light on this? One last question: what calibers have Remington's Models 760/7600 rifles been chambered for?

Rechambering Model 760s in 35 Remington to 358 Winchester and 35 Whelen has long been a popular conversion for those rifles. You may also have to switch the detachable magazine in your rifle for one made for the 243 Winchester or 308 Winchester (available through any Remington dealer). Even though the rim diameter of the 35 Remington case is slightly smaller than that of the 308 Winchester, the bolt face counterbore diameters of most rifles built by Remington in those two chamberings usually measure about the same. This applies to all Model 760 rifles as well as XP-100 handguns and Model 600 carbines I have examined through the years. I mention this because it is likely that the bolt of your rifle will work with the 358 Winchester without modification. Your gunsmith can determine if this is true by simply measuring its counterbore diameter with a caliper. The 1:16 inch rifling pitch of your rifle will work fine with the 358 Winchester cartridge.

Since its introduction in 1952 Remington's Models 760/7600/Six/76 family of centerfire pump guns has been manufactured in 222 Remington, 223 Remington, 244 Remington, 243 Winchester, 6mm Remington, 257 Roberts, 270 Winchester, 280 Remington, 300 Savage, 308 Winchester, 30-06, 35 Remington and 35 Whelen. At present only the 243, 308, 270, 280 and 30-06 chamberings are catalogued by Remington while the carbine version (18-1/2-inch barrel) is available only in 30-06.

1903-A3 Springfield Safe to Shoot?

I recently inherited a rifle which I am unfamiliar with and hope you can answer some questions about it. Its receiver has the following markings: US, Smith-Corona, Model 03-A3, 4782247. The rifle appears to be in 30-06. Is it safe to fire with modern ammunition?

Your rifle was manufactured by L.C. Smith-Corona Typewriters, Inc., one of several manufacturers of 1903 and 1903-A3 rifles for the U.S. Government during World War II. If its barrel is original it is chambered for the 30-06 cartridge. The numbers on its receiver make up its serial number. The 1903 Springfield was adopted by the U.S. Army in 1903 and served until being replaced by the M1 Garand in 1936. If your 1903-A3 is in good serviceable condition, it will safely fire modern factory ammunition. But to be on the safe side, the rifle should be checked over by a good gunsmith before it is fired.

How Do You Zero Your Big-Game Rifles?

Seems like every hunter has his own idea about how to zero his rifle. What do you prefer?

It depends on the rifle and what it will be used for. When hunting potentially dangerous game such as Cape buffalo, I zero my rifle dead on at 100 yards simply because that's the maximum distance I will shoot one of those animals. For about everything else, I prefer to zero three inches high at 100 yards. When shooting a flat-shooting cartridge such as the 270 Winchester, that allows me to hold dead center of the vital area and not worry about holding over or under out to about 325 yards. When using a woods cartridge such as the 30-30 Winchester, I can hold dead center out to 200 yards.

Why Are Bullets Keyholing?

I recently bought a Model 70 in 25-06 and it cuts perfectly round holes in a paper target when shooting Winchester factory ammo with the 120-gr. PEP bullet. But as you can see on the target I've enclosed, the Remington 120-gr. pointed Core-Lokt and Sierra 117-gr. spitzer boattail bullets tumble when fired from the same rifle. I've tried loading those two bullets to maximum velocity with several powders, including IMR-4350, and my results are the same. Why are those bullets keyholing?

Had you examined the holes made in the target you sent to me a bit more closely, you might have noticed that the Winchester bullets were also tipping a bit as they punched through, although not as severely as the Remington and Sierra bullets. I have not compared the lengths of those three but if the Winchester is shorter than the Remington and Sierra bullets, that would explain why it is a bit more stable when fired from your rifle. A rifle will, on occasion, escape from the factory with an incorrect rifling twist rate for its chambering and it would appear that the twist in your rifle is too slow for the longer 25-caliber bullets. Correct rate of twist for the 25-06 is 1:10 inches and if you find it to be slower than that you have the answer to your bullet instability problem. If your barrel does prove to have the wrong twist rate I'm sure U.S. Repeating Arms will replace it with another with the correct rate of twist. Or if you decide to stick with that barrel, it will likely produce acceptable accuracy with the shorter 100-gr. bullets.

Does Longer Barrel Reduce Velocity?

I'm in the market for a long-barrel lever action rifle in 357 Magnum. According to a salesman I talked with in a gun shop, some lever actions in this caliber are made with barrels in the neighborhood of 18-1/2 inches because a longer barrel reduces the velocity of the 357 Magnum. He also stated that the cartridge is more accurate in the short carbine-length barrel. Sounds ridiculous to me. Was he off track?

The salesman you spoke with was right on target in the velocity department. It is true that optimum barrel length for a cartridge of extremely high expansion ratio (i.e., the ratio of interior case volume to barrel volume) such as the 357 Magnum is usually somewhere between 16 and 20 inches. A longer barrel can actually reduce velocity simply because the bullet is still traveling through the barrel after pressure has dropped off to a relatively low level. The velocity decrease seldom amounts to enough to make a practical difference ballistically, but it is there. The same holds true for other high expansion ratio cartridges such as the 38 Special, 44 Magnum and the 22 Long Rifle.

I find a lever action rifle with a long barrel easier to shoot accurately due to its longer sight radius, better balance and heavier weight. To me, the slight loss of velocity is a tradeoff I'm willing to take. As for accuracy, I believe your source of information is off track. Some of the most accurate 22 rimfire target rifles made by Remington, Anschutz and others have barrels measuring anywhere from 20 to over 30 inches in length.

Why Is Federal Fusion Ammo Priced So Low?

I recently bought two boxes of Federal 308 ammunition loaded with the 150-grain Fusion bullet. That's a premium-grade bullet with a bonded core and yet a box of the ammo cost no more than Federal ammo loaded with nonbonded bullets and considerably less than ammo loaded with bonded-core bullets by other manufacturers. It is absolutely the most accurate ammunition I have tried in my Tikka rifle. How can Federal sell premium-grade ammo at standard-grade prices?

The Fusion bullet is made by electrochemically forming a copper jacket around a lead core molecule by molecule. This manufacturing process is more cost efficient than forming a jacket and a core in separate operations and then joining them together. A bullet made in this manner is potentially accurate mainly because a high level of jacket thickness concentricity is easily attained.

How About My H&R Ultra Wildcat?

I recently bought a gorgeous little bolt action varmint rifle at a gun show and it is in near mint condition. Built by Harrington & Richardson during the 1960s (or so the previous owner said), it is chambered for the 17-223 cartridge. RCBS handloading dies came with the rifle. Do you think the barrel is factory original? If it is original why did H&R not chamber it for the 17 Remington rather than the 17/223 wildcat? Is it not unusual for a major firearms company to chamber one of its rifles for a wildcat cartridge? Where can I find load data for the 17-223?

The Harrington Richardson Model 317 Ultra Wildcat was built around the Sako L461 action and introduced in 223 Remington and 17-223 in 1968. If the barrel on your rifle has all the factory markings, it is original. The rifle was introduced during a time when various 17 caliber wildcat cartridges were at their peak in popularity and the 17-223 (223 Remington case necked down) was one of the more popular. Remington did not unveil its 17 Remington cartridge until 1971, three years after your rifle was introduced.   While it is unusual for a major manufacturer to offer a firearm chambered for a wildcat cartridge, it has happened more than once. Back when Browning's High Power model rifle was built on the Sako L461 action, it became available in 22-250 in 1965, almost two years before Remington decided to transform that cartridge from a wildcat to a factory-loaded number. Load data

The 7mm STW needs a relatively quick rifling twist rate in order to stabilize heavy 160- and 175-grain pointed bullets in flight.

for the 17-223 can be found in the Hodgdon Data Manual. You can also begin load development for your rifle by using starting loads listed for the 17 Remington in the Hodgdon and Hornady manuals.

Browning Rifle Made in Finland?

Enclosed are some photos of my father's Browning bolt-action rifle in 222 Remington. As you can see, the inscription stamped on its action and barrel reads "Made In Finland" and yet several gun dealers have told me Browning rifles were never manufactured in that country. Please help us solve this mystery.

Prior to the introduction of the Japanese-made A-Bolt rifle, Browning High Power rifles (as they were then designated) were built around barreled actions made by companies in a couple of other countries. Rifles chambered for the larger cartridges, 270 Winchester through 458 Winchester Magnum, were on the Belgium-made FN Mauser action. The barreled actions of rifles chambered for smaller cartridges, 222 Remington through 222 Remington Magnum, were made by the Finnish company of Sako. The action of your father's rifle is designated by Sako as the L461 and is basically identical to the one that company used in building its own rifles until late 1996 when it was superseded by the new Model 75 action. Brownings with the FN Mauser and Sako actions are some of the finest rifles ever built.

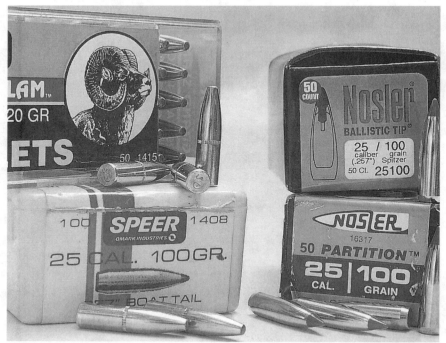

Heavy bullets with their longer bearing surfaces wear out barrels no more quickly than light bullets.

Do Heavy Bullets Wear Out Barrels?

I shoot rifles in 270 Winchester and 30-06 Springfield. I am interested in handloading 150-gr. bullets for the 270 and bullets weighing 200 grains for the 30-06 but have been told that heavier bullets will wear out the barrel of a rifle faster than lighter bullets. Is this true or is my leg being pulled?

Bullet weight has absolutely no influence on bore wear so long as chamber pressures to which the various weights are loaded are close to equal. The bore of a barrel is eroded by hot gases and the amount of wear that can be attributed to the passage of bullets is so insignificant it can be ignored.

How Do I Calculate Residual Energy?

Most of my handloading manuals list energy for rifle bullets of standard weights, but only in 100-yard increments. If an 180-gr. bullet fired from my 30-06 is still traveling at 2210 fps at 260 yards, how do I calculate its energy at that range?

Energy of a bullet is easily calculated if its weight and velocity are known. The simplest way I know to do it is to multiply bullet weight by velocity squared and then multiply what you get by 0.000002218. To come up with the amount of energy a 30-caliber bullet fired from your 30-06 will deliver at the range you mentioned, you would multiply 180 (bullet weight) by 4,884,100 (velocity squared) and then multiply what you get (879,138,000) by 0.000002218 (constant). Doing so would give you 1949.92 foot-pounds of energy.

Was 30-30 Winchester the First Smokeless Cartridge?

I received a Winchester Model 94 as a birthday present. The rifle seems quite old and has "30 WCF" roll-marked on its barrel. I have been told the Model 94 was the first rifle chambered by Winchester for a cartridge loaded with smokeless powder. Is this correct?

The 30 WCF (Winchester Central Fire), or 30-30 as it is more commonly known today, and the 25-35 Winchester were the first smokeless cartridges developed specifically for sporting use and offered by Winchester in a repeating rifle. Prior to the introduction of the Model 94, Winchester offered the Model 1885 single-shot rifle in 30 U.S. Army (30-40 Krag), making it the first sporting rifle made by Winchester for a smokeless cartridge.

Is 1909 Argentine a Good Mauser?

I just bought a military surplus 1898 Mauser and it has the following inscription on the left side of its receiver; "Mauser Modelo Argentino 1909—Deutsche Waffen-Und Munitionsfabriken Berlin." An insignia on its receiver ring depicts a human handshake inside a wreath with the sun rising over its top side. Is this a good rifle? What can you tell me about it and the cartridge it is chambered for? I want to shoot the rifle and could use handload data as well as a source for factory ammo.

Your Model 1898 Mauser was manufactured at the DWM arms factory in Berlin for the army of Argentina. The insignia on its receiver ring is the Argentine coat of arms and its presence makes your particular rifle somewhat rare since for a time the Argentine government required that the insignia be ground off the receivers of those rifles before they were exported to other countries. Of all the '98 Mausers sold on the war-surplus market, I consider the Argentine Model 1909 to be one of the very best.

Your rifle is chambered for the 7.65mm cartridge. Other countries such as Belgium, Turkey and Peru adopted the 7.65mm and Mauser rifles of that caliber were used in the Chaco War between Bolivia and Paraguay. In addition to the Mauser bolt-action rifle, several machine guns and the Belgium FN Model 1949 automatic rifle were chambered for the cartridge. Both Remington and Winchester once loaded the ammo with softnose bullets for hunting but at present it is available only from Norma and RWS. Cases can be formed by running 30-06 brass through a 7.65mm full-length resizing die and trimming to a length of 2.10 inches. Bullets of .311 to .312 inch in diameter (same as for the 303 British and 7.7mm Japanese cartridges) are available from Hornady, Speer and Sierra. The Hornady manual also has loads listed under the heading of 7.65mm Belgium Mauser. This cartridge sits about midway between the 308 Winchester and 30-06 in performance.

What Happens to Fruit Cakes?

I realize you are just a simple writer and you probably don't know much about nothing 'cept guns, but since your magazine offers to answer our questions free of charge, I figure I don't have much to lose by asking you one that's bugged me since I was knee high to a crawdad. So here it is. What happens to fruitcakes that don't get eaten every year?

There is a big fruitcake recycling center in Cleveland and another in Kansas City. Very little of the tons of fruitcakes produced each year is actually eaten by anyone except magazine editors, their assistants, art department people and those unusual fellows who sell advertising space in magazines. The fruitcake has taken its lumps through the years, but all jokes aside, I can tell you with all seriousness that it is far more useful than most people think.

When soaked in pine tar, fruitcakes make excellent fire logs and drilling a hole through their middle transforms them into near-indestructible go-cart wheels. I've also seen those with a hole in the middle used as barbells by people in health clubs and when stacked about 15 high they make a nice chimney for a barbecue pit. I've even heard of a Midwestern town with streets paved with fruitcakes and they have also been used in the construction industry as substitutes for adobe and concrete blocks. Other common uses include door stops, airplane wheel chocks, boat anchors, patio tables, bird houses, roofing shingles, foot warmers, fertilizer pellets, and transmission gears for Dodge trucks. Faced with a severe lead shortage during the latter months of World War Two, the U.S. Marines loaded thousands of fruitcakes into artillery pieces and fired them at enemy troops with devastating effect; others were melted down and made into 50-caliber bullets.

Where Do l Find a Magazine for My Remington Model 740?

Where can l find a spare magazine for a Remington Model 740 in 280 Remington?

By checking with your local Remington dealer, I believe you will find that the detachable magazines made for the later Model 742 and Model 7400 Remington autoloaders will fit your Model 740. Your dealer should be able to order a magazine for the 280 Remington but if it is not available, a magazine made for the 30-06 and 270 Winchester will work just as well.

How Good Is the 338-378 Weatherby Magnum?

l have decided to add to my battery the ultimate bolt-action rifle for hunting elk, moose, and brown bear. l have decided on the 338-378 Weatherby Magnum. What rifle do you recommend? What velocities can l expect from this cartridge?

As I write this, Weatherby is the only major supplier of rifles and ammunition to offer the 338-378 Magnum. It is available in the Weatherby Mark V and several factory loads are offered. The first rifle I worked with several years ago was a custom job built on the Weatherby Mark V action. It belonged to the late NASCAR driver Dale Earnhardt and had a 24-inch barrel. Using a maximum charge of IMR-7828, I managed to push the Nosler 210-gr. Partition along at 3400 fps. The Sierra 250-gr. spitzer boattail moved out at 3200 fps. I later worked with a Weatherby Mark Accumark with a 26-inch barrel and it produced about the same velocities.

Is the 444 Marlin a Good Moose Cartridge?

l am getting mighty serious about buying a Marlin lever-action rifle in 444 caliber. Is it a good moose cartridge? Will the Remington 265-gr. factory load get the job done? If l decide to handload the cartridge what bullet and powder should l use?

Remington has discontinued the 265-gr. loading of the 444 Marlin and offers only a 240-gr. load. It is an excellent choice for use on deer-size game but the Cor-Bon load with a 280-gr. bonded-core bullet at 2200 fps is even more effective on larger game such as moose and elk. The Cor-Bon load would also be my choice for all-around use on all game ranging in size from deer to moose. The Hornady 265-gr. Light Magnum loading of the 444 is also quite good but it is not as fast as the Cor-Bon load, nor is its bullet capable of penetrating as deeply on the larger game. You might also try handloading the 444 Marlin with the Nosler 250-gr. Partition or the Swift 280-gr. A-Frame. I took a nice barren ground caribou with the latter loaded to 2200 fps in a Marlin Model 444 lever action. A number of powders have the correct burn rate for this cartridge but my favorites are H4198, H322, IMR-4198 and Reloder 7.

How Little Should a Mountain Rifle Weigh?

I am planning a trip for sheep in the mountains of Alaska and have decided to stick with the grand old 270 Winchester for that hunt. I will soon be shopping for a rifle to be used exclusively for high-country hunting and would appreciate your comments on what it should weigh. What about barrel length? Jack O'Connor once wrote that anything longer than 22 inches was too long for sheep hunting. Do you agree?

Eight pounds has long been the accepted maximum for a mountain rifle and that's still not bad when talking gross weight, which includes not only the rifle but its scope, a carrying sling and a magazine full of cartridges. The development of lightweight synthetic stocks (and not all synthetic stocks are lightweight) along with actions made of titanium or actions that are lightened by gunsmiths now make it possible to climb the mountain with an even lighter load. When some factory rifles are fitted with scopes and slings of reasonable weights, they will tip the scale somewhere between 6-1/2 and 7-1/2 pounds, even with scope, sling and a magazine full of cartridges. Some of those rifles that spring to mind are the Super Big Game Master and Ultra Lightweight versions of the Weatherby Mark V (both on the standard action), the short-action Remington Model 700 Titanium, the Tikka T3 Lite in standard (non-magnum) chamberings, the Browning A-Bolt Titanium and the Model 20 from New Ultra Light Arms.

As for barrel length on a mountain rifle, I like either 22 or 24 inches for standard calibers such as the 270 Winchester, 280 Remington and 30-06 and 24 to 26 inches for the 257 Weatherby Magnum, 7mm STW, 300 Remington Ultra Mag and others of that breed. I have used all of those barrel lengths when hunting in mountain country and never felt that either was too short or too long. A rifle with a long barrel can still be quite light. I have a custom rifle in 7mm STW built on the Remington Model 700 action by Lex Webernick and it has a 26-inch barrel. That rifle wears a Leupold 3-9X Compact scope and weighs only a few ounces over six pounds.

Eight pounds is a good maximum for a mountain rifle replete with scope, sling and magazine full of cartridges but several of today's factory rifles are even lighter.

Does Ammunition Grow Too Old to Use?

My father gave me a good supply of 30-06 factory ammunition for use in my Remington Model 700. Also included were several hundred rounds of reloads. Since I don't shoot a lot it will take me many years to use up all that ammo, but dad says not to worry because it will last forever if stored in a cool, dry area. Do you agree with his opinion?

Forever is a mighty long time, but properly stored factory ammunition will last for many years. In 1994 I bought a Savage Model 99 rifle in 22 Hi-Power and the previous owner included several boxes of very old ammo in the deal. After pulling bullets from several cartridges to make sure the powder had not gone bad, I fired about 40 rounds in the rifle. Every single round fired and accuracy was excellent. I later used three more of the cartridges to take two javelina and a nice little whitetail buck, all at ranges between 100 and 200 yards. That ammo, by the way, was factory-loaded during the 1920s.

Reloads are another matter. After reloads have aged for a few years, propellant fouling on the inside of the case neck will sometimes bond the bullet to the neck of the case. While the bond is seldom tight enough to cause any damage, it probably does increase chamber pressure when the cartridge is fired. Assuming that the mouth of the case is not crimped into a cannelure on the bullet, there is a quick fix. Seating the bullet slightly deeper into the case will break the bond between the two.

Does Barrel Length Influence Muzzle Brake Efficiency?

A friend tells me a muzzle brake does a better job of reducing recoil and muzzle jump on a rifle with a short barrel than on one with a long barrel. He says he knows this to be true but is unable to explain why. Do you know the answer?

To understand why your friend's statement is true, you must first understand that the ability of a muzzle brake to reduce recoil and muzzle jump is greatly influenced by the velocity of propellant gas flowing through its ports. When a powder charge ignites, pressure quickly builds to its maximum when the bullet is no more than a couple of inches or so from the chamber and gradually decreases as the bullet travels farther down the bore. If we look at the pressure curve on a graph, we see a line rising sharply toward maximum pressure and then descending at a slower rate as pressure within the barrel drops.

Let us say that pressure is at 60,000 psi while the bullet is still near the chamber, drops to 10,000 psi when the bullet has traveled 20 inches down the bore, and drops on down to 4,000 psi as the bullet nears the muzzle of, say, a 26-inch barrel. It should now be easy for you and your friend to see that if the barrel is shortened to 20 inches and fitted with a muzzle brake, propellant gas will escape through its ports at much higher velocity than if the brake is attached to the end of the 26-inch barrel.

When Was the Ruger Deerstalker Introduced?

I have a Ruger 44 Magnum autoloader called the Deerstalker. I bought the little carbine new in 1970 but have never used it a great deal. When was this model introduced? Is my old gun as good as the 44 caliber carbine Ruger makes today? Is the new one more accurate than the old one? What load should I use when hunting deer and wild hogs in heavy brush?

When introduced in 1961, the Ruger carbine had "Deerstalker" roll-engraved on the side of its receiver but complaints from Ithaca, a manufacturer of shotguns that had previously trademarked the name "Deerslayer," prompted Ruger to later change the name to 44 Carbine. I prefer the old Ruger autoloader over the new one because it is lighter and more aesthetically appealing to my eyes. At a list price of $108 back in the bad old days, it was also represented more gun for the dollar than the new Ruger at about six times that price. As for accuracy, the old and new models are plenty good for shooting deer out to 100 yards which is about as far away as the 44 Magnum should be used on deer anyhow. When hunting deer and hogs with your Ruger, factory ammo loaded with a 240-gr. jacketed bullet will get the job done. Never fire ammunition loaded with lead bullets in your carbine as lead will accumulate in its gas port and eventually cause it to malfunction.

Can I Rechamber Rifle in 257 Roberts to 257 Improved?

I have a Browning BLR in 257 Roberts and would like to have it rechambered to 257 Ackley Improved. Can this be easily done?

Rechambering a rifle barrel can often require far more effort and expense than simply removing the barrel and reaming out its chamber for another cartridge. Chamber dimensions can vary considerably from rifle to rifle for the same cartridge and a 257 Roberts chamber reamed by one gunsmith or rifle manufacturer might differ a bit from the same chamber reamed by another gunsmith or manufacturer. Should the diameter of the reamer used for rechambering happen to be a bit smaller than the diameter of the existing chamber mouth, the shank of the barrel will have to be shortened to allow the reamer to clean out the old chamber, and then new threads will have to be cut. When a barrel is shortened at its breech end, nothing from that point forward fits anymore. This includes the barrel in its channel in the stock, dovetails in the barrel used for attaching the forearm (in the case of some lever-action rifles). As you can see, the price of a seemingly simple rechamber job can grow into quite a large investment.

Should I Shoot Grandfather's Winchester Model 1886?

My grandfather gave to me a number of firearms, one being a Winchester Model 1886 in 45-70 Government. It is in excellent condition. The action is tight, the bore is spotless, and most of the bluing and color-casehardening remain. I have fired a few rounds of factory ammunition in the rifle and it is quite accurate. When did Winchester manufacture the Model 1886 and how many were made? Should I continue shooting the rifle or is it too valuable for that?

Winchester manufactured the Model 1886 from 1886 to 1935, the year it was replaced by the Model 71. Around 200,000 were made. Whether or not you should

How Should a Rifle Be Carried in a Saddle Scabbard?

I am headed west for my first elk hunt and my outfitter says I will be spending lots of time in the saddle. Since I will be hunting with a rather expensive custom rifle, I had a friend who owns a saddle shop make for me a heavy-duty leather scabbard replete with suede lining that will go easy on the finish of my rifle. In the hunting magazines I have read through the years I have seen scabbards attached to the saddle in various positions and I hope you can tell me which is best.

Your outfitter or the guide you will be hunting with will surely have his own ideas about how your scabbard should be attached to the saddle of the horse you will be riding. Since they will probably have years of experience, whatever position they come up with will be fine so long as it feels comfortable to you when you are sitting in the saddle and your rifle is positioned with its scope up. Attaching the scabbard to the saddle in a position that allows the rifle to ride upside down should not be done since the weight of the rifle is on the scope and its mounts.

A rifle should always be carried in a saddle scabbard with its scope up.

continue shooting your grandfather's old rifle is a question only you can answer. It all boils down to whether you enjoy using the gun more or less than owning it as a collectible. I have no interest in owning a firearm I cannot enjoy shooting but there are those who had rather collect than use. I seriously doubt that shooting a few rounds of factory ammo in your Model 1886 will subject it to enough wear to depreciate its value.

What Can You Tell Me about My Marlin Model 36?

I recently purchased a Marlin lever-action rifle in 30-30 Winchester. The barrel is roll marked "Model 36 ADL, 30-30 Caliber." What can you tell me about my rifle?

Marlin introduced the Model 36 in 1937 as the successor to the Model 1893. Several variations were available: standard with 20-inch barrel and seven-round magazine, Sporting Carbine with 20-inch barrel and six-round magazine, and ADL grade with 24-inch barrel, curved grip with cap, checkered walnut, and a leather sling with quick-detachable swivels. When Model 36 production resumed after World War II, it was available in 30-30 and 32 Winchester Special. During 1946 and 1947, Marlin redesigned the rifle and renamed it the Model 336. The major changes made in the new model were the substitution of a cylindrical bolt for the old square bolt and the use of stronger steel.

Is the 35 Remington Enough Cartridge for Elk?

One of my favorite rifles for hunting deer in wooded country is an old Marlin Model 336 in 35 Remington. I live in the heart of Roosevelt elk country and while I have never hunted an animal that large with my Marlin, I am tempted to do so due to its light weight. What are your thoughts on the 35 Remington as an elk cartridge?

The 35 Remington packs enough punch for elk at extremely close range, and that's the hitch. If you restrict your shooting inside 100 yards and turn down all except broadside shots into the lung area, the 35 Remington loaded with a good 200-gr. bullet will work on elk. Under other conditions, the great little deer cartridge leaves a lot to be desired for shooting such a large animal. I would sure hate to spot a big bull across one of your Oregon logging slashes and have nothing more potent in my hands than a rifle in 35 Remington. If you do decide to hunt elk with a Marlin lever action, the 450 Marlin, 45-70 and 444 Marlin are better choices than the 35 Remington.

Where Do I Find Info on the 338-378 KT?

Where do I find information on a wildcat called the 338-378 KT. What action should be used in building a rifle in this caliber?

The 338-378 KT (Keith-Thompson) is formed by shortening the 378 Weatherby Magnum case by 1/4 inch and necking it down to 338 caliber. The big wildcat kicks a

250-gr. bullet out the muzzle about 300 fps faster than the 338 Winchester Magnum but is not as fast as the 338-378 Weatherby Magnum.

The best commercial action to use in building a rifle in 338-378 KT is the Weatherby Mark V. Form dies and reloading dies are available from RCBS and Redding. The 338-378 KT is a fine cartridge but no logical reason remains for building a rifle for it since Weatherby offers ammunition and unprimed cases for the standard 338-378 Magnum.

Why No Rifles in 8x57mm Mauser?

I am a fan of vintage bolt-action rifles and cartridges. I especially enjoy shooting a Mauser sporting rifle in 8x57mm Mauser. The 8mm is a good cartridge with excellent potential for the game fields when good handloads are used. I would like to own a modern bolt-action rifle in this caliber, but I don't want to go the expensive custom route. Do you think Remington or Ruger will ever revive the 8x57mm by offering it in the Model 700 or Model 77?

On several occasions through the years I recommended to anyone at Remington who would listen that the limited-edition Model 700 Classic rifle be offered in 8x57mm Mauser. It finally became available in 2004 but only during that year. Another way to come up with a modern rifle of American make in 8x57mm Mauser is to simply rebarrel a Remington Model 700, Ruger Model 77, Winchester Model 70 or any one of several other rifles. Start with one of those rifles in 30-06 and rebarreling is all you will have to do.

How Do I Get an Ultralight Rifle in 7mm BR Remington?

I am intrigued by the idea of owning a lightweight deer rifle in 7mm BR Remington. It would seem that an XP-100 action with an 18-inch barrel would work nicely. Is it possible to convert the XP-100 action to a repeater, complete with box magazine? What rifling twist rate do you recommend when using bullets weighing from 100 to 140 grains in the 7mm BR?

Converting the old single-shot XP-100 action to a repeater would cost a fortune and makes no sense anyhow since the more recent XP-100 repeating action could be used instead. Fact of the matter is, the XP-100 repeater is nothing more than the Remington Model Seven action with a different name so that action could be used as well.

I recommend a rifling twist rate of 1:9 inches for any 7mm cartridge because it will stabilize a bullet as long as the 175-gr. spitzer boattail and yet it is not too quick for lighter bullets.

How Can I Restore Accuracy of a 1898 Krag?

I have a clean '98 Krag sporter but its rifling seems worn to the point where accuracy is quite poor. I am aware of the inherent limitations of this rifle but don't want to give up its extremely smooth action. Any suggestions on how I can go about restoring its accuracy?

If you have not given the bore of your Krag a good cleaning, I suggest that you do so before attempting to restore its accuracy in some other manner. Try removing all powder fouling by scrubbing the bore with a 30-caliber bronze brush and a good solvent such as Shooter's Choice or Hoppe's No. 9. Then remove all bullet jacket fouling with J.B. Nonimbedding Bore Cleaner, a product available from Brownells. If the barrel of your rifle has never been thoroughly cleaned, the procedure I have described may take an hour or so to remove all the fouling.

If a thorough cleaning fails to restore the accuracy of your rifle, you could have it rebarreled to its original 30-40 caliber. Another option is to have the original barrel rebored and rechambered to the 33 or 35 Krag. Those cartridges are easily formed by necking up 30-40 brass with reloading dies available from Redding and RCBS. The 35 Krag duplicates the performance of the 35 Winchester, a cartridge once available in the 1895 Winchester rifle. Another possibility is to have the rifle rebarreled to 405 Winchester and feed it ammunition loaded by Hornady.

Which Chambering for Third Rifle?

I hunt deer a lot in Mississippi with two rifles, a Model 700 Mountain Rifle in 7mm-08 and a Browning A-Bolt in 30-06 Springfield. Up until now those rifles are all I have needed but I plan to start hunting in other states. I have already booked a whitetail hunt in Texas and another hunt for mule deer in Colorado. I am looking to add a third rifle to my battery and while I have already decided on a Strata Stainless from Rifles, Inc., I cannot decide on its caliber. What should it be chambered for?

To be perfectly honest, if whitetail and mule deer are the largest animals you plan to hunt in other states, the two rifles you already own are all you actually need. They will also work quite well on larger game such as elk and moose but if you feel a need for more power then by all means go for it. One of my favorite big-game rifles is a lightweight job built on the Remington Model 700 action by Rifles, Inc. Chambered to 7mm STW, it has a 26-inch barrel and weighs around six pounds. If you prefer a larger caliber, that same rifle in one of the 30- or 33-caliber magnums would be an excellent choice, assuming that you can handle the recoil.

Why Do Unfired Primers Have Indentations?

I recently bought a M1 Garand and enjoy shooting it very much. The rifle appears to be in excellent condition but anytime I decide to unload it by removing a live round from its chamber, the primer has a shallow indentation that appears to have been made by the firing pin. Is this a normal characteristic of the Garand or is mine in need of repair?

When the bolt of the M1 Garand speeds forward to its locked position, it is normal for its floating firing pin to travel forward and make light contact with the primer. This is no cause for alarm. Military specifications for 30-06 ammunition called for primers with extremely hard cups to avoid the possibility of a slam-fire, a term used to describe the firing of a round as it is shoved into the chamber by the bolt. The likelihood of experiencing a slam-fire with a well maintained Garand in serviceable condition is rare but it can happen in some of the old battle-weary rifles. Even then certain precautions can prevent it from happening. First of all, never manually load a round into the chamber and then allow the bolt to travel forward unrestrained; all cartridges should be fed from the magazine. When preparing handloads, always full-length resize cases to the point where they offer absolutely no resistance to being chambered by the bolt.

While commercial primers have proven to be suitable for use in handloads for the Garand, it is important to clean primer pockets thoroughly and seat primers slightly below the surface of the case head. The precautions I have mentioned along with keeping the chamber and bolt face of the rifle clean will usually prevent slam-firing in the grand old Garand.

What Are Owl, Bunny and Rabbit Ear Bags?

While recently zeroing my new varmint rifle at the gun club I overheard a couple of benchrest shooters talking about the various styles of sandbags used in competition. If memory serves me correctly, they were describing them as owl-ear, bunny-ear and rabbit-ear bags. I intended to ask what they meant but got busy and let them slip away before I had a chance to do so. What did those fellows mean by their descriptions of sand bags?

The two vertical projections atop a leather sandbag between which the stock of a rifle rests are commonly referred to as ears by manufacturers who make the bags and by shooters who use them. The owl-ear style is quite short and is designed to be strapped to the cradle of an adjustable front rest where it is used to support the forearm of the rifle. That type of bag is available with its ears spaced far apart for wide forearms and closer together for narrow forearms. Sandbags designed to support the buttstock of a rifle are considerably taller and usually come in two styles. The rabbit-ear style has tall ears and is best used with a buttstock that has no cheek rest. The ears of the bunny-ear bag are intentionally made shorter to prevent their interfering with a buttstock that does have a cheek rest. Sinclair International is the best source I have found for leather sandbags of various styles.

Who Builds Super Lightweight Rifles in 300 Ultra Mag?

I plan to have a super lightweight mountain rifle chambered for Remington's 300 Ultra Mag and want to keep it within a seven-pound maximum weight limit with scope and mount. I also want the rifle to be capable of shooting minute-of-angle for three shots with big-game bullets. Who can build such a rig for me?

Lex Webernick of Rifles, Inc. has built for me three rifles in 257 STW, 6.5 STW and 7mm STW and all fit your criteria perfectly. My rifles are built on Remington Model 700 actions and weigh less than 6-1/2 pounds complete with scope. Lex makes his own fiberglass stocks and they weigh only 15 ounces. My rifles have 26-inch barrels and will average just under minute-of-angle with a variety of loads.

How Do I Improve Model 700 Accuracy?

Regardless of whether I shoot factory ammo or handloads in my Remington Model 700 in 7mm-08, the best accuracy I can squeeze from it is 1.5 to 2.0 inches for five shots at 100 yards. I want minute-of-angle or better accuracy but am wondering if I am asking too much of a production rifle. What do you think? Would the installation of a heavy barrel improve accuracy? And what do you think about pillar-bedding the action and free-floating the barrel?

The accuracy you are squeezing from your Model 700 really isn't all that bad for a production rifle with a standard-weight barrel and from a practical point of view it is plenty good for hunting big game. Pillar-bedding the receiver and free-floating the barrel might help, but there are no guarantees. The installation of a heavy barrel can improve accuracy considerably but only if the barrel is match-grade to begin with and it is installed by someone who knows how to handle the job properly.

In Which Direction Do I Shim a Scope?

I recently received my very first 22 rimfire rifle as a gift from my Dad. I have adjusted its scope as far as it will go but my rifle is still shooting low. I once read that I could shim up the base of the mount to compensate but I haven't figured out in what direction to move which end of the scope in order to shift my aim in the require direction. Please explain.

Simply remember that the rule for shifting point of aim in relation to point of bullet impact by physically moving one end of a scope is the same as when adjusting the front and rear open sights on a rifle; move the rear end of the scope in the direction in which you want point of bullet impact to change in relation to point of aim or move its front end in the opposite direction for the same effect. Since your problem is with point of bullet impact being too far below point of aim, you would elevate the rear end of the scope by shimming.

Does Off-Center Firing Pin Strike Affect Accuracy?

I noticed that the firing pin indentation on the primers of cases fired in my Ruger 77/22H in 22 Hornet are not perfectly centered. Why is this? Does it have any affect on accuracy?

The firing pins of most rifles strike the primer of a cartridge a bit off center. This is due to the fact that when building rifles on a mass-production basis, it is virtually impossible to end up with the receiver, barrel, chamber, bolt and firing pin tunnels all in perfect alignment. The slight misalignment has no affect on accuracy.

Who Can Rebarrel Marlin 336 to 7mm STE?

I would like to have a Marlin 336 rebarreled for your 7mm Shooting Times Easterner. Who can do the work for me? What bullets do you recommend? Is the 7mm STE enough cartridge for game as large as elk?

Harry McGowen of McGowen Barrels did an excellent job of rebarreling a Marlin 336 to 7mm STE for me. Since that rifle has a tubular magazine, only flatnosed bullets should be loaded in this cartridge, which rules out everything but the 120-gr. Nosler and 139-grain Hornady bullets of that type. While I am sure the 7mm STE would work on elk, the woods are full of better elk cartridges. It is at its best when used on deer-size game.

How Do I Measure Group Size?

I recently read that it is common for benchrest competitors to shoot five-shot groups that measure .200 inch and smaller with rifles in 6mm PPC. How is it possible for a group to measure less than the diameter of a .243-inch bullet?

Group size is commonly measured from center to center of the two bullet holes that are farthest apart. Therefore, if all five bullets precisely entered the same hole in the target, the group would measure zero or .000 inch. This has never happened in registered benchrest competition but several shooters have come mighty close. The easiest way to determine the size of a group is to measure from the inside edge of one hole to the outside edge of the other with a caliper. If the group is too small for that method, measuring from outside to outside and subtracting one bullet diameter gives the same results. For example, if a group fired with a 6mm caliber rifle and its .243-inch bullet measures .436 inch outside to outside, its size for record would be .193 inch.

Is There a 338-08?

Through the years I have read a number of magazine articles written on the 308 Winchester and its various offspring but have never seen anything published on that case necked up for 338 caliber bullets. Does the 338-08 exist? If so, where can I get load data? Which bullets would be best for hunting big game? I have a Remington Model 700 in 308 Winchester. Who could install a barrel in this caliber on it?

The 338-08 wildcat does exist and it is an excellent choice for a short-action rifle like your Model 700. You can begin load development by reducing starting loads shown in various handloading manuals for a particular bullet weight in the 358 Winchester by 10 percent. For all-around use of this cartridge on game ranging in size from whitetail deer to moose and elk, I would load it with the Nosler 210-gr. Partition. Other good choices are the Sierra 225-gr. spitzer boattail, Hornady 225-gr. spirepoint, Speer 225-gr. spitzer and the 200-gr. X-Bullet from Barnes. Try Shilen Barrels for the rebarrel job.

Can I Rebarrel for the 6x45mm?

I have a rifle in 223 Remington and would like to have it rebarreled to 6x45mm. Is this feasible? I would use the rifle mostly for punching paper and shooting coyotes out to 200 yards or so. My choices in bullets would be those weighing from 70 to 90 grains. Who makes reloading dies for the 6x45mm? Are cases difficult to form? Where can I get load data? If I decide to try this cartridge on deer, which bullet should I use?

Rigby and Remington .416s Compared?

I plan to buy a bigbore rifle for an upcoming hunt in Zambia and am torn between the 416 Remington Magnum and the 416 Rigby. Which should I choose?

Bullet weight and the velocity of those two cartridges are the same so their performance on game is the same. Due to its larger case, the 416 Rigby is loaded to lower chamber pressure than the 416 Remington Magnum but having used both in the heat of Africa, I can say first-hand

I took this Cape buffalo with a Kimber rifle in 416 Rigby but the 416 Remington Magnum offers the same performance in a smaller package.

that this is important only those who spend much of their time debating the number of angels who can pirouette on the head of a thumbtack. In the United States, both Remington and Federal load the Remington cartridge while only Federal loads the Rigby. You are more likely to find a box of 416 Remington ammo in a gunshop in Anchorage, Alaska, than a box of 416 Rigby. You will also spend considerably less money on a box of 416 Remington cartridges than on a box of 416 Rigby cartridges. I love both and anytime I am overcome by nostalgia I choose the Rigby cartridge, but from a practical point of view the Remington cartridge wins out.

Any good gunsmith can rebarrel your rifle to 6x45mm. Reloading dies are available from Redding and RCBS. Cases are easily formed by running 223 Remington brass through a 6x45mm full-length resizing die equipped with a tapered expander button. The Hodgdon handloading manual has plenty of loads for that cartridge with bullets ranging in weights from 60 to 100 grains. The use of bullets as heavy as 90 grains will require a rifling twist no slower than 1:10 inches, although I prefer a 1:9 twist for this cartridge. Your best bets for deer bullets are the 85-gr. Nosler Partition and the Barnes X-Bullet of the same weight. Muzzle velocity of the 6x45mm loaded with a bullet of that weight runs 2800 to 3000 fps in a 22-inch barrel.

A Left-Hand 1903 Springfield?

Enclosed is a photo of a 1903 Springfield stock I own. It is in mint condition and as you can see, it has a cutout on the left-hand side that appears to have been put there for clearance of the bolt handle. Does this mean the 1903 Springfield was made with a left-hand action?

The cutout on the left-hand side of your 1903 Springfield stock was put there for clearance with a magazine cutoff lever located on that side of the receiver. With the lever in its upward position, the bolt feeds cartridges from the magazine in a normal fashion. Pushing the lever downward into its cutout in the side of the stock allows the bolt to be operated by manually loading a round in the chamber but prevents it from picking up a cartridge from the magazine. This design feature of the '03 Springfield rifle came about as a result of requests from U.S. military leaders for a battle rifle that could be operated as a single-shot with cartridges held in reserve in its magazine until an increase in firepower was needed to fend off a charge by enemy troops.

Do You Have Information on the Mark I Springfield?

I recently purchased a 1903 Springfield Mark I and unlike other Springfields I have seen, it has a narrow slot milled through the left-hand side of its receiver. The dealer from whom I bought the rifle said it had been modified for something he called the Pedersen automatic conversion. What can you tell me about it?

Originally designated by the U.S. Government as "Automatic Pistol, Caliber .30, Model Of 1918" (in an effort to keep its development secret during World War I), the Pedersen Device (as it is now commonly called) consisted of a blowback-operated, semiautomatic mechanism designed to temporarily replace the bolt of the 1903 Springfield rifle. The slot in the left-hand side of the receiver of your rifle is the ejection port for the device; a 40-round magazine was attached to the opposite side of the receiver. So converted, the Springfield fired a short, rimless, straight-walled cartridge loaded with a 129-grain 30-caliber bullet which exited the barrel of the rifle at 1300 fps. As tactical battlefield theory behind development of the Pedersen Device went, a doughboy would, after first engaging the enemy from long range with his 30-06 caliber bolt-action Springfield, replace the bolt of his rifle with the semiautomatic device, leap from his trench and lay down a barrage of suppressive fire as he made his way across no-man's land. The war ended before any Pedersen

Devices could be used in battle and except for only a few survivors (like the one in the Remington firearms museum in Ilion, NY) all were destroyed by Uncle Sam.

How Many Chamberings Were Available in Winchester M64?

I recently bought a Winchester Model 64 lever action rifle with a 24-inch barrel in 30-30 and plan to use it for hunting deer and black bear. I like the looks of this particular Winchester more than the Model 94 carbine with its short barrel and full-length magazine. What other chamberings were offered in this rifle and when was mine made?

I agree with your opinion; with its long and graceful barrel, curved-grip buttstock, hand-filling forearm, two-thirds magazine and quick-detach carrying sling swivels, the Model 64 is a much more handsome deer rifle than the Model 94 saddle carbine and I always thought it made a nice companion piece to the Winchester Model 71 which has similar styling. Two variations were available, Sporting Rifle with plain stock and Deer Rifle (my favorite) with checkered stock. The Model 64 was also manufactured in a carbine version with 20-inch barrel but rifles with the longer barrel outsold it by a considerable margin. In addition to 30-30, it was also available in 219 Zipper, 25-35 and 32 Special. The Model 64 was introduced in 1933, discontinued the first time in 1957, reintroduced in 1972 and discontinued a final time in 1973. The serial number on your rifle indicates its year of manufacture as 1934.

Will 7mm STW Work in Browning Stalker?

I plan to have my Browning Composite Stalker in 7mm Remington Magnum rechambered to 7mm STW but am concerned that since the inside length of its magazine box measures a bit shorter than the 3.60 inches maximum of the 7mm STW cartridge it may not work. Do you have any suggestions?

The 3.60 inches you mention is the recommended maximum overall length for the 7mm STW and all factory loads I have measured are somewhat shorter. I just checked the overall lengths of seven factory loads and they ran as follows:

Remington 140-gr. PCL, 3.585"

Remington 140-gr. AF, 3.580"

Federal 150-gr TBBC, 3.580"

Federal 160-gr. BTSP, 3.495"

Winchester 140-gr. BST, 3.550"

Winchester 160-gr. FS, 3.215"

You didn't mention the actual inside length of your magazine box but if it is too short to handle the above cartridge lengths you can switch it out for a magazine box made for the 375 H&H Magnum (available from Browning).

The barrel of a rifle in 257 STW should be no shorter than 26 inches.

How Do I Zero My Rifles?

Although new to deer hunting I already own two centerfire rifles, a Winchester Model 94 in 30-30 with a 4X scope and a Remington Model 700 in 270 with a 3-9X scope. I'll use the 30-30 for woods hunting and the 270 when hunting over cultivated fields in the Southeast. Several of my friends zero their rifles dead on at 100 yards but it seems to me that by doing so they are handicapping themselves on shots at longer ranges. At what range do you prefer to zero your big-game rifles?

Regardless of whether I am hunting in the woods with a cartridge in the 30-30 class or in open country with a flat-shooting cartridge such as the 270 Winchester, I prefer to zero a rifle three inches high at 100 yards. When zeroed in that manner most 170-gr. loadings of the 30-30 will be no more than four inches low at 200 yards which would allow me to take a deer out to that distance with a dead-center hold behind the shoulder. When that same load is zeroed dead on at 100 yards the bullet is down nine to 10 inches at 200 which is low enough to either shoot under a deer with the dead center hold or even worse, only break its leg. The same type of zero with a flat-shooting cartridge such as the 270 allows a dead on hold out to about 325 yards since the bullet is down by no more than five inches or so at that range. On the other hand, zero the 270 dead on at 100 yards and it is down by close to a foot at 300 yards.

What Barrel Length for 257 STW?

I plan to build a rifle in 257 STW and need your assistance on choosing the right barrel length. Should I go with a 28- or 30-inch barrel or will your new cartridge produce its maximum velocity in a 26-incher?

The 257 STW is capable of pushing a 100-gr. bullet along at 3700 feet per second (fps) in a 26-inch barrel and while I have yet to try it in a longer barrel it should gain somewhere in the neighborhood of 40 to 50 fps for each inch of barrel length increase. I personally consider a bolt action rifle with a barrel longer than 28 inches a bit ungainly although a 30-inch barrel is none too long for single-shot rifles such as the Ruger No. 1 and Browning 1885. Either of those rifles with a 30-inch barrel would have an overall length of about 46 inches or about the same length as a Remington 700, Weatherby Mark V or Winchester 70 with a 26-inch barrel.

What Rifle for 9.3mm Wildcat Conversion?

I am about to embark upon my first wildcat cartridge project and plan to neck up the 300 Weatherby Magnum case for 9.3mm bullets. What rifle would be best for this conversion? What rifling twist rate should I specify for the barrel? How do I come up with starting load data when developing loads for my rifle?

A Weatherby Mark V chambered for the 300 or 340 Weatherby Magnum can be converted to your 9.3mm wildcat by simply rebarreling with no other modification required. A Mark V in 257, 270 or 7mm Magnum can also be used but its magazine box will have to be replaced with one available from Weatherby for the longer 300 and 340 cartridges and the stop groove in the bottom of its bolt body will need to be lengthened in order to increase bolt travel a bit. For that matter, any rifle chambered for the 300 and 340 Magnums as well as other cartridges on the full-length Holland & Holland style belted case such as the 7mm STW, 300 H&H, 8mm Remington and 375 H&H can be rebarreled. A rifling twist rate of 1:10 or 1:12 inches is plenty fast for stabilizing the heaviest 9.3mm bullets available.

If I were to develop loads for the wildcat you have in mind I would begin with starting loads listed for the 9.3x64mm Brenneke in the handloading manual available from A-Square (11774 Highway 42, Bedford, KY 40006).

Why Is the Bullpup Rifle Not More Popular?

Through the years I have seen the bullpup-style bolt action rifle written up in various publications but it never seems to catch on. Its extremely short overall length allows a compact rifle with no sacrifice in barrel length and other than muzzle blast being quite close to a shooter's ears I see more advantages than disadvantages in this design. Why has it not gained greater acceptance among hunters and target shooters?

The bullpup-style bolt action rifle never caught on for the same reason I have always refused to have any part of one – when shouldered in the firing position its action is positioned alongside the shooter's face. If a primer should blow or a case separate during firing, the fellow pulling the trigger stands a good chance of being injured from escaping propellant gas and residue.

What Is a Sleeved Action?

I recently saw a benchrest rifle in 222 Remington advertised for sale and it was described as having a sleeved action. What is a sleeved action?

Back before custom benchrest actions became available it was common practice to glue tight-fitting, thick-walled steel or aluminum sleeves around the receivers of various turnbolt actions. Adding the sleeve makes the receiver more rigid and increases its bedding surface area. The idea got its start back in the 1950s and works best when applied to actions with cylindrical receivers such as Remington's 40X, 722 and 700.

How Much Velocity Increase per Inch of Barrel?

How much velocity can I expect to gain by replacing the 20-inch barrel of my rifle in 30-06 with a 22- or 24-inch barrel?

Depending on a number of factors including the powder used, you should gain anywhere from 25 to 40 feet per second for each increase in barrel length with your rifle in 30-06 Springfield.

Can I Rebarrel 224 Weatherby Magnum to 22-250?

I recently bought a Weatherby Varmintmaster in 224 Magnum and want to use it for shooting woodchucks at long range. The rifle averages half-minute-of-angle with factory ammunition so I have grown extremely fond of it but since the ammo and unprimed cases are quite scarce I would like to have it rebarreled to 22-250. Would this be a practical conversion? Would I gain much performance in the field by going with the 22-250?

In addition to rebarreling you will need to have the bolt face of your rifle opened up for the larger head diameter of the 22-250 case. Back when the Varmintmaster was in production it was available in 22-250 so Weatherby may have a magazine box and follower for that cartridge which you will also need. Whether or not the conversion can be considered practical is for you to decide but if it were my rifle I would either trade it for a Varmintmaster in 22-250 or order a supply of 224 Magnum cases through any Weatherby dealer and leave things as they are. As for your second question, since the 22-250 is only about 100 feet per second faster than the 224 Weatherby Magnum you would never notice the difference in the field.

How Do I Tighten Rifle Action Screws?

What is the proper action screw tightening sequence when reassembling a bolt-action rifle after taking it apart for cleaning?

Good question. The correct answer varies from rifle to rifle. For a stock with conventional bedding I like to first tighten the front screw and then only snug up the rear screw. If the stock has pillar bedding I tighten both screws the same in no particular order. Please note that these are rules of thumb and it can take a bit of experimenting with some rifles before the correct amount of action screw torque is found for best accuracy.

Which Action and Barrel for 257 STW?

I am interested in building a long-range rifle in 257 STW and would like your recommendations on the action and barrel. What velocities can I expect with 100- and 120-gr. bullets from a 26-inch barrel?

My rifles in 257 STW were built around the Remington Model 700 action. They also have Shilen barrels (205 Metro Park Blvd, Ennis, TX 75119). Any modern action long enough to handle other full-length belted magnums such as the 300 Weatherby and 8mm Remington works fine with the 257 STW. When loading 100- and 120-gr. bullets to maximum you should be able to push them to respective muzzle velocities of 3700 fps and 3500 fps with a 26-inch barrel.

Who Can Modify Siamese Mauser Action?

I would like to have a Siamese Mauser action converted and rebarreled to 45-70 Government. Do you know of a gunsmith who specializes in this work?

The barrel-making company of E.R. Shaw, Inc. specializes in the work you are looking for. That company will modify the Siamese Mauser action for reliable feeding of the 45-70 cartridge and install one of its own in-the-white barrels. This company, by the way, manufactures about 100,000 centerfire, rimfire, shotgun slug and muzzleloading barrels each year. You can obtain a price list by writing to E.R. Shaw, Inc., Dept. ST, 53112 Thoms Run Rd., Bridgeville, PA 15017.

How Do I Zero My 257 STW?

I recently had a rifle built in 257 STW and it has averaged 0.678 inch for the last 10 three-shot groups I fired with the Nosler 100-gr. Ballistic Tip. When pushed along by a maximum charge of Reloder 22 that bullet exits the muzzle of a 26-inch barrel at an average of 3718 feet per second. I plan to hunt pronghorn antelope with my new rifle and would appreciate if you will give me your recommendation on how it should be zeroed for extremely long-range shooting.

I still prefer to sight-in long range rifles three inches high at 100 yards. Zeroed in that manner, the trajectory of a 100-gr. Ballistic Tip fired from your rifle at 3700 fps would be approximately as follows: four inches above line of sight at 200 yards, two inches above at 300 and four inches below line of sight at 400 yards. Zeroing your rifle in this manner would enable you to hold dead center on a pronghorn's vital area out to 400 yards or so and connect, assuming your hold is good and your allowance for wind conditions is correct.

Should I Replace My 25-06?

I am using a rifle in 25-06 for summertime varminting and am not exactly wild about its level of recoil for that application. I have experience with the 223 Remington but am not impressed by its long range potential on woodchucks. Would the milder-kicking 22-250 give me the range of the 25-06 I am now using?

It depends on how far away your targets are. Regardless of what the ballistics charts have to say, I find that when ranges are really long (like 500 yards and beyond) I average fewer shots per varmint with a fast-stepping 6mm or 25 caliber cartridge than when using any cartridge of 22 caliber. This assumes that the rifle is capable of long range accuracy and heavy enough to dampen recoil. I have a varmint rifle in 6mm-284 built on the short Remington 700 action by Lex Webernick of Rifles, Inc. It has a heavy Shilen barrel, McMillan stock and Leupold 7.5-30X scope, weighs 19.5 pounds and will consistently keep five Nosler 70-gr. Ballistic Tips inside half-minute-of-angle. On several prairie dog shoots I have alternated between this rifle and heavy-barrel rifles in 22-250 and 220 Swift. In doing so I was careful to make side-by-side comparisons by firing all under the same wind conditions and the outcome was consistently the same—I scored more long range kills with the 6mm than with either of the 22 caliber rifles.

If your rifle in 25-06 is relatively light I'm sure you would find a rifle in 22-250 more fun to shoot and it should hold its own with the larger caliber out to 300 yards or so. Beyond that, you might be better off to simply replace the barrel of your rifle with a heavier one of the same caliber.

Rebarrel 7mm STW to Smaller Caliber?

I have a Remington Model 700 in 7mm STW and while it is a great cartridge I would like to rebarrel the rifle for something that damages less meat. What do you think about a 6mm on the same case?

Necking the 7mm STW case down to 6mm would not totally solve your meat damage problem because velocity would still be high, and high speed combined with soft bullets is what tears up the eating part. Any high velocity cartridge will damage more meat on close shots than slower cartridges and this is the price we must pay for a flatter trajectory and more downrange punch. The damage can be minimized by using a bullet that holds together and penetrates rather than flying to pieces. If you shoot factory 7mm STW ammo try one or more of the following loads: Remington Safari Grade with the 140-gr. Swift A-Frame, Federal Premmium with the 150-gr. Trophy Bonded Bear Claw, Winchester Supreme with the 160-gr. Fail Safe and Speer Nitrex with the 145-gr. Grand Slam. If you handload try those bullets along with Nosler Partitions or Barnes X-Bullets in 150- and 160-gr. weights.

Problems with Side-Mounted Scope?

My eyes are not what they once were so I want to install a scope on my M1 Garand. Since that rifle requires the use of a side-mounted scope my friends say I will find it difficult to sight in. They also say that if I am lucky enough to get the rifle zeroed at close range it will place its bullets off to the side of a target at longer range. Are they correct?

Even though side-attached scope mounts fasten to the side of the receiver of a rifle, those I have used actually position the scope over or at least close to the center of the receiver. For this reason that type of mount works just as well as one that attaches to the top of the receiver. You didn't mention which brand of mount you intend to use but even if the one you have decided on does not hold the scope in precise alignment with the axis of the barrel, your line of sight will still be close enough to the path of the bullet for long range shooting when the scope is properly zeroed.

Where Can I Get 7mm STE Chamber Reamer?

Please supply me with any information you might have on your 7mm Shooting Times Easterner. Also, where can I find the chamber reamer?

I developed the 7mm STE as a high-performance cartridge for late-production Winchester 94 and Marlin 336 rifles. Either rifle in 307, 356 or 444 caliber can be converted by rebarreling. The 7mm STE is the 307 Winchester case necked down for

.284-inch bullets and fireformed to minimum body taper and a 40-degree shoulder angle. The Nosler 120-gr. and Hornady 139-gr. flatnose bullets are ideal for this cartridge since both were designed for use in rifles with tubular magazines. Maximum velocities for those two weights in my Marlin 336 with its 22-inch McGowen barrel are 2900 and 2700 fps. Hodgdon's latest reloading manual has plenty of data on the 7mm STE for several powders, including two of my favorites, W760 and H414. Reloading dies can be ordered through any Redding or RCBS dealer and you can get a chamber reamer from JGS Precision Tool Mfg. in Coos Bay, Oregon.

Argentine Mauser Action Rebarreled to 25-06?

I would like to install a barrel in 25-06 on a Model 1898 Argentine Mauser action. Do you consider that particular action suitable for such a conversion?

I consider the Argentine version to be as good as they come as '98 Mauser actions go and I wouldn't hesitate to outfit one with a barrel in 25-06 so long as the gunsmith who does the work is qualified and satisfied with the condition of the action.

A Finnish-Made Browning?

The action on a Browning bolt action rifle in 284 Winchester I bought back in 1970 is marked "Made In Finland." Could it have been made by Sako?

Back when your rifle was built the actions of all Browning rifles chambered for cartridges ranging in length from the 222 Remington to the 284 Winchester were made by the Finnish firm of Sako. Rifles chambered for longer cartridges were built around FN Mauser actions.

Which Rifle and Cartridge for Dual-Purpose Use?

I own a half-dozen rifles in calibers ranging from 22 Long Rifle to 300 Winchester Magnum but not a single one has all the characteristics I need. The new rifle I'm looking for has to be chambered for a factory cartridge and it must be capable of delivering enough energy to bag deer-size game out to 300 yards. It must also be comfortable to shoot and capable of target-grade accuracy at long range. I plan to used the rifle mostly for long-range target shooting and then give it to my son once he is old enough to start hunting deer. What factory rifle and cartridge do you recommend?

I am afraid you are searching for something that does not exist. A rifle that's ideal for long-range target shooting is likely to be far too heavy for a youngster's first deer rifle. Your best bet is to buy two rifles. For serious long-range target shooting with a factory rifle, you won't go wrong in choosing a Remington 40-XB chambered for the 300 Winchester Magnum or perhaps a smaller cartridge such as the 260 Remington or 308 Winchester. When shopping for your son's first deer rifle, you are likely to make him much happier by taking a close look at lightweight rifles such as the Remington Model 700 Mountain Rifle, Browning Micro Medallion and Ruger Model 77RL Ultra Light, all in 243 Winchester.

Building a Custom '03 Springfield

I have a high-number 1903-A3 Springfield built by Smith-Corona and would like to have a custom rifle built around its action. What chamberings is it suitable for? Who can refinish the action, drill and tap it for a scope and install a new barrel?

Many '03 Springfield actions have been modified for use with medium-length belted magnums such as the 300 Winchester Magnum, 338 Winchester Magnum and 358 Norma Magnum and they work quite well with those cartridges when the work is properly done. If it were my project, however, I would stay with the 30-06 or one of its offspring such as the 6mm-06, 25-06, 6.5-06, 270 Winchester, 338-06 or 35 Whelen. If you mount a scope on the action its bolt handle will have to be reshaped to clear the objective housing of the scope or it can be replaced with an aftermarket bolt handle. That work along with the other modifications you mentioned is performed every day by dozens of gunsmiths across the country with a good example being Shilen Rifles.

Information on Schultz & Larsen Model 65?

I recently acquired a Schultz & Larsen Model 65DL in 308 Norma Magnum and its workmanship is excellent. What can you tell me about this rifle?

You're right about the excellent quality of the Schultz & Larsen Model 65. It never really caught on among American hunters due to a couple of unpopular design details, one being locking lugs at the rear of its bolt rather than at the front. Its magazine was designed to be loaded from the bottom, something else that was not in its favor. About 25 years ago I worked with a Model 65 as well as an earlier Model 60, both in 7x61 Sharpe & Hart, and found them to be fine rifles and extremely accurate. At that time they were imported from the Schultz & Larsen factory in Otterup, Denmark by Norma Precision of South Lansing, New York. In addition to the 7x61 S&H and 308 Norma Magnum, the Model 65 was offered in 358 Norma Magnum and several American chamberings such as 243, 270, 30-06 and 264 Winchester Magnum. The importation of Schultz & Larsen rifles to the U.S. began during the 1950s and ceased during the early 1970s. When discontinued, the Model 65DL sold for $485 while the Weatherby Mark V (which was its equal in quality) sold for $300, another probable reason why the rifle disappeared from the market.

What Do 22 Rimfire Barrel Markings Mean?

I have been shooting and handloading for 30 years but a friend recently asked me a question that had never crossed my mind. How does a rifle marked "For 22 Short, Long and Long Rifle" differ from one that simply has "22 Long Rifle" or 22 Long Rifle Only" stamped on its barrel? Can a 22 Short or 22 Long cartridge be fired without damage to a rifle marked in the latter manner? And would doing so be safe?

As a rule, the three-cartridge marking on a repeating rifle in 22 rimfire means it is capable of functioning with all three cartridges. Some rifles are designed to feed

Most bolt-action rifles chambered for 22 Long Rifle can handle 22 Shorts and Longs, too, though feeding from the magazine may be a problem.

only the 22 Long Rifle, thus the reason for the single-cartridge marking you refer to. While it is safe to fire the 22 Short and 22 Long cartridges in a rifle marked "22 Long Rifle," the shorter rounds may not feed properly from its magazine, in which case they would have to be manually fed directly into the chamber.

Who Can Repair Model 94 Front Sight?

I recently inherited my father's old Winchester Model 94 and find that it shoots to the left. It does that because its front sight was installed at an angle at the factory. I shipped the rifle to the customer service department of U.S. Repeating Arms but it was returned to me along with a note indicating that the rifle was too old to be repaired under warranty. Any suggestions?

Any good gunsmith who is experienced in general repairs should be able to correct the sight on your rifle.

Convert Siamese Mauser to 45-70?

I have a Siamese Mauser in 8x52mm Rimmed and would like to know how much work is involved in converting it to handle the 45-70 Government cartridge. What will have to be done besides rebarreling and opening up the bolt face a bit? Will the barreled action fit into one of the laminated wood or synthetic stocks made for the Model '98 Mauser? Do you consider this a worthwhile project or would I be better off to sell the rifle and buy a Ruger No. 1 in 45-70 caliber?

In addition to rebarreling and increasing the diameter of the recess in the bolt face, the space at the front of the cartridge feed lips of the Siamese Mauser receiver will have to be widened a bit to allow the fatter 45-70 case to travel from magazine to chamber. This is most definitely a job for a gunsmith who is experienced in this type of conversion because if the feed rails are opened up excessively, the receiver is ruined. Except for the slightly larger diameter of its receiver ring, the Siamese Mauser action is virtually identical to the large-ring '98 Mauser action. Consequently, a stock inletted for the former can be made to fit the latter with only slight modifications. As to whether or not the conversion is worth its cost, only you can decide but as dollars invested go, you would probably be ahead financially to sell the Siamese Mauser and buy a Marlin New Model 1895 or Ruger No. 1 in 45-70 caliber.

Convert Weatherby Rifle to 358 STA?

I have an old Weatherby rifle built on the FN Mauser action in 300 Magnum and would like to convert it to your 358 Shooting Times Alaskan. Can I have its barrel rebored and rechambered or will I be better off to simply have it rebarreled?

First of all let me mention that some of the old Weatherby rifles built around FN Mauser actions have considerable collector value. If yours is in excellent to new condition you might want to consider selling it and buying a more modern rifle for the 358 STA. If the barrel of your rifle is heavy enough, it can be rebored to 35 caliber and rechambered to 358 Shooting Times Alaskan, although doing so may cost more than a rebarrel job.

Which One-Rifle Battery for Africa?

I will soon be headed to Zambia where I'll be hunting lion, cape buffalo and various antelope. A shotgunner at heart, I am not really a rifle enthusiast and would like to take just one rifle for the entire hunt. What outfit do you recommend?

If you were hunting only the various antelope, my recommendation would be any good rifle chambered for the 270 Winchester on up to one of the 300 Magnums but since lion and buffalo are on your agenda, I'll have to recommend the 375 H&H Magnum as an excellent do-it-all cartridge. A good bolt-action rifle in that caliber is enough gun for those animals and it shoots flat enough for bagging antelope out to 300 yards or so. In the factory ammo department, you won't go wrong with Federal or Winchester loaded with the Trophy Bonded or Fail Safe bullet. As for a scope, I would choose a top-quality brand with 1X to 1.5X at the lower end of its magnification range and no more than 6X at the top end. Excellent examples are the Leupold 1.5-5X Vari-X-III, Burris 1.5-6X Signature and Zeiss 1.25-4X Diavari. When set on their lowest power, those scopes have respective fields of view of 66, 70 and 105 feet, making them good choices for use on a rifle to be used for hunting potentially dangerous game.

Quicker Rifling Twist Equals Increased "Buzz Saw" Effect?

I plan to have a custom rifle in 300 Winchester Magnum built for shooting whitetails and pronghorn antelope at long range. I had about decided on a barrel with a 1:12 inch rifling twist rate when a friend mentioned that any expanding bullet fired from the quicker 1:10 twist will do more damage to game since it is spinning faster. He called it the "buzz-saw" effect. It makes sense to me that the jagged and sharp edges of an expanded bullet would do more damage when rotating faster but I decided to get your opinion on the subject before changing my mind about the rifling twist rate of the barrel I will order.

Your friend's understanding of bullet rotation is far off course. When exiting the muzzle of a barrel with a 1:12 inch rifling twist rate, a bullet is revolving one complete turn for each foot of its forward travel. In other words, given an animal with a chest cavity measuring 12 inches thick, the bullet will rotate exactly one time during its trip through that area. Increasing the rifling pitch to 1:10 inches will cause the bullet to rotate 1.2 times while traveling through that same chest cavity. Perhaps you can now see that regardless of the rifling twist rate of a barrel, the "buzz-saw" effect sometimes touted by hunters and cartridge developers simply does not exist. Forward velocity and not rotational velocity is what determines the effectiveness of an expanding bullet.

Any Factory Rifles in 6x45mm?

I'm considering buying my daughter her first deer rifle and have about settled on the 6x45mm chambering due to its extremely light recoil. Do you consider it adequate for use on deer? Does any company offer a factory rifle in this chambering? How about loading data?

Some years back a gunsmith friend of mine built a rifle in 6x45mm for his son and the lad went on to take a couple dozen deer with it before growing into a more powerful rifle. The youngster did, however, turn down all shots beyond 200 yards and he used only one load, the Nosler 85-gr. Partition at about 2900 feet per second. I own a Kimber Model 82 in that chambering and have taken enough close-range whitetails with the outfit to prove to myself that it is adequate when that little Nosler is placed where it should go. The only company I'm aware of that currently offers a rifle in 6x45mm is Cooper Arms. The 6x45mm case is easily formed by necking up the 223 Remington case. Load data listed in the Hornady handloading manual for the 6x47mm cartridge (222 Remington Magnum case) can be used in the 6x45mm as well.

Ballistic Tips in Lever-Action Rifles?

My cartridge of choice for deer hunting is the 30-30 Winchester and my favorite deer rifle is an old 1940s vintage Winchester 94 that belonged to my father. The rifle is in excellent condition and more accurate than I can shoot. In the past I have mostly handloaded various 150-gr. flatnose or roundnose bullets but am intrigued by the possiblity of trying the Nosler 125- and 150-grain Ballistic Tips. Do you see any problem with my doing so as long as I never load more than one cartridge in the magazine?

Using cartridges loaded with pointed bullets in a rifle with a tubular magazine is a safe practice so long as the magazine never contains more than one cartridge during firing. Through the years I have fired hundreds of 125-gr. Ballistic Tip bullets in various 30-30 lever actions and find accuracy to almost always be better than with the various 150- and 170-gr. roundnose bullets. When loaded to 2500 feet per second or so, the Nosler bullet is also quite deadly on deer. When using ammo with pointed bullets in a lever action rifle, I prefer to manually load one round directly into the chamber and either leave the tubular magazine empty or load it with ammo with blunt-nosed bullets. As a rule, when the 30-30 cartridge is loaded with a pointed bullet, its overall length is too long to allow it to feed from the tubular magazine to the chamber. This is due to the extremely long ogive of pointed bullets as compared to those with round or flat noses.

Rifling Twist Rate or Velocity More Important for Bullet Stability?

When it comes to stabilizing extremely long VLD-style bullets in flight, is rifling twist rate of the barrel or bullet velocity the primary consideration?

Both are important, but rifling twist rate is the more influential of the two. If the twist rate is too slow to stabilize an extremely long bullet, it is unlikely that any small arms cartridge of conventional design will produce enough velocity to stabilize it. On the other hand, the correct rifling twist for a particular bullet length will spin it to stability, even at relatively low velocities. Let's take the Sierra 80-gr. MatchKing in the 223 Remington as an example. When exiting a barrel with a rifling twist rate of 1:7 inches at a velocity of 2600 feet per second (fps) the bullet is spinning at a rate of 4457 revolutions per second (rps) which, according to Sierra, is fast enough to stabilize it in flight. On the other hand, if that same bullet were fired at, say, 3000 fps in a rifle in 22-250 with a 1:14 inch twist, bullet spin would be reduced to 2571 rps which is too slow to stabilize it in flight. In order to spin the bullet as fast in the 22-250 with a 1:14 twist as in the 223 with a 1:7 twist, it would have to exit the muzzle at well over 5000 fps which, as we all know, is not now possible. So as you can see, a small difference in rifling twist rate has far greater influence on bullet spin than a great difference in forward velocity.

Marlin 336 From 30-30 to 307 Winchester?

I wish to improve the ballistics of my Marlin Model 336 in 30-30 by having it rechambered to 307 Winchester. Would doing so be safe?

Several years ago when Marlin decided to build a short production run of Model 336s in 356 Winchester, a company official informed me that the barrels installed on those rifles underwent a special heat treatment that allowed them to safely handle higher chamber pressures than were recommended for barrels used in building Model 336s in 30-30 caliber. And since the 356 Winchester and the 307 Winchester in which you're interested are loaded to the same chamber pressures, I'll have to recommend against the rechamber job.

The Remington Model 700BDL I used to take this buck in 2003 was built in either 1962 (the year it was introduced) or in 1963 (the year I bought it).

When Was Your Remington 700 Built?

A Remington Model 700 BDL in 7mm Remington Magnum has been in a number of your articles through the years. It has to be rather an old rifle and I am wondering when it was built.

I bought that rifle in 1963 and since the Model 700 and the equally new 7mm Remington Magnum were introduced in 1962, it had to have been built during one of those years. I have taken lots of game with that rifle and even today it is still quite accurate. During the 2003 season I carried it on a hunt for mule deer in Colorado with Eddie Stevenson and used the Remington Premier factory load with the 140-gr. Core-Lokt Ultra bullet. Back home, my old Model 700 had averaged around an inch for five shots at 100 yards with that load. Incidentally, my rifle has a stainless steel barrel but back then Remington applied a black finish to that type of barrel because in those days no hunter would have been caught dead in the woods with anything but a blued steel rifle.

Can Butchered Rifle Be Salvaged?

I recently bought a rifle in 300 Magnum and paid practically nothing for it because a previous owner had butchered it badly. He had started to shorten its barrel by four inches but seems to have changed his mind just before the blade of his saw actually cut through the barrel wall. In an attempt to color-case or perhaps blue the bolt he heated it red hot and then allowed it to slowly cool down. What can I do to salvage the rifle?

First of all, do not fire that rifle in its present condition! Heating the bolt to an extremely high temperature may have weakened its locking lugs to the point where they could shear off during firing. Your best bet is to return the rifle to its manufacturer where its bolt can be checked for proper hardness. If the bolt is ruined (and I'm betting it is) it can be replaced. As for the barrel, pressure with any cartridge is considerably lower near the muzzle than at the chamber area so if the saw cut is no more than a third of the way through the wall of the barrel it should be safe to use as is. If the saw cut is deeper than that, it should be extended all the way through (in which case you'll end up with a 300 Magnum with a rather short barrel), or the barrel should be replaced.

Are Autoloaders Accurate Enough for Varmint Shooting?

I want to purchase a semiautomatic rifle in 223 for long-range varmint shooting but am not familiar with either the reliability or accuracy potential of the Ruger Mini-14 and other rifles currently available. I also like the AR-15 rifle but know nothing about its accuracy. Also, it looks to me like a scope attached to the carrying handle of the AR-15 is too high for comfortable shooting. What options do you recommend?

The Ruger Mini-14 is quite reliable but as a rule it is not accurate enough for long-range varminting in its factory-original form. Clark Custom Guns offers an accuracy package for the Ruger that includes the installation of a heavier match-grade barrel. The one I tried some time back averaged close to minute-of-angle with some loads. Match-grade versions of the AR-15 rifle made by Les Baer, Bill Wilson and others are even more accurate, with some capable of shooting five bullets inside half an inch at 100 yards on a regular basis. If you buy a flat-top version of the AR-15 (sans carrying handle), the scope will be positioned no higher than on any other type of rifle.

Which One-Rifle Battery for Alaska?

I'll soon be relocating to Alaska and prior to heading north I want to buy one rifle that can handle all big game that state has to offer. I am torn between a bolt-action rifle chambered for a belted magnum in 7mm, 300 or 338 caliber. What would you choose if you had to do it all in Alaska with one rifle that shoots readily available factory ammo?

Based on your criteria, I would choose a bolt-action rifle with a stainless steel barreled action and a synthetic stock in 338 Winchester Magnum or 340 Weatherby Magnum. When loaded with the right bullet, both cartridges are excellent choices for all Alaskan game, from blacktail deer and moose to coastal brown bear. And since both cartridges are quite popular in Alaska, you are sure to find an excellent variety of factory ammo in most gun shops there. I would also outfit the rifle with a top-quality variable-power scope with a maximum magnification of 4X to 7X and somewhere between 1X and 2.5X at the lower end of its range.

Where Do I Get Martini Scope Mount?

I have noticed in several of your articles through the years a custom single shot rifle in 222 Rimmed built on the Martini Cadet action. The rifle has a Unertl target scope attached to its barrel and I would like to use the same type of mount on my Martini. Where did you get that mount?

The mount you refer to is actually a solid steel quarter rib attached to the barrel of my Martini. The half-inch wide rib begins at the front of the loading port of the action, extends 10-1/4 inches down the barrel, and accepts Unertl rings. The gunsmith who built that rifle back in the 1960s has long since retired but anyone who owns a milling machine and knows how to use it could duplicate its rib. A couple of other details you might not have noticed on my rifle are a transverse safety button at the front of its trigger guard and a flush-contoured operating lever. When the action is closed the lever fits inside a metal trough inletted into the front of the grip of the stock.

Are 22 Hornet Rifles Inaccurate?

A writer who I believe is no longer in the business once wrote an article about what he described as "an inherently inaccurate pair." He was referring to the 22 Hornet and 257 Roberts. Through the years I have worked with enough accurate rifles in 257 Roberts to know the writer is at least half-full of hogwash but I have never shot a rifle in 22 Hornet. Do you have any experience with that cartridge?

I once collected rifles in 22 Hornet of both American and foreign make and shot them a lot. I can tell you from actual experience that the writer you read is more than half-full of hogwash. The most accurate 22 Hornet I currently own is a custom job built on the Winchester Model 54 barreled action by the old Hart Arms Co., of Cleveland, Ohio. It will average just under 0.60 inch for five shots at 100 yards with a load consisting of the Winchester case, Federal 205M primer and a maximum charge of H110 powder behind either of the following three bullets — Hornady 35- and 40-gr. V-Max, and Nosler 40-gr. Ballistic Tip. I also have two other rifles in 22 Hornet that will consistently shoot inside an inch, a Kimber Model 82 Super America and an Anschutz 1700D. A Savage Model 40 I recently accuracy-tested was almost as accurate as those two rifles.

Excessive Bore Fouling in Swedish Mausers?

I own a number of Swedish Mauser rifles in 6.5x55mm and have noticed that each has a tendency to quickly collect severe copper fouling in its bore during

A laminated wood stock on a hunting rifle has both advantages and disadvantages.

firing. Is this due to the relatively quick rifling twist rate of their barrels or is there another reason?

In addition to having worked with several 6.5 caliber Swedish Mausers, I own a custom Remington Model Seven in 6.5 American with a Lilja 1:8 inch twist barrel and have never noticed that the barrels of either of those rifles copper-fouled more than normal. If the bores of your rifles are relatively smooth you shouldn't be experiencing excessive fouling either. If you haven't tried thoroughly cleaning the barrels of your rifles with J.B. bore cleaner (available from Sinclair International and Brownells), I suggest that you give it a try.

Synthetic vs. Laminated Wood Stocks?

Seems like more and more companies are offering rifles with laminated wood stocks. How does that material compare with a regular wood stock and a stock made of synthetic?

Due to the weight of the glue used to hold its layers of wood together, a laminated stock is usually heavier than a synthetic and even heavier than a stock of natural wood. A laminated stock is as strong as and in some cases even stronger than a synthetic stock and it is friendlier to the touch on a cold morning. Many shooters (including this one) consider a laminated stock to be more pleasing to the eye, especially if it is brown in coloration like the one worn by the Remington Model 673 Guide Rifle. Where weight in a rifle is an issue, synthetic is better than laminated wood, but where it is not I prefer the looks and field of the laminated stock. I prefer the lightest synthetic stock available on a sheep rifle but had rather have a laminated stock on a heavy-barrel rifle used for shooting varmints at long range.

Need a Portable Reloading Bench?

Sometime back you responded to an apartment-dweller who was in need of a sturdy reloading bench that could be taken down or folded for storage under the bed or in a closet. Several years ago I found myself in that same situation and solved my dilemma by purchasing a Work Mate Bench made by Black & Decker. The bench is very strong and leaving a reloading press mounted on it doesn't interfere with its folding up for storage. To increase the size of its work area during use, I simply clamp a small piece of plywood in its vise. I also find it easier to mount other items such as a case trimmer and powder measure to small pieces of plywood so they can be quickly and easily attached to or removed from the vise. The Work Mate is available at many hardware and home improvement stores.

I'm sure your tip will be appreciated by others who are cramped for space. Thanks very much for taking the time to write.

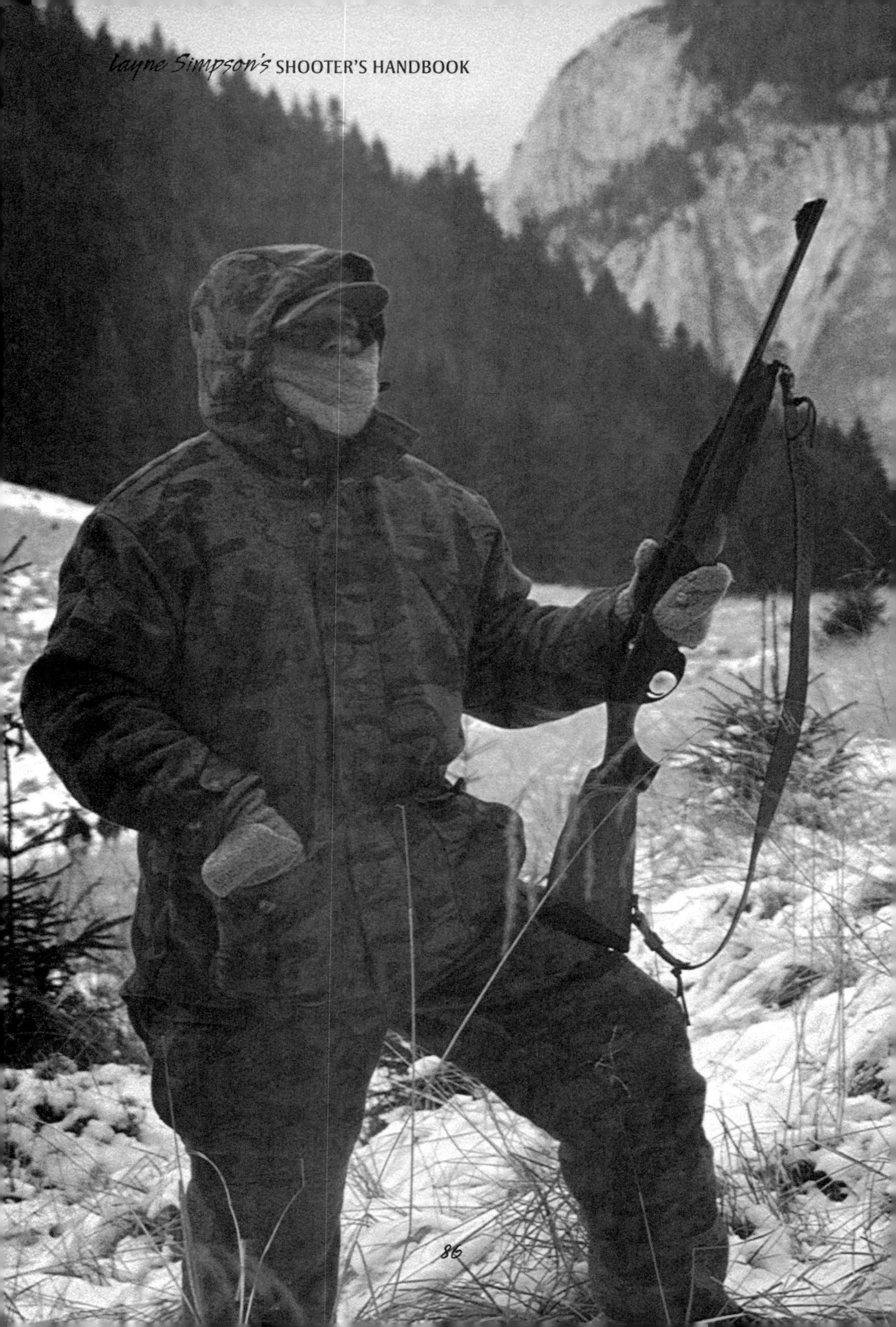

It took some mighty good boots to keep my feet warm on this mid-winter hunt in the Transylvania mountains of Romania.

Best Subzero-Weather Footwear?

I realize your writing is mostly devoted to the shooting sports and you seldom ever touch on such things as hunting clothing but I hope you will make an exception just this one time and help me out with a problem. I often hunt deer from treestands in subzero temperatures and am usually able to keep everything but my feet reasonably warm. Since you have hunted all over the country I'd like to know which boots are the warmest you have ever worn?

The warmest boots I currently own are made for ice fishing and available from Sorel. They are all rubber and in addition to having the latest in space-age insulation, they also have removable insulated bootees or liners and air bob-style soles. They are the best I have found for sitting in extremely cold weather but their weight and bulk rule them out for walking more than short distances.

How Do I Reduce Recoil?

I suffer from a joint problem that makes me quite sensitive to recoil. I bought a Browning Eclipse in 300 Winchester Magnum and plan to use it on everything from deer to elk. Its BOSS reduces recoil some and I plan to have a Pachmayr Decelerator recoil pad installed but even then, recoil is likely to be a bit much. What else can I do to my rifle to reduce its kick?

The easiest and least expensive way to reduce recoil is to increase the weight of the laminated wood stock of your rifle. This can be done by drilling several large holes deep into its buttstock and filling them with lead shot prior to installing the new recoil pad. Additional weight can be added by drilling shallow half-inch holes in the barrel channel of the stock and gluing in a row of 50-caliber lead bullets that can be found at most muzzleloader supply shops.

Aftermarket Stock for Ruger 96/44?

My wife (bless her) bought me a Ruger Model 96/44. It is a very nice little carbine, one that should prove about perfect for the deer hunting I do, but it could use three improvements. One is cut checkering on the wrist and forearm of its stock. That would make it easier to hang onto when shooting with cold, wet hands. The Ruger also needs sling swivels, as any hunting rifle does. Lastly, its curved steel buttplate makes the gun less than comfortable to shoot, a

Perceived recoil can be reduced in several ways.

problem a good recoil pad would solve. Do you think Ruger will ever make these improvements to its little woods gun? Or perhaps even better, is an aftermarket stock with those features available?

I wouldn't be surprised to someday see a "Deluxe" version of the Ruger 96/44 become available with the features you desire but your guess is as good as mine as to when it might happen. Sorry, but at this time I know of no sources of aftermarket stocks for that rifle. Another possibility is to dress up the factory stock. You could have a gunsmith install Uncle Mike's quick-detach sling swivels on it, or you might consider doing the job yourself with tools available from that company. Replacing the curved steel buttplate with a recoil pad can be done but it is likely to be rather expensive due to the shape of the stock in that area. As for checkering the stock, try Sherry Abraham out in Mulino, Ore., who, I am told, was the head checkerer for Kimber before that firm relocated to New York. You can contact her at 503-632-4010. She might also know someone in her area who can install a recoil pad on the stock.

7mm STW Rifles?

I have long been a fan of the 280 Remington cartridge but have decided to shop around for a rifle in 7mm STW. What options in rifle models do the major manufacturers offer in this caliber?

More variations of the Sako Model 75 are catalogued in 7mm STW than any other rifle: Hunter, Deluxe, Super Deluxe, Synthetic/Stainless, Euro, Battue, Carbine and Varmint. Remington offers the 7mm STW chambering in its Sendero and BDL Stainless Synthetic variations of the Model 700. From Remington's custom shop you can get the 40-XB in that caliber as well as three versions of the Model 700-KS Mountain Rifle, African Plains Rifle and Alaskan Wilderness Rifle. As Model 70 variations from U.S. Repeating Arms go, you have a choice of the Ultimate Classic and Custom Sporting Sharpshooter II from that company's custom shop or standard production Model 70s such as the Classic Sporter (with or without the BOSS) and Classic Laredo (fluted or nonfluted barrel). As Weatherby rifles go, you can buy the Mark V Accumark in 7mm STW.

Where Can I Get a Steel Triggerguard for the Model 70?

After drooling all over a photo of your custom Winchester Model 70, I decided to have a custom rifle built just like it. I want to use a current Winchester Model 70 action but since a custom rifle deserves more than its aluminum trigger guard I'd like to know where you got the one made of steel for your rifle.

The steel trigger guard on my rifle came from Brownells and you are correct – any custom rifle deserves its quality. For the benefit of others who simply want to replace the aluminum trigger guards on their factory Model 70s with steel, I'll mention that it drops right in with no modifications to the action or stock required. Four options are available: in-the-white (no finish), high-gloss or bead-blasted blued finishes, and stainless steel with a brushed finish.

Who Makes Strap-On Recoil Pad?

While at my gun club a few days ago l noticed a fellow shooting a rifle in 458 Winchester Magnum from a benchrest. When l asked him how he was able to tolerate the recoil he pointed to a thick recoil pad strapped to his shoulder. l checked the gunshop where he said he had purchased the item a couple of years previous but a salesman there had never heard of it. Any idea where l could find such a device?

The strap-on recoil shield that fellow was wearing on his shoulder was probably made by PAST. It is available in four thicknesses with the Field, Magnum and Mag Plus being ambidextrous. The thickest of the four, the Super Mag, is designed to ease the pain of shooting extremely powerful belted magnums such as the 458 Winchester and 460 Weatherby and is available only for right-hand shooters. PAST also makes its Black Powder and Heraean Shield models, the latter an ambi design made to be worn beneath clothing by women. The company also offers other excellent products such as padded leather shooting gloves, shooting vests for trap, skeet and sporting clays, turkey vests and range bags. A catalog is available from PAST Sporting Goods.

Parts for Remington 788

In a past issue of your magazine a reader asked about parts for the Remington Model 788 rifle in 30-30 and 44 Magnum calibers. Please be advised that a number of replacement parts are custom-made for that rifle (using original Remington specifications) by Russell Sports, Dept. ST, Box 40, Ozark, AL 36361. Also, Buddy's Custom Guns has extractors for Model 788 rifles in 30-30 and 44 Magnum.

Thanks very much for some information I'm sure owners of Model 788 rifles in those calibers will be happy to have.

Who Made 358 STA Stock?

Sometime back l saw a photo of your custom Remington Model 700 in 358 Shooting Times Alaskan and really liked the looks of its synthetic stock. Who made it?

As synthetic rifle stocks go for big-game rifles go, the one on my 358 STA is my all-time favorite style. Made by McMillan, it is called the Griffin & Howe pattern.

A Rifle Built for Smith & Wesson?

Sometime back l added a used rifle to my battery and would like some information on it. It is a Smith & Wesson Model 1700LS in 30-06 caliber. What can you tell me about it?

Your rifle was built for Smith & Wesson by the Japanese firm of Howa during the 1980s. Three grades of stocks were available and they ranged in quality from the least expensive standard Model 1500 to the mid-priced Model 1500 Deluxe to the most expensive version, the Model 1700LS, which listed for $479.95 in 1985. The action of your rifle is basically the same as the one Howa once built for the Weatherby Vanguard series of rifles. A S&W Model 1500 in 270 Winchester I once owned was extremely accurate and would average around three-quarters of an inch at 100 yards with the Nosler 130-gr. Ballistic Tip seated atop a maximum charge of H4831.

History of Mauser 22 Rimfire?

I recently acquired a bolt action single-shot rifle in 22 rimfire and its previous owner said that his father took it from a female sniper in Germany during World War II. The receiver is marked "ERMA" as well as "Waffenfabrik-Erfurt Modell E36." What can you tell me about this rifle?

Your rifle was manufactured during the late 1930s or early 1940s by the German firm of ERMA. Sporter and military versions were produced, the latter with an extended stock and handguard. Other German firms including Mauser, Simson, Gustloff, Geco and Walther also produced basically the same rifle. If your rifle is the military version it was built for training purposes for use by the German army. It was once common for the military powers to adopt 22 rimfire rifles to be used for that purpose. In the United States we had the 1922 Springfield, a 22 caliber version of the 1903 Springfield. Great Britain also adopted a 22 rimfire version of its Lee Enfield.

Remington M7600 in 358 Magnum?

I hunt elk in Oregon. During hunting season the weather here is extremely wet so I was interested when you mentioned that in addition to being as accurate as most bolt action big-game rifles, Remington's Model 7600 pump gun with its enclosed receiver is also quite weatherproof. Soon after reading your article I bought one in 35 Whelen and find it to be perfect for most of the hunting I do. I would, however, like a bit more velocity for shots at long range. Since the Model 7600 is also chambered for high-pressure cartridges such as the 270 and 308 I'm wondering if maybe it can be converted to 358 Norma Magnum. What do you think?

While the Model 7600 is probably strong enough to handle the 358 Norma Magnum, the difficulty of converting one to that cartridge would make its cost prohibitive, not to mention extremely impractical. In addition to rechambering, the bolt face would have to be opened up and modifying the magazine to handle the larger belted case would be an absolute nightmare, even if it could be done.

Your best bet for a velocity increase is to have your rifle rechambered for the 35 Brown Whelen, an improved version of the 35 Whelen. The velocity potential of that cartridge is only about 150 fps shy of what is practical with the 358 Norma Magnum and rechambering is the only modification that would need to be made to your Model 7600. Reloading dies for the 35 Brown Whelen are available from Redding and RCBS and starting loads listed in various handloading manuals for the 35 Whelen can be used for load development.

We Had One Too

Sometime back you wrote about a barrel-attachment device that enabled German troops to fire their submachine guns around the corner of a building without exposing themselves to the target. You might be interested in knowing that the U.S. Army also had such a device for the 45-caliber grease gun. I don't know when it was adopted but our reserve Recon Company in San Bernardino had several in its armory in the early 1960s.

Thanks for the additional information. I'm sure the military weapons enthusiasts among our readers will be quite interested.

How Should I Check the Accuracy of My Rifle?

I am new to deer hunting and am a bit confused over how I should check out the accuracy of my Ruger Model 77 in 243 Winchester. When shooting a group should I allow the barrel to cool down between each shot or between each group of shots? How many shots should I fire in each group?

The most important thing to know about a big-game rifle is where it places its first bullet from a cold barrel. This is what you are accomplishing when allowing the barrel of your Model 77 to cool down between shots. As for checking the accuracy of your rifle, it is best to fire three shots as rapidly as possible since that more closely simulates what might happen in the field should you miss with your first shot. You would then allow the barrel to cool down completely prior to firing the next group. There are those who prefer to fire five-shot groups but I let each rifle decide. If a rifle proves to be incapable of consistently shooting 100-yard groups measuring less than 1-1/2 inches I will fire five shots per group. If it is capable of shooting groups measuring less than 1-1/2 inches I fire only three shots. Firing three-shot groups uses less ammo, heats up the barrel more slowly and will tell you everything you need to know about the accuracy of a good big-game rifle.

When Was My Kodiak Rifle Made?

I recently bought a semiautomatic rifle in 22 WMR made by Kodiak Arms. Its quality is excellent and it has proven to be reliable with a variety of ammunition. What level of accuracy should it be capable of? When was my rifle made?

The Kodiak Model 260 was introduced in the early 1960s and it was the first semiautomatic rifle of American manufacture to be offered in 22 WMR. A steel inertia block housed in the forearm of the rifle and connected to its bolt by a couple of steel rods enables it to handle the increased backthrust of the 22 WMR cartridge (as compared to the 22 Long Rifle cartridge, for which the same basic rifle was also built). I never had the opportunity to fire a Kodiak Model 260 but do recall that a friend who owned one was extremely proud of his. His rifle wore a Weaver K8 scope and if memory serves me correctly, it would average two to three inches for five shots at 100 yards with Winchester ammo.

How Do I Stop Cases from Swelling Up in a British Enfield?

When 303 factory ammunition is fired in my British Enfield, a case emerges from the chamber all swelled up in front of its rim. On top of that, fired primers have backed partially out of their pockets. Is that normal for an Enfield or is it a sign that my rifle is worn out?

Your rifle is showing signs of excessive headspace and I recommend that you stop shooting it until the condition is corrected. This is one of the biggest weaknesses in the Enfield rifle design but fortunately its designers allowed for it by making the head of the bolt easy to replace. They also designed a series of interchangeable bolt heads that vary by .003 inch in length. First you should have a gunsmith determine to what degree headspace is excessive in your rifle. If, for example, it needs to be snugged by, say, .006 inch, you will have to round up a bolt head that much longer than the one now in your rifle. Extra bolt heads for the Enfield rifle are not as easily found as they once were but you might luck out and find a dealer in military surplus parts who advertises in *Gun List* or *Shotgun News* who has just what you need.

What Cartridges Has Savage 99 Been Chambered for?

I have never had a lot of interest in collecting rifles but the recent acquisition of a 1950s vintage Savage Model 99 in 250-3000 Savage has gone a long way toward sparking my interest in doing so. If I decided to round up a Model 99 in every chambering it has been made in, how big would my collection be?

According to my research the Savage 99 has been offered in 15 different standard-production chamberings. Beginning with the smallest caliber and working up, they are the 22-250 Remington, 22 High Power, 243 Winchester, 25-35 Winchester, 250-3000 Savage, 7mm-08 Remington, 284 Winchester, 30-30 Winchester, 303 Savage, 300 Savage, 308 Winchester, 32-40 Winchester, 358 Winchester, 38-55 Winchester, 375 Winchester and the 2-1/2-inch 410 shotshell. The 410 chambering was commonly offered as an extra-barrel option for Model 99 takedown rifles and also in a cased two-barrel set with the other barrel chambered for the 300 Savage cartridge.

Who Can Rebarrel My Marlin 336 to 7mm STE?

I plan to have a Marlin Model 336 rebarreled for your 7mm Shooting Times Easterner. What other lever-action rifles can be converted? I read your original article on the cartridge in Shooting Times but have misplaced it. Who can rebarrel my rifle? Where do I find load data? How fast is the 7mm STE with various bullet weights?

My Marlin 336 was originally in 356 Winchester and was rebarreled by Harry McGowen of McGowen Rifle Barrels, 5961 Spruce Lane., St. Anne, IL 60964. Harry did an excellent job for me and I'm sure he will do the same for you. Any modern Marlin 336 or Winchester 94 of current production in 30-30 Winchester, 307 Winchester, 356 Winchester or 444 Marlin can be converted to 7mm STE by rebarreling. Load data for the Nosler 120-gr. and Hornady 139-gr. flatnose bullets

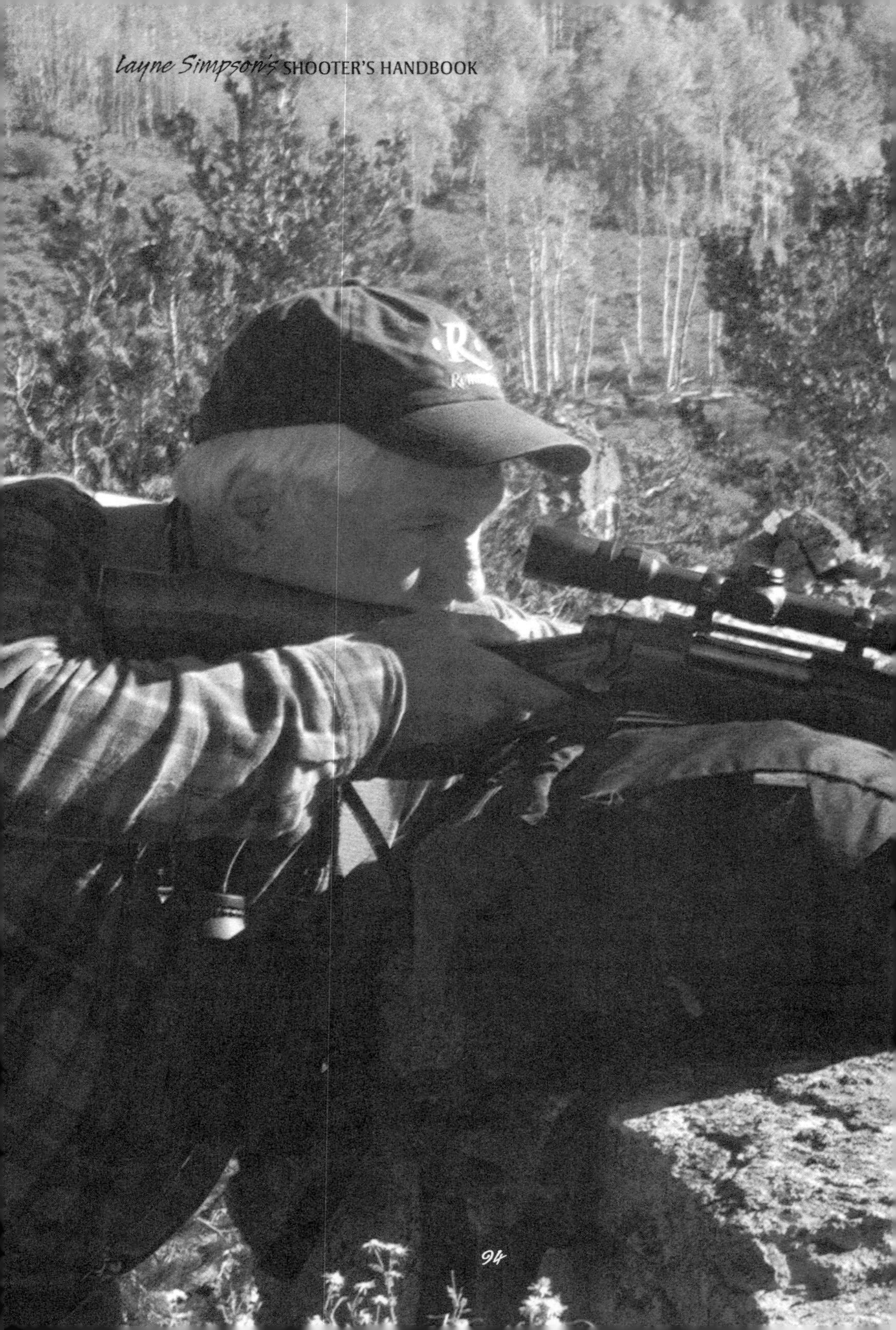

How Much Do I Compensate When Shooting Uphill and Downhill?

As a big-game hunter I realize that a bullet does not drop as much when fired either uphill or downhill at a sharp angle as it does when fired from a rifle that is held perfectly horizontal. How do I figure out how much I should compensate for this difference in trajectory?

When the barrel of a rifle is positioned either above or below the horizontal, the effect of gravity on the trajectory of a bullet in relation to the line of sight is lessened. For this reason, the amount you would need to compensate for when shooting either uphill or downhill depends on the angle of the barrel when the bullet is fired. Multipliers that can be used to adjust the slant range of the target for angles up to 45 degrees are as follows:

Up or Downhill Slope Angle In Degrees	Slant Range Multiplier
5	.99
10	.98
15	.96
20	.94
25	.91
30	.87
35	.82
40	.77
45	.70

When shooting uphill or downhill at, for example, a 30-degree angle, and the slant range to the target is, say, 300 yards, you would hold as if the target were 261 yards away on the horizontal. Increase the slope to 45 degrees and you would hold on that same target as if it were 210 yards away. At reasonable ranges all of this can be ignored so long as you are zeroed properly, hunt with a flat-shooting rifle and use a dead-center hold on the target. For example, if the 270 Winchester loaded with a 130-gr. spitzer at 3100 fps is zeroed three inches high at 100 yards it will place its bullet about three inches high at 210 yards and about an inch low at 300. As you can see, with a dead-center hold on of the vital area of a deer you will hit your mark regardless of whether the animal is standing 300 yards away on the horizontal or the same distance away at a downhill (or uphill) angle as great as 45 degrees.

are available in the Hodgdon reloading manual. Starting loads shown for the 139-gr. bullet can also be used for the new Speer 130-gr. flatnose bullet. Maximum velocities in the 22-inch barrel of my rifle are 2900, 2800 and 2700 fps, respectively, for the 120-, 130- and 139-gr. bullets. When the 120-gr. Nosler is zeroed three inches high at 100 yards it is about two inches high at 200 yards and about eight inches low at 300 where it is still packing almost 1100 foot-pounds of energy.

When Was My Ithaca Lever-Action 22 Made?

I recently bought a Ithaca lever-action rifle in 22 WMR that looks a lot like the Winchester Model 94. When was it made and what did it cost?

Ithaca introduced its 22-caliber lever-action repeater during the early 1970s and it was manufactured until about the mid-1980s. It sold for $99.95 in 1975 and was built to compete with the Marlin 39A, Browning BL-22 and Winchester 94/22 which were also around in those days.

Is the Scout Rifle Concept Really a New Idea?

I am puzzled by those who seem to consider the so-called scout rifle with its forward-mounted scope a new and novel idea. Back in the 1960s I owned a Winchester Model 94 equipped with a Redfield extended eye relief scope mounted on its barrel. I really didn't like the concept back then and still don't today.

Mounting a long eye relief scope out on the barrel of a rifle is a very old idea. I have no idea who was first to try it but do know that some of the Model 1898 rifles used by German snipers during World War II had that type of scope attached out on the barrel at the rear sight. In addition to the Winchester Model 94, the Redfield Frontier scope you mentioned was also available for the Remington Model 600 bolt-action carbine.

What Advantage Short-Action Rifle?

So much ado is being made over bolt-action rifles with short actions I decided to give a Winchester Model 70 in 7mm WSM a try. It is a nice rifle but I have yet to discover anything I can do with it that I couldn't do equally well or perhaps even better with my old long-action Model 700 in 7mm Remington Magnum. Am I missing something here?

From a practical point of view the only advantage a short-action rifle has over one with a long action is it is a bit lighter and ever so slightly shorter overall. The short Model 70 action is about three ounces lighter and about an inch shorter than the long Model 70 action. Whether or not this is important is for the fellow who is buying the rifle to decide. Some say the shorter bolt travel of the short action makes it quicker to operate but I have hunted extensively with rifles with actions of both lengths and have yet to discover this to be true. The thing that appeals most to me about a short-action bolt gun is its balance point is often just enough farther toward the rear to make it handle and feel somewhat better than the same rifle with a long action.

Why Is Weatherby Mark V So Much Lighter in 30-06?

I am shopping for a Weatherby Mark V rifle and am a bit confused by the weights I have seen listed for it. According to what I have read, the Mark V Ultra Lightweight (which I intend to buy) weighs 6-3/4 pounds in 300 Weatherby Magnum but only 5-3/4 pounds in 30-06 Springfield. Please explain how this can be.

Weatherby rifles chambered for all magnum cartridges except the 240 Weatherby are built around the original magnum-size Mark V action. Those chambered for the 240 Weatherby Magnum and all standard cartridges from the 243 Winchester up through the 338-06 A-Square are on the newer standard-size Mark V action. Since the standard action is smaller, it weighs about 3/4-pound less than the magnum action. This, plus the use of a barrel of slightly lighter contour on the standard rifle, allows Weatherby to build it a pound lighter than the magnum rifle.

Who Built My Weatherby Mark XXII?

I have a Weatherby Mark XXII autoloader in 22 Long Rifle. In addition to being the most handsome rifle I own it is also one of the more accurate. Engraved on its receiver is "Made In Italy." Who made this rifle for Weatherby?

Your Weatherby Mark XXII (pronounced Mark 22) was built sometime between 1964 and 1971 by the Italian firm of Beretta. From the time of its introduction in 1964 until it was discontinued in 1988 the Weatherby autoloader was also manufactured in the United states by Mossberg (during 1981 and 1982) and by three Japanese companies, KTG (from 1967 to 1971), Nikko (1972-1980) and Howa (1984-1988). Like your rifle, all Mark XXIIs made by Beretta and KTG have a detachable box magazine while that style as well as another with a tubular magazine were built by the three other manufacturers. With a stock that just about duplicated the looks of Weatherby's Mark V centerfire rifle in those days, the Mark XXII can only be described as the classiest 22 rimfire autoloader ever built.

What Bullet For My M1903 Mannlicher-Schoenauer?

My favorite deer and black bear rifle is Model 1903 Mannlicher-Schoenauer in 6.5x54mm that belonged to my great-grandfather. I would like to reload a supply of cases I have accumulated through the years and hope you will advise me on what bullet I should use.

Any bullet measuring .264-inch in diameter from Nosler, Swift, Hornady, Speer and Sierra is the correct size for your rifle. If you have a scope on your carbine or if it has adjustable sights, the Nosler 125-gr. Partition would be an excellent choice for deer but for bear I would move up in weight to the 140-gr. Partition. If your rifle wears no scope and its sights are not adjustable for elevation, it was likely regulated at the factory with a 160-gr. bullet and may not shoot bullets of lighter weights to point of aim. Should that be the case, roundnose bullets of that weight from Hornady and Sierra are your only choices as far as American manufacturers go.

What Type of Firearm was Daisy Ammo Made for?

I am a 73-year-old hunter who knows a bit about firearms but someone recently gave me some ammunition that has me stumped. Made by Daisy, it is 22-caliber and the bullet has a pad of light-colored material at its rear end rather than a brass case. What can you tell me about this most unusual ammo and the firearm it was designed for?

The V/L caseless ammunition you have was introduced during the late 1960s by air rifle maker Daisy/Heddon of Rogers, Arkansas. It was named after its developer Van Langenhoven. The pad of material fastened to the base of the 22 caliber projectile is a special propellant which is ignited by a jet of hot air produced by the Daisy Model 002 single-shot rifle in which the ammo is fired. Pulling the trigger of the cocked rifle allows a spring-powered piston located inside its receiver to move quickly forward to compress air trapped inside a special chamber but something else also takes place when the trigger is pulled. The designer of the system knew that when air is compressed quite rapidly it heats up and can reach temperatures as high as 2000 degrees Fahrenheit. So, in addition to causing the air inside its chamber to become almost instantly compressed that same

The fixed sight of my Model 1903 Mannlicher-Schoenauer requires that I shoot only 160-grain bullets in it.

pull on the trigger also releases a small high-speed jet of the heated air, allowing it make contact with the propellant charge at the base of the caseless ammo and thereby igniting it. A check valve in the end of the chamber prevented the propellant gas from flowing in the wrong direction. Contrary to how my description might sound, the entire firing process took place rather quickly as locktime of the rifle was measured by Daisy at less than six milliseconds. Muzzle velocity of the 29-grain lead bullet was rated at 1150 fps which just about duplicated the performance of 22 Short ammunition. While a novel idea, the entire system is probably best described as the answer to a question no one had ever asked or even cared about.

Did Sako Make the Marlin Model 322?

I just bought a Marlin Model 322 bolt-action rifle with a 24-inch heavy barrel in .222 Remington. The action is marked "Sako Riihimaki" and "Made In Finland." Why did Marlin have Sako build this rifle?

Marlin produced its Model 322 rifle from 1954 until 1956 and only the action was made by Sako of Riihimaki, Finland. Back in those days a number of companies built rifles around Sako actions, another being Browning. Your rifle is built on the Sako L46 action and was introduced by Marlin in 1954. Sako has not manufactured that action since 1964 so some of its parts are not easy to find. You most definitely do not want to let that detachable magazine go astray! Incidentally, a similar Marlin rifle called the Model 422 replaced the Model 322 in 1956 but it was dropped in 1958. One difference between the two is the Model 322 has Marlin's Micro-Groove rifling whereas the Model 422 is rifled with the more conventional six lands and grooves.

Can a Model 70 in 264 Magnum Be Rechambered to 6.5 STW?

A Winchester Model 70 in 264 Magnum I now own was purchased by a friend in 1962. The bore of the rifle is in excellent condition but extensive nicks, dings and wear on its wood and metal prevent it from having any collector value. I have decided to have its metal refinished in electroless nickel and intend to replace its stock with one made of fiberglass from McMillan. Another thing I would like to do is have the rifle rechambered to your 6.5 STW. Will it work? How fast will the 6.5 STW be in my rifle when loaded with a 140-gr. bullet?

Just as a rifle in 7mm Remington Magnum is easily rechambered to 7mm STW, so it goes with converting a rifle in 264 Winchester Magnum to 6.5 STW. You will have to switch out the magazine box in your rifle for one made for the 300 H&H Magnum or 375 H&H Magnum but other than that and rechambering nothing else needs to be done. Rifles chambered for any cartridge can vary considerably in velocity but the 6.5 STW should safely reach 3300 fps with 140-gr. bullets in your 26-inch barrel. I recently shot a Rifles, Inc. Model 700 with a Shilen barrel of the same length and it averaged just over 3350 fps with a maximum but safe charge of Reloder 25 behind the 140-gr. Nosler Partition.

Load for Savage Model 20?

I recently inherited a Savage Model 20 in 250-3000 Savage and would like to use handloads with 120-gr. bullets in it. Is the rifling twist of its barrel fast enough to stabilize a bullet that long?

I doubt if the rifling twist of your barrel is quick enough to stabilize a 120-grain bullet but there two ways to find out for certain. One way is to actually shoot that bullet weight on paper. Another way is to check its rifling twist rate yourself. If the twist turns out to be slower than 1:10 inches it probably won't work with any pointed bullet weighing much over 100 grains.

Which Rifle Bipod Is Best?

I shoot groundhogs a lot in West Virginia and want to purchase a folding bipod for my Weatherby rifle in 220 Swift. Which of the many models available will best suit my needs?

Folding bipod designs come and go but the original Harris bipod which is made in Kentucky is still the best available in my book. Another company has tried to copy the design but a close look reveals they fell short on quality. Since you will most likely be resting your rifle on uneven ground, the "S" version of the Harris bipod with its swiveling top is your best bet.

Made in Kentucky, the original Harris bipod is still the best available.

What Can You Tell Me about My Marlin Model 336?

I recently bought a Marlin Model 336 in 30-30 but unlike all other Marlin deer rifles I have seen, it has a 24-inch barrel, short magazine, checkered stock and detachable sling swivels that appear to have been factory-installed. The rifle is like new and shoots two-inch groups at 100 yards with factory ammo. What can you tell me about it?

The Marlin you have is a Model 336A-DL and is but one of several similar Model 336 variants built in 30-30, 32 Winchester Special and 35 Remington. Your rifle is one of 39,290 Model 336As built from 1953 to 1980. All have 24-inch barrels, two-thirds length magazines and buttstocks with curved grips but only the DL (Deluxe) version left the factory with checkered buttstock and forearm. The Model 36A was obviously Marlin's answer to Winchester's Model 64 lever action since the two share similar styling. I am quite fond of that style of rifle and hope to see both companies bring those two models back to their lines someday.

How Can My Browning Be in 22-250?

My father recently gave me a Browning Safari Grade rifle in 22-250. He swears he bought the rifle in 1961 but according to my research Remington did not introduce the 22-250 cartridge until 1967. How can my dad's old varmint rifle be chambered for a cartridge that didn't exist when it was built.

Remington did not introduce the 22-250. Instead, in 1967 the company domesticated a wildcat that had been around since the 1930s. As odd as it might sound today, Browning began offering the 22-250 chambering in its rifles at least seven years before Remington domesticated it. Back then, owners of those rifles formed cases by necking down 250 Savage brass to 22 caliber. RCBS also offered a set of form dies designed to make 22-250 cases from 30-06 brass.

How Do l Remove Grease from Military Surplus Rifles?

A friend and l recently bought a couple of '98 Mauser rifles and both arrived covered with a thick coat of heavy grease. The bores of their barrels are also full of the messy stuff. How do we remove it?

I recently received a mint-condition Persian Mauser from Samco Global Arms and after completely disassembling the bolt and removing the barreled action from the stock I degreased all the parts with Shooters Choice Shotgun and Choke Tube Cleaner (from Ventco Industries, 16770 Hilltop Park Place, Chagrin Falls, OH 44023). Any good solvent will do but in addition to dissolving the grease, that product's aerosol can makes it easy to spray into nooks and crannies of the bolt body and receiver. An old tooth brush was also used to apply the solvent and paper towels were used to wipe off the metal. For removing grease from the bore I first sprayed solvent in from its breech and muzzle ends and then mopped it out by pushing through dry cotton patches with a cleaning rod. I performed the entire job out of doors and wore protective rubber gloves.

Which Barrel Length Should l Choose?

l want to buy a light and compact walk-around type varmint rifle in 22-250. l had pretty much decided on a Ruger Model 77 with a 22-inch barrel and then my dealer showed me a Remington Model Seven with a 20-inch barrel. l actually prefer the Remington but am concerned about velocity loss with its shorter barrel. l realize I'll lose some bullet speed by going with two inches less barrel but since the maximum range l usually shoot seldom exceeds 150 yards, is it enough to make any practical difference in the field? I'm not seeking any endorsement for one brand of rifle over another—just your opinion on velocity loss with the shorter barrel.

Due to variations in chamber and bore dimensions among rifles, it is possible for a 20-inch barrel to deliver the same (or higher) velocities than a 22-inch barrel but assuming that everything is equal (and it seldom is), you will give up anywhere from 40 to 60 feet per second by going with two inches less barrel.

A rifle like this Cooper in 17 Remington is very accurate and shoots flat, and almost nonexistent recoil makes it fun to shoot.

A Varmint Rifle in 17 Remington?

I own a rifle in 17 HMR and while it is a great close-range varmint rifle, it begins to run out of steam on prairie dogs at about 125 yards. I am trying to convince myself that I need a rifle that shoots flatter and hits harder and am about convinced the 17 Remington is the next cartridge for me. What rifle should I buy?

The 17 Remington is great fun to shoot simply because its almost total lack of recoil will allow you to see your bullet strike the target right there inside the scope. Contrary to all the hoopla about the 204 Ruger, the 17 Remington is still the fastest gun in the west. It is loaded by Remington with two bullet weights, the original 25-gr. hollowpoint at 4040 fps and the more recent 20-gr. AccuTip at 4250 fps. Zero either load two inches high at 100 yards and its bullet is just about dead on point of aim at 300 yards. The most accurate rifle in this caliber I have ever shot is the Cooper and therefore it is the one you should buy. With my handload and the 30-gr. Berger bullet, my Cooper seldom shoots five-shot groups larger than half an inch at 100 yards.

What Propellant for Inline Muzzleloader?

I recently bought a Thompson/Center 50-caliber inline muzzleloader and a variety of saboted bullets from various manufacturers. I must now decide which propellant to use. What do you recommend?

Most who hunt with 50-caliber inline muzzleloaders use either Pyrodex Pellets or Triple 7 pellets. Thompson/Center approves the use of three 50-gr. pellets of either propellant for a total charge weight of 150.0 grains. Some muzzleloaders are quite accurate when burning that much powder behind some saboted bullets. Other rifle/bullet combinations do not shoot accurately unless a plastic sub-base available from MMP is placed between bullet and powder during the loading process.

Where Can I Get a Remington Model 760 in 35 Whelen?

Seems like I'm always a day late and a dollar short and now I have waited for Remington to discontinue the 35 Whelen chambering in its Model 760 pump gun before deciding that I absolutely cannot live without one. Assuming that my luck in finding one on the used gun market doesn't change for the better, what are my alternatives?

While Remington did not make a great number of Model 760s in 35 Whelen, I'll be surprised if you don't eventually find a used one gathering dust in some gunshop. Failing that, you could round up a Model 760 in 35 Remington, have it rechambered to 35 Whelen, shorten the tail on its bolt carrier for the longer cartridge and buy a detachable magazine made for either the 35 Whelen or the 30-06 Springfield. Another (and considerably more expensive) possibility is to have a rifle in 270, 280 or 30-06 rebored and rechambered to 35 Whelen although I know of no one who does that type of work on the Model 760.

Advantages of Single-Shot Rifles?

I realize single-shot rifles of dropping-block design like the Ruger No. 1 and Dakota Model 10 lack the firepower of the various types of repeating rifles, but other than being the most handsome of all sporting rifles, what other advantage does the single-shot rifle offer to the hunter?

The short action of the single-shot rifle allows the use of a long barrel for maximum velocity while keeping the overall length of the rifle quite manageable. I consider this to be its most worthwhile advantage. As an example, I have a Ruger No. 1S with a 26-inch barrel which was rechambered from 7mm Remington Magnum to 7mm STW. At 42-1/2 inches, it is almost two inches shorter than my Remington Model 700 with a 24-inch barrel in the same caliber. In other words, the Ruger single-shot could wear a 28-inch barrel and be no longer than a bolt gun with a 24-inch barrel.

Who Makes a Match-Grade Autoloading Rifle in 22 WMR?

A custom-modified H&K semiautomatic rifle in 22 WMR I once owned was capable of shooting five shots close to an inch at 100 yards with Winchester ammo but I foolishly sold it. During the past six months I have seriously bench-tested 22 WMR autoloaders made by several different companies and while all are nice rifles and plenty accurate for hunting, neither is capable of equaling the accuracy of the discontinued H&K rifle. Does anyone today make a super-accurate, match-grade 22 WMR semiautomatic?

It might be possible to install a match-grade barrel with minimum-dimension chamber on the Remington or Ruger autoloader and come up with a 22 WMR capable of duplicating the accuracy of the custom H&K rifle you owned. The only autoloader I know of that will do just that out of the box is available from the Carroll, Iowa, firm of Volquartsen Custom. It uses the rotary magazine Ruger makes for its autoloader, but the receiver of the Volquartsen rifle is precision-machined from stainless steel rather than aluminum. It also has a match-grade, air-gauged barrel, is guaranteed to average

A single-shot rifle like the Dakota Model 10 I used to take this nice pronghorn offers one big advantage over the repeaters.

3/4-inch or smaller groups for five shots at 100 yards with good ammunition. I have a Volquartsen switch-barrel rifle with barrels in 22 WMR and 17 HMR and it is superbly accurate. The same company also offers fine-tuned Ruger 10/22s in 22 Long Rifle and 17 Mach 2 capable of averaging less than half an inch at 50 yards. Also available from Volquartsen is the easily installed TG/2000 match-grade trigger housing/magazine release/adjustable trigger system for the Ruger 10/22.

How Good Is the Springfield M1A?

I have a Springfield, Inc., M1A target rifle with a 308-caliber air-gauged barrel, match-grade trigger, upgraded gas assembly, heavy match stock and Springfield 6x scope. I waited for years to own just such an outfit and while I don't shoot competitively I enjoy punching paper with an accurate rifle. What is your opinion of Springfield's rifle? Sometime back you mentioned that you also shoot a Springfield match-grade M1A. How do you go about putting together a handload for it?

I have a very high opinion of all Springfield, Inc., firearms and am especially fond of a M1A match rifle much like yours. Mine is the Super Match version with heavy Hart barrel and fiberglass stock, and it wears a Leupold 6.5-20x scope. With the right load, it will shoot five bullets well under an inch all day long and my guess is yours will do as well. The most accurate load I have come up with to date for my rifle consists of the Federal case, Federal 210M primer, 44.0 grains of VARGET and the Sierra 168-gr. MatchKing or Nosler's 168-gr. J4 Competition bullet. When preparing a fired case for reloading, I first resize its neck only with a Redding bushing-style neck sizing die which contains a titanium nitride bushing .0025 to .003 inch smaller than the outside neck diameter of a loaded round. I then resize the body of the case with a Redding body-sizing die. Bullets are seated .010 inch shy of contact with the rifling with a micrometer-adjustable competition seating die, also made by Redding. Muzzle velocity averages around 2630 fps and five-shot, 100-yard groups seldom exceed .600 inch in size.

Why Marlin "New Model" 1895?

In several of your articles you have referred to the rifle Marlin currently catalogs as its 45-70 caliber Model 1895 as the New Model Marlin 1895. Please explain why you do this.

On several occasions I have explained in print why I use that description of the Marlin rifle and when it comes to matters of safety, I don't mind repeating myself. The rifle Marlin now catalogs as the Model 1895SS is actually the Model 336 which, due to its use of more modern, heat-treated steel alloy, is (in my opinion) better capable of withstanding high chamber pressures than the original Model 1895 introduced by Marlin during that year and discontinued around 1917. I consider this an especially important point to be stressed anytime high-pressure loadings of the 45-70 like those shown in various handloading manuals are mentioned. In other words, whenever I refer to such loads in print I want to make sure each and every reader understands they are intended for the current Marlin rifle in 45-70 and not for the one built close to 100 years ago. It might also be of interest to note that I did not originate the term "New Model 1895." Some of Marlin's first 1972 advertisements for its new 45-70 lever action rifle described it in exactly that manner; it is also described the same way by author William S. Brophy in his excellent book, *Marlin Firearms*.

SECTION TWO

Shotguns

How Far Will Lead Shot Travel?

When our gun club was built during the early 1950s it was out in the country, but it is now surrounded by a large residential area. The rather close proximity of those homes prompts me to ask this question: how far will lead shot fired from shotguns travel before hitting the ground?

The maximum range of lead shot will vary depending on a number of factors such as its initial velocity, shot size, wind velocity and direction, air density and the actual density of the lead used in forming the shot. All else being equal, when both exit the muzzle at the same velocity, large shot will travel farther than small shot because it is heavier and therefore loses its momentum more slowly. This is why most gun clubs prohibit the use of shot sizes larger than No. 7-1/2 for trap and skeet shooting.

Many years ago a French military officer by the name of Journee discovered that the approximate range of lead shot could be calculated by multiplying its diameter in inches by a constant of 2200. The diameter is obtained by the commonly used method of subtracting shot size from a constant of 17 to come up with a fraction of an inch. This gives us .11 inch for No. 6 shot and when that is multiplied by 2200 we come up with an approximate maximum range of 242 yards for that size shot when it is accelerated to common shotshell velocities and fired from a gun with its barrel elevated at an angle of 30 degrees. Using the same method to calculate the maximum range of the smaller No. 9 shot, we multiply .08 times 2200 and arrive at 176 yards.

Most gun clubs limit lead shot sizes to no larger than No. 7-1/2 due to the greater distances large shot can travel.

What Are Bore Diameters of Various Gauges?

I am a bit confused by the bore diameters of shotguns of various gauges. I recently read in one publication that the industry standard for the 12 gauge is .729 inch and in an article in another magazine the author stated the bore of the gun he had tested was .735 inch. What's going on here?

Standard bore diameters in the industry are .775 inch for the 10 gauge, .729 inch for the 12 gauge, .670 inch for the 16 gauge, .615 inch for the 20 gauge and .550 inch for the 28 gauge. Since .410 inch is the nominal bore diameter for the 410 shotshell it is correctly described as 410-caliber. The bores of shotgun barrels made in America are usually held close to those dimensions during their manufacture but the minimum-maximum tolerance range the various companies work within result in barrels that vary a bit. I have measured 410 barrels that measured as tight as .405 inch and as loose as .415 inch, but all delivered excellent patterns due to the fact that the concave base of the modern plastic shotshell wad is flexible enough to seal off powder gases during firing, even in an oversized bore. An extreme example of this takes place when a shotshell is fired in a barrel intentionally reamed to a considerably larger diameter than is standard for that gauge. This is commonly called overboring or backboring and the barrels of some 12-gauge guns will measure as large as .740 inch or more. The gun being described by the author of the article you read either had a backbored barrel or his measurement was a bit off.

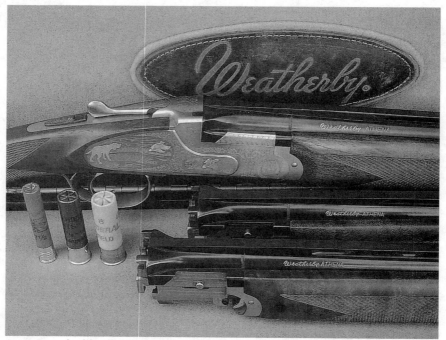

An over-under like this 20-gauge Weatherby Athena with extra barrels in .410 and 28 gauge is extremely versatile.

What Are the Advantages of Over-Under Shotguns with Extra Barrels?

I have noticed that Weatherby and Beretta offer over-under shotguns with an extra set of barrels in a different gauge. Other than the obvious advantage of costing less than two shotguns of different gauges, what other advantages are offered by that concept?

As you said, cost is the biggest advantage. As an example, the Beretta EELL Diamond Pigeon grade shotgun in 20 gauge with an extra set of 28-gauge barrels costs only 20 percent more than a gun with one set of barrels in either gauge and only about 60 percent as much as two guns in the two gauges. There is another advantage as well. If both sets of barrels are weighted properly, the gun will feel the same regardless of which barrels are being used. Several other companies also offer the extra-barrel option. The 20-gauge Weatherby Athena, for example, is available with two extra sets of barrels in 410 and 28 gauge.

How Should I Close a Double-Barrel Shotgun?

The author of an article I recently read emphasized that closing a double-barrel shotgun and allowing its top lever to slam to the locked position subjects the gun to unnecessary wear. He advocated easing the toplever to its locked position with the thumb. I have been shooting side-by-sides and over-unders for years and it has always been my practice to close the barrels and allow the toplever to snap into the locked position on its own. Three of my guns, a Winchester Model 21, a Browning Superposed and a Fox Sterlingworth, have seen over half a century of hard use in my hands and in my father's hands before me and while they still lock up tight as a tick the article has me wondering if maybe I should change my evil ways. What is your opinion on the subject?

When closed in the manner prescribed by the author of the article you read, the locking bolts of some modern double-barrel shotguns will not travel all the way to their locked position and this can subject the gun to unnecessary wear and possible damage when it is fired. Moreover, owner's manuals published by some shotgun manufacturers recommend that the toplever be allowed to snap smartly into the locked position on its own as the gun is closed. Slowing toplever travel with the thumb works fine on those guns so long as you remember to always give the lever a final nudge to make sure it seats all the way home prior to shooting the gun. It also depends on the gun. The toplevers of L.C. Smith and Fox doubles (which share the same rotary locking bolt design) have a tendency to snap violently to the locked position when the barrels are closed so in their case I make it a point to ease them closed with my thumb. Out of habit, I usually do the same when shooting any vintage double because some of them were made of softer steels than shotguns made today. The important thing to remember about any double is its barrels should be closed gently and not slammed to the closed position.

How Do l Measure the Amount of Choke in My Shotgun Barrels?

l own several shotguns and have been told that markings on them may not agree with the actual amount of constriction in their barrels. How do l measure choke constriction? What is the accepted amount of constriction for a specific choke designation?

The amount of choke in a barrel is easily measured with a bore gauge available from Brownells. It is basically a micrometer designed to measure the inside diameter of a tube and it comes in either dial indicator or digital styles. The one I have is called the Skeet's Shotgun Bore Gauge and it accurately measures the diameters of the chamber, forcing cone, primary bore and choked section of a barrel. To arrive at the amount of choke in a barrel simply measure its bore and choke diameters and then subtract the latter from the former. For example, if the bore of a 12-gauge gun measures .730 inch and the choke measures .700 inch the barrel has .030 inch of constriction which is Full choke by American standards. The following chart from Briley Manufacturing shows standard constrictions for the various choke designations.

BRILEY MANUFACTURING CHOKE CONSTRICTIONS		
	10/12/16 GAUGE	20/28 GAUGE	410 BORE
Light Skeet	.003	.003	.003
Skeet	.005	.005	.005
Improved Skeet	.007	.007	.007
Improved Cylinder	.010	.009	.008
Light Modified	.015	.012	.010
Modified	.020	.015	.012
Improved Modified	.025	.018	.014
Light Full	.030	.021	.016
Full	.035	.024	.018
Extra Full	.040	.027	.020

Should Shotgunner Hold High for Long-Range?

Rifle shooters are taught to hold higher to compensate for bullet drop when shooting at long range but l never see this mentioned by those who write about shotguns. Should the shotgunner hold high when shooting at long range?

As a rule, shotgunners need not be concerned with holdover for two reasons. For one, the shotgun is a close-range firearm and shot does not drop enough to really matter at the ranges at which it is used. For example, when a No. 8 lead pellet exits the muzzle at 1200 fps, it drops less than an inch at 20 yards and only about two inches at 30 yards. At the longer ranges at which game such as ducks and turkey are sometimes taken, drop is greater but holdover is still unnecessary since shot dispersion or actual pattern diameter increases as the range is increased.

Do Briley Full-Length Subgauge Tubes Really Work?

I have read about the subgauge tubes made by Briley Manufacturing and they sound like an excellent way to increase the versatility of shotgun. Are patterns shot with them are as good as those shot from a regular barrel without the tube installed?

Patterns fired with Briley subgauge tubes are as good and sometimes even better than those fired from barrels of the same gauge without the tubes installed. But you don't have to take my word for it; just ask the scores of top-ranked skeet shooters who win hundreds of tournaments each year with various 12-gauge over-under shotguns equipped with Briley tubes in 410, 20 and 28. I have Briley tubes in my skeet and trap guns and I also have them in a number of my hunting guns. Two pairs of tubes I have for my 20-gauge Browning Superposed allow me to also shoot 28-gauge and 410 shells in it. For my No. 1 grade AyA double in 28 gauge, I have 410 tubes. Those tubes are used only in those guns whereas Briley's Companion tubes can be used interchangeably in more than one gun of the same gauge. I use the same sets of 20-gauge and 28-gauge Companion tubes in my Fox Sterlingworth and Remington Model 3200 doubles. Briley's Companion tubes are a few ounces heavier than the Ultralight fitted tubes but they offer the advantage in working in more than one gun so long as their gauge is the same.

Will We Ever Get a Shotgun with Electronic Ignition?

I have a Remington EtronX rifle in 243 Winchester I and use it for both varmint shooting and deer hunting. I have hunted with my rifle in rain, snow and freezing cold and have yet to have a problem with it. Since Remington seems to have perfected the electronic ignition concept, do you think that company will be first to introduce a shotgun with the same type of ignition? I would really like to have a 20-gauge over-under of that type.

While I have received no official word on the subject from Remington either way, I would be surprised to see the company eventually introduce a shotgun with electronic ignition. I say this because the EtronX rifle has been less than a commercial success. I do, however, believe the concept has some merit, especially when applied to shotguns used for shooting trap and skeet. An over-under of that type is certainly possible, but so are autoloaders and slide actions. Actually, electrical ignition in a shotgun is far from new as the British experimented with the idea as far back as the nineteenth century. Later, during the 1950s, a French maker introduced a side-by-side double called the SMFM Electrique. It used a standard shotshell that differed only by its special primer.

What Shot Sizes for Hunting and Clay Target Shooting?

What shot sizes do you recommend for hunting rabbits and various game birds? I also plan to shoot skeet and trap with a new autoloader I just bought. What size shot do you use for those games?

Through the years I have settled on the following shot sizes for various applications. Some recommendations may not be exactly what is needed under special circumstances but, day in and day out, they have worked for me. A couple of clarifications are in order. The shot sizes I have recommended for body shots on turkey gobblers are to be used only where it is legal to use shot sizes that large on those birds. My recommendations for lead shot also apply to nontoxic shot with densities similar to that of lead. Tungsten-Matrix from Kent Cartridge and bismuth from Bismuth Cartridge are examples. Steel shot should be two sizes larger than shown for lead. For example, whereas I once used No. 4 lead shot on ducks I now use No. 2 steel.

	Close To Medium Range	Longer Range
Woodcock, snipe, rail & other small shore birds	9	8-1/2
Quail, doves (early season)	8	7-1/2
Quail, doves (late season)	7-1/2	7-1/2
Mountain quail	7-1/2	6
Grouse: ruffed, sharptail, spruce, ptarmigan	7-1/2	6
Pheasant	6	5
Sage grouse	5	4
Cottontail rabbit, squirrel	5	4
Swamp rabbit	4	4
Turkey; for shots to head & neck only	6	5
Turkey; for shots to body	2	BB
Skeet	9	NA
Trap	8	7-1/2
Sporting Clays	9	7-1/2

Origin of the Monte Carlo Stock

I recently purchased a Perazzi trap gun with a Monte Carlo stock. How did that style of stock get its name?

The Monte Carlo style of shotgun stock gets its name from the famous European country of Monaco, which is world-renowned for its live pigeon shooting. Competitors who often had a lot of money riding on each shot preferred the parallel comb of the original Monte Carlo design because vertical eye-to-barrel lineup remains the same regardless of whether the cheek is positioned forward or rearward on the stock. This style of stock is becoming quite popular with clay target shooters today and hunters are also taking a serious look at it.

Why Two "Spreader" Shells in Box of 12-Gauge Ammo?

While attending a recent gun show I purchased several old boxes of ammunition from a dealer who specializes in vintage collector-quality items. One box of 12-gauge shells I bought were Winchester target loads from the 1930s. Of the 25 shells in the box, 23 had the same markings but two were marked "Brush Load." What does that mean?

The brush load (or spreader load as it is more commonly called) has been offered by Winchester, Remington and Federal off and on for many years. Its purpose is to throw a pattern of larger diameter than a standard load. Winchester used an X-shaped cardboard divider in the shot charge while Remington divided the shot charge into three layers with thin cardboard wads. Both systems had the same effect and caused pellets in the charge to disperse more quickly after leaving the muzzle. Back when your box of 12-gauge target loads was loaded by Winchester, it was common for skeet shooters to use spreader loads when shooting at station eight because both targets there are much closer when shot than at other stations; the larger pattern spread of the spreader load made those targets a bit easier to hit. This is why vests worn by skeet shooters today have shell loops on the pocket for two shells--they were put there so the two spreader-load shells could be kept separate from the shells carried in a pocket of the vest. Even though skeet shooters seldom use spreader loads anymore, the tradition refuses to die among manufacturers who make those vests.

The spreader load is an excellent idea simply because it will produce patterns of about Improved Cylinder diameter when fired from a gun with Full choke. My 12-gauge Fox Sterlingworth is choked Modified and Full and anytime I hunt where shots at birds are likely to be within 30 yards, I shoot a regular load in the right barrel and a spreader load in the left barrel. This gives me the downrange performance of Modified and Improved Cylinder chokes. If the shooting really gets close, I slip spreader loads into both chambers and my gun becomes Light Skeet and Improved Cylinder. Spreader loads in various shot sizes are available in 12, 16, 20 and 28 gauges from Magnum Performance Ballistics. That company also offers Poly-Wad spreader inserts to those who handload their own shells. The smallest available is 28-gauge but it can be trimmed by hand enough to work in the 410 shotshell.

How Are Shotguns Pattern-Tested?

I keep reading about the importance of pattern-testing shotguns but no one seems to go to the trouble of explaining why or how it should be done. What do you have to say about the subject?

Pattern-testing is best performed by the old-fashioned method of shooting a sheet of paper and then evaluating the shot pattern. Sheets of paper measuring about 40 inches square are fastened to a cardboard or plywood backboard, which is nailed or bolted to a couple of six-foot 2x4s. The ends of the 2x4s are sunk into the ground. If you are only interested in how a gun/choke/load combination compares to the industry standards, you would shoot the target from a distance of 40 yards, count the number of holes in the paper that can be contained by a 30-inch circle and divide what you get by the number of pellets in the load you fired. You can cut open a shotshell and actually count the number of shot inside, but the information contained in the chart below is close enough. Let us say the writing on the box of shells you wish to test indicates the shotshells inside are loaded with 1-1/4 oz. of #7-1/2 lead shot. According to the first chart, that charge weight of that size shot contains approximately 431 pellets. When you count the number of holes within the 30-inch circle you drew on the paper target you shot, you came up with 241. Dividing 241 by 431 gives us 56 percent. According to the pattern percentages chart on page 118, the combination of gun, choke and load you fired is delivering Improved Cylinder choke performance. Had you counted 297 pellets in the 30-inch circle your gun would be delivering close to 70 percent, which is rated as Full choke.

Pattern testing can be as simple or as complicated as the shotgunner chooses to make it.

All of this is well and good but it does not reveal information that is useful to many hunters. The New England hunter who kills most of this ruffed grouse at no more than 25 yards off the muzzle of his gun could care less how it performs at 40 yards. This is why I prefer to allow the type of shooting I will be doing determine how I pattern-test a particular gun and load. Most of the shots I get at quail and other game birds range from 15 to 30 yards so when checking out a gun or load, I do all of my pattern testing at those distances. I also often use a steel pattern plate rather than paper target because in addition to telling me all I want or need to know, it saves a lot of time. Rather than being concerned about pattern percentages, I am more interested in how large in diameter the pattern is and how uniformly the pellets within it are distributed.

APPROXIMATE NUMBER OF PELLETS PER LOAD (Lead Shot)

SHOT CHARGE (Oz.)	9	8-1/2	8	7-1/2	SHOT SIZE 6	5	4	3	2	1	BB
1/2	293	248	205	173	112	86	68	53	44	35	30
5/8	366	311	256	216	139	108	85	66	55	44	37
11/16	402	342	281	237	153	118	94	73	61	49	41
3/4	439	373	307	259	167	129	102	80	66	53	44
7/8	512	435	358	302	195	151	119	93	77	62	52
1	585	497	409	345	223	172	136	106	88	71	60
1-1/8	658	559	460	388	251	194	153	120	99	80	67
1-1/4	731	621	511	431	279	215	170	133	110	89	74
1-3/8	804	683	562	474	307	237	187	146	121	98	82
1-1/2	878	746	614	518	335	258	204	160	132	107	89
1-5/8	951	808	665	561	362	280	221	173	143	116	97
1-3/4	1024	870	716	604	390	301	238	186	154	125	104
1-7/8	1097	932	767	647	418	323	255	200	165	134	112
2	1170	994	818	690	446	344	272	213	176	143	119
2-1/8	1243	1056	869	733	474	366	289	226	187	152	127
2-1/4	1316	1118	894	756	492	378	307	240	196	161	134

NOTE: Pellet count for Tungsten-Matrix and bismuth is only slightly lower.

APPROXIMATE NUMBER OF PELLETS PER LOAD (Steel Shot)

SHOT CHARGE (Oz.)	6	5	4	3	2	1	BB	BBB	T	TT
7/8	236	182	144	118	94	---	---	---	---	---
15/16	295	230	180	149	117	---	---	---	---	---
1	314	243	189	155	125	---	---	---	---	---
1-1/8	335	274	212	175	141	116	80	---	---	---
1/1-4	---	---	237	194	156	129	89	76	67	56
1-3/8	---	---	260	212	170	141	97	84	73	62
1-9/16	---	---	300	247	195	161	112	97	81	71
1-3/4	---	---	---	---	215	177	125	108	92	82

INDUSTRY STANDARD PATTERN PERCENTAGES

CHOKE	PERCENTAGE
Cylinder	40
Skeet	50
Improved Cylinder	55
Modified	60
Improved Modified	65
Full	70

Is the 20 Gauge Enough Gun for Turkey Gobblers?

My son is now old enough to go turkey hunting with me but he is bothered by the recoil of 12-gauge guns, even when one of the 2-3/4 inch loads is used. Several companies offer 20-gauge turkey guns but I am not sure they offer the performance needed for the job. What do you think?

When teamed up with enough choke, the various three-inch 20-gauge turkey loads offered by Winchester and Remington with 1-1/4 ounces of lead shot and the Federal load with its 1-5/16 ounces of shot are plenty effective on gobblers out to 35 yards. Some combinations offer adequate pattern density to saturate a gobbler's head at even greater distances. When the Remington 20-gauge turkey load with 1-1/4 ounces of No. 6 Hevi-Shot is combined with around .040 inch of choke constriction it will usually extend the range by another 5 to 10 yards over lead shot. I find .025 to .030 inch to be the optimum amount of choke constriction to use with lead shot and .040 inch seems to be about optimum for Hevi-Shot. If you are unable to find chokes with those

I have taken five subspecies of turkey with 20-gauge shotguns (eastern, Osceola, Rio Grande, Merriam's and Gould's). This Gould's bird fell victim to a Remington 870 wearing a Kahles 2-7X scope and Remington ammo loaded with 1-1/4 oz. of No. 6 HeviShot.

constrictions for the gun you buy for your son, either Briley or Hunter's Specialties will likely have what you need. Incidentally, I took my first Osceola and Gould's gobblers with 20-gauge shotguns, the former with a Browning BPS and Winchester's 1-1/4-oz. loading of No. 5 lead shot, the latter with a Remington Model 870 and Remington ammo loaded with 1-1/8 ounces of No. 6 Hevi-Shot.

You might be interested in knowing that the 20-gauge turkey gun is no longer considered just for kids as many experienced turkey hunters have switched to it. For several years now I have used nothing but 20-gauge guns when hunting turkey and with them I have taken the Super Slam which consists of five sub-species: eastern, Merriam's, Rio Grande, Osceola and Gould's.

Which Type of Shot Delivers the Most Energy?

With the availability of so many different types of shot such as steel, lead, Hevi-Shot and bismuth, I often wonder how their performance compares. Which type of shot delivers the most energy to the target?

I will take the easy way out in answering your question with the following chart. Since the densities of bismuth, Tungsten-Matrix and Tungsten-Iron are similar to the density of lead, shot made of those materials deliver about the same amount of energy to the target.

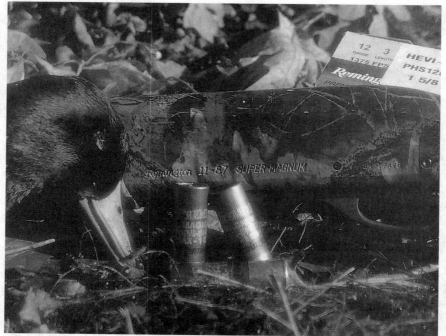

Slightly more dense than lead, Hevi-Shot delivers more downrange energy than any other type of shot in common use.

TYPE SHOT	SHOT SIZE	MUZZLE VELOCITY (FPS)	RETAINED ENERGY PER PELLET (FT. LBS.)	
			40 Yards	60 Yards
Lead	9	1300	0.7	0.5
Lead	8	1300	1.2	0.8
Lead	7-1/2	1330	1.4	0.9
Lead	6	1330	2.5	1.7
Lead	5	1330	3.6	2.5
Lead	4	1330	4.8	3.4
Lead	2	1330	8.0	5.8
Lead	2	1240	7.3	5.4
Hevi-Shot	7-1/2	1325	1.6	0.9
Hevi-Shot	6	1325	2.8	1.7
Hevi-Shot	5	1325	3.9	2.5
Hevi-Shot	4	1325	5.3	3.5
Hevi-Shot	2	1325	9.1	6.2
Steel	6	1365	1.3	0.2
Steel	4	1365	2.4	1.4
Steel	2	1275	4.1	2.4
Steel	2	1365	4.4	2.6
Steel	BB	1275	8.3	5.2
Steel	T	1300	12.5	8.0
Steel	TT	1300	15.0	9.9

Does a Fired Case Protect the Firing Pin During Dryfiring?

I often dry-fire my shotguns and have been told that keeping a fired case in the chamber while doing so will protect the firing pin from possible damage. Is this true?

Placing a fired case in the chamber while dry-firing a firearm is better than nothing at all but the pre-indented primer does not cushion the blow of the firing pin as well as snap caps that are designed specifically for the job. A snap cap is a dummy shell made of plastic, aluminum, brass or other material with its primer pocket filled with

Why Doubles Only in Skeet Shoot-Offs?

I recently watched the highlights of a skeet tournament on television and several shooters ended up with perfect scores. At the end of the match the winners were chosen by process of elimination in shoot-offs but rather than shooting regular rounds of skeet they shot doubles only. Why did they do that?

Years ago the winners of tournaments were determined by shoot-offs in regular rounds of skeet but once competitors progressed to the point where perfect scores were quite common, that method became too time consuming. A good example of what could happen took place at the end of the 1968 National Skeet Shooting Association championships in Kansas City when competitors Al Buntrock and Tommy Heffron broke 1050 straight targets without a single miss in a shoot-off while attempting to determine the winner of the 12-gauge event. At that point weary tournament officials decided the best thing to do was to declare the two shooters co- champions for that year and both agreed. Marathon shoot-offs of that nature eventually convinced NSSA officials that doubles, which is more difficult than regular skeet, was a better way to break ties in determining tournament winners.

Skeet doubles are shot during tournament shoot-offs to speed up the game.

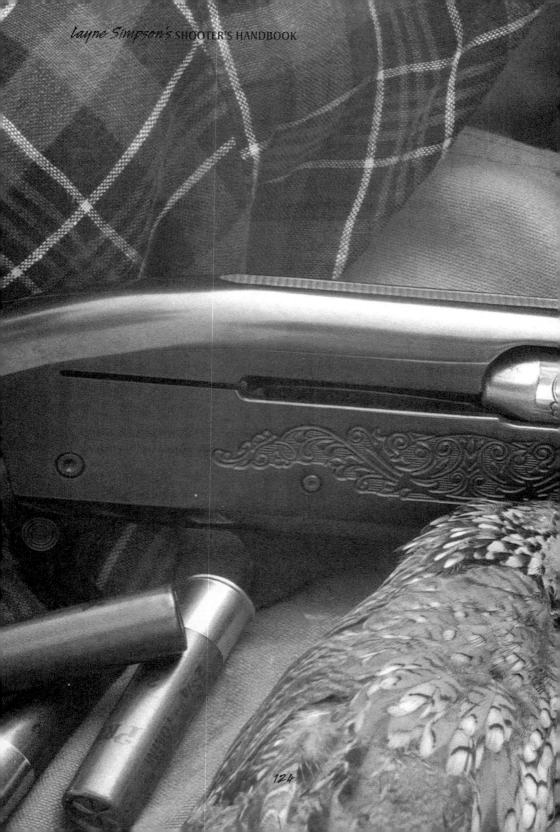

What Shotgun for My Daughter?

My daughter is one of the best natural shots I have seen on both clay targets and birds and she has been shooting shotguns for only two years. She is, however, quite sensitive to recoil. What is the softest-shooting shotgun larger than the 410 that would serve her for casual skeet shooting as well as hunting quail and doves and yet not be too heavy?

Pound for pound, the softest-shooting shotgun available today in a bore size larger than 410 is the Remington Model 1100 in 28 gauge. I occasionally use one for hunting quail and while at seven pounds it is not the lightest shotgun available, it is light enough and its weight combined with the mild-kicking 28-gauge shell puts recoil at a level anyone should be able to handle. The various 3/4-oz. target loads available from Remington, Winchester and Federal are excellent choices for skeet while field loads offered by those same companies work great on doves and quail.

The Remington Model 1100 in 28 gauge generates very little recoil.

125

a durable shock-absorbing material. Those made for use in rifles and handguns of various calibers as well as the standard shotgun gauges are available from Brownells. For use in occasional dry-firing, you can make your own snap cap by filling the primer pocket of a shotshell hull with silicone bathtub sealant (available at most hardware stores) but the commercial snap caps are better for extensive dry-firing.

Who Made the First Lever-Action 410?

I recently bought a Marlin Model 410 shotgun and it is a fun little gun. I was torn between it and the Winchester Model 9410 but bought the Marlin because it feels better and its action is smoother. Which of those companies was first to build a 410-bore lever action?

Marlin introduced the original Model 410 lever-action on the Model 36 rifle action in 1929. That gun was dropped from production in 1932 but Marlin brought the 410 chambering back on its Model 336 action in 2003. Through the years a few gunsmiths have converted Winchester Model 94 rifles to handle the 410 shotshell but it was not offered as a factory chambering until the introduction of the Model 9410 in 2002. Actually, Savage beat Marlin and Winchester to the punch by offering a 410 barrel for its Model 99 takedown rifle in 1925. That company also offered a cased Model 99G/TD with barrels in 410 and 300 Savage. Like those of the Marlin and Winchester rifles, the Savage 410 barrel was chambered for the 2-1/2 inch shell. Unlike the Marlin and Winchester, the Savage rifle had to be used as a single-shot when its 410 barrel was installed since its rotary magazine would not handle the shotshell.

Who Invented the Rifled Shotgun Slug?

The various sabot slug loads are quite popular but I'm still convinced the old rifled lead slug drops deer and black bear quicker, especially if the range does not exceed 75 yards. Who invented the rifled slug which is available in shotshells loaded by Federal, Winchester and Remington?

The American version of the rifled slug was invented by Karl M. Foster and this is why it is often referred to as the Foster-style slug. After experimenting with various shapes for several years Foster came up with a final design that was quite similar to what we have today. He showed his slug to Remington officials in 1932 and they turned it down. About a year later he presented it to Winchester and in June of 1936 that company introduced Foster's slug in 16 gauge only but soon followed up with other gauges as well. It wasn't long before Remington was also loading the same type of slug in various gauges and Federal eventually followed suit.

Rifled slugs loaded in America today differ from Foster's original design only in that they are swaged rather than cast. Up until that type of slug came along, the only single-projectile shotgun ammo available to American hunters was loaded with a round ball and it had a reputation for horrible accuracy. This made the introduction of ammo with the Foster-style slug even bigger news back in the 1930s than the sabot slug load was many decades later.

How Do I Stop Shotgun Butt from Slipping from My Shoulder?

I recently bought a Trojan-grade Parker shotgun in excellent condition. I like the gun but its butt occasionally slips downward from my shoulder and ends up at my armpit when I fire it. What modifications do I need to have made to the gun to prevent this from happening?

It is impossible for me to say for sure without actually examining your gun, but I'd say its stock does not have quite enough down-pitch for you. Simply installing a good recoil pad would go a long way toward solving your problem since its surface would not be as likely to slip from your shoulder as the hard rubber buttplate on your gun. If you choose one of the thinner pads available, the buttstock may not have to be shortened since length of pull on many of the old shotguns is a bit short anyway. A good gunsmith can increase the amount of pitch in your stock by sawing, at an angle, a bit of wood from its butt. You can determine how much additional pitch is needed by temporarily placing paper shims beneath the buttplate at the heel of the stock (business cards work fine). My guess is, if the gunsmith starts his cut at about 1/8 inch thick at the toe of the stock and tapers to zero at the heel, you will feel a world of difference when shooting the gun. What you and your gunsmith should be striving for is the precise amount of pitch that creates full and uniform contact between the butt of the stock and your shoulder.

Shotguns with More than Two Barrels?

Single- and double-barrel shotguns have long been quite common but has any company ever made one with more than two barrels?

Back before pumps and autoloaders became common, several British and European manufacturers came up with different ways of increasing the firepower of double-barrel shotguns. One maker introduced a gun with three side-by-side barrels while another offered a four-barrel gun with a pair of side-by-side barrels stacked atop another pair. Those guns offered the hunter more shots between reloads than was possible with the double-barrel gun but the extra barrels made them quite heavy, not to mention the extremely high cost involved in building a gun that places the shot charges from four barrels to the same point at 40 yards.

One of the more interesting methods of increasing the firepower of the side-by-side double was developed by Belgium gunmaker Charles Leve. The Leve gun has only two side-by-side barrels and with its sliding breech it looks a bit like the French-built Darne. With two shells in its chambers and two more stowed in recesses in the frame immediately below the chambers of the barrels, it can be fired four times quite rapidly, or so I have read. After the two shells in the barrels have been fired, the breech is opened, causing those spent cases to be ejected and allowing spring-loaded carriers to elevate the other two shells to alignment with the chambers of the barrels. Closing the breech chambers those two shells.

What Are Pitch and Cast-Off?

I keep reading about pitch and cast-off in shotgun stocks but I am not exactly clear on what they mean. Please explain.

Cast-off is best described as an offset of the centerline of the butt of the stock to the right of the centerline of the barrel of a shotgun. On a double-barrel gun it would be the relation between the centerlines of the rib and buttstock. A stock cast in the opposite direction for a left-hand shooter is said to have cast-on. The amount of cast at the toe of a stock can differ from the amount at its heel. As is commonly seen on guns built in England, my Westley Richards double has a bit of cast-off in its stock. Some shooters believe it makes a gun point more naturally but you cannot prove it by me. None of my other doubles has cast-off in its stock and I shoot them as well as the Westley Richards.

The amount of pitch in a stock is easily measured by standing the butt of a shotgun flat on a level floor and sliding it against a wall. With the top of the receiver touching the wall, measure from the wall to top of the barrel or rib at the muzzle. The amount of down-pitch in stocks will vary from gun to gun but in most factory guns it will usually measure from 1/2 to 3 inches with around 1-1/4 inches being the most common. My 28-gauge AyA double is a No. 1 grade, which means its stock dimensions were made to order for its first owner. I am the second owner of the gun and while I cannot for the life of me imagine why, it came from the factory with about an inch of up-pitch in its stock. In other words, the direction of pitch was exactly the opposite of what is usually seen. Each time I fired the gun its butt would slide downward on my shoulder and end up at my armpit. I sent it to David and Cathy Yale for the installation of a leather-covered recoil pad along with instructions to introduce two inches of down-pitch into the stock during installation of the pad. This is done by cutting the stock at the proper angle prior to installing the recoil pad.

12-Gauge Handload for Cowboy Action Shooting?

My wife and I are just now getting into cowboy action shooting and the shotgun we have chosen is the Winchester Model 1897 slide action. I have a Lee shotshell loader and would like to come up with a handload that is extremely light in recoil. What do you recommend?

I recommend the same soft-kicking 12-gauge load I use for 16-yard trap, for the first shot in trap doubles, for skeet shooting and for sporting clays. It is also an excellent choice for wingshooting, especially on quail and doves. The recipe can be used in the Winchester AA, Remington STS and Federal Gold Medal plastic hulls. It consists of the Winchester 209 primer WAA12L plastic wad, 15.5 grains of Hodgdon's Clays and 7/8 oz. of shot. With the light shot charge and a muzzle velocity of 1050 fps, that load generates extremely light recoil and most guns I have tried it in print nice, uniform patterns out to 30 yards. You mentioned the Winchester 97 pump gun. I recently horse-traded for one with a 30-inch barrel and decided to try it with my light-recoil load at 16-yard trap. The first 50 rounds I fired in the gun (with No. 9 shot) smoked 48 targets, which is not bad considering I had not previously fired the gun a single time.

Why Wooden Dowel for Winchester Shotgun?

A Winchester Model 1897 slide-action shotgun I recently bought at an estate sale came with a leather case and a number of other accessories including a long wooden dowel with "Winchester" engraved on its side. Do you have any idea what it was used for? How many Model 97 shotguns were manufactured?

Due to a Presidential Proclamation signed in 1935, the capacity of any repeating shotgun used for hunting migratory birds in the United States had to be limited to three rounds. Beginning that year, Winchester shipped with each Model 97 shotgun a wooden plug to be used in reducing its magazine capacity from five to two rounds. Approximately 1,024,700 Model 97s were built from 1897 until that model was discontinued in 1957.

Are Ejectors Necessary on a Double-Barrel Shotgun?

I am new to shotgunning and am in the market for a vintage shotgun to be used for hunting quail. While at a recent gun show I turned down a great buy on a L.C. Smith 20-gauge double because it was a non-ejector gun. A friend tells me doing so was a mistake simply because many of today's experienced wingshooters find automatic ejectors on a double to be of limited usefulness. Do you agree with his opinion?

I own both ejector and non-ejector side-by-side doubles and except when shooting a clay target game called the flurry, I had just as soon have a non-ejector gun. When shooting skeet, trap and sporting clays I save my fired hulls for handloading and find manually plucking them from the chambers of a double without ejectors to be just as convenient as catching them as they are automatically ejected. Same goes for most of the hunting I do but for another reason as well–I prefer to not litter the landscape with plastic hulls that remain on the scene practically forever. I would never let the fact that a double-barrel shotgun does not have automatic ejectors prevent me from buying it. In fact, I recently had a choice between two otherwise identical 1930s vintage side-by-sides in 410 and bought the non-ejector gun.

Okay to Shoot Modern Loads in Browning Super-Tubes?

I recently bought a 12-gauge Browning Superposed shotgun built during the 1960s. It came in a leather case along with a set of original Browning subgauge tubes in 20, 28 and 410. Should I observe any special precautions when shooting this gun in order to avoid damaging it?

Unlike modern, full-length subgauge insert tubes like those make by Briley and Kohler that extend all the way out to the muzzle of the shotgun barrels for which they are made, the Super-Tubes extend only about two-thirds of the way down the barrels of your Browning. As shotshells are fired, carbon builds up in the bores of

Can I Duplicate the 410 3/4 Oz. Factory Load by Handloading?

While attending a gun show sometime back I purchased two boxes of Remington and Winchester three-inch 410 shotshells loaded with 3/4 oz. of #8 shot. As I am sure you already know, 3/4 oz. is the standard shot charge loaded today in the 28-gauge shotshell. On a recent quail hunt I tried the 410 shells in my Weatherby Athena over-under and their performance seemed better than anything I had previously used in that gun. According to my local dealer, Remington and Winchester no longer offer that load; do you know of any other company that does? If such a load is not available commercially is it possible for me to duplicate it by handloading?

Winchester introduced its 410-bore Model 42 pump gun along with the three-inch version of the 410-bore shotshell in 1933. From its beginning, the three-inch 410 was loaded with 3/4 oz. of shot, a practice continued by both Winchester and Remington until the adoption of the plastic wad with integral shotcup during the 1960s made it necessary to reduce the shot charge to 11/16 oz. The handload I have used for years to duplicate

The 3-inch 410 is easily handloaded with 3/4 oz. of shot.

those old factory loads first appeared in the *Lyman Shotshell Handbook*. It consists of the Federal three-inch plastic hull, Winchester 209 primer, 16.5 grains of Hodgdon's H110, Winchester WAA41 wad and 3/4 oz. of shot for a muzzle velocity of about 1200 fps. W296 can also be used but the Lyman manual recommends reducing the charge to 15.5 grains. Remington and Winchester three-inch plastic hulls can be substituted but the shotcup petals of the WAA41 wad may have to be trimmed back in order to make room for the entire shot charge. Squeezing 3/4 oz. of shot into the 3-inch 410 requires vibrating the hull by hand as the shot is poured in but it can be done and pattern quality is usually quite good when magnum-grade, high-antimony shot is used.

the 12-gauge barrels, just forward of the muzzles of the insert tubes. Anytime the tubes are removed, this ring of carbon must be cleaned out with brush and solvent as failure to do so can result in bulged barrels in that area when 12-gauge shells are fired in the gun with the tubes removed. The fact that some owners of Superposed shotguns failed to follow this procedure in the past probably explains why Browning decided to discontinue production of its Super-Tube option just as it was beginning to catch on with skeet shooters. As for other precautions, you should never fire loads with steel shot in your Browning and it is also a good idea to refrain from firing anything but 2-3/4 inch target loads in its subgauge tubes. It might also interest you to know that anytime Browning installed Super-Tubes in one of its 12-gauge Superposed shotguns, its inertia trigger was converted to mechanical to assure that it operated properly when shooting the light-recoiling 410 shotshell.

Who Can Fix the Trigger of My Parker Shotgun?

A year or so ago I bought a Parker BHE-grade 12-gauge shotgun with a single-selective trigger. Quite often both barrels fire simultaneously when I pull its trigger and while I have had two different gunsmiths examine the gun, neither was able to solve its problem. Any suggestions?

I recently acquired a 28-gauge Parker and like your gun, it doubled almost every time I pulled its trigger. I solved the problem by having its trigger replaced by Miller Single Trigger Mfg. Co. of Millersburg, Pennsylvania. The shop was started back in the 1920s by Elmer Miller and eventually became world-renowned for replacing single triggers in top-quality American-built doubles such as the Parker, L.C. Smith, Ithaca, A.H. Fox, Lefever, Iver Johnson Skeet-er and Winchester Model 21 as well as the better doubles produced by various English, German, Italian and Spanish makers. The Miller brothers took over the operation from their father and ran it until selling out to Doug Turnbull at Turnbull Restorations.

Why Are Chokes Reversed in Winchester Model 21 Barrels?

My Winchester Model 21 was built during the 1930s and its right barrel has a tighter choke than the left barrel, something I have verified by measurement and by shooting the gun at the pattern board. This is the reverse of what I have always seen in side-by-side doubles and I hope you have some explanation for it.

Back when your Model 21 was built, side-by-side doubles were enjoying some popularity in the clay target games. In those days skeet shooters called for targets from the low-gun start position and as a result, when shooting doubles the outgoing target, which was the first target taken, was usually broken at longer range than the incoming target. And since the right barrel of a side-by-side double is customarily fired first, it made sense to have a bit more choke in that barrel. This prompted Winchester, Parker, L.C. Smith, Iver Johnson and other makers of side-by-side skeet guns to offer the option of reversed chokes. Considering all of this I'd say the original owner of your Model 21 was a skeet shooter. In today's version of skeet the shooter is allowed to shoulder his gun before calling for the target and since this allows him to break the outgoing target of a pair at about the same range as he breaks the incomer he has no need for more choke in one barrel of his gun than in the other.

Why Was "Y" Added to the Serial Number of this Beretta?

While recently examining a friend's Beretta over-under shotgun I noticed that the letter "Y" appears to have been added at the end of its serial number. Does this have any significance?

From time to time Beretta sells some of its higher grade shotguns that have undergone various stages of wear from being displayed at trade shows and while on loan to distributors, firearms writers and others. Those firearms are sold only after undergoing rigorous safety testing and inspection by trained technicians. Upon passing inspection, an inverted letter "Y" is added to the serial number to indicate that the gun was fired after it left the factory and may exhibit minor cosmetic flaws. There are three possible levels of grading in the Beretta certification policy. A "Y1" added to its serial number means the gun may have minor dings, dents and/or scratches in its finish. The "Y2" stamp means that any dings, dents or scratches the gun might have suffered are more apparent. A gun given the "Y3" stamp may also be missing some of its original accessories. Regardless of how a particular gun is identified, its service life will be the same as a factory-new gun.

What Medicine for Troublesome Chipmunks?

My vegetable and flower gardens are being devastated by an infestation of chipmunks. We have great neighbors all around our property and even though they have suggested to my husband and me that we shoot the little pests, we hesitate to do so with a rifle for safety reasons. As shotguns go, even the 410 bore is too loud. During a typical evening stroll through the gardens, ranges from me to running targets are usually from five to 10 yards so I thought about using an air gun but nixed the idea when it dawned on me that a ricocheting pellet might make one of my neighbors friendly no more. Any suggestions?

Assuming that your neighbors will tolerate its relatively low noise level, a 22-caliber rifle with a smoothbore barrel like the Marlin Model 25MG Garden Gun in 22 WMR would solve your problem. That gun along with a supply of CCI 22 WMR shotshells should rid your gardens of those marauding chipmunks and be great fun to boot.

Longest Shotgun Barrel?

Shotguns with barrels as long as 34 inches are popular among clay target shooters but most shotguns made for hunting have shorter barrels. What is the longest barrel a U.S. manufacturer has offered on a modern shotgun? Do long barrels greatly improve the effective range of shotshells? What is your favorite barrel length?

Back in the 1970s Marlin manufactured a Winchester Model 12 look-alike pump gun called the Model 120 and it was available with a 40-inch barrel. As far as I know, it holds the barrel length record among modern shotguns. Marlin later offered the Goose Gun variation of its Model 55 bolt action with a 36-inch barrel. Very little velocity is gained by increasing shotgun barrel length much beyond 28 inches but longer barrels have become popular in trap and sporting clays circles because some shooters prefer the way they handle. Another advantage to a longer barrel is that it puts muzzle blast a bit further away from the shooter's ears. I prefer 26-, 28- and 30-inch barrels on hunting guns and like 32- or 34-inch barrel on a trap gun but consider anything longer unwieldy, poorly balanced and too muzzle-heavy.

Is Parker Shotgun Safe to Use with Modern Loads?

I inherited a 12-gauge Parker shotgun from my grandfather back in 1953 and while its stock bears the marks of heavy use and only about 25 percent of its bluing is left, its "Vulcan Steel" barrels are near perfect with no pits in their bores. I hunted upland game birds with the gun for several years but stopped doing so when it dawned on me that modern high-velocity ammunition might damage it. Should I resume using the old Parker or would hanging it on the wall be the wiser thing to do?

Parker usually stamped "Vulcan Steel" on the barrels of its VHE grade shotguns which should indicate that your gun is one level higher than the standard Trojan grade. More important, its barrels are fluid steel and assuming lockup of the action is still tight, your fine old double is quite suitable for use with today's 2-3/4 inch smokeless ammunition. In my opinion, firearms in serviceable condition should be used and not retired, so if it were my Parker I would resume taking it afield. Out of respect for its vintage, I would refrain from feeding it anything heavier than the various 3-1/4 dram equivalent field loads available from the major shotshell manufacturers. If I could get by with even lighter 2-3/4 and 3 dram target loads that's what I would use. And, of course, you should never shoot steel shot in your Parker.

Where Can I Have a Custom Gun Case Built?

I'd like to have a compartmented gun case built to my specifications, one that would hold my double-barrel shotgun along with various accessories for it. Just as important as interior design would be the ability of the cases to withstand rough treatment during airline transit. Who can build such a case for me?

I too travel a lot by commercial airline with firearms, and my guns and accessories stay safe and secure inside cases built by Americase. In the unlikely event that you don't find what you're looking for among dozens of sizes and interior configurations illustrated in their catalog, the company will build whatever you need to your exact specifications.

Where Can I Find the Nominal Diameters of Lead Shot?

Where can I find the nominal diameters of lead shot of various sizes? My grandfather once told me that his favorite shot size for hunting quail was #10 but I never see it for sale at any of the local gun shops. Is it still available?

Charts published in ammunition catalogs by various shotshell manufacturers usually give the nominal diameters of shot of various sizes. You can also come up with the same information by subtracting the shot size in question from 17. As an example, subtracting 8 from 17 gives us 9 which is the nominal diameter of #8 shot in thousandths of an inch (.09-inch). Subtracting 6 from 17 gives us 11 (or .11-inch) which is the nominal diameter of #6 shot. This method works on shot sizes from #1 to #12. The #10 shot your grandfather mentioned was once mildly popular among quail hunters in the Deep South but after trying it I found it to be acceptably effective on quail out to no more than 15 yards. Too many birds struck beyond that range were able to fly away wounded. For this reason I prefer to use shot no smaller than #8-1/2 when hunting Gentleman Bob and consider 7-1/2s and 8s even better.

What Is a Carrier Barrel?

I recently read where some makers of over-under shotguns offer a "carrier barrel" option but no further description was given. What type of barrel was the author referring to?

Many of today's serious skeet shooters prefer a 12-gauge over/under with full-length insert tubes in 20, 28 and 410. While that type of setup enables them to use the same gun in all four events some believe doing so puts the shooter at a slight disadvantage since the gun weighs about 3/4 pound more with the tubes than without. A shotgun with the carrier barrel option comes with two sets of over/under barrels, one of standard weight. The other set of barrels are lightened during manufacture to the point where they weigh the same with a pair of subgauge tubes installed as the standard barrels alone weigh. Unlike the standard-weight barrels, the carrier barrel set is intended for use only with subgauge tubes and cannot be used for firing 12-gauge shells. To my knowledge, Krieghoff and Kohler are the only companies presently offering this option although other manufacturers of high-quality over/unders are likely to eventually follow suit.

Why Do Some Shotguns Have Two Beads?

Since the proper use of a shotgun in wingshooting requires that it be pointed instinctively rather than aimed, I have long wondered why the rib on the barrels of my Remington Model 332 has two beads, one out near the muzzle and the other about halfway back on the rib. Do you have the answer to this?

When shouldering a new shotgun to check it out for proper fit, some shooters use the twin beads to determine if the comb of the stock has the desired amount of drop and thickness. Ideally, (for me at least) when a field gun is shouldered and my eye is looking down its rib, the top of the rear bead will be aligned with the bottom of the front bead. Shotgunners refer to this as a figure-8 sight picture and it indicates correct comb height for my style of shooting. Some shotgunners prefer to see the two beads in perfect alignment while others want to view the rear bead several bead-heights below the front bead. How the two beads align can also indicate whether or not comb thickness is correct. If a right-handed shooter sees the rear bead aligned to the left of the front bead it means the comb of the stock is too thin. Just the opposite bead alignment indicates the comb is too thick. The beads can also be used to check for the correct amount of cast-off in a custom stock.

While I have just described the primary purpose of two beads on the rib of a shotgun, I must also mention that some shooters use them to aim a shotgun when firing slug loads. Before it became fashionable to mount adjustable sights and scopes on slug guns I used to do just that and anyone who tries it for the first time is almost always surprised at how accurate such a seemingly primitive sight system can be out to 75 yards or so. Turkey hunters also use the two beads for aiming and clay target shooters who shoot from the high-gun position often use them to check for proper gun mounting before calling for the bird.

Who Can Install Chokes in My Old Double-Barrel?

According to a gunsmith I know, the barrels of my Ithaca double are too thin at the muzzle to allow the installation of screw-in chokes. Nor does he want to install chokes in my Navy Arms double-barrel muzzleloader. Do you know of anyone who would give me a second opinion on both jobs?

Briley Manufacturing has developed a line of screw-in chokes specifically for shotguns of all types with thin-wall barrels. Sometime back I had them install a set of seven chokes in a 1960s vintage Krieghoff 32 and the workmanship is flawless, not to mention how much more versatile that gun is now. A friend of mine had a set installed in his old Winchester 1897 pump gun and he raves about their performance. Briley can also install screw-in chokes in your muzzle loading shotgun. If you go that route be sure to specify chokes with a slight bell at the muzzle as it makes the insertion of wads much easier.

What Is Safe Way to Carry an Old Hammer Gun in Field?

I get a real kick out of hunting with the old classic firearms and only last year took my best whitetail buck of all time with a Winchester 94 chambered for the 450 Marlin cartridge. The latest addition to my vintage firearm battery is a J.W. Laird 20-gauge, breech-loading, side-by-side double with exposed hammers. I plan to use it for all of my quail hunting but no one around here can tell me the safe way to carry such a firearm in the field when it is loaded.

Vintage double-barrel, breech-loading shotguns with exposed hammers are presently enjoying a resurgence of interest mainly because fine old English game guns like your J.W. Laird are now being imported into the U.S. in respectable

The Briley bunch are experts at installing screw-in chokes in old doubles.

There is more than one safe way to carry a hammer gun in the field.

numbers. There are two safe ways to carry a loaded hammer gun in the field. One way is to walk in to flush a covey of quail with both chambers loaded and hammers at full cock but with the action broken open. To fire the gun you simply close the action, shoulder the gun, swing through the target and pull the trigger, all in one smooth motion. A second method and the one I prefer to use is to leave the loaded gun closed but have both hammers down in their safety notches; as a bird flushes I cock both hammers with one sweep of my thumb as I shoulder the gun.

Did Browning Superposed Once Have Two Triggers?

My favorite shotgun is the old Browning Superposed and I own several, the oldest bought by my father back in the early 1940s. All of my guns have single triggers but I recall seeing a photo of one with two triggers. When was that type of trigger system available?

John Browning's Superposed shotgun was introduced in America in 1931 and for quite some time thereafter it was available with either single or double triggers. The single trigger was available in two versions, selective and nonselective. A fourth option designed by Val Browning and called the Twin-Single Trigger consisted of two nonselective triggers, either of which could be used for single-trigger operation. Pulling the front trigger fired the lower barrel first and pulling it again fired the upper barrel. The rear trigger worked just the opposite; its first pull fired the upper barrel while the second pull fired the lower tube. Two triggers that worked in the reverse order were also available. The Twin-Single Trigger gave shotgunners the instant barrel selectivity of two triggers along with the advantages of a single trigger.

How Do I Control Solvent Spray?

I followed your advice on cleaning shotguns and now scrub the bore of my 12-gauge Beretta AL391 every 100 rounds or so with a brush and solvent. It is, however, quite messy as the brush sprays solvent all over the floor of my shop each time it exits the muzzle. Any ideas on how to avoid this?

After removing the barrel from your Beretta but prior to beginning the cleaning process, attach a medium-size plastic zip-lock bag over its muzzle with a rubber band. The bag will catch not only solvent spray from the brush but dirty patches as well. The bag can be used for several barrel cleanings before needing to be discarded.

Light or Heavy Shotgun?

I am new to wingshooting and cannot decide between two over-under shotguns for hunting mourning doves and bobwhite quail. Both guns have 28-inch barrels. One weighs 6-1/2 pounds while the other is rated almost two pounds heavier. I realize the heavier of the two will be more comfortable to shoot but does it have other advantages I may be not be aware of?

Assuming both guns are properly balanced, the lighter of the two will have a slight edge for close going-away shots on flushing quail simply because less weight makes for a quicker-handling gun. On the other hand, you may average fewer shots per bird when taking passing shots on doves with the heavier and slightly longer gun. This is due to the fact that a heavier shotgun swings more smoothly and once you get its momentum built up during a swing-through, you are less likely to stop swinging the gun as you squeeze its trigger. This is one of the reasons why skeet shooters favor shotguns weighing in the neighborhood of 8-1/2 pounds.

Which Shooting Tournament Is Biggest?

Seems like each time I pick up a gun magazine some writer is saying this event or that tournament is the biggest and fastest growing of all shooting sports and yet when the number of participants are revealed at the end of the article they seem quite small in number to me. Tell me, what shooting match has the most actual participants each year?

The shooting sport with the most participants in the U.S. is trap. Membership in the Amateur Trap Association (ATA) is around 90,000 of which roughly 40 percent participate in registered events on a regular basis. This is why as major shooting tournaments go, the Grand American World Trapshooting Tournament (more commonly called the "Grand") ranks No. 1 in participation. More than 7,000 participants usually attend the Grand.

A Lever-Action Double-Barrel Shotgun?

I recently saw on television what appeared to be a lever-action, double-barrel shotgun. It looked the same as any other double but its side-by-side barrels did not hinge downward as is common for that design. Instead, the barrels remained fixed while the standing breech section of the receiver moved straight to the rear when operated by a lever. Where was such a gun made?

The side-by-side double you saw may have been the French-built Darne. Once imported by Stoeger in 12, 20 and 28 gauges, it is a top-quality shotgun. Just as you described, its barrels remain stationary while the sliding breech, which is operated by a lever located in the upper tang of the receiver, moves to the rear for loading, unloading and the removal of fired cases. During one my past wingshooting safaris in Uruguay, the owner of the farm where I stayed owned a trim little Darne in 28 gauge. It weighed only slightly over five pounds and was a delight to hold.

How Do American and English Shot Sizes Differ?

During a recent vacation in London I bought a very nice Webley & Scott side-by-side double in 12 gauge with 2-1/2 inch chambers. It was built prior to World War II and weighs only six pounds. I also brought back a few boxes of English shotshells with #7 shot and in addition to patterning beautifully in my gun the load is quite effective on bobwhite quail and mourning dove. I want to reload the fired cases with US-made lead shot of the same diameter but have been told that shot made here differs in diameter from English shot. If so, what size American shot is the same diameter as the English 7s I've been using? What I would really like to see is a chart illustrating shot size diameters for the two countries. Also, can you tell me where to find load data for the 2-1/2 inch 12-gauge shell?

The Hodgdon shotshell data manual contains a few loads for both the two and 2-1/2 inch shells with cases made by shortening American-made 2-3/4 inch hulls. All the recipes generate chamber pressures commonly considered to be quite acceptable for the old lightweight British game guns. I have been shooting one of the Hodgdon loads in shortened Winchester AA hulls with a Winchester 209 primer, WAA12R plastic wad, and an ounce of either #8s or #9s pushed to 1200 fps by 20.5 grains of Universal powder. Pattern uniformity is excellent and recoil extremely mild, even in a lightweight gun. You might also be interested in knowing that factory-loaded 2-1/2 inch shells are now available here in America from Magnum Performance Ballistics.

As you can see in the below chart, nominal diameter of the #7 lead shot you've been shooting is .095 inch, same as for American 7-1/2 shot. Of the various shot sizes shown, only No. 9s made in the two countries share the same diameter.

	DIAMETER (INCH)	
SHOT SIZE	AMERICAN	ENGLISH
2	.15	.13
4	.13	.12
5	.12	.11
6	.11	.10
7	.10	.095
7-1/2	.095	.09
8	.09	.085
8-1/2	.085	----
9	.08	.08

What Other Combination Guns Were Built?

At a recent gun show I examined a German-made drilling with two barrels in 16 gauge and a third barrel chambered for the 8x57mm Mauser. The owner of the gun mentioned that other types of combination guns have also been made but he did not elaborate. Please describe some of the others.

I have not examined a specimen of all the various combination gun configurations made but in addition to the drilling, I have seen a *Buchsflinte* (one rifle barrel and one shotgun barrel), a *Doppelbuchsdrilling* (one shotgun barrel hanging beneath two rifle barrels of the same caliber) a *Bockdrilling* (one shotgun barrel and two rifle barrels of different calibers) and a *Vierling* (two shotgun barrels with two rifle barrels for different calibers). No doubt, many other combinations have been built on both a production and custom basis by the West German firms of Krieghoff, J.P. Sauer & Son, F.W. Heym and others. They have also been made by firearms manufacturers in other countries, such as Franz Sodia of Austria and BRNO of Czechoslovakia. Of course, the combination guns most commonly seen by Americans in recent times are the Savage Model 24 and Springfield M6 Scout.

How Do I Install a Model 1100 Shell Feed Latch?

I always field-strip my Remington Model 1100 shotgun after each hunting season and give it a thorough cleaning. I have done this many times through the years without experiencing any problems, but I finally have one. When I removed the trigger assembly from the receiver, a long thin metal bar (almost as long as the receiver) dropped out. The bar obviously fits inside a groove inside the receiver but I have yet to figure out what holds it in position. I'm sure a good gunsmith could fix my shotgun but I live many miles from the closest one. Can you help?

The long metal stamping is called a shell feed latch and it is a component part common to Remington's entire family of Models 1100/11-87/878/870/58/48 shotguns. I have been shooting several of those models since the 1960s and during that time have had a feed latch come loose in only two guns so it is not a common occurrence. During assembly at the factory, the part is staked into its slot in the receiver with a special tool from Brownells. The same thing can be accomplished with a hammer and screwdriver but you'll need the help of another person.

Before reinstalling the latch, examine it carefully to make sure it is not broken and then place it back into its slot in the receiver. Make sure its front tip is positioned between the side of the magazine tube and the receiver. Then align the hole in the latch with the rear trigger assembly hole in the receiver and install the rear trigger assembly crosspin to hold it in position. At this point you might need assistance from a second pair of hands. With the receiver resting atop a padded surface (to prevent scratching its finish), press the rear end of the latch into its slot until its top surface is flush with the receiver. While holding it in that position, let your assistant use a hammer and the Brownells tool to stake it in place by upsetting metal from the inner surface of the receiver against both sides of the latch. If you decide to use a screwdriver rather than the tool from Brownells, use its sharp corner to upset the metal. I'd like to take credit for coming up with this home repair, but truth of the matter is, my old quail-hunting buddy, Jay Bunting of Remington, taught me how to do it.

Will Slug Loads Damage Screw-In Chokes?

I have a Winchester over-under combination gun with 12-gauge and 30-06 barrels. I would like to shoot rifled slugs in the smoothbore barrel, but I fear they may damage its screw-in chokes. Would the various sabot loads be safer to use in my gun than the all-lead Foster-style load?

Even though Sabot slugs compress very little as they travel through a shotgun barrel, they should not harm the barrel of your shotgun so long as you do not use a choke constriction tighter than Improved Cylinder. The old Foster-style rifles slug is swaged from extremely soft lead so it can be fired through any choke without damaging the barrel. Due to variations in actual diameter, 12-gauge Foster-style slug loads from different manufacturers often require different choke constrictions for best accuracy. Several years ago I shot three different loads in a Remington Model 870 with screw-in chokes. The Federal slug was most accurate with the Full choke, the Remington slug was most accurate with Modified and the Winchester was most accurate with Improved Cylinder.

Should I Use Steel Shot in My Winchester Model 97?

I have a 12-gauge Winchester Model 1897 pump gun in excellent condition and I would like to hunt ducks with it. Will it handle loads with steel shot okay? When did Winchester manufacture the Model 97? What else can you tell me about it?

Never fire shells loaded with steel shot in your Model 97 as it was made long before shot of that type came into use. You can, however, use waterfowl loads containing other types of nontoxic shot such as bismuth from Bismuth Cartridge and Tungsten-Matrix from Kent. Winchester introduced the Model 97 in November 1897 in 12 gauge and only in a solid-frame version. The takedown option was first offered in October 1898, and the 16-gauge chambering was introduced in February 1900. The Model 97 was the first shotgun built by Winchester in 16 gauge. By the time the grand old scattergun was discontinued in 1957, approximately 1,024,700 had been built.

Is Remington's SP-10 Better than Ithaca's Mag-10?

I enjoy hunting turkey and waterfowl with an Ithaca Mag-10 shotgun I have owned for many years. After experiencing several problems with that gun, I was on the verge of buying a new Remington SP-10 but put my purchase on hold after being told it is nothing more than a copy of the Ithaca. Is what I heard true or is it nothing more than rumor?

While it is true that Remington purchased the manufacturing rights to the Ithaca Mag-10, it was totally redesigned to the point where about the only things it and the Remington SP-10 have in common is they are gas-operated autoloaders capable of using the same size shotshell. For many years I have hunted waterfowl with one of the first SP-10s built so take it from someone who knows, it is one tough shotgun. The SP-10 is also totally reliable and shoots beautiful patterns with both lead and the various types of nontoxic shot. It is my favorite waterfowl gun because it throws the same amount of steel shot as a shotgun chambered for the 3-1/2 inch 12-gauge shell and yet the SP-10 is much more comfortable to shoot.

Unusual Safety on L.C. Smith

I recently acquired an Ideal grade 12-gauge L.C. Smith shotgun and am puzzled by its tang safety. When the safety is placed in its middle position a small "s" appears to indicate that it is on safe. Now for the interesting part; the safety can be removed from its "On" position to either of two "Off" positions by either pushing it all the way forward or by pulling it all the way to the rear. This is the first three-position safety I have seen on a shotgun. Was it standard on all L.C. Smiths?

The three-position safety was originally standard equipment on all L.C. Smith shotguns and then later offered as an extra-charge option. This explains why some guns have that type of safety while others like those in 16-gauge and 410 I currently own have two-position safeties. Here's how the two types of safeties work.

When the selector switch of the two-position version is in its extreme rearward position the safety is engaged; pushing it forward moves it to its "Off" or "Fire" position. In its factory-original condition, that type of safety also automatically returns to its "On" position when the top lever is pushed to the side for loading the gun. With the three-position type, the safety is engaged when its switch is in the mid position and disengaged when placed in either its full-forward or full-rearward position. Now here's the difference between those two positions. When the switch is in its forward "Fire" position the safety is automatically engaged and the switch it returned to its mid position when the top lever is pushed to the side to open the barrels. When the safety is in its rearward "Fire" position it stays there until the shooter manually moves it to its engaged position. L.C. Smith officials obviously figured that such a dual-function design would appeal to clay target shooters who prefer the non-automatic safety as well as those hunters who prefer the automatic safety.

Some L.C. Smith shotguns have safeties designed for clay target shooters.

L.C. SMITH

16 GA.

N EAGLE

ELLS

KELESS POWDER

RTRIDGE CO.

Y. U.S.A.

Is the 12-Gauge Slug Load Enough for Bear?

I plan to hunt black bear in Maine and have been told the shooting will be no farther away than 50 yards. I am leaning toward the use of my Browning Gold shotgun with a slug barrel, a 4X scope, and the Winchester or Remington slug load. The fellows who will accompany me on the bear hunt are trying to convince me to buy a rifle in 30-06 and leave my shotgun at home. Should I listen to them or should I take the gun I have used when hunting deer for several years?

I believe you will be better off taking the gun you are accustomed to hunting with. For the ranges you mentioned, your Browning with its magazine filled with slug loads is plenty of gun for black bear.

What Happened to the 16 Gauge?

I would like to buy a top-quality, 16-gauge side-by-side double-barrel shotgun for my grandson but am having difficulty finding one. Can you help? Why was this chambering dropped by American manufacturers?

As I write this, the best buys in top-quality 16-gauge doubles are a used Fox Sterlingworth or a field grade L.C. Smith. It is still possible to find either in good hunting condition at an affordable price. When shopping for a Sterlingworth, look for a Philadelphia gun made during the 1920s with ejectors, double-triggers and 28-inch barrels. Of all the 16-gauge doubles made, the Sterlingworth is my favorite, mainly because Fox scaled its receiver to size rather than building on the 12-gauge frame as other gunmakers chose to do. Something else I like about those guns is they often have straighter stocks than others built during that period. My 12-gauge Sterlingworth was built in 1923 and its stock has very little more drop than seen on stocks made today. Many Fox guns of that vintage have chambers that measure 2-1/2 or 2-5/8 inches but this is no problem since several companies including Estate Cartridge and Gamebore offer 2-1/2 inch shells. If the gun is not of collector quality you can have its chambers lengthened for 2-3/4 inch shells.

When I was a youngster growing up in the Deep South during the 1950s, the 16 gauge was second in popularity only to the 12 gauge and considerably more popular than the 20 gauge. As you have discovered, times have changed. The 20 now rivals the 12 in popularity in some areas, the 28 is gaining more fans each day, and yet, sadly enough, the 16 appears to be on its last legs. Most American manufacturers have abandoned the 16 simply because guns chambered for it no longer sell in great numbers.

How Much Velocity Will a Shorter Barrel Lose?

The 32-inch barrel of my Marlin 10-gauge bolt-action shotgun makes it too muzzle-heavy and gives it poor handling qualities. I mostly feed the gun rifled slugs and buckshot. How much velocity will I lose if I have the tube shortened to a more manageable 22 inches?

You will lose only 75 to 100 feet per second in velocity by chopping 10 inches from your barrel. This is an insignificant loss in performance when weighed against what should prove to be a drastic improvement in handling qualities. If you shorten the barrel by that much it will no longer have any choke constriction, which may work out okay with slug loads but I doubt if you will be happy with the patterns it shoots with buckshot. An easy solution to that problem is to have any good gunsmith who specializes in shotgun work install screw-in chokes after the barrel has been shortened. For just about any work on shotguns, I highly recommend Briley Manufacturing.

Do Rifled Slugs Really Spin?

Does the rifling on a slug cause it to spin in flight?

If the Foster-style rifled slug actually does spin, it is not enough to stabilize it during flight. A slug is relatively stable in flight simply because its center of gravity is located forward of its center mass, same as with a badminton cock or a sock with a rock placed in its toe. The primary purpose of the rifling on the skirt of a slug is to allow the slug to squeeze through the choke constriction of a barrel without damaging it.

How Do I Mount a Scope on My Remington 870?

I want to equip my 20-gauge Remington Model 870 slug gun with a scope. What type of mounting system should I use?

Since the receiver of the Model 870 is steel rather than aluminum as seen on some shotguns, you can drill and tap it and use a mount made by several companies such as Burris and Weaver. If you prefer a less permanent attachment system, the receiver-attached mount from Aimtech is easily installed or removed by simply pushing out the two trigger assembly pins of the Model 870. The Aimtech mount is available for many other brands and models of shotguns as well. The 20-gauge Remington Model 870 I used when hunting Gould's turkey in Mexico wore a Kahles 2-7X scope held in place by an Aimtech mount.

What Steel Shot Size for Ducks and Canada Geese?

I plan to use my 12-gauge Weatherby Orion over-under shotgun for hunting waterfowl. What size steel shot should I choose for ducks and Canada geese?

When shooting ducks over decoys I prefer #2 steel shot but I switch to #1s for pass shooting at longer ranges. For Canada geese, I like BBs for close work and BBBs for the longer shots.

What Barrel Length for Turkey Gun?

I have been shopping for a new 12-gauge turkey gun and the various available barrel lengths have me a bit confused. One of the pump guns I looked at had a 30-inch barrel while a couple of the autoloaders had barrels measuring 24 and 26 inches. The dealer who showed me the guns says short barrels are as efficient as long barrels. Is he correct? What is your favorite turkey gun? What are some of the longer shots you have made on gobblers?

The L.C. Smith I am hunting quail with is my favorite 410 shotgun. Art Wheaton at left holds his 410-bore Parker.

Favorite 410 Shotguns?

I know you are a big fan of small-gauge shotguns. What 410 shotguns are your favorites for wingshooting?

One of my favorite 410 guns is a 1940s vintage, field grade L.C. Smith with 26-inch barrels choked Skeet and Improved Cylinder. Just over 6,000 L.C. Smith shotguns were made in 410 and mine just happened to be built during the year I was born. My other favorite 410 double was built during the 1930s. It is a Iver Johnson Skeet-er and its 26-inch barrels are choked Skeet and Skeet. I shoot both of those doubles as well as any other shotguns I own and have used them successfully when hunting a variety of game birds, including pheasant at ranges out to 30 yards. My other favorite 410 is a Winchester Model 42 pump gun. It is a skeet gun with ventilated rib and Cutts Compensator but I use it more for hunting than for breaking clay targets. Another favorite 410 side-by-side is not actually a 410 gun. It is a No.1 grade AyA in 28-gauge that I had fitted with a pair of Briley Ultralight subgauge tubes in 410. It is possible that I shoot that gun even better than the L.C. Smith and Iver Johnson Skeet-er.

Your dealer is correct about barrel lengths. It was long ago proven that the optimum length for squeezing maximum velocity from modern shotshell loads is around 24 inches. While a longer barrel often improves the handling of a shotgun for certain types of shooting, and it positions muzzle blast a bit farther from the shooter's ears, it does not increase muzzle velocity by a significant amount. A short barrel can also deliver patterns that are equal in density and uniformity to those fired by the longest of barrels.

I usually let the type of country in which I hunt turkey determine which shotgun I will use. For mountain hunting in thickly wooded areas where the terrain is extremely steep, I usually choose an extremely light 12-gauge Remington Model 870 Special Field with a 21-inch barrel. I have bagged over two dozen gobblers with that gun. My most serious turkey gun is a 12-gauge Remington Model 870 with a 28-inch barrel. I seldom shoot at a gobbler until it is 30 yards or closer to the toes of my boots but with that gun and Winchester ammo loaded with two ounces of #5 shot, I once bagged a big gobbler at a measured 68 yards. Other turkey guns I have hunted with and really liked are the Beretta AL391, the Browning Gold and the Benelli.

How Many Different Shotshell Lengths and Gauges?

I want to start a small collection made up of samples of the various gauges and lengths of shotshells manufactured in the United States. How many have been made?

I have never seen a complete listing of what you need but the following information I obtained from a Winchester price list published during the early 1900s should get you started.

Gauge	Shell Lengths (Inches)
4	4
8	3, 3-1/4, 3-1/2, 4
10	2-5/8, 2-3/4, 2-7/8, 3, 3-1/8, 3-1/4
12	2-1/2, 2-5/8, 2-3/4, 2-7/8, 3, 3-1/8, 3-1/4
14	2-9/16
16	2-1/2, 2-9/16, 2-5/8, 2-3/4, 2-7/8, 3
20	2-1/2, 2-5/8, 2-3/4, 2-7/8, 3
24	2-1/2
28	2-1/2, 2-7/8
32	2-1/2

Add the 2-, 2-1/2- and 3-inch 410, the 2-3/4-inch 28 gauge, the 3-1/2-inch 12 gauge, the 3-1/2-inch 10 gauge, all arriving on the scene after that list was published, and the various rimfires, and you would have an interesting shotshell collection.

Turkey guns like these from Benelli come with a variety of barrel lengths.

Who Makes Strap-On and Slip-In Recoil Pads?

While at my gun club a few days ago I noticed a fellow pattern-testing a 12-gauge shotgun by shooting it from a benchrest. When I asked him how he was able to tolerate the recoil of those 3-1/2-inch magnum loads, he pointed to a thick recoil pad strapped to his shoulder. I checked the gunshop where he said he had purchased the item a couple of years before but a salesman there had never heard of it. Any idea where I can find one?

The strap-on recoil pad you saw was probably made by PAST which is a part of Battenfield Technologies. The pad is available in four thicknesses with the Field, Magnum and Mag Plus being ambidextrous. Thickest of the four, the Super Mag is designed to ease the pain from shooting extremely powerful rifles and shotguns and it is available only for right-hand shooters. PAST also makes Black Powder and Herean Shield models, the latter an ambidextrous design made to be worn beneath clothing by women. Another type of recoil pad slips into a pocket sewn into hunting and shooting clothing and is available from several sources, including Beretta, Browning and Bob Allen. That type of slip-in pad is better for wingshooting than the strap-on pad because it fits inside the shirt or jacket rather than on the outside. Phyllis uses one on the inside of her Beretta upland jacket and clay target vest and would not leave home without it.

The lightweight recoil pad worn by Phyllis on the inside of her shooting shirt reduces kick considerably.

What Can You Tell Me about My Davenport Shotgun?

I recently acquired a 12-gauge side-by-side double made by the W.H. Davenport Firearms Co. of Norwich, Connecticut. Its metal is in excellent shape but the buttstock is missing. What can you tell me about my shotgun? Any idea where I might find a new stock for it?

The W.H. Davenport Firearms Co. began in 1880 and made inexpensive single- and double-barrel shotguns up until the 1920s. Some of the doubles sold for as little as $12. I know of no source of parts for those guns and while you could have a stockmaker make a stock for yours I doubt if the value of the gun would justify the financial investment.

Which Shotshell Is Best for Goose Hunting?

I am a goose hunter and shoot steel shot. I plan to buy a new shotgun but cannot decide between a 10-gauge gun or one chambered for the 3-1/2-inch 12-gauge shell. How do the effective ranges of those two compare?

Once the use of steel shot became mandatory I came to really appreciate the 10-gauge shotshell. When the 3-1/2-inch 12-gauge shell came along I figured there was no way it could equal the performance of the 10 on the larger waterfowl, but a season or two in the field proved me wrong. Even so, I still prefer the 10 gauge for waterfowling with steel shot, not because it outperforms the 3-1/2-inch 12 gauge but because Remington's gas-operated SP10 is so much more comfortable to shoot than any gun chambered for the extra-long 12-gauge shell. I like the 3-1/2-inch 12 for turkey hunting because autoloaders chambered for it are lighter than the SP10 and not as many shots are fired in the field, but for waterfowling with steel shot where more shots are usually taken during a day's hunt, I'll take the Remington SP10 over any other gun made at this time.

What Size Shot for Valley and Mountain Quail?

Sometime back my grandfather gave to me a Remington Model 11-48 autoloader in 28-gauge and I want to use it for hunting valley and mountain quail. What loads, chokes and shot sizes do you recommend?

I once had the pleasure of hunting valley quail for five days in California and I used a Weatherby Athena over-under with 28-inch barrels in 28 gauge and 410. When hunting with the 28 gauge, I used an Improved Cylinder choke in the bottom barrel and Modified up top and that combination proved to be ideal for the areas I hunted. I found #7-1/2 shot to be more effective than #8s, probably due to the fact that I was hunting late in the season and all the birds I shot were fully mature. The valley or the California quail, as it is also called, is about the same size as the bobwhite quail; the mountain quail is a few ounces heavier. When hunting those I have found #7-1/2s to work fine.

Choosing the right firepower is important when high-flying Canada geese are the targets.

Where Can I Find Better Performing 9mm Rimfire Shotshells?

I desire to place my childhood garden gun, a bolt action chambered for the 9mm rimfire shotshell, back into service but I am experiencing frustratingly poor performance from ammunition made by the Italian firm of Fiocchi. It is the only ammunition I have managed to locate here in Belgium. Are you aware of any other company that manufactures this ammo? Alternatively, I wish the 9mm rimfire cases could somehow be reloaded for better performance. Any ideas?

During the 1920s Winchester loaded the 9mm rimfire shotshell and even offered an inexpensive bolt-action single-shot shotgun for it called the Model 36. Winchester has not manufactured the ammo in many years and I know of no American company that does so at present. The 9mm rimfire contains slightly less than 1/4 oz. of shot which is less than half as much as is loaded by U.S. manufacturers in the 2-1/2 inch 410 shotshell. For this reason, even if you do find another source of the ammo I'll be surprised if it proves to be a better close-range pest load than the one you are now using. The centerfire version of the 9mm shotshell may also still be commonly available in Europe and it probably could be reloaded. Whether or not your shotgun would be suitable for the rimfire to centerfire conversion is a decision only a competent gunsmith should make.

Where Do I Find Choke Tubes for Cutts Compensator?

I recently bought a 410 Winchester Model 42 and it has a Cutts Compensator attached to the muzzle of its barrel. Was the Model 42 available from the factory with the Cutts installed or was it an aftermarket installation? I have fallen in love with the little pump gun but the only choke tube I have for it is marked "Full" and for hunting I need a bigger pattern than it throws. Where can I find Improved Cylinder and Modified tubes for my gun?

Winchester began offering the Cutts Compensator on its Model 42 skeet guns in 1954 but not many shooters bought that option, making it somewhat rare. If your gun does not have a choke designation stamped on its barrel just forward of the receiver, its Cutts was most definitely installed at the factory. If the choke is stamped on the barrel of your gun it was either returned to the factory for the installation or the Cutts was installed by a gunsmith. Cutts choke tubes in 20 and 12 gauges are available from Brownells but tubes for the 16, 28 and 410 are becoming rather difficult to come by. I know this to be true since my Model 42 skeet gun wears a Cutts and the only tubes I have for it are Spreader and Full; thus far I have had no luck finding Improved Cylinder and Modified tubes. A good gunsmith could ream out your Full tube to less choke but considering how scarce the tubes are, I would continue the search at least for awhile. Another possibility is to have Briley Manufacturing make a tube for your gun.

Who Made My 10-Gauge Shotgun?

I am a duck and goose hunter and use the 10-gauge shotshell a lot here in France. Can you tell me who made a 10-gauge side-by-side double called the Matador III? I believe it was once imported to your country by Ventura Imports of Seal Beach, California.

The Matador side-by-side double was made by the Spanish firm of AyA and it was once available in 10, 16, 12, 20, 28 gauges as well as 410. An economy grade shotgun, it no longer is being manufactured but several higher grades of AyA shotguns are still being brought into the US by various importers.

How Many Trap Shooting Clubs?

You mentioned that you were one of over 7000 shooters who were registered at the one hundredth anniversary Grand American trap shoot held in Vandalia, Ohio in 1999. That event has more participants than any other shooting sport and is second only to the runners' marathons held in Boston, New York and a few other places as far as single-day, individual-participant events go. How many gun clubs in the United States offer trap shooting? How can I learn more about the sport?

I have no idea how many gun clubs across the country offer trap shooting but I do know that just about every state in America has several. New York, Kentucky, Michigan, Wisconsin, Ohio, California, Texas, Iowa, Pennsylvania and Illinois are the states with the most trap-shooting clubs. In all, close to 500 clubs in those states alone have one or more trap fields. Add the number of trap fields in all the other states in the U.S. and it is easy to see why it is such a huge sport. You can obtain information on the sport and a membership application by writing to the Amateur Trapshooting Association.

How Do You Rate The 17 Hornady Mach 2?

I enjoy hunting small game such as rabbits and squirrels. I like the looks of the Classic autoloading rifle from Thompson/Center which is available in 17 Mach 2. How do you rate the performance of that cartridge in the field? What are its disadvantages?

I first used a T/C Classic in 17 HM2 while hunting huge fox squirrels in Kansas. It wore a Nikon 3.5-10X scope. I found that outfit to be quite effective out to 60 yards or so when a shot to the body of a squirrel was taken, but beyond that distance shots to the head were required for quick, humane kills.

The superb accuracy and flat trajectory of the T/C rifle and the Hornady ammo I was using made head shots quite easy out to 80 yards (when the wind was not blowing). The biggest disadvantage of the 17 HM2 is a box of ammo costs three to 3-1/2 times the price of the most expensive 22 Long Rifle high velocity ammo. This is neither here nor there to most hunters because, typically, not a great deal of

HIGH
BRASS
HB

28
GAUGE

2¾
INCHES

MAX.
DR. EQ.

X28H7½

1
OZ.

7½
SHOT

WINCHESTER X
SUPER-X ™

**28 GA. 2¾ IN.
MAX.** DR. -1OZ.-7½

HIGH
BRASS

WARNING: Keep out of reach of ch

Pheasant and Dove Loads for 28 Gauge?

I am the proud owner of a spanking new Remington Model 1100 Sporting in 28 gauge and after accumulating a supply of empty Winchester AA hulls while shooting skeet, I am ready to start reloading. You have written a great deal about wingshooting with the 28 and I'd like to know your favorite handload for bobwhite quail and mourning doves. I don't reload enough shotshells each year to justify the purchase of a progressive reloader so I'm in the market for a single-stage rig; which one is bolted to your reloading bench? I would also be interested in your opinion of various 28-gauge factory loads. And one last thing; do you think any other manufactures will start offering the 28 gauge in an autoloader?

I use the same 28-gauge load with high-antimony, target-grade shot when hunting doves and pheasant with the 28 gauge as I do for skeet but use I #9 shot for clay targets, #8s for doves and #6s for pheasant. The combination I choose most often consists of the Winchester AA hull, the Winchester 209 primer, 13.0 gr. of Hodgdon's Universal powder, Winchester AA28 plastic wad, and 3/4 oz. of shot. I recently chronographed that load in three of my guns, a Remington Model 1100 with 26-inch barrel, a Browning Superposed with 26-1/2 inch barrels and a Parker VHE with 26-inch tubes. Muzzle velocity averaged just over 1200 fps in all of them. Pattern quality of that load is excellent and Universal powder leaves very little residue in the barrel. The single-stage reloader I use for developing a new load for the 410 is a Du-O-Matic 375C built by Ponsness Warren. The same machine is also available in 28 gauge. The MEC 600 Jr. would also suit your needs.

When hunting doves and quail with 28-gauge factory ammo, I especially like the AA target load from Winchester and the STS target load from Remington, both loaded with 3/4 oz. of #8 shot. The Federal Premium field load with the same size shot is also an excellent choice. For pheasant, I prefer to move up in payload to the Winchester Super-X load with an ounce of #6. The Franchi 48AL autoloader is available in 12 gauge and I will not be surprised to see Beretta eventually offer the 28 in its AL391.

The Winchester Super-X 28-gauge load with an ounce of shot is excellent pheasant medicine.

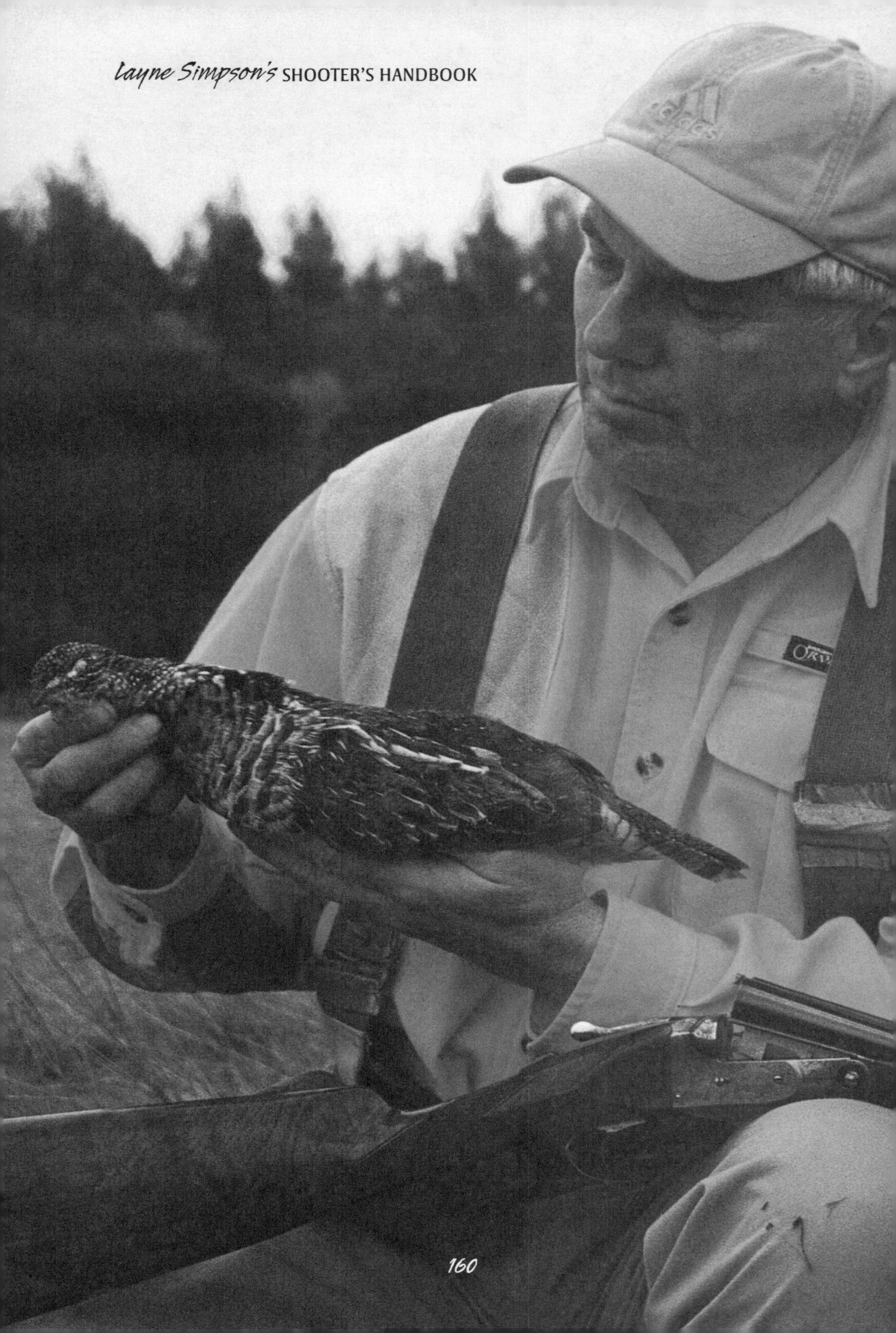

The "Quail-1" and "Quail-2" chokes of this Parker are great for close-range shooting of ruffed grouse.

What Are Parker Reproduction Q-1 and Q-2 Chokes?

Several months ago I bought a 20-gauge Parker reproduction side-by-side shotgun and its choke markings are "Q-1" for the right barrel and "Q-2" for the left. Never having heard of those designations and not having the proper tools to measure the bores of my shotgun to determine actual choke constriction, I'm hoping you can shed some light on the subject.

As a rule, the "Quail-1" choke designation on the barrel of a 20- or 28-gauge Parker reproduction double indicates around .004 inch of constriction which would be midway between Light Skeet (.003-inch) and Skeet (.005-inch). The "Quail-2" barrels usually run anywhere from .007 to .010 inch, or in the neighborhood of Improved Cylinder.

ammo is used on game. Ammo cost does rule out a lot of plinking, an American pastime which will always belong to the 22 rimfire. Muzzle blast of the 17 HM2 seems louder and sharper than that of the 22 Long Rifle so you will want to wear ear protection when shooting it.

What Barrel Length for 3-1/2" 12-Gauge?

I plan to buy a Beretta 391 or a Browning Gold chambered for the 3-1/2-inch 12-gauge shell but cannot decide between the available 26-, 28- and 30-inch barrel length options. Which of those barrel lengths squeezes optimum performance from magnum loads? Another question. Why don't manufacturers list velocity and energy figures on shotshell boxes?

Increases in the length of a shotgun barrel produce only a few feet per second higher velocities per additional inch so choosing between the three lengths you are considering boils down to other factors. First of all, I don't care for a 26-inch barrel on a magnum 12 due to the muzzle blast. If I were buying a 3-1/2-inch magnum for waterfowl hunting I would choose the 30-inch barrel simply because it swings smoother on passing shots. For turkey hunting I would go with the 28-inch barrel because it is a bit handier in the woods. The 28-inch barrel length is also my pick for all-around use.

While some manufacturers currently include velocities on the boxes of certain loads only, the information can be found on all loads in ammunition catalogs published by Federal, Remington, Winchester, Kent and others. Since so many shot sizes are available in shotshells and since energy figures differ for each shot size and velocity range I doubt if we will ever see that info printed on shotshell boxes. The information is, however, available in the *Shotshell Handbook* from Lyman Products Corp.

Steel Shot in Browning Over/Under?

I have a Browning 12-gauge over/under shotgun made in Belgium during the early 1950s. Is it suitable for use with steel shot?

Your Browning Superposed was manufactured long before the use of steel shot was mandated for waterfowl hunting. Since it was not designed for use with steel, the only nontoxic shot loads you should use in it are bismuth from Bismuth Cartridge and tungsten-matrix from Kent.

Why Is Winchester Model 59 So Light?

Sometime back I was given a 12-gauge Winchester Model 59 shotgun and I am amazed at how light it is. How was Winchester able to keep the heft of a full-size autoloader at less than seven pounds? When was it manufactured?

The Model 59 was produced from 1959 until 1965 and Winchester rated it at 6-1/2 pounds. An aluminum receiver along with a composite Win-Lite barrel built by wrapping 500 miles of glass fiber around a thin steel tube are what made the shotgun so light. Experimental Model 59s were also made in 20 and 14 gauge and I still have one of the latter aluminum-cased shells in my collection, but production guns were made only in 12 gauge. The Model 59 was the first American-made gun available with screw-in chokes inside the barrel, a system referred to by Winchester as the "Versalite." Despite the fact that Winchester's glass-barrel Model 59 is one of the most dynamic handling ruffed grouse and quail guns ever built, it never won any popularity contests and fewer than 85,000 were made.

Why Use the 20 Gauge in 12-Gauge Skeet?

Sometime back you mentioned that many registered skeet shooters now shoot both the 12- and 20-gauge events with 12-gauge over/unders but their guns have subgauge tubes chambered for the 20-gauge shell. It appears to me that shooting the smaller shell in the 12-gauge event would put those who do so at a disadvantage when competing against others who are shooting 12-gauge guns. Also, why do they shoot a 12-gauge gun with 20-gauge tubes when they could be shooting lighter guns originally chambered for the 20-gauge shell?

Since the longest shots in skeet seldom exceed 25 yards, it only takes a shooter a few rounds with the two gauges to discover that he breaks as many targets with the 7/8 oz. of shot from the 20 as with the 1-1/8 oz. from the 12. This, along with the fact that it is not uncommon to shoot several hundred rounds per day in a tournament, prompts many skeeters to choose the milder-recoiling 20 for both the 20- and 12-gauge events. One of the reasons skeet shooters prefer a tubed 12-gauge gun over one chambered the 20-gauge shell is its heavier weight reduces recoil. Another reason they do so is because the heavier gun swings more smoothly during a sustained lead and its greater momentum during the swing encourages correct follow-through. Some skeet shooters are now taking the low-recoil idea a step further by shooting the 28-gauge in its event as well as the 20- and 12-gauge events. I recently started doing just that when it dawned on me that my overall average was just as good with the 28 as when using the larger bores.

Which Slug Gun Should I Buy?

I'll soon be moving to a state where only shotguns and slug loads are allowed for hunting deer. In browsing through brochures from various companies I see that prices of slug guns range from just under $2000 for a bolt action model said to be capable of shooting one-inch groups at 100 yards to various pumps and autoloaders that sell for less than $500. Since I have already sold several of my deer rifles I can afford to buy the more expensive gun but I question whether or not a super-accurate slug gun is actually needed for hunting. What is your opinion on this?

If you plan to do a lot of serious target shooting with slug loads the bolt-action match gun you mentioned might be the way to go although I have shot less expensive bolt guns like the Browning A-Bolt and Marlin 512 Slugmaster that occasionally came mighty close to minute-of-angle accuracy with some saboted slug loads. When looking at the slug gun as a hunting arm from a practical point of view, any model that will average four inches or less at 100 yards is plenty accurate for shooting deer anywhere within the effective range of most slug loads. And since you are more interested in the slug gun for hunting than for target shooting I believe you would be quite happy with one of the various bolt actions, pumps and autoloaders offered by companies such as Remington, Browning, Marlin, Benelli, Beretta and Ithaca. Some of the money you save by buying one of those guns could go toward the purchase of practice ammo and a good scope.

How Do I Open Up Choke in Shotgun Barrel?

My father recently gave me his favorite Winchester Model 12 shotgun and its barrel is choked too tightly for the hunting I do. I'd rather not have screw-in chokes installed in the barrel and hope you can advise me of an alternative or two.

The choke in the barrel of your shotgun can be reamed out to less constriction but it should be done only by a gunsmith who has both the proper tools and the experience in this type of work. To perform the job properly, a long extension must be used to insert a special reamer through the breech end of the barrel and into its choked section at the muzzle. After the choke has been reamed out to the desired constriction, any reamer marks should be removed by polishing. A second option is to leave the barrel as is and shoot special spreader loads available from Magnum Performance Ballistics. Available in 12, 16, 20 and 28 gauges, a plastic Polywad insert in the shot column causes the pellets to disperse widely enough as they exit the muzzle to produce Improved Cylinder patterns from a Full Choke barrel. The inserts are also available for handloading.

How Do I Tame Recoil at the Bench?

I live in a state where only shotguns can be used for hunting deer. I own several shotguns and enjoy accuracy-testing slug loads from various manufacturers in them at the benchrest. Due to the heavy recoil of those guns I am ready to quit shooting long before I am ready to go home. How do you survive the poundings of all those guns you test at the bench?

When shooting a hard-kicking gun over sandbags, I place a "sissy bag" between the butt of the gun and my shoulder. Nothing more than a sausage-shaped leather bag filled with sand, it is available from Sinclair International. Another recoil-tamer I have been using lately is called the Lead Sled. It consists of a heavy steel tray with front and rear rests for supporting the stock and forearm of a rifle or shotgun. When two 25-pound bags of lead shot are placed in the tray the Lead Sled tames any shotgun you might want to attempt to shoot. A great idea, it is available from Battenfield Technologies.

Which Choke and 28-Gauge Load for Quail?

On several occasions you have mentioned hunting quail with various shotguns in 28 gauge. I recently bought a Beretta over-under chambered for the little cartridge and a friend with whom l hunt bought a Remington Model 1100 Sporting 28. We do not handload and are hoping you will recommend a factory load for our guns. What chokes do you prefer when hunting quail?

When hunting on preserves where liberated quail usually hold tight to a dog's point and flush at close range any of the target loads with 3/4 oz. of #9 shot are plenty effective. Excellent examples are the Remington Premier STS, Federal Gold Medal and Winchester AA skeet loads. I really like those loads for close-range work at 25 yards and less. When using a double-barrel shotgun I prefer Skeet choke in its first barrel and Improved Cylinder in the other. When hunting wild quail, I switch to Improved Cylinder and either Light Modified or Modified chokes simply because those birds have a tendency to flush farther away from the gun. I also switch to heavier shot and have enjoyed great success with Remington's Premier STS loaded with #8s and Federal's Gold Medal Target with #8-1/2s. The Winchester Super X Game Load with an ounce of 7-1/2s or 8s is also a very effective load, especially at the tail end of the season when the birds are more heavily feathered.

Is Magnum Shot Better than Chilled Shot?

I reload all my 12, 20 and 28 gauge shotshells for shooting trap and skeet. Each time l visit my dealer to stock up on several 25-pound bags of shot l am reminded that the harder magnum variety is more expensive than chilled shot. l usually buy the more expensive stuff because l have been told it produces more uniform patterns. Do you agree?

Magnum shot costs a bit more than chilled shot and for some applications it is worth it.

An over-under like this Browning Cynergy is quite versatile.

Is Over-Under a Good All-Around Shotgun?

I'm in the market for a new shotgun and had about decided on a Beretta over-under when a friend informed me that a double-barrel shotgun is not as versatile as an autoloader. According to him, a good 12-gauge auto with a variety of screw-in chokes has the entire shotgunning spectrum covered, something a double-barrel gun cannot do. What do you think?

While your friend is correct about the versatility of an autoloader with screw-in chokes, I'll have to disagree with his opinion on the over-under double. In fact, if I had to dispose of every shotgun in my battery except one, the survivor would be a 12-gauge over-under. The gun would have a set of subgauge tubes that would allow me to also shoot the 20- and 28-gauge and 410 shells. For the barrels of the gun and its six insert tubes I would have screw-in chokes with constrictions ranging from Skeet to Full. With such an outfit I would have all the gun I might need for upland wing shooting, rabbit hunting, waterfowling, skeet, trap and sporting clays. So equipped, that Beretta you have your eye on would be just as versatile. The 12-gauge autoloader does have the edge as a deer gun since it can also be equipped with a rifled barrel for shooting sabot slugs but this should matter only to those who live in areas where the use of rifles is not allowed for hunting deer.

Back before the introduction of shotshells with plastic wads and their integral shotcups, magnum shot, which is harder due to its higher antimony content, could usually be counted on to produce denser patterns simply because its greater hardness enabled it to be shoved through the barrel of a shotgun with less deformity than was the case with softer chilled shot. This is still true but to a lesser degree since today's plastic wad columns do a great job of protecting the shot charge from damage during firing. Some deformation still occurs with both types of shot and while it is usually a bit less with magnum shot, the difference is seldom great enough to make a big difference in pattern quality on the skeet field where targets are usually broken at less than 25 yards. I'd just as soon have one as the other when shooting skeet but I prefer magnum shot when shooting trap where shots are taken a longer ranges and an improvement in pattern quality can result in fewer lost targets. I prefer magnum shot in loads used for hunting various game birds for the improvement in pattern quality and the greater penetration of the harder shot.

How Do We Fix Ithaca Slug Gun Accuracy?

Friends and I own three Ithaca Model 37 Deerslayer shotguns, all built during the 1960s. According to a local gunsmith, their bores measure .705 inch, which is .024 inch smaller in diameter than is standard for 12-gauge guns. Regardless of whether the brand of ammo we shoot is Winchester, Remington or Federal, all Foster-style slugs leave terrible leading in the barrel and this results in poor accuracy. A call to the plant manager at Ithaca revealed that .705 inch was the standard bore diameter for Model 37 slug guns years ago but since our guns were made while his company was under previous ownership, he can do nothing about it. We are looking for a solution to this problem and hope you have a recommendation.

I discussed your letter with my friend Chuck Webb at Briley Manufacturing who is more knowledgeable of shotguns than anyone else I know. He says a .705-inch bore diameter is quite acceptable when top accuracy is desired with 12-gauge Foster-type slug loads in a smoothbore barrel. But the barrel has to be cleaned frequently and all leading removed. Chuck also suggests that you and your hunting pals try sabot slug loads in your guns. I might add that Ithaca pioneered the 12-gauge slug gun with its Model 37 Deerslayer. The one I owned years ago was the most accurate firearm of its type I had fired until fully rifled barrels and sabot slug loads came along. Through experimentation, Ithaca engineers found that 12-gauge smoothbore barrels with about 25 points of choke constriction (between Modified and Full) produced the best accuracy with Foster-type slugs. This resulted in the introduction of the Deerslayer barrel with a bore measuring just over .700 inch from the end of its forcing cone to the muzzle.

Years ago I experimented with various Foster-style slug loads and found that accuracy was best in a variety of guns when their bores were kept free of leading. This may mean cleaning the bore thoroughly every five rounds or so with a wad of 0000-grade steel wool attached to the end of a cleaning rod. Soaking the steel wool with a good solvent such as Bore Scrubber from Birchwood Casey or Hoppe's No. 9 also helps. If, by chance, you find that your guns continue to shoot poorly, even with clean barrels, my advice is to have screw-in rifled chokes installed in them and stick with sabot slug loads.

Which Barrel for Sabot Slug Loads?

In one of the areas in which I intend to hunt deer next season, I will be restricted to the use of a shotgun with slug loads. The terrain is brushy and heavily wooded and 75 yards would be an exceptionally long shot. I already hunt waterfowl and upland game with a Remington 11-87 shotgun in 12 gauge with interchangeable chokes and want to use it for hunting deer as well. Will a screw-in rifled choke get the job done or should I bite the bullet and spend the extra money for a fully rifled barrel?

I once tested the accuracy of various sabot slug loads in several shotguns and found that out to 50 yards, most were about as accurate when fired in smoothbore barrels with rifled screw-in chokes as when they were fired in fully rifled barrels. When increasing the range to 100 yards I found all loads to be more accurate in fully rifled barrels but even when fired at that range from the smoothbore/rifled choke combination, all loads were still plenty accurate for bringing home the venison. Considering that most shots in the area you will be hunting seldom exceed 75 yards, I believe you should give a screw-in rifled choke a try in your Model 11-87 before spending money on another barrel.

When Will You Write a Shotgun Book?

I have enjoyed your articles on shotguns for many years. When will you write a book on the subject?

I already have. The name of the book is *Shotguns and Shotgunning* and it was published in 2003 by K-P Books (715-445-2214), the publisher of this book.

SECTION THREE

Handguns

What Are Prot-X Bore Bullets?

I recently purchased several boxes of 44-caliber bullets at a gun show and the box was marked "Prot-X Bore by Lakeville Arms." What can you tell me about them?

The Proto-X Bore bullet in 357-, 44- and 45-caliber was available in the 1950s and 1960s from Lakeville Arms of Lakeville, CT. Developed by company owner Jim Harvey, it is a rather soft cast bullet with a zinc base. The base was supposed to prevent leading by scraping the bore clean as the bullet passed through it, but those I handloaded many years ago in the 357 Magnum leaded about as badly as conventional cast bullets. Another bullet developed by Harvey and called the Jugular Xpress did eliminate leading since its jacket prevented the lead core from making contact with the bore. It came along several years before the major bullet makers offered jacketed handgun bullets designed to expand. Harvey was also a pioneer in the development of lightweight handgun bullets and loaded his 106-gr. jacketed hollowpoint to 1800 feet per second in the 357 Magnum.

What Is the 357 Atomic?

My father recently gave to me a Great Western single-action revolver in 357 Atomic. Was it a special cartridge developed by that company? What did my gun cost back in the good old days?

Your revolver is chambered for the standard 357 Magnum. Great Western called it the 357 Atomic in an effort to boost sales. During the mid-1950s your revolver had a list price of $75 compared to $87.50 for the Ruger Blackhawk in 357 Magnum.

The 50 AE in France

I recently bought an L.A.R. Grizzly pistol in 50 AE and have discovered that jacketed bullets for it are extremely expensive here in France. I'd like to cast my own bullets but cannot locate a mould. Is there a source in the United States? If so, the address, telephone and FAX numbers would be most helpful to me.

Try NEI Handtools, Inc., 51583 Columbia River Hwy, Scappoose, OR 97056. Tel:503-543-6776; FAX:503-543-6799. NEI may already have the mould you're looking for in stock but if not, the shop will make one to your exact specifications.

Custom Aftermarket Parts for Double Eagle?

I own a Colt Double Eagle in 45 ACP and would like to make a number of custom modifications to it. Do any of the aftermarket parts made for a 1911-style pistol such as Colt's Government Model fit the Double Eagle as well?

Most aftermarket parts made for the top assembly of 1911-style pistols will work with your Double Eagle. They include the barrel, full-length recoil spring guide, recoil spring, extractor, firing pin and firing pin spring. A Series 80 slide will also work on your frame if a notch is machined into the rear end of its right-hand rail for clearance with the top-

This Alaska moose took only about four steps after I shot it with a revolver in 44 Magnum.

Will the 44 Magnum Work on Moose?

I have hunted a lot with a 44 Magnum revolver and find it to be plenty powerful for taking deer out to 100 yards or so. I would like to use the same outfit on a moose hunt, but since some writers recommend nothing less than a rifle in 338 Magnum for that animal, I am wondering if I would be undergunned. What do you think?

I have proven to my own satisfaction that when the right bullet is placed where it must go at relatively close range, a revolver in 44 Magnum will work on moose. A few years back I used a Smith & Wesson Model 629 to bag one of the best moose I have taken in Alaska. After taking a shot to the lungs at about 65 yards, the bull took about six steps and stood there a few seconds before discovering it was supposed to be dead. The load I used consisted of just enough H110 powder to push the Nosler 260-gr. hollowpoint along at maximum speed.

end of the disconnector. As for the lower assembly, the ejector, slide catch, magazine latch and magazine well funnels are the same for the two guns.

Is 500 S&W Magnum Better Than 454 Casull?

I plan to hunt elk with a handgun and want to move up in power from the 44 Magnum I have used quite successfully on deer for several years. I was considering a Freedom Arms revolver in 454 Casull, but the introduction of the 500 S&W Magnum now has me undecided. Would the big 500 be a better choice?

For my own hunting use the 500 S&W Magnum two strikes against it and one is the 72-ounce weight of the S&W Model 500 revolver. The other is recoil, around 50 foot-pounds compared to 35 for the 454 Casull and 16 for the 44 Magnum. This is why I prefer the 454 Casull.

A 400 Cor-Bon Barrel That Works?

In addition to being a 30-year veteran of law enforcement, I am also a competitive shooter. Several of us have become interested in the new 400 Cor-Bon cartridge since 1911-style pistols in 45 ACP can be converted by merely switching barrels. I recently tried a so-called "drop-in" barrel in this caliber in two different Colt Gold Cups, a Colt Combat Elite and a Springfield 1911-A1, all 45 caliber guns, of course. The barrel worked in none of those guns. Where can I get a genuine drop-in barrel in 400 Cor-Bon?

There are a number of sources for 400 Cor-Bon barrels but the only one I have any experience with is Nowlin Custom Manufacturing. I recently tried a Nowlin barrel in that caliber in four 45 caliber 1911-style guns—a custom Colt Government Model built by Bill Wilson; and three factory-original guns, a Springfield 1911-A1, a Kimber Classic and a Colt Government Model. The barrel dropped right into those guns and worked without a hitch. In fact, its fit in the custom Colt was as good as the 45-caliber barrel installed by Bill Wilson when he built the gun. Accuracy was excellent as well.

Do Titanium Firing Pins Improve Accuracy?

I've read that the installation of lightweight titanium firing pins in rifles and handguns improves accuracy by decreasing locktime. Is this fact or fallacy?

Installing a titanium firing pin does shorten locktime. I was once extremely high on firing pins made of this material but after trying them in a couple of match-grade AR-15 rifles and several extremely accurate 1911-pattern pistols, I became convinced they are incapable of improving the mechanical accuracy of a firearm by a noticeable amount. Using a titanium firing pin in a pistol chambered for the 9x23mm Winchester can actually result in misfires due to the thick cup of the small rifle primer loaded in that cartridge. Same goes for major-power loadings of the 38 Super in which small rifle primers are commonly used.

Where Do I Find More Powerful 45 Colt Ammo?

Do you know where I can find 45 Colt ammo that's more powerful than the stuff loaded by Winchester, Remington and Federal?

The most powerful 45 Colt factory ammo I'm aware of is loaded by Cor-Bon. Two loadings are available. One is the standard load with a 200-gr. JHP at 1100 fps and the other load is identified by Cor-Bon as the 45 Colt Magnum. According to Cor-Bon officials, the latter load is intended only for the Ruger Super Blackhawk and Freedom Arms Casull in 45 Colt. It is loaded with a 300-gr. JHP at 1300 fps.

How Do I Reduce 45 ACP Recoil?

I have been shooting in Limited Class USPSA competition for about two years and would like your opinion on the effectiveness of various shock-absorber type recoil spring guides that are available from several sources that offer aftermarket parts for the 1911 pistol. Do they actually reduce recoil and muzzle jump as claimed?

I have tried the item you described from two different sources and if they were any better at reducing recoil and muzzle jump than a regular full-length steel recoil spring guide rod, I could not detect it. In my experience, a spring guide made of tungsten is more effective with the five-ounce version from Brownells and Wilson Combat the best I have found for dampening recoil and muzzle rise. It uses a special large-diameter recoil spring and its installation requires a slight enlargement of the recoil spring tunnel in the slide. The modification is easily done with a tool called the Reverse Plug Reamer from Brownells or you can have it installed by a gunsmith. Brownells also offers a smaller drop-in unit and while it weighs a couple of ounces less, its installation requires no modification to the slide of the gun.

How Do I Get the Lead Out?

I have been shooting cast bullets in my handgun and its bore has accumulated severe leading deposits. How do I get the stuff out?

The quickest way to remove the leading from your barrel is to scrub it with a special kit made for just that purpose. One is called the Hoppe's Lead Remover and is made by Penguin Industries, maker of Hoppe's No. 9 solvent. Available for 38/357, 40/10mm, 44 and 45 caliber handguns, it can be purchased at any well-stocked gun shop or sporting goods store. Another option is called the Lewis Lead Remover and is available from Brownells. Both kits consist of a short cleaning rod with a special tip that accepts patches made of brass mesh. The patches are hard enough to scrape away the lead deposits but not hard enough to harm the barrel. The patches work even better when coated with a past-like product called J.B. Nonimbedding Bore Cleaner (also available from Brownells).

The lead can also be removed by wrapping a small swatch torn from a copper cleaning pad around a bore brush and pushing it through the barrel. This item is

The 38 Super is plenty accurate in a barrel that headspaces it properly.

Is 38 Super Inaccurate?

I have the opportunity to buy a used custom Colt Government Model in 38 Super built by Bill Wilson but have been told the cartridge is neither accurate nor very popular. Since you have a great deal of experience with that cartridge, would you please comment on this?

For many years the 38 Super has been the No. 1 choice among Unlimited class USPSA competitors. I have used it in competition since 1992 and after firing many thousands of rounds of major-power loads, it has become one of my favorites. The accuracy problem associated with the 38 Super was caused by a design detail in Colt pistols and not by the cartridge. In older Colts the rim of the cartridge was required to headspace on a tiny shoulder cut into the hood of the barrel. Due to variations in the dimensions of cases, headspacing with that system was neither positive nor uniform. Aftermarket barrel manufacturers eventually solved the problem by cutting a shoulder at the front of the chamber so the 38 Super case could headspace on its mouth, same as rimless cartridges such as the 45 ACP and 9mm Luger. Springfield Armory was the first manufacturer to make that change in factory barrels and was also the first to change to a full-support chamber in barrels of that caliber. Colt and other manufacturers eventually started cutting the headspace shoulder in their barrels.

When fired in custom guns I find the 38 Super to be extremely accurate and quite capable of averaging two inches or better at 50 yards with either jacketed or cast bullets. One of the custom Government Model pistols used by the legendary Ruby Fox to win High Woman at the 1996 bullseye matches at Camp Perry was built by my friend Bob Marvel and chambered for the 38 Super.

Why Custom M1911 instead of a Colt Gold Cup?

I am a great fan of the 45-caliber 1911 pistol and have long been puzzled by the absence of Colt's Gold Cup in discussions on guns for personal protection. I have owned one for years and it has proven to be totally reliable with a variety of ammo. I have read many articles about the various 1911 modifications offered by pistolsmiths, changes that can add up to more than the cost of a Gold Cup. So why not simply buy a Gold Cup and forego the custom route?

The Colt Gold Cup is a fine handgun but due to its price, standard guns with custom modifications tailored to the individual shooter are still preferred by many. And you don't have to be rich to own one. You can certainly spend a lot more money on a custom 1911 pistol but it is possible to have the really important modifications made to a standard 1911 and end up with a better personal defense gun for the same or less money than you would pay for a Gold Cup. If I had to choose between the two, I'd rather have a plain-Jane Colt 1911-A1 with a good trigger job, high-sweep beavertail grip safety and an extended thumb safety than a box-stock Gold Cup. As for accuracy, there probably wouldn't be a great deal of difference between the two. While Gold Cups built as late at the 1970s were often quite accurate, the later ones are seldom any more accurate than Colt's standard Government Model.

Many shooters prefer a custom 1911 pistol for many reasons.

Regardless of the load, the 357 Magnum is too light for bear.

Which 357 Magnum Load for Deer?

I plan to hunt whitetail deer with a six-inch revolver in 357 Magnum. I realize most hunters consider this cartridge underpowered for deer but the whitetails here in Florida are quite small and my shooting will be restricted to close range. I hunt from a wheel chair and am able to assume a stable position in order to place my shots carefully. I am quite proficient with my revolver and have used it to take several feral hogs. For deer, I will use ammo loaded with 125- or 158-gr. hollowpoint bullets. Which do you recommend?

While you can include me among those who consider the 357 Magnum less than ideal for hunting deer, I also realize deer can be taken with it if the right bullet is put in the right place and the range does not greatly exceed 50 yards. The 125-gr. hollowpoint may open up quicker but the 158-grain is more likely to exit a lung-shot buck and in doing so, leave a good blood trail should the animal decide to run off. Actually, whatever load you have been using on wild hogs should perform about the same on deer.

A good pistolsmith can easily modify case ejection angle.

Can Case Ejection Angle Be Altered?

Is it possible to change the case ejection angle of a 1911-style autoloading pistol?

The angle at which fired cases are ejected from an autoloading pistol is usually accomplished by reshaping the nose of its ejector. This is a common modification for the 1911-style pistol when it is fitted with a low-mounted electronic sight. The modification should be performed only by a pistolsmith who is experienced in working on that particular firearm.

Starting with a Caspian frame and slide, I built my own 1911 in 38 Super for IDPA competition.

What Gun for IDPA Enhanced Pistol Division?

I recently joined the International Defensive Pistol Association and from all I have read, the Enhanced Pistol class is the one for me. What gun do you use to shoot IDPA?

The 1911 pistol I shoot in the Enhanced Pistol division of IDPA is one I built under the watchful eye of masterpiece pistolsmith Don Fraley. Starting with a Caspian frame and barstock slide, I put the gun together from scratch while spending a week in Fraley's shop. Chambered for the 38 Super cartridge, it will consistently shoot five bullets inside three inches at 50 yards. I shot that gun in the IDPA Invitational, a match held in Columbia, Missouri and then later shot it in the first IDPA Nationals.

commonly used to scrub pots and pans in the home and you should be able to find it in the kitchen department of most any food store. Be sure the pad is solid copper and not copper-coated steel which can scratch the bore of a barrel.

What Electronic Sight and Mount for Ruger Super Blackhawk?

I have a Ruger Super Blackhawk in 44 Magnum and plan to use it for hunting deer in areas where shots seldom exceed 75 yards. I have already decided to purchase an electronic sight but cannot decide between the various brands, models and options. Should I go with one of the easily installed "no-gunsmithing" mounts?

The many models and variations of electronic sights available make choosing among them a tough thing to do but you won't go wrong so long as you stick with names such as C-More, Burris, Tasco, Weaver, Bushnell, Leupold and Aimpoint. When using that type of sight on a hunting gun, I prefer one with a tube no larger in diameter than 30mm. When hunting deer and larger game such as elk and moose, I like for dot subtension to be in the eight to 12 minute-of-angle range. If you decide to go with a tubeless sight your options boil down to making a choice between the lighter weight and lower profile of the C-More and the interchangeable reticle patterns of the Bushnell HoloSight. If you plan to shoot your revolver a great deal, stay away from the so-called no-gunsmithing mount as it will not hold up under a steady pounding of heavy 44 Magnum loads. The very best mount I have ever used on hard-kicking revolvers is the one installed by SSK Industries.

How Do I Clean a Glock Magazine?

I have owned a Glock pistol for several months and absolutely love it. There is one thing about it I have not figured out—how in the world do I disassemble its magazine for cleaning?

The floorplate of the Glock magazine is held in place by the integral stud of an internal retaining plate (which is under pressure from the magazine spring). It is an excellent design and the reason why a Glock magazine won't fly apart even when dropped on a hard surface while fully loaded. Field stripping the magazine is quite easy once you have done it a time or two. If you are right-handed, hold the empty magazine bottomside up in your left hand with its front surface facing you. Slightly depress the internal floorplate retaining plate by inserting a thin metal rod into the hole in its center and then pull the floorplate toward you by applying pressure on the rod. Breaking the floorplate loose can sometimes take a bit of muscle so it helps to lock the thumb of the right hand (the one holding the rod) over the back of the left hand for leverage. When buying a takedown rod at your favorite hardware store, keep in mind that applying sufficient leverage is quite difficult if it is much shorter than six inches. A metal file can be used in lieu of the rod if its handle is small enough to enter the hole in the floorplate. When removing the spring from the body of the magazine for cleaning, note which end goes up and how the spring attaches to the follower. Doing this will ensure proper reassembly.

Field-stripping the Glock magazine for cleaning isn't difficult but does take some practice.

Which Pistol Holds Endurance Record?

I own a H&K USP in 45 ACP and like it a lot. The narrator of a H&K video I watched stated that the model I have has proven capable of firing many thousands of rounds without a single stoppage or component part failure and may eventually go for the durability record. What pistol holds that record?

Most reputable firearms manufacturers thoroughly test new autoloading pistols before introducing them to the market but if one of them has officially established a level of reliability and durability for others to attempt to match or exceed, I am not aware of it. I do know from personal experience that it is possible for some top-quality autoloaders to digest 10,000 rounds without a single malfunction or parts failure. Sometime back I experienced just that with a Glock 17 in 9mm Luger. As far as personal records go, I have fired over 50,000 rounds of full-power loads in each of two custom 1911-pattern pistols, both in 38 Super. Other than installing new recoil and firing pin springs in those guns every 5,000 rounds, the only part that had to be replaced was one extractor.

Which Cartridges for XP-100 Switch-Barrel?

In several of your articles, you have mentioned a custom XP-100 with interchangeable barrels in several calibers. What do you consider to be a good battery of barrels for such a firearm? Is your XP-100 the old center-grip style or the later version with rear grip? What are some of its details? Who built it?

The possibilities for a switch-barrel firearm are virtually endless. My custom XP-100 is the old center-grip style which I greatly prefer over the rear grip version. Built by Jarrett Rifles, it has three 15-inch Shilen barrels in 22-250 Improved, 7mm-08 Improved and 358 Winchester. Those three chamberings make it suitable for hunting everything from varmints to deer to moose and elk. It also has quick-detach scope mounts and three Burris variable-power scopes in 1.4-4X, 2-7X and 3-9X magnification ranges.

Which 1911 Compact Pistol?

I recently acquired my concealed carry permit. The Model 1911 in 45 ACP is my favorite handgun and I own a couple of full-size versions of it. Since I am quite familiar with this type of pistol I want to stay with it for concealed carry but need something lighter and more compact. What is your favorite handgun for this application and what do you recommend I look at?

At the moment I have two favorite concealed-carry handguns, a Glock Model 27 in 40 S&W and a Kimber Model 1911 Ultra Carry in 45 ACP. The Glock is my wintertime gun and I carry it in a lightweight Kramer belt holster. The entire outfit---gun, holster and 10 rounds of ammunition weighs 29 ounces. During summer, I often carry the Kimber in a Galco fanny pack. That gun has an aluminum frame and weighs 30 ounces with eight rounds of ammo. An extra seven-round magazine adds another eight ounces to the fanny pack. Other compact 1911 pistols worthy of a serious look are the Colt Lightweight Commander, Ed Brown Cobra Carry, Kimber Pro Carry, Para-Ordnance Para Companion and Springfield Compact Lightweight. Wilson Combat also offers several compact versions of the 1911 pistol and I highly recommend them as well.

The 243 Winchester As a Pistol Cartridge?

I want to start hunting with a long-range handgun. Being a bit sensitive to recoil, I am considering a custom Remington XP-100 in 243 Winchester. As a hunter, what is your opinion of that cartridge in a handgun? What velocity is it capable of in a short barrel? Do you have any favorite loads?

I have taken whitetail deer and pronghorn antelope with a Springfield SASS in 243 Winchester. While the 243 has worked okay for me, it is most definitely the minimum cartridge that can be considered adequate for shooting deer-size game at long range. Shots should be restricted to no more than 200 yards. The fastest 243 Winchester 100-gr. factory load I have checked in a 14-inch barrel averaged just over 2600 fps but some fell below 2500 fps. My favorite deer load for this cartridge in a short barrel consists of the Winchester case and WLR primer, 45.0 grains of H4350 and the Nosler 85-gr. Partition bullet for an average of 2751 fps. That load works nicely on deer and antelope, as does the Nosler 95-gr. Partition pushed to 2600 fps by 44.0 gr. of the same powder. I have not tried the Barnes 85-gr. XBT on deer but it too should work quite well.

Should I Use Shock Buffer in Colt Officer's ACP?

I have long used disposable shock buffers in my Colt Government Model pistols to prevent battering between the slide and frame. I recently bought a Colt Officer's ACP and installed a full-length recoil spring guide and rear-entry plug in it with the intention of using a buffer in that gun as well. Then I read a magazine article in which the author warned against using a shock buffer in the Officer's ACP. What do you think about all of this?

Shortly after acquiring my first Colt Officer's ACP I installed in it a full-length recoil spring guide, a rear-entry plug and began using shock buffers from Wilson Combat. To date I have fired close to 3000 rounds in that gun and have yet to experience any problem caused by the use of shock buffers. I do, however, replace the buffer every 500 rounds in that gun.

Reading Glasses for Handgun Shooting?

I am responding to a reader's letter to you concerning the use of bifocals when shooting handguns. I solved my problem by going to the store and buying a pair of reading glasses. They enable my eyes to focus on close objects, such as the sights on a handgun. When I wear the glasses, the sights are sharp and clear while the target is a bit fuzzy which is how the two are supposed to appear anyhow, even with perfect vision. One thing is certain, I am able to shoot a handgun much more accurately when wearing those reading glasses.

I also wear inexpensive reading glasses when shooting handguns with open sights and even use them when competing in USPSA and IDPA action pistol matches. You are correct about the target being a bit fuzzy but it is more important for the sights to be in focus than the target. I learned through trial and error that choosing the correct magnification is important (2X is correct for me). To decide which magnification is right for your eyes, visit the store and while wearing a pair of reading glasses, fully extend your arm in a horizontal position with its thumb pointed toward the ceiling. Start with a low magnification (1.25 or so) and keep trying glasses with higher magnification until your thumb is clearly in focus. That pair of glasses will prove just right for shooting most handguns.

Can I Convert from 38 Super to 9mm Luger?

I have a Series 70 Colt Government Model pistol in 38 Super and would like to convert it to fire the 9mm Luger cartridge. Is this a practical conversion? If so, what parts besides a new barrel and bushing will I need?

Converting your Colt to fire the 9mm Luger cartridge is indeed practical and the only other part you may have to replace in your gun is its magazine. While the original magazine would work fine with the 9mm handloaded to the same overall length as the 38 Super, it might not reliably feed the shorter cartridge. An interior filler plate in the factory 9mm magazine positions the cartridge toward the front for smooth feeding. By installing a 9mm barrel, you will end up with a switch-barrel gun capable of shooting that cartridge as well as the 38 Super.

Best Hog Loads for 357 and 41 Magnum?

My hunting partner and I are headed to Arkansas where we will hunt wild boar with a Colt Python and a Ruger Blackhawk. What 357 Magnum and 41 Magnum loads should we use?

When loaded with the CCI shot load this custom Ruger Single Six in 22 WMR is good close-range snake repellent.

WINCHESTER
SUPER-X™

22 WINCHESTER
MAGNUM
FULL METAL JACKET

50 RIMFIRE
CARTRIDGES

WARNING: Keep out of reach of children.
Read all Warnings on carton.

22 WMR Shot Load on Diamondbacks?

I plan to move to another state, and I will be spending a lot of my time outdoors. Since the area is known for its diamondback rattler population, I would like to carry a revolver loaded with shot cartridges. Would the CCI 22 WMR shot load be a good choice or would I be better off to carry a revolver in 38 Special or 357 Magnum and use shot loads in it?

I also spend a great deal of time in diamondback rattler country. Keeping the diamondbacks company are cottonmouths, copperheads, timber rattlers and the occasional pygmy rattler. Long ago I decided that the best protection against being bitten is common sense combined with a good pair of snake-proof boots or chaps. I never wander around the countryside shooting snakes at will. After all, they were here long before we came along. I will bump one off, but only if it is endangering a companion or me by hanging around where it should not be. After pattern-testing various shot loads in a variety of handguns I find the CCI 22 Long Rifle and 22 WMR loads to be far superior to 38 Special and 44 magnum shot loads from the same company. Out to five yards or so, the finer shot loaded in the 22 caliber cartridges saturates a close-range target with much greater density than the larger but fewer pellets loaded in the larger cartridges.

The very best 357 Magnum hunting load I have used is Winchester Supreme with the 180-gr. Partition Gold bullet. Muzzle velocity in a six-inch barrel is just under 1200 fps. I have taken several wild hogs with that load and its performance was quite good. For the 41 Magnum I recommend Federal's Premium load with the 250-gr. CastCore bullet at 1250 fps.

Should I Fire 38 Super Ammo in My Star Autoloader?

I recently purchased a Star Model A autoloading pistol in 9mm Largo. I have been told that I can fire any ammo from the old 38 ACP to the 38 Super in my gun. Is this correct?

The CCI Blazer 9mm Largo load which is loaded to a maximum chamber pressure of 30,000 psi is the proper readily available commercial ammunition for your Star pistol. It comes close to duplicating the performance of Winchester and Remington 38 Super factory loads. While 38 Super ammo might function in your gun, it is loaded to higher chamber pressures and for that reason I don't think it should be done. If you handload, 9mm Largo cases are available from Starline. You can also handload Winchester 9x23mm or Starline 9mm Super Comp cases to duplicate 9mm Largo velocities but 9x23mm Winchester factory ammo should not be fired in your gun due to the extremely high chamber pressure it develops. As for load data, you can begin developing loads for your gun by reducing starting loads shown in various handloading manuals for the 38 Super by 10 percent. Maximum loads for the 9mm Largo usually run about 10 percent below 38 Super maximum loads.

Will 1911 Slide Work on Colt's Double Eagle?

I noticed in your series of articles on building a custom 1911 pistol, a photo of an extensively modified Colt Double Eagle. I am especially interested in the Commander slide worn by your gun. Did its installation require a lot of work?

Double Eagle and 1911 slides are not interchangeable due to the different designs of their disconnectors. Even so, a good gunsmith can fit a 1911 slide to the Double Eagle frame by milling a disconnector slot in the right-hand rail of the slide. The gun you saw in my article has an extra Commander top assembly fitted to its frame in that manner and it works perfectly. Many parts of the Double Eagle and Model 1911 pistols are interchangeable, including their barrels, barrel bushings, recoil springs, recoil spring guides, firing pins, firing pin springs, extractors and firing pin retainers. The lower assemblies of the two guns share the same slide latch and magazine catch.

6mm BR in Remington XP-100?

What is your opinion on rebarreling a Remington XP-100 pistol to 6mm BR Remington? The short fat cartridge should perform rather well in a 14-inch barrel. I also believe the same cartridge in the short-action Remington Model 700 rifle and Model Seven carbine would be excellent outfits for varmint shooting. Factory ammunition loaded with a 60- or 70-gr. Power Lokt bullet would also be nice.

Converting a single-shot XP-100 in 7mm-08 Remington, 308 Winchester or 35 Remington to 6mm BR Remington is a rather painless project since switching barrels is the only modification required. An XP-100 with a good match-grade barrel in 6mm BR would be capable of excellent accuracy and due to its light recoil it would be great fun to shoot.

Where Do I Get Powder Measure for C&B Revolver?

I have a modern reproduction of a famous 44 caliber cap and ball revolver and plan to shoot Pyrodex P in it. Since I do not own a powder scale, how do I measure out the correct powder charge?

Since you did not state what make your revolver is, my first suggestion is that you write to its manufacturer and ask for recommended powder charge weights for it. Most gunshops that handle blackpowder firearm accessories have adjustable powder measures designed to be used with cap and ball revolvers. The brass measure made by Michael's of Oregon is a good one.

Spitzer Bullets in 30-30 Contender?

I recently bought a T/C Contender in 30-30 Winchester and plan to use it when hunting whitetail deer. The only load data I have found specify the use of roundnose or flatnose bullets which are required when the 30-30 is loaded for rifles with tubular magazines. Since my Contender is a single shot, pointed bullets can be safely used in it. Where do I find load data for that type of bullet in the 30-30?

When handloading the 30-30 for the Contender pistol, you can substitute spitzer bullets of the same weights as roundnose and flatnose bullets specified in load data published by various sources. For example, if the data calls for a 150-gr. flatnose bullet, you can safely use those same loads with a spitzer of the same weight in your Contender. If the data specifies the use of a 170-grain flatnose, you can substitute a 165-gr. spitzer. When doing this it is extremely important that you begin your load development with the starting powder charges recommended by the data source you are using.

Will 7mm-08 Remington Work in the T/C Contender?

I would like to have a custom 21-inch barrel in 7mm-08 Remington built for my T/C Contender carbine. Is the Contender strong enough to handle that cartridge or should I forget that project and buy a Remington Model Seven in 7mm-08 instead?

Extremely high operating pressures combined with a relatively large case head surface area make the 7mm-08 more cartridge than the Contender was designed to handle. Since you obviously like single-shots built by Thompson/Center firearms, I suggest that you take a serious look at the Encore rifle in 7mm-08 Remington from that company.

Should Norma 44 Magnum Ammo Be Fired in Handguns?

I recently bought several boxes of 44 Magnum factory ammo. It was loaded quite a few years ago in Sweden by Norma with a 240-gr. Power Cavity bullet. Printed on each box is "Special Carbine Load." Does this mean I should not fire the cartridges in my 44 Magnum revolver?

Many years ago, back when Ruger introduced its original 44 caliber Deerstalker autoloading carbine, it was discovered that firing ammunition loaded with plain lead bullets in it would foul the gas port in its barrel and cause it to malfunction. The statement printed on the boxes of Norma ammunition you bought indicates that due to the jacketed bullet it is loaded with, the ammo is suitable for use in the Ruger autoloader. It is also suitable for use in any 44 Magnum revolver. Incidentally, the original Norma 44 Magnum load gained quite a bit of notoriety back in the late 1950s when it was used by a Californian, Robert Petersen, to take the first brown bear and polar bear ever taken with that cartridge. If memory serves me correctly, Petersen used a Smith & Wesson Model 29 revolver.

Will Longer Barrel Increase 9mm Luger Velocity?

I'm thinking about replacing the four-inch barrel of my S&W Model 59 with a five-inch barrel. Will the longer barrel increase the velocity of the 9mm Luger cartridge enough to notice or should I leave well enough alone?

If you replace the factory barrel of your pistol with a properly fitted, top-quality custom barrel, you should see an improvement in accuracy. If an increase in velocity is what you are after, increasing barrel length by only one inch will not make enough difference to notice.

What Combination Is Best for USPSA Open Class Competition?

I want to start shooting in USPSA action pistol competition but my eyes are a bit too old to focus on the open sights of a Limited class gun. I have decided to get into Unlimited class competition and since I will be having a custom gun in 38 Super built, I would like to know what combination of gun and sight is the most popular. What powder and bullets are best for major-power loads in the 38 Super?

As I write this the most popular combination among Unlimited class competitors is a 38 Super race gun built on the STI International modular frame and wearing a C-More Serendipity electronic sight. The gun I am presently using in competition has all of that plus a Caspian Arms slide and a Schuemann hybrid barrel with four-chamber compensator. My gun was built by Texas pistolsmith, Benny Hill. When fired from a Ransom Rest it averages around two inches for five shots at 50 yards.

The most popular bullet weights for the 38 Super are 124 and 125 grains. A few competitors use 115-gr. bullets (which I consider too light) and a few others use bullets weighing 135 to 150 grains. As a rule, major-power loads with the heavier bullets seem to generate less recoil in a compensated gun but muzzle-jump is a bit less with the lightweights. I am presently shooting a 125-gr. bullet but I have won more matches with 150-gr. bullets than with any other weight. The most popular 38 Super powders among USPSA competitors are relatively slow in burn rate. My personal favorites are HS7 and AA-7 with bullets weighing up to 135 grains and HS6 for the heavier weights.

Where Do l Find Load Data for 250-grain Bullet in 45 ACP?

I bought a big supply of Speer 250-gr. lead bullets with a diameter of .452 inch. Problem is, I want to shoot those bullets from my Colt Gold Cup but cannot find load data for that bullet weight in the 45 ACP. Can you recommend a load?

The Speer bullets you have were made for use in the 45 Colt. The Speer reloading manual has no data for that bullet in the 45 ACP but it does contain loads for a 260-grain jacketed bullet. Some of the 45 ACP starting loads listed by Speer for that bullet are 5.4 grains of W231, 5.8 grains of Unique, 5.3 grains of Green Dot and 4.6 grains of Red Dot.

Which Vaquero Barrel Length Should l Buy?

I plan to buy a Ruger Vaquero in 45 Colt but cannot decide between the 5-1/2 and 7-1/2 inch barrels. How much difference in accuracy and velocity can I expect from those two barrel lengths?

Depending on the 45 Colt load used, the 7-1/2 inch barrel should produce anywhere from 40 to 80 fps higher velocities than the 5-1/2 inch barrel. Assuming barrels of equal quality, length has no bearing on the mechanical accuracy of a revolver but due to the heavier weight and longer sight radius of the gun with the 7-1/2 inch barrel, most shooters would find it easier to shoot accurately. The shorter barrel also has an advantage or two; in addition to being more compact, many shooters believe a single-action revolver with a 5-1/2 barrel balances and feels better in the hand than one with a longer barrel.

Why No New Semiautomatics in 10mm Auto?

I am very interested in the 10mm Auto cartridge and consider it to be one of the more important developments in handgun cartridges to come along in many years. Why do more handgun manufactures not offer this chambering?

The 10mm Auto made a very big splash when it came on the scene in 1983 and I know one writer who predicted it would make all other autoloading cartridges obsolete. Time has proven him quite wrong. Fine cartridge though the 10mm is, it is now a dying a rapid death. There are two reasons for this, one being the fact that the 40 S&W, which is small enough to work in semiautomatics originally designed around

Which Cartridges for the T/C Contender?

I plan to buy a new barrel for my T/C Contender and will use it for hunting deer. I have already decided on a 10-inch barrel but cannot decided between the 30-30, 35 Remington or 375 Winchester. I am also considering a wildcat chambering offered by SSK Industries called the 309 JDJ. Which do you prefer?

The three factory-chambered cartridges you mentioned are excellent choices for hunting deer in wooded terrain but for all-around use I would choose the 30-30 simply because it shoots a bit flatter at long range. For example, when the Sierra 135-grain SSP exits the muzzle of a 14-inch barrel at 2300 fps and is zeroed three inches high at 100 yards, it is about dead on point of aim at 150 yards and only four inches or so low at 200. Regardless of which of the three cartridges you decide on, you will be much better off with the 14-inch barrel than with the 10-inch barrel due to the higher velocity possible with it. Two of the best deer bullets I have tried in a 14-inch 30-30 are the Nosler 125-gr. Ballistic Tip and the Sierra 135-gr. SSP, both loaded in the neighborhood of 2300 to 2400 fps. Powders that work in rifles chambered for the 30-30, 35 Remington and 375 Winchester work equally well in a Contender chambered for those cartridges.

As for the 309 JDJ, I consider it to be superior to either of the three other cartridges you are considering. I have a 14-inch SSK Industries barrel in this caliber and have used it on a variety of game up to the size of Alaskan caribou with complete satisfaction. For the benefit of those who are not familiar with the 309 JDJ I will add that its case is formed by necking down the 444 Marlin case for 30-caliber bullets. Anyone who buys a barrel in this caliber should have the T'SOB scope mount installed by SSK.

I used a barrel in 309 JDJ from SSK Industries to take this caribou with my Contender pistol.

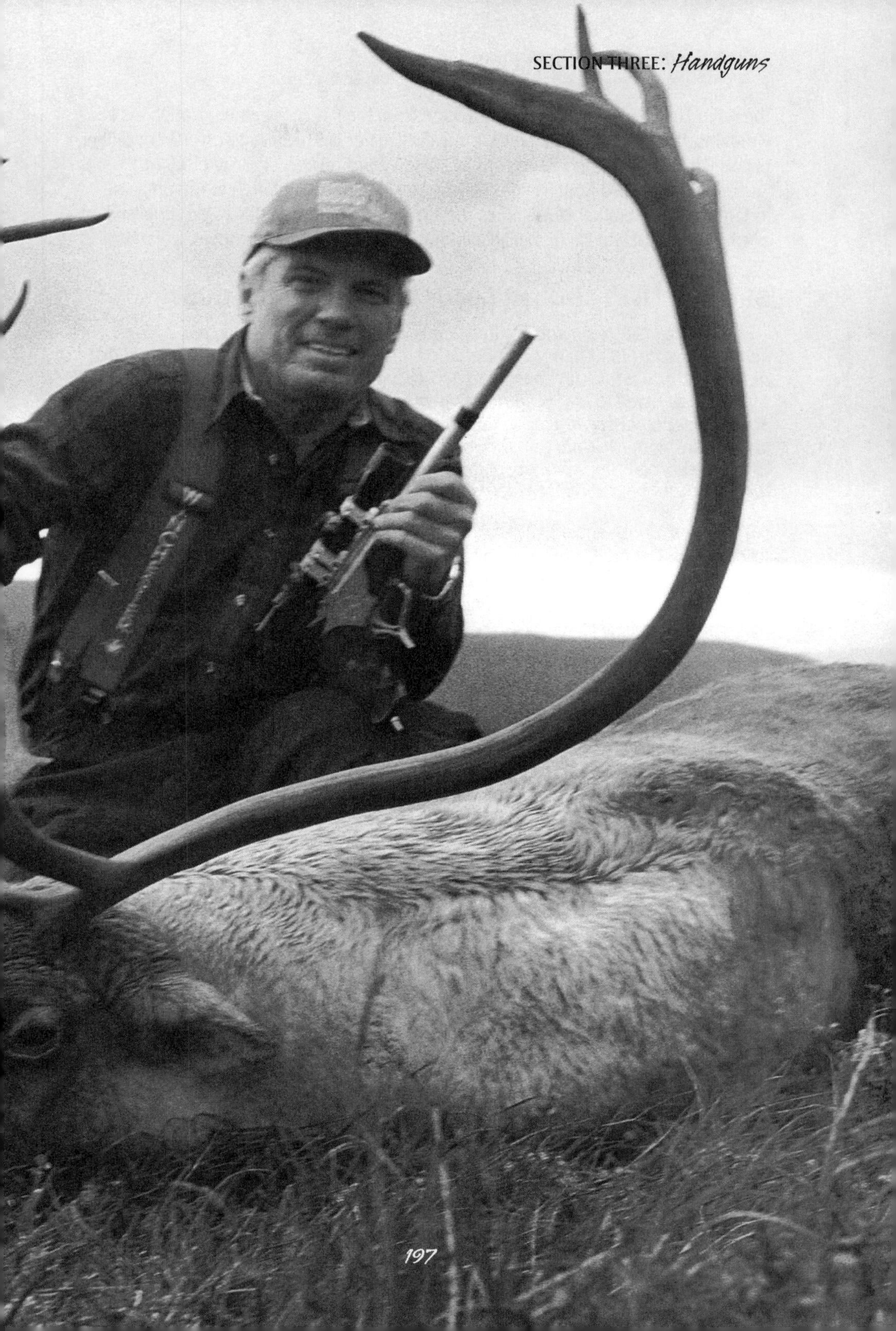

the 9mm Luger cartridge, rooted the 10mm from the law enforcement trough. As I write this, the Kentucky state police is the only major U.S. agency to use 10mm caliber pistols while all the others issue guns in 40 S&W, 9mm Luger, 357 Sig or 45 ACP. Secondly, while a few hunters consider the 10mm powerful enough to use on game as large as deer at rather close range, most handgun hunters prefer single shots and revolvers, both of which are available in much better big-game cartridges.

Should I Use Hardball Loads in My Colt Gold Cup?

Throughout the year I shoot a light charge of Bullseye behind a cast 200-gr. semiwadcutter bullet in my Colt Gold Cup. I recently used that gun in a bowling pin match, and while my speed and accuracy were good enough, my light 45 ACP target loads failed to knock some of the pins completely off the table. As a New York resident, I am restricted in the number of handguns I can own, so I would like to stick with the Gold Cup for bowling pin competition. Will the installation of a heavier recoil spring in my pistol enable me to use more powerful hardball loads without pounding it to pieces?

By all means, you should switch to a heavier recoil spring when shooting hardball loads in your Gold Cup. They are available in a variety of weights from several sources, including Brownells and Wilson Combat. Try a 22-pound spring in your Gold Cup, and if that's too much tension, try a 20-pounder. You can also protect the frame and slide from battering by installing an inexpensive shock buffer from Wilson Combat. The buffer will probably need replacing about ever 500 rounds or so when heavy loads are used.

Most Accurate 22 Rimfire Handguns?

One of the things I enjoy most in life is plinking, casual target shooting and hunting small game with 22 rimfire handguns. My son and I spend a lot of our free time doing just that. Of the various standard-production and affordable guns available today, which do you consider to be the most accurate in the three categories?

In the double-action revolver category, I consider the Smith & Wesson K-22 Masterpiece to be the most consistently accurate. I own two and while the trigger on the one built during the 1990s is not as smooth as on my 1950s gun, it is just as accurate. In single-action revolvers, nothing else I am aware of will come close to the accuracy of the Freedom Arms Model 83 Varmint Class. Other revolvers might occasionally match its accuracy with a particular load but no other revolver is as accurate with a great variety of loads. In the single-shot category, it is a toss-up between the G2 Contender from Thompson/Center, the Maximum from M.O.A. Corporation and the XL from RPM.

Are Grooves in Colt Gold Cup Chamber Factory-Original?

I recently bought a Colt Gold Cup with "National Match Automatic 38 Special Mid Range" stamped on the left-hand side of its slide. Immediately after arriving home with my new acquisition I field-stripped it and was surprised to see deep grooves cut into the wall of its chamber. Did the gun leave Colt that way or was it modified after it left the factory? What purpose does the grooving serve?

The chamber wall of the barrel of your pistol was actually threaded to a depth of about 3/4 inch and it was an option offered by Colt during the 1960s. When a cartridge is fired in your gun and the wall of its case expands outward against the wall of the chamber, the grooves grip the case and actually hold the slide and barrel together long enough for the bullet to exit the barrel before unlocking of the breech begins to take place. This was thought to improve the accuracy of the pistol. You should never fire heavy 38 Special loads in your Gold Cup as it was designed for use only with 148-gr. hollowbase wadcutter bullets loaded to 700 fps or so. If you handload, Speer and Hornady offer that style of bullet. If not, match-grade ammunition loaded with the same style of bullet is available from Winchester, Federal and Remington.

A Revolver That Also Fires Shotshells?

In a spaghetti western I recently watched, one of the good guys packed a most unusual revolver that had a shotgun barrel beneath its rifled barrel. Was that revolver a figment of the imagination of some Italian prop man or was it for real?

The firearm you saw was probably a reproduction of the LeMat revolver. It was designed by Jean Alexandre Francois LeMat who, during the American Civil War, was a colonel on the staff of the Governor of Louisiana. Of percussion design, the revolver was made in 36- and 46-caliber and had a nine-shot cylinder. The cylinder revolved around a .63 smoothbore barrel which was usually loaded with buckshot. The pivoting hammer nose could be quickly set to fire either of the two barrels. Its effectiveness at close range in the hands of Confederate troops earned the LeMat the nickname of "grapeshot revolver."

Why Is Smith & Wesson K-38 Single-Action Only?

I recently bought a fine old Smith & Wesson K-38 Masterpiece and unlike any other revolver of that model I have ever examined, it cannot be operated double action. Do you think some gunsmith who specialized in building revolvers for target shooting converted my S&W to single-action only?

During the early 1960s, Smith & Wesson began to offer the K-38 Masterpiece in single-action only to target shooters. Its advantage over the standard K-38 when both were fired single action was a shorter hammer fall which resulted in slightly quicker locktime. A conversion kit also offered by S&W at the time could be used by a gunsmith to convert older K-38 revolvers to single-action only.

Which Deer Cartridge and Load for the Contender?

I plan to buy a T/C Contender with a 14-inch barrel. I had about decided on the 44 Magnum when it dawned on me that even though most of my shots at deer are rather close I do occasionally get an opportunity as far away as 200 yards. What chambering do you recommend for the type of deer hunting I

How Can I Shrink the Grip of a M1911?

I would like to have a custom 1911 pistol built around a Caspian frame and slide I recently bought but the grips of all 1911s I have handled are too fat for my hand and my finger has a problem reaching the trigger. What can be done to slim down the grip of John Browning's fine old autoloader?

Using extremely thin wood grip panels is one way to shrink the handle of the 1911 and the nicest I've seen are available from Wilson Combat. Identified in the Wilson catalog as part No. 433G for full-size Colt, Springfield and Kimber pistols and No. 433O for the Colt Officer's ACP and Springfield Compact, they come with short grip screws and bushings that replace the factory screws and bushings. Installing a straight mainspring housing in lieu of the arched version (also available from Wilson) makes the grip feel a bit smaller, as does cutting 30-line checkering into the frontstrap or carefully thinning the frontstrap just a bit. Sounds like the gun you intend to have built should also wear one of Wilson's short triggers rather than the more commonly seen long version.

Thin grips can slim down the bulk of the 1911.

223 vs. 22-250 in a Handgun?

Sometime back I purchased an old-style Remington XP-100 with the center-grip style of stock and it has become one of my favorites for long range sniping at woodchucks. It is currently chambered for the 223 Remington and while my handgun is extremely accurate I'd like to have it rebarreled for a flatter-shooting cartridge. What do you recommend?

The two flattest-shooting XP-100 pistols I own are chambered for the 220 Swift and 22-250 Improved. Either cartridge will push a 50-gr. bullet out the muzzle of a 15-inch barrel at 3500 to 3600 fps which is 500 to 600 fps faster than is possible with the 223 Remington in the same length barrel. Both are capable of excellent accuracy in good barrels. One of my XPs has a rather heavy Shilen barrel while the other wears a Hart Barrel; both have on a number of occasions shot five bullets into less than half an inch at 100 yards. Any competent gunsmith who specializes in rebarreling should be able to install a new barrel chambered for either cartridge on your XP-100 action and open up its bolt face for their larger rim diameter.

Built by Jarrett, this custom XP-100 in 223 shoots half-inch groups at 100 yards.

Remington
MODEL XP-100

do? I will be shooting handloads and hope you will be of some assistance in choosing a good deer load.

Among the various chamberings T/C offers in its 14-inch Contender, the 30-30 is my favorite for the type of hunting you do. An excellent load I have used to take several deer is the Nosler 125-gr. Ballistic Tip seated over 29.0 grains of H4198. A couple of other great 30-30 loads for the Contender are 33.0 grains of H335 and the Hornady 130-gr. SSSP and 33.0 grains of A-2015BR behind the Sierra 135-gr. Pro-Hunter. Either of those loads should clock 2200 to 2300 fps in a 14-inch barrel.

Where Do I Get Handgun in 45 Super?

I recently read your article on the 45 Super and I was so impressed by the velocities you attained, I must have a 1911 pistol chambered for the cartridge. I also like the idea of being able to fire 45 ACP and 45 Super ammo in the same gun. I am now ready to do just that but rather than converting a pistol as you did, I would prefer to buy one built from scratch for the 45 Super. Does any company offer what I am looking for? Is factory ammo still available?

You're in luck as 1911-style pistols chambered for the 45 Super cartridge are available from Springfield, Inc., and STI International. Both are long-slide guns with six-inch barrels and the Springfield barrel and slide are ported. I haven't worked with the STI gun but I have shot the Springfield and found it to be extremely accurate with both 45 Super and 45 ACP ammunition. Triton no longer offers 45 Super ammo but excellent unprimed brass is available from Starline. Reloading dies made for the 45 ACP also work with the 45 Super.

Should I Use My 3″ Colt Python?

Several years ago I bought a Colt Python with a 3″ barrel and contacted Colt to obtain information on it. I was told my gun is a limited-edition Combat Python (of which only 500 were made) but since all those guns were supposed to have 2-1/2 inch barrels she figured my gun was probably a "factory mistake". I would very much like to shoot the gun but am not sure I want to devalue it with practice and holster wear. With Colt no longer making the Python I am reluctant to use it but would dearly love to do so. Should I use it, sell it or store it in my gun safe?

I'm afraid you have asked the wrong person whether or not you should use that Python. I say this because I am a firm believer in using guns rather than collecting them. I own several valuable firearms and I'm sure my using them is not exactly increasing their value but I enjoy being afield with them a lot more than collecting them or saving them for someone else to enjoy after I have moved on to that big quail covert in the sky.

Perhaps this little story will help you make up your own mind. There was this fellow who owned a 28-gauge Parker shotgun worth somewhere in the neighborhood of $25,000. An avid quail hunter, he used to dream about using the fine little double in the field. About every time he and one of his friends crossed paths he would eventually get around to saying, "one of these days me and old Bell will hunt bobwhite with that little Parker." His attitude was always rather puzzling to some of us since he thought nothing of driving through the brambles and boonies in a pickup truck he had paid as much for as his Parker was worth. Unfortunately, the fellow never got around to using his Parker simply because he was too concerned that doing so would depreciate its value. To end a sad story on an even sadder note, the fellow died without ever experiencing the joy of being in the field with his beloved Parker a single time. It was inherited by a son who had absolutely no interest in either hunting or guns and who sold it within months after taking possession of it. The moral to my story? Enjoy using that Colt Python now while you can or sell it and buy something you will enjoy using.

How Often Should I Clean My 1911 Pistol?

I just bought a Kimber Super Match in 45 ACP and plan to use it and cast bullet handloads in IDPA competition. How often should I clean my new gun?

Back when I competed in USPSA Limited Class on a regular basis, I shot Bull-X cast bullets in a 1911-style pistol built by STI International and cleaned it every 600 to 700 rounds. My regular routine was to shoot 100 to 150 rounds during a club match with a clean gun and then later fire another 500 rounds during practice prior to cleaning the gun. Immediately after a practice session I would field strip the gun for cleaning and lubrication in preparation for the next match. In other words, I always made it a point to start each match with a clean and properly lubricated gun. At each 5000 round mark or just prior to a major tournament (whichever came first) I would completely disassemble the gun for thorough cleaning and lubrication and to examine it for any excessively worn parts. Three of my 1911 pistols continue to function perfectly and are still accurate after exceeding 50,000 rounds each, so my cleaning program obviously works.

Who Can Install New Barrel on a Ruger Blackhawk?

I own a Ruger Blackhawk revolver in 45 Colt. The idea of replacing its 4-5/8 inch barrel with a longer and heavier barrel interests me but I know of no gunsmith who will take on the job. Can you recommend one?

If I owned that Blackhawk and wanted it rebarreled, I'd send it to Mag-Na-Port International or SSK Industries. Through the years both shops have done nothing short of top-quality work for me and they back up what they do with a no-hassle guarantee.

Why Is Barrel Link Missing on Modern Pistols?

I've noticed that unlike John Browning's 1911 pistol design with its linked barrel, most of today's autoloading pistols have linkless barrels. Please explain what purpose the barrel link serves and why it is missing from most other pistols.

During the firing cycle of the 1911 pistol its barrel link pulls the breech end of the barrel downward, thereby disengaging its locking lugs from their recesses inside the roof of the slide. In some guns with poorly fitted barrels the link also pushes the barrel back into lockup with the slide at the end of the firing cycle but on a properly fitted barrel its underlug bearing on the top of the slide latch shaft serves that purpose. The 1911 has proven to be one of the most durable of pistol designs which is why it dominates practical pistol competition where handguns are fired more rounds and subjected to more punishment with heavy loads than in any other shooting sport. But the fact remains, anytime a moving part can be eliminated from any machine the possibility of parts breakage is reduced. John Browning designed his High Power pistol with its linkless barrel after designing the 1911 so he might agree, but he might also point out that another factor in favor of the linkless barrel from a manufacturer's point of view is it is less expensive to produce and takes less skill to install properly.

Laser Sight for Combat Matches?

A need to wear eye glasses rules out the use of open sights for me when shooting in combat pistol matches. Would installing a laser sight on my Glock 17 solve my problem?

A laser sight works fine during low light conditions but all I have tried were worthless when competing in bright sunlight because the dot becomes impossible to see on light-colored targets. Your best bet for action pistol matches is to install an electronic red-dot sight on your Glock.

Should I Shorten 10mm Cases to 40 S&W Length?

I would like to shorten my supply of 10mm Auto cases so they can be used in my 40 S&W autoloader. Do you see any potential problem with this?

I see two problems with your plan. First of all, when trimming the 10mm case to the same length as the 40 S&W case you end up with a case with a heavily tapered wall. As a result, when a bullet is seated, its base can expand the diameter of the case to the point where it won't enter the chamber of a gun. The second problem has to do with case capacity. Due to its extremely thick wall, the shortened 10mm case won't have as much capacity as a 40 S&W case with its thinner wall and this rules out the use of load data published for the 40 S&W cartridge.

How Do I Calculate CCI Stinger Muzzle Energy?

The CCI Stinger 22 rimfire cartridge is loaded with a 32-gr. bullet and has a muzzle energy rating of 191 foot-pounds in a 22-inch rifle barrel. How do I calculate the muzzle energy of that load when it is fired in a 2-1/2 inch handgun barrel?

You will first need to use a chronograph to determine the actual muzzle velocity of the Stinger load when it is fired in the short barrel of your handgun. Then multiply bullet weight by velocity squared and multiply what you get by .000002218 to arrive at muzzle energy. For example, if the load chronographs, say, 1100 fps in your handgun, its muzzle energy would be 86 ft-lbs. I once chronographed the velocities of 14 CCI 22 rimfire loads in six different barrel lengths and the Stinger load clocked 1055 fps in a two-inch barrel.

Is Ruger Old Army Suitable for Deer Hunting?

I recently bought a 44 caliber Ruger Old Army cap and ball revolver and am absolutely amazed at its accuracy. Is it powerful enough to use on deer? If not, what game besides varmints is it suitable for?

As you have already discovered, the Ruger Old Army will hold its own in an accuracy contest with most modern revolvers but I'll have to classify it as too weak for use on deer. Even when exiting the muzzle of the Ruger at 1050 fps or so, a round ball generates only about 350 ft-lbs of energy which places it in about the same performance class as the old low-velocity loading of the 44 Special. I have taken several wild boar with cap and ball revolvers but I hunted with hounds and got plenty close before pulling the trigger; the longest shot I recall taking was inside 12 yards. I have also taken javelina at close range with the same type of handgun which probably isn't saying a lot since I also once stalked on foot and bagged one of those neat little animals with Kevin Howard's Walther PPK and Winchester's 95-gr. SXT loading of the 380 ACP. I wouldn't hesitate to use the Ruger Old Army on a treed cougar but that's about the size of it as far as game size goes.

Single-Action Revolver More Comfortable to Shoot?

I intend to start hunting deer with a handgun and am in the market for a revolver in 44 Magnum. Even though I am not overly sensitive to recoil, I will be practicing a lot with my new gun so it makes sense to me to buy whichever of the two types is most comfortable to shoot. Which will be less punishing to my hand, a single-action or double-action revolver?

It depends on two things: the particular revolver being shot and the person shooting it. I, for example, find the Ruger Super Redhawk in 44 Magnum to be considerably more comfortable to shoot than the Ruger Super Blackhawk in the same caliber. Between those two revolvers I prefer the looks of the single action but had rather shoot the double-action. On the other hand, I find the single-action Freedom Arms Casull to be more comfortable to shoot than either of the Rugers. It all has to do with variations in grip size and shape and the size and strength of the shooting hand. Would your opinion be the same as mine after shooting those three guns? Maybe, maybe not. If at all possible, your best bet is to perform your own side-by-side perceived recoil tests with the two types of handguns in order to decide which you prefer.

Should I Prevent Dents on Ejected Cases?

I recently bought a 1911-pattern pistol in 45 ACP and some of the spent cases ejected from it end up with a small dent on the side. This doesn't happen to all the cases but it does happen often enough to cause concern on my part. Is this a common occurrence with autoloading pistols? Should anything be done to my gun to prevent it from happening?

Long-distance diagnosis can become a guessing game but I'd say those cases are picking up dents by striking the edge of the ejection port in the slide as they are ejected from your gun. This is a common occurrence among autoloading pistols and is no cause for alarm so long as it has no effect on functioning. Having the ejection port of a 1911-style pistol lowered and flared is the usual cure for dented cases but if you are experiencing no malfunctions with your gun my suggestion is to leave it as is.

Why Did the 10mm Auto Bite the Dust?

I often see Colt and Smith & Wesson pistols in 10mm Auto for sale and am puzzled by the lack of acceptance of this cartridge. Are pistols of this caliber known to have any type of problems that might have doomed the 10mm? How does its recoil compare to that of the 45 ACP?

The 10mm Auto never achieved the success it deserves for two reasons. For one, the majority of those who buy 1911-pattern pistols still prefer the 45 ACP and I don't see that ever changing. Secondly and even more influential, unlike the 40 S&W which has become quite successful, the 10mm Auto cartridge is too long to work in the dozens of autoloaders which were originally designed to handle the shorter 9mm Parabellum. Due to its extremely high chamber pressures the 10mm subjects a firearm to a bit more stress than milder cartridges but I have seen two Colt Delta Elite pistols exceed 10,000 rounds each with no parts breakage. My guess is a top-quality 1911-style pistol in 10mm will last just as long as the same type of pistol in which major-power 38 Super handloads are used and the service life of those guns will exceed 50,000 rounds. To answer your other question, while the 10mm Auto does generate a bit more recoil than the 45 ACP, the difference is not enough to explain its failure in the handgun market.

Which Lubricant for Ruger?

I read your article on the Ruger P95 but still have one question in mind: what lubricant do you recommend for a pistol with a synthetic frame?

So many excellent firearms lubricants are available on the market it is becoming difficult to go wrong with any of them. Some I have used on various guns with complete satisfaction are Ultima-Lube, Tetra Gun G, All Weather Grease from Shooter's Choice, Outers' Gun Slick and Brownells' Action Lube Plus. Applying only a very small amount is the key to using any light lubricating grease on a firearm; I prefer to moisten my fingers with just a trace and then rub it over areas that are subject to wear.

Ruger 41 Magnum Enough for Bear?

I have two questions I hope you will answer for me. I plan to use a 6-1/2 inch Ruger Blackhawk in 41 Magnum for hunting black bear with hounds and would like to know what factory load you recommend for it. Also, I have a Weatherby Vanguard in 300 Weatherby Magnum and am wondering if it is suitable for rebarreling to 358 Shooting Times Alaskan.

If I were to hunt black bear with 41 Magnum factory ammo I'd take a serious look at two loads, Federal's recipe with the 250-gr. CastCore bullet at 1250 feet per second (fps) and Cor-Bon's load with a 265-gr. LBTF at about 1300 fps. If your Weatherby Vanguard is in good serviceable condition it is an excellent candidate for rebarreling to 358 STA.

Use 9x23 Winchester in 9mm Largo Gun?

I recently bought a Destroyer carbine in 9mm Largo. Is it strong enough to handle the 9x23 Winchester cartridge?

While 9x23 Winchester ammo can be fired in any firearm chambered for the 9mm Largo I must recommend against the practice simply because the Winchester cartridge is loaded to far higher chamber pressures. Your best bet in ammo for the Destroyer carbine or any other firearm chambered for the 9mm Largo is the factory loaded version of that cartridge available from CCI/Speer.

Which Rust-Resistant Finish for Handguns?

I realize that many types of handgun finishes rate high in rust resistance but nobody ever gets around to comparing their durability. What is the most wear-resistant finish available for carbon steel concealed-carry handguns?

Most of the new finishes are tough enough to do an excellent job of resisting metal surface wear during concealed carry but some are more resistant to metal against metal wear. An example is the wear that can occur between the surfaces of the slide and frame or the slide and barrel hood of an autoloader. The most durable finishes I have tried are chrome plating or variations of same. Unlike the shiny plating we used to see on the bumpers of 1955 Buicks, the type applied to firearms forms a molecular bond with the steel and won't chip or peel off. One of the best such finishes I have used on both handguns and rifles is NP3 from the Robar Co. While not as resistant to wear as hard chrome, Armor-Tuff from Wilson Combat seems to be living up to its name as well.

220-Grain Bullets in 40 S&W?

One of the handloading manuals I have recommends against the use of bullets heavier than 200 grains in the 40 S&W and yet I've noticed that among USPSA action pistol competitors, 220-gr. cast bullets have become quite popular in that cartridge. In using a bullet that heavy, are those fellows loading the 40 S&W to dangerously high chamber pressures? Why don't they simply switch to the larger 10mm Auto case?

Those who use 220-gr. cast bullets in the 40 S&W for Limited class USPSA competition are using 1911-style guns such as the Edge from STI International. The magazine of that gun allows the 220-gr. bullet to be seated out to an overall length considerably greater than the 40 S&W is commonly loaded to. Whereas that cartridge is usually loaded in the neighborhood of 1.125 inches overall, the longer magazine of the 1911 allows the length to be increased to 1.225 inch and even a bit longer. For my STI Edge, I load 220-gr. cast bullet atop a light charge of Hodgdon's

454 Casull vs. 44 Magnum Recoil?

I realize the perception of recoil is a subjective thing but I'm wondering how you would compare the level of recoil generated by the 454 Casull to that of the 44 Magnum when both are fired in revolvers of the same type and weight? Who makes the best 454 caliber handgun?

I have fired Freedom Arms single-action revolvers in both the calibers you mention and to me, perceived recoil of maximum-velocity 300-gr. loads in the 454 Casull is about twice as heavy as the same bullet weight loaded to maximum speed in the 44 Magnum. Even with that said, I must add that I don't find the 7-1/2 inch Freedom Arms revolver in 454 to be at all uncomfortable to shoot for the first 20 rounds or so. After that, the same gun in 44 Magnum is much more fun to shoot. As to who makes the best 454 caliber handgun, I believe very few would argue the fact that the Freedom Arms Premier is the finest made by anybody, anywhere. In fact, I consider it to be the finest revolver of any type and any caliber made anywhere in the world.

My two favorite big-bore revolvers: a custom 45LC/454 Freedom Arms and a custom Ruger.

Clays for an average muzzle velocity of 825 fps. Chamber pressure is actually lower than when lighter bullets are seated to 1.125 inches overall and loaded to the same power factor level. Perceived recoil is also extremely light, which, of course, is why we use that bullet. USPSA competitors choose the 40 S&W over the 10mm Auto simply because cases are considerably less expensive. As an example, sometime back I bought 25,000 once-fired, law enforcement-surplus 40 S&W cases for about 20 percent of the cost of the same number of new 10mm Auto cases.

What Ruger Super Single Six Mods?

You recently mentioned a Ruger Super Single Six that had been modified by Mag-Na-Port. What modifications did you specify and how did they improve the overall usefulness of that gun? For what applications do you consider the little Ruger single action best suited?

Since it is impossible for me to describe all the modifications Mag-Na-Port performed on my Super Single Six in this column, I'll keep it to the point by saying that the most important from a standpoint of improving my performance with that gun is the trigger job. And when it comes to fine-tuning the trigger of any Ruger Single action revolver, nobody does it better than Mag-Na-Port. Its capability of shooting both the 22 Long Rifle and 22 WMR cartridges makes the Super Single Six one of the more flexible small game handguns I own. It is an excellent choice for woods-roaming and I have used it to take a number of rabbits, squirrels and the occasional close-range groundhog.

Old vs. New Remington XP-100

I would like to see Remington update its XP-100 and put it back into production. Other than its rear-grip fiberglass stock and repeating action, how does the current XP-100 differ from the old one? Which gun do you prefer?

Technically speaking, Remington did not reintroduce an updated version of the original XP-100. Rather, the company introduced a new pistol on the Model Seven rifle action and gave it the old name. Actually, the "new" XP-100 isn't all that new. Several years before Remington ceased to produce the old XP-100, its custom shop started offering a repeating version with a rear-grip fiberglass stock on the Model Seven action. I have one of those guns in 7mm-08 and it is identical to the standard-production XP-100 repeater Remington once built. In answer to your question of which XP-100 I like best, I still prefer the original version with the center-grip stock simply because it is a bit more compact and it handles and feels so much better in the field. The later version does, however, have a much better bolt release and its trigger is easier to fine-tune. A friend of mine who is an old XP-100 fan likes the new one because it is a repeater but I've hunted with both and had just as soon have the old single-shooter.

Mag Spring Loses Tension?

I keep a Ruger P85 in my home for personal protection and prefer to leave its magazine fully loaded. How long can the magazine remain in that condition before its spring becomes too weak to push ammo up for feeding?

If the magazine of an autoloading pistol has a good spring to begin with, it can be left fully loaded indefinitely without the spring losing enough tension to cause malfunctions during feeding. Several of my Glock 17 magazines have been in a fully loaded condition for well over a decade and they work just as well now as they did when I first acquired them. I do, however, believe it is a good idea to occasionally test magazines stored in that manner during practice sessions.

Likes 10.9mm Ruger Magnum

You once wrote an article on loading the 44 Magnum with bullets seated out for long-cylinder revolvers such as the Ruger Super Redhawk. To differentiate between ammo loaded in that manner and standard loads you referred to it as the "10.9mm Ruger Magnum." One of those loads with the Hornady 300-gr. JHP-STP averages 1350 fps in the 7-1/2 inch barrel of my Super Redhawk. I have used that load to take a number of deer and black bear here in Pennsylvania but until recently had been unable to recover a single bullet due to complete penetration. During the past season I placed one of those bullets into the chest of a whitetail as it stood facing me. The bullet ranged lengthwise through the body and came to rest in one of the animal's rear hams for an amazing four feet of penetration. It expanded to over 50-caliber and retained 293 grains of its original weight. Expansion of the bullet was picture-book perfect. Thanks for a great big-game load!

My thanks go out to you for going to the trouble of reporting on the performance of that 10.9mm Ruger Magnum load. I'm sure the folks at Hornady will be as pleased as I am to hear about the excellent performance of their 300-gr. bullet.

Scope Mount for Ruger Super Blackhawk?

I have a Ruger Super Blackhawk with a 7-1/2 inch barrel and plan to use it for hunting deer in areas where shots seldom exceed 75 yards. Having already decided on an electronic sight, I don't know which brand or model to buy and am hoping you can help me with this decision. I also want to have the gun drilled and tapped and a permanent mount installed. Which mount do you recommend?

The many models and variations of electronic sights available make choosing among them tough but here are a few guidelines you might keep in mind. When mounting a tube-type sight on a hunting gun I personally prefer one with a tube no larger in diameter than 30mm. When hunting deer and larger game such as elk and moose, I like for dot subtension to be in the eight to 12 minute-of-angle range. If you'd rather go with a tubeless sight, your options boil down to choosing between the lighter weight of the C-More Railway and the interchangeable reticle patterns of the Bushnell HoloSight. As permanent mounts for revolvers go, the best I have used are the T'SOB from SSK Industries and the mount available from Weigand Combat.

Either shop will take care of the entire job, including drilling and tapping the topstrap of your Super Blackhawk. Since the bases of both mounts are the Weaver-style you can utilize the mounting rings that come with various tube-type sights and they are equally compatible with the integral base of the C-More Railway sight.

How Do l Unload a Glock?

When unloading my Glock pistol l remove its magazine, retract the slide to unload the chamber, allow the slide to move forward and then with the muzzle pointed in a safe direction, pull the trigger on an empty chamber. A friend says l should simply remove the magazine and lock back the slide. Who's right, him or me?

When preparing an autoloader for long-term storage, I prefer your procedure because it leaves all springs in the gun in a relaxed position. On the other hand, some handgun owners feel more comfortable when storing an autoloader with its magazine removed and slide locked back since doing so makes the firearm easy to identify at a glance as totally unloaded.

Who Offers Pistol in 260 Remington?

l would like to have a long range pistol in 260 Remington. l could round up an XP-100 and have it rebarreled, but prefer to not go the custom route. Does anyone offer a factory gun in 260 Remington? If so, how accurate is it?

The M.O.A. Maximum is available in 260 Remington. I own the first one built in that caliber and it is quite accurate. The extremely heavy barrel on mine is 1.125 inches in diameter and 14 inches long. Wearing a Burris 3-9X LER scope, the gun averages .70-inch at 100 yards with Remington's 140-gr. factory load and less than half an inch with several bullets, including the Sierra 120-gr. Matchking and Nosler's Ballistic Tip of the same weight. The Maximum is capable of even better accuracy; a friend owns one in 6mm BR that will consistently keep five bullets inside a quarter inch. His gun is equipped with a Burris 6-24X scope. The M.O.A. Maximum has interchangeable barrels and is available in about every factory and wildcat chambering you can think of, from 22 rimfire to 375 H&H Magnum.

New Barrel for Dan Wesson?

l would like to have a custom barrel installed on my Dan Wesson 44 Magnum revolver. Whom do you recommend for the job?

Three shops come to mind for two reasons; either should be able to handle the job and all have done excellent revolver rebarrel work for me in the past. They are Mag-Na-Port International, SSK Industries, and Weigand Combat Handguns.

SECTION FOUR

Cartridges & Shotshells

How Are Cartridges Named?

How have the various ammunition manufacturers gone about choosing names for their cartridges through the years?

Various approaches have been used through to name cartridges. Some make sense and others don't. Here are but a few of the many examples. Some cartridges have actual bullet diameter or the groove diameters of their barrels in their names. Examples are the 243 Winchester, 257 Roberts, 264 Winchester Magnum, 284 Winchester, 308 Winchester, 358 Winchester and 458 Winchester Magnum. The 300 Savage, the 350 Remington Magnum, the 450 Marlin and the various 300 Magnums are examples of cartridges named for the bore diameters of their barrels. When introduced, the 250-3000 Savage was loaded to 3000 fps with a 25-caliber bullet. The 30-06 is a 30 caliber cartridge adopted by the U.S. Army in 1906. The 25-06 is the 30-06 case necked down to 25 caliber. The 6mm BR Remington was designed for bench rest shooting. The 45-70-500 is a 45-caliber cartridge loaded with 70.0 grains of black powder and a 500-gr. bullet. The 257 Roberts is similar to a 25-caliber cartridge designed by Ned Roberts while the 35 Whelen was designed by James Howe and named in honor of Townsend Whelen. The "STW" as in 7mm STW is short for "Shooting Times Westerner." Some cartridges share the same bullet diameter but you would never know it by their names. The 218 Bee, 219 Zipper, 220 Swift, 221 Fire Ball, 222 Remington, 223 Remington, 224 Weatherby Magnum and 225 Winchester are all loaded with bullets measuring .224-inch in diameter. The 30-378 Weatherby Magnum is the 378 Weatherby Magnum case necked down for a 30-caliber bullet. The case of the 7x57mm Mauser is 57mm long and it is loaded with a 7mm bullet. Some names are probably chosen because they roll more smoothly off the tongue than the alternatives. The 44 Remington Magnum is loaded, not with a true 44 caliber bullet but with a bullet measuring .429-inch in diameter. Some cartridges get certain names because the other name was already taken. The 340 Weatherby Magnum, as an example, is loaded with a .338-inch bullet, same as the 338 Winchester Magnum which was introduced earlier.

How Good Is the 308 Winchester?

The most accurate big-game rifle I own is a Sako Model 75 in 308 Winchester. I plan to do a lot more hunting than in the past and while I would like to use my Sako, I am wondering if I might be better off with a more powerful chambering such as the 300 Winchester Magnum or 300 Remington Short Action Ultra Mag. Just how good is the 308 Winchester as a big-game cartridge? Which is the best factory load?

In the hands of those who can shoot them accurately, more powerful cartridges are better choices for shots at extremely long range, especially at larger game such as elk and moose. But most hunters take most of their big-game animals inside 300 yards and the 308 Winchester is plenty of cartridge for that. Through the years I have used various rifles in 308 to take game such as deer, caribou and black bear so I speak from personal experience. Any good factory load with a bullet weighing 150 or 165

I took this magnificent red stag in New Zealand with a Kimber rifle in 308 Winchester.

grains will get the job done on deer-size game but for larger game or for all-around use on all game ranging in size from deer and antelope to black bear, moose and elk, you will not find a better choice than Federal's Premium High-Energy load with the Nosler 180-gr. Partition at 2740 fps.

Why Hangfires with My 30-378 Weatherby Magnum Handloads?

I recently bought a Weatherby Mark V rifle in 30-378 Magnum and while it is superbly accurate with factory ammo, I am experiencing occasional hangfires with my handloads. What am I doing wrong?

You did not mention which components you are using in your handloads, but your misfire problem suggests to me that you have chosen the wrong primer. A friend of mine purchased a custom rifle in 30-378 Weatherby Magnum. It was built on the Weatherby Mark V action by a gunsmith who enjoys a reputation for building super accurate rifles. The best three-shot accuracy he was able to squeeze from his rifle with handloads was four to five inches at 100 yards. He brought the rifle to me and the very first group I fired measured 0.62 inch. The handload I used to fire that group consisted of the Weatherby case, 110.0 grains of Retumbo and the Nosler 180-gr. Ballistic Tip bullet. Most important of all, I used the Federal 215 primer whereas my friend had been using a standard-force primer. The 215 primer was developed by Federal upon special request by Roy Weatherby who used it in his then-new 460 Magnum cartridge. It is the best primer for use in that cartridge as well as the 30-378, 338-378 and 416 Weatherby Magnums. The Federal 215 is also an excellent choice for other large-capacity cartridges such as the 7mm STW, 7mm Ultra Mag, 300 Weatherby Magnum and 300 Ultra Mag.

Should I Choose the 204 Ruger or 223 Remington?

I plan to buy a new varmint rifle and am trying to decide between two cartridges, the 204 Ruger and the 223 Remington. Capable of delivering a muzzle velocity of over 4200 fps with a 32-gr. bullet, the 204 is faster but the 223 has the advantage of being available in more different loadings from various companies. Which is the better choice for varmint shooting?

Both are excellent choices and while it is true that the 204 is faster, the 223 makes up the difference by being loaded with a heavier bullet. When the 223 Remington is loaded with a 40-gr. bullet at 3700 fps, it is almost a dead-ringer for the 204 Ruger in performance. When zeroed two inches high at 100 yards, the 40-gr. Ballistic Silvertip loaded by Winchester will strike the target about three inches below the line of sight at 300 yards where it will deliver just over 450 foot-pounds of energy. When zeroed the same, the 32-gr. bullet of the 204 will strike about two inches low at 300 yards where it will deliver around 440 foot-pounds. The 40-gr., 224-caliber bullet has a slightly higher ballistic coefficient (221 versus 185), but since the 32-gr., 20-caliber bullet starts out faster, drift in a 10 mile per hour crosswind is almost identical for the two cartridges at about eight inches. Like I said, there really is not a lot of difference in the performance of the 204 Ruger and 223 Remington.

17 HMR or 22 WMR for Turkey?

My home state allows the use of rifles for hunting turkeys. I want to switch from a shotgun to a rifle and will call them in close before shooting. I have a rifle in 22 WMR but am wondering if the newer 17 HMR would be a better choice. Where is the best place to hold on a turkey when shooting it with a rifle?

The 22 WMR loaded with a 40-gr. jacketed hollowpoint bullet works great on gobblers out to 40 yards or so. Only three days before writing this I took a Rio Grande gobbler in Texas with a Winchester Model 9422M and the Winchester 40-gr. factory load. I placed the crosshairs in my scope about one-third of the bird's body length back from its breast and dead center. One shot at about 30 yards did the trick. I have not taken a gobbler with the 17 HMR but I do have serious doubts about its 17-gr. bullet being as effective on shots to the body as the 40-gr. bullet of the 22 WMR. As for where to the crosshairs should be placed, I like the broadside shot described above. If the bird is close enough and your rifle is accurate enough, a hold on the head or neck is deadly. If the bird is facing you but not in full strut, a hold at the juncture of its chest and neck will work and it won't damage much of the breast meat. A shot to the center of the back on a walking-away bird is also quite effective but the bullet may penetrate to the breast and spoil a few gobbler McNuggets.

Pros and Cons of Winchester Super Short Magnums?

What are the pros and cons of the latest breed of 22, 6mm and 25 caliber super short magnum cartridges from Winchester? I already own rifles in 220 Swift, 240 Weatherby Magnum and 257 Weatherby Magnum and would like to know how the performance of those cartridges compares with the latest from Winchester.

When the 223 WSSM and 220 Swift are loaded to similar chamber pressures, there really is not a great deal of difference in their performance. The Hodgdon handloading manual shows the 220 Swift capable of reaching a muzzle velocity of 3840 fps with a 55-gr. bullet. That same source shows the 223 WSSM capable of pushing a 55-gr. bullet along at 3890 fps. As you can see, there is no practical difference in the performance of the two cartridges. The performance of the 243 WSSM falls about midway between the 243 Winchester on the slower side and the 240 Weatherby Magnum on the faster side. When the three cartridges are loaded to maximum with 100-gr. bullets, the Hornady manual shows respective maximum velocities of 3000, 3060 and 3202 fps for the 243 Winchester, 243 WSSM and 240 Weatherby Magnum. Moving on to the 257 WSSM, it was designed to duplicate the performance of the 25-06 Remington and that puts it 300 to 400 fps slower with a 100-gr. bullet than the 257 Weatherby Magnum. The primary advantage offered by

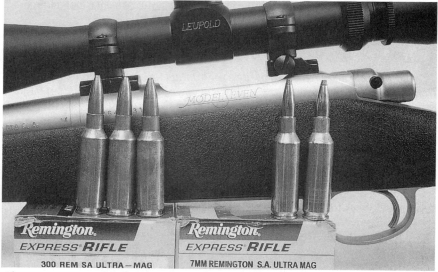

Short magnums pack a lot of punch into a short package.

the super-short magnums is their ability to squeeze into bolt-action rifles with super-short actions. This can reduce the overall weight of a rifle by several ounces.

Best 30-06 Factory Load for Pronghorn?

I plan to take my wife on a hunt for pronghorn antelope in Wyoming in the near future. She will use my Ruger Model 77 in 30-06 with a Tasco 3-9x scope. My wife is a bit sensitive to recoil and since I don't handload I'm counting on you to help me choose the lightest-kicking factory load available. I realize I'm putting you on the spot but I would prefer that you recommend a single factory load from a specific company.

One of the most comfortable 30-06 factory loads I have tried and one of the most effective I have used on deer-size game is the Sako 123-gr. pointed softnose. It is one of the fastest and flattest shooting 30-06 big-game loads available and its bullet is constructed for optimum performance on deer and other game similar in size. Sometime back I tried the ammo in three rifles, a Remington Model 700 Mountain Rifle with 22-inch barrel a Sako Model 75 with a 24-inch barrel and a Ruger No. 1B with 26-inch barrel. Average muzzle velocities in those rifles were 2968, 3037 and 3107 fps, respectively. Respective average accuracy was 1.28, 1.34 and 1.46 inches. If your local dealer doesn't already carry Sako ammunition, he can order it from its importer, Stoeger Industries, at 5 Mansard Ct., Dept. ST, Wayne, NJ 07470.

How Do the Short and Long Magnums Compare?

My wife and I have been hunting elk successfully for many years with rifles in

7mm Remington Magnum and 300 Weatherby Magnum. A couple of friends who hunt with us carry rifles in 300 Winchester Magnum. We handload for our rifles and use various premium-grade bullets weighing 160 and 175 grains in the 7mm Magnum and 180 and 200 grains in the 300 Magnums. My son says the cartridges our rifles are chambered for are old hat and we would be better off retiring them and buying new rifles chambered for the short 7mm and 30 magnums from Remington and Winchester. Are those cartridges all that much better than the ones we are using? Of all the short and super-short magnums introduced during the past few years, which do you consider to be the most useful?

From a performance point of view, the short magnums offer no advantage over the cartridges you and your group are now using. In fact, since you prefer the heaver bullet weights for elk, you are better off sticking with the longer magnum cartridges. This is due to the fact that the short-action rifles in which they are chambered require the heavier bullets to be seated quite deeply into the cases of the short magnums and that takes a drastic toll on their powder capacity. When loaded with 160- and 175-gr. bullets, the 7mm Remington Short Action Ultra Mag and the 7mm Winchester Short Magnum are capable of producing velocities of approximately 2900 fps with the 160-gr. bullet and 2800 fps with the 175-gr. bullet. The 7mm Remington Magnum is capable of reaching the same velocities with those bullet weights while the 7mm Weatherby Magnum is about 100 fps faster. The 300 SAUM and 300 WSM are capable of pushing 180- and 200-gr. bullets along at 2900 fps and 2800 fps, respectively. Those velocities are easily exceeded by at least 100 fps with the 300 Winchester Magnum and a good 200 fps with the 300 Weatherby Magnum.

Of the short and super-short magnums introduced during the past few years, the 270 WSM makes the most sense to me. While the others more or less duplicate what we already had, the 270 WSM is an improvement on the 270 Winchester and is capable of pushing the 130-gr. bullet about 200 fps faster. More important, the 270 WSM will reach about the same velocity with a 150-gr. bullet as the 270 Winchester loaded with a 130-gr. bullet.

Have Ammo Makers Throttled Back?

While at a recent gun show I bought 10 boxes of 300 Winchester Magnum factory ammunition at a very good price. The ammo was loaded by Winchester and I was told that even though it was over 25 years old, it had been stored properly and was as good as new. The near-mint condition of the cartridges and their boxes seemed to bear this out. Loaded with the 150-gr. Power Point bullet, the ammo proved to be extremely accurate in my Sako Fiberclass rifle. It clocks 3392 fps on my chronograph and 3374 fps on a friend's chronograph. Now for the really interesting part. Those same chronographs register averages of 3255 fps and 3238 fps for current-production Winchester, Remington and Federal 150-gr. 300 Magnum loads. Why is the old ammo so much faster than the new stuff? Are the ammo makers loading today's ammunition to lower velocities than they were in the good old days?

In order to reduce the chamber pressures of factory ammunition, U.S. ammo manufacturers have throttled back the velocities of most all centerfire cartridges during the past few decades. Back when the 300 Magnum ammo you bought at the gun show was produced, it was rated at a muzzle velocity of 3400 fps by Winchester. Today, Winchester, Remington and Federal 150-gr. loadings of that same cartridge are rated at 3290 fps and usually average a bit slower than that in standard-production rifles with 24-inch barrels. This conservative attitude toward the loading of ammunition was brought on by a liberal society in which individual citizens are no longer held responsible for their own foolish mistakes.

What Is the 240 Cobra?

I have an old custom rifle on the Pre-64 Winchester Model 70 action with "240 Cobra" stamped on its 26-inch barrel. I believe P.O. Ackley made the barrel. The rifle is in excellent shape and has a gorgeous claro walnut stock with cut checkering and a checkered steel buttplate. I originally bought the outfit with the intention of having it rebarreled to 270 Winchester but its barrel is in such good shape I've decided to shoot it as is. What can you tell me about its chambering? Do you have any load data for it?

The 240 Cobra is a wildcat designed by Homer Brown and was probably the most popular 6mm cartridge in existence prior to the introduction of the 243 Winchester and 244 Remington during the 1950s. It is quite simply the 220 Swift case necked up for 243-inch bullets and fireformed to less body taper and a 30-degree shoulder angle. The case is easily formed by running 220 Swift brass through a 240 Cobra full-length resizing die with a tapered expander button and fireforming in the chamber of the rifle with a slightly reduced load. Handloading dies are available from RCBS and Redding.

When developing loads for your rifle, begin by reducing starting loads shown in various handloading manuals for the 243 Winchester by 10 percent. Years ago I owned a rifle in 240 Cobra and found it to produce virtually the same velocities as the 243 Winchester and 244 Remington with all bullet weights. It is an excellent cartridge for both varminting and hunting medium-size game such whitetails and pronghorn antelope.

I'm glad to see you preserve that old custom rifle in its original condition and chambering. All too many fine rifles of yesteryear have been lost forever because their actions were salvaged for a more modern project.

264 Magnum Case Necked Down to 25 Caliber?

Necking down the 264 Magnum case to 25 caliber should produce a cartridge with performance identical to that of the 257 Weatherby Magnum with the advantage of less expensive and more readily available cases. Do you think having a rifle in 257 Weatherby Magnum rebarreled for such a cartridge would be worthwhile?

While the 264 Magnum case necked down to 25 caliber would duplicate the 257 Weatherby Magnum in performance, you could buy quite a nice supply of 257 Magnum cases for what you would have to pay for a having a new barrel installed plus the cost of a chamber reamer and special-order handloading dies for the 25-264 wildcat. If you must use cases other than those manufactured by Norma for Weatherby, a less expensive option would be to leave your rifle in 257 Magnum and buy a set of case forming dies from RCBS or Redding to use in forming that case from 264 Winchester Magnum or 7mm Remington Magnum brass.

Is the 16 Gauge Dead?

Why did American manufacturers drop the 16-gauge chambering? It always seemed to me to be the perfect bore size for most of the upland shooting I do. Can you assist me in locating a shotgun of this gauge?

Some very fine 16-gauge side-by-side doubles are being imported from other countries. They include the AYA boxlock and sidelock guns (Armes de Chasse, P.O. Box 827, Chadds Ford, PA 19317), the Merkel Model 47 (GSI, Inc., P.O. Box 129, Trussville, AL 35173), the Arietta sidelock (Wingshooting Adventures, 4320 Kalamzoo Ave. SE, Grand Rapids, MI 49507), and the Garbi Model 100 (Moore & Co., 8727 E. Via de Commencio, Suite A, Scottsdale, AZ 85258). Possibly the finest 16-gauge double currently made in the U.S. is the A.H. Fox reproduction from Connecticut Shotgun Mfg. (P.O. Box 1692, New Britain, CT 06051).

When I was a youngster growing up in the Deep South, the 16 gauge was second in popularity only to the 12 gauge and considerably more popular than the 20 gauge. As you have discovered, times have changed. The 20 now rivals the 12 in popularity in some areas, the 28 is gaining more fans each day and yet, sadly enough, the 16 appears to be on its last legs. This is why most American shotgun manufacturers have abandoned it.

Which Long-Range Deer Cartridge?

Mexican government regulations are getting even more strict on the use of rifles of 7mm caliber and larger so I am in the market for a long-range cartridge to use when hunting deer. I am particularly interested in a 6.5mm on the 8mm Remington Magnum or 300 Weatherby Magnum case. Any ideas?

A wildcat called the 6.5-300 WWH (Weatherby/Wright/Hoyer) has been around for several decades and once enjoyed a bit of popularity among 1000-yard benchrest shooters. It is formed by necking down the 300 Weatherby Magnum case. Years after the 65-300 WWH was introduced I developed a similar cartridge on the 8mm Remington Magnum case called the 6.5 STW. Either cartridge will generate velocities about 200 fps higher than the 264 Winchester Magnum. Handloading dies for the two cartridges are available from Redding and RCBS.

I used a T/C Encore rifle and a 26-inch barrel in 6mm-06 to take this pronghorn buck in New Mexico.

Where Can I Get a 6mm-06 Rifle?

I have a Sako Model 75 in 243 Winchester and while I like it a lot, I yearn for more speed. I once read about a cartridge called the 6mm-06 and it sounded like just what I am looking for. Where can I get a rifle chambered for it? How do I form the case? How does its performance compare with other cartridges of its caliber?

A gunsmith who specializes in rebarreling rifles can install a barrel in 6mm-06 on any good turnbolt action so long as its magazine is long enough to handle the 30-06 family of cartridges. The Thompson/Center custom shop also offers that chambering in barrels for the Encore. I have a medium-heavy barrel for my Encore rifle and it is quite accurate. I used that barrel to take a pronghorn buck in New Mexico with the Swift 90-gr. Scirocco bullet loaded to 3400 fps.

The 6mm-06 was originally developed by necking down the 30-06 case for a 6mm caliber bullet, but I prefer to neck down 25-06 cases available from Federal, Winchester and Remington. The 6mm-06 is a wildcat cartridge so it requires handloading. Those who prefer to stick with factory ammunition can get exactly the same performance by buying a Weatherby Mark V rifle in 240 Weatherby Magnum. I also have one of those and find velocities of the two cartridges to be identical, which makes sense considering their near-identical powder capacities. Maximum velocities of the 6mm-06 and 240 Weatherby Magnum are about 200 feet per second faster than for the 243 Winchester, 6mm Remington and 243 WSSM.

Which 41-Caliber Bullet for Deer?

I am new to handgun hunting and plan to go after deer with an 8-3/8 inch S&W Model 57 in 41 Remington Magnum. Although this cartridge is less powerful than the 44 Magnum, I figure it is enough for whitetails. I have read about the use of extremely heavy (over 300 grains) hard-cast bullets in the 44 Magnum on big game rather than lighter bullets of jacketed hollowpoint design. Do you agree with this practice? If yes, where can I find really heavy 41-caliber cast bullets? If no, what bullet should I use?

The 41 Magnum is plenty of cartridge for deer. While you are correct about some handgun hunters preferring to use extremely heavy cast bullets for greater penetration on game such as moose and elk I personally don't care for them on smaller game. Jacketed hollowpoint bullets are a better choice for deer simply because they are more likely to expand and open up a larger wound channel. And besides, the extra penetration of an extremely heavy cast bullet is not needed for an animal of that size. Load one of the 210-gr. jacketed hollowpoints from Nosler, Sierra, Hornady or Speer to about 1450 fps with a maximum charge of W296 and you'll have an excellent deer load for your 41 Magnum revolver.

If you decide to take on larger game with the 41 Magnum, Federal's Premium load with a 250-gr. CastCore bullet at 1250 fps should be an excellent choice. Another possibility is Cor-Bon's load with a 265-gr. cast bullet at 1325 fps.

How Fast Is the 300 Jarrett?

My gunsmith has a very nice custom sporter in 300 Jarrett. He says the cartridge is formed by necking down the 8mm Remington Magnum case and then fireforming to the improved shape. How does its velocity compare to the 300 Weatherby Magnum? On another subject, can you tell me why the chambers of Weatherby rifles are freebored?

The 300 Jarrett (which is basically the 358 Shooting Times Alaskan necked down) has virtually the same powder capacity as the 300 Weatherby Magnum. Consequently, their velocities are about the same when both are loaded to the same chamber pressures. If you buy the custom sporter from your gunsmith and someday find yourself on a hunt with no ammunition, keep in mind that 300 Weatherby and 300 Holland & Holland Magnum factory ammo can be fired in a rifle chambered for the 300 Jarrett.

Freeboring is the removal of a short section of the rifling just forward of the chamber, leaving the bore smooth in that area. This allows the bullet to travel freely for a greater distance prior to engaging the rifling than in a chamber with a standard-length throat. The result is a slight delay in peak pressure, which allows the use of a slightly heavier powder charge than can be used in a chamber with a standard throat length. Contrary to once-popular opinion, a rifle with a freebored chamber does not always produce higher velocities than a rifle with a standard chamber.

Which Chambering for Third Rifle?

I hunt deer a lot in Mississippi and own two rifles, a Remington Model 700 Mountain rifle in 7mm-08 and a Browning A-Bolt in 30-06 Springfield. Those are the only rifles I have needed in the past but I plan to start hunting in other states. In fact, I have already booked a whitetail hunt in Texas and a mule deer hunt in Colorado. I'm looking to add a third rifle to my battery but cannot decide on the caliber. Can you help?

To be perfect honest, if whitetail and mule deer are the largest animals you plan to hunt in other states, the two rifles you already own are all you actually need. They will also work quite well on larger game such as elk and moose but if you feel that you need a heavier caliber then by all means go for it.

Another 358 STA Fan?

After reading your articles for many years and collecting a lot of great ideas I finally had my dream rifle built, a Model 70 chambered for your 358 Shooting Times Alaskan. The rifle has a Shilen 24-inch stainless steel barrel with a 1:12 inch twist and a fiberglass stock. Most of the loads I've tried came from your introductory article in the September, 1992 issue of Shooting Times *but a favorite load I recently came up with pushes the Speer 250-gr. Grand Slam along at just over 2950 fps for excellent accuracy. It should work quite well on moose and Yukon grizzly. Now for my question. Have you tried the Barnes 275- and 300-gr. bullets on heavy game at close range?*

Thanks for your comments on the 358 Shooting Times Alaskan. While I included the Barnes 275- and 300-gr. bullets in my load data chart in the article you referred to, I have yet to bag a big-game animal with either at close range. My guess is those bullets would work fine although they are not likely to offer as much penetration as the Barnes 250-gr. X-Bullet, especially if heavy bone is struck. Incidentally, the Nosler 250-gr. Partition is also an excellent bullet for the 358 STA.

Which Cartridge for Japanese Arisaka?

I have a military surplus Japanese Arisaka rifle in 6.5x50mm caliber. Would it be practical to have the rifle rebarreled to another caliber?

Rebarreling your Japanese Arisaka to another cartridge would be a poor investment simply because its resale value would probably not be increased by the modification. If your rifle is in excellent condition its collector value would actually be decreased by the conversion. If it were my rifle I would either sell it, trade it on another more modern rifle or simply shoot it as is. The 6.5x50mm Japanese cartridge is still loaded by the Swedish firm of Norma and available in the U.S. If you decide to handload the cartridge, 6.5mm bullets of various weights are available from Nosler, Speer, Hornady and Sierra. Reloading dies are manufactured by Redding and RCBS and *Hodgdon's No. 26* data manual contains plenty of load data for the cartridge.

Degree of bullet deflection isn't determined by velocity of the projectile but by distance from the deflecting object to the target.

Does Faster Bullet Deflect More?

Given two bullets of the same weight but at different velocities, will the faster one deflect more when contacting brush?

When everything including caliber, weight and construction are the same, I find that velocity has little to do with how much bullets deflect when striking small limbs and twigs. Any bullet is subject to deflecting off-course when traveling through brush and whether or not it strikes the target is greatly dependent on the distance the target is from the point of deflection. If the target is no more than five yards or so behind the screen of brush and the bullet does not fly to pieces (as a varmint bullet is inclined to do) it is likely to strike the target even though it may have started to tumble. As the target is positioned farther and farther away from the point of deflection, chances of it being struck by the bullet become quite slim.

In 2004, Remington made a run of limited-edition Model 700 Classic rifles in 8x57mm Mauser.

Why No 8x57mm Mauser?

The fact that firearms publications seem to have completely written off the fine 8x57mm Mauser cartridge disturbs me. I have taken several deer with a '98 Mauser in that caliber and find it to be an excellent performer. The best buck I've taken, a South Carolina nine-pointer, ran only 30 yards before piling up after being struck through the lungs by a Hornady 150-gr. spire point which exited the muzzle at close to 2700 fps. Why don't I see more written on one of my favorite cartridges? I recently noticed that Midway is selling 8mm caliber 185-gr. bullets made by Remington. Since none of my handloading manuals lists loads for that bullet weight, can you come up with a starting load for it?

With the exception of a short run of Model 700 Classic rifles in 8x57mm Mauser built by Remington during 2003, that cartridge has been totally ignored by American rifle manufacturers. This is why I seldom write about the 8mm Mauser. Of course, enough letters like yours to various gun companies could change that. Reducing a starting load listed in one of the handloading manuals for a 170-gr. bullet by a couple of grains would be a safe way to begin load development for the Remington 185-gr. bullet in your rifle. As an example, the 12th edition of Speer's manual lists 49.0 grains of IMR-4064 as a starting load for the 170-gr. spitzer. When substituting a 185-gr. bullet you would start with 47.0 grains of the same powder.

Which Has Greater Penetration?

The 9mm Luger cartridge is faster but the 45 ACP shoots a heavier bullet. Which offers the greater penetration?

The penetration of a bullet is influenced mainly by its sectional density, its construction, its impact velocity and the type of medium into which it is fired. If all those factors are the same, the penetration of bullets fired from the 9mm Luger and 45 ACP will be the same. As examples, the Speer 147-gr. 9mm TMJ and 230-gr. 45 caliber TMJ bullets have almost identical sectional densities of .167 and .162, respectively, and their construction is basically the same. If those two bullets impact the same type of material at identical velocities, their penetration will be basically the same.

Why Was It Named 303 British?

Why was the 303 British named that when its bullet diameter is a nominal .311 inch?

Through the years it has been popular among cartridge designers to use the bore diameter of the rifle barrel in identifying their creations. This is true for the 303 British just as it is for the 250 Savage, 270 Winchester, 280 Remington, 300 Winchester Magnum and others. Correct bullet diameters for those cartridges are .257, .277, .284 and .308 inch. On the other hand, some cartridges have the nominal bullet diameter or barrel groove diameter in their designations. Good examples are the 224 Weatherby Magnum, 243 Winchester, 257 Roberts, 308 Winchester, 358 Winchester, 416 Remington Magnum and 458 Winchester Magnum. Then we have cartridges the designations of which refer to neither bore, groove, nor bullet diameter. Among others, that group would include the 220 Swift, 225 Winchester, 340 Weatherby Magnum, 44 Remington Magnum and 460 Weatherby Magnum.

How Do I Prepare A Rifle For Cold Weather Hunting?

Should I do anything special to my rifle before hunting during extremely cold weather?

Oil inside the bolt of a rifle can become thick enough at low temperature to cushion the blow of the firing pin on the primer of a cartridge and cause a misfire. Removing all trace of oil from inside of the bolt and around the firing pin and its spring will prevent this. Cover the lenses of your scope with caps and place a piece of plastic electrical tape over the muzzle and you are ready for snow.

Why Are 8x57mm Mauser Factory Loads So Light?

I recently purchased a Model 1898 Mauser in 8x57mm caliber. I plan to hunt deer with the rifle but am sorely disappointed by the fact that factory ammo is rated at an extremely slow 2360 fps with a 170-gr. bullet. This is 260 fps slower than the smaller 308 Winchester is rated at with a 180-gr. bullet. It is also 340 fps slower than the 180-gr. 30-06 factory load, the performance of which the 8x57mm Mauser is capable of duplicating with handloads. Why do the ammunition companies load the 8mm Mauser so light?

The ammo companies load the 8x57mm Mauser to relatively low chamber pressures for two important reasons. One is respect for the thousands of war-surplus rifles of that caliber still in use, many of which are close to 100 years old. Even more important, some of the Mauser rifles still floating around are chambered for the 8x57J which was loaded with a bullet of .318 inch diameter. Since the more modern 8x57JS cartridge is loaded with a .323-inch bullet, it could generate excessive chamber pressures if accidentally fired in a rifle chambered for the old 8x57J, so American manufactures have no choice but load it light.

Will 375 JDJ Work in Marlin Model 444S?

Is it possible to rebarrel a Marlin Model 444S for the 375 JDJ wildcat? I would use flatnose bullets.

Even though the 375 JDJ is the 444 Marlin case necked down, its overall length is too great for the Marlin action. With the Hornady 220-gr. flatnose bullet seated to its cannelure in the 375 JDJ case, it measures 2.735 inches overall or .165 inch longer than the 444 Marlin cartridge. I came up with a 375-caliber wildcat that will work in the Marlin action years ago and called it the 370 Winchester. It is the 356 Winchester case necked up for a 375-caliber bullet. Using form dies available from Redding, the case can also be made from 444 Marlin brass.

Should I Rechamber My 225 Winchester?

I have a Winchester Model 70 in 225 Winchester. The rifle is in excellent condition and has proven to be quite accurate with the few factory cartridges I have managed to find for it. I like the cartridge but since I am having a difficult time finding the ammo or unprimed cases for reloading, a friend has suggested I have the rifle rechambered to 22-250. Should I do it? Also, would rechambering my rifle reduce its collector value or affect its accuracy?

The poor 225 Winchester never had a chance. First, it was introduced in 1964, the year Winchester decided to do terrible things to its Model 70 rifle. And as if that alone were not enough, the 225 received its final deathblow about a year later when Remington decided to start factory loading the 22-250. Despite the fact that Winchester stopped offering the 225 chambering in 1972, it will do anything the 22-250 will do in the varmint fields.

If your rifle belonged to me I would purchase a good supply of 225 ammunition and unprimed brass (both still available from Winchester) and leave it as is. I doubt if Model 70s in that caliber will ever have hordes of collectors chasing after them, but you never know. Of those that were made, many have been rebarreled for other calibers, just as you are thinking about doing.

A rifle in 300 H&H Magnum is an excellent choice for long-range target shooting and for big-game hunting.

One 300 H&H Magnum Load for Deer and Elk?

I have a Remington Model 700 in 300 Holland & Holland Magnum and can only locate Winchester ammo loaded with the 180-gr. Silvertip bullet. Is that a good load for elk as well as long-range shots at deer? My rifle wears a Weaver 2.5X scope. Do you think I need more magnification for hunting?

Your questions would have been much easier to answer had you mentioned the type of country you hunt in. On a combination hunt where both deer and elk are on the menu, the Winchester 180-gr. load would be a good choice. The same goes for hunting elk only. On a deer-only hunt, the same load would work fine if most of your shooting will be at close to medium ranges. For shots at deer beyond 300 yards I would prefer a 150-gr. bullet. Its trajectory is a bit flatter than a 180-gr. bullet but more important, it will open up quicker on deer-size game at long range where impact velocity has dropped off considerably.

When hunting deer and elk in open country I prefer a variable-power scope with 7X, 8X or 9X at the upper end of its magnification range and 2X, 2.5X or 3X at the opposite end. When set on its lowest magnification, such a scope has a field of view wide enough for shooting at close range in heavy timber and when set on a higher magnification is all you need for long-range shooting.

Who Created the 270 Helldiver?

About 30 years ago I bought a Wallack barrel, fitted it to a '98 Mauser action and made my own stock for it out of a nice piece of walnut. The barrel came already chambered for the 270 Helldiver which is basically the 257 Roberts Improved case necked up. I have determined beyond doubt that it is not the same cartridge as P.O. Ackley's 270-257 Improved. Through the years I have combed through many books in libraries and have written letters to several experts (including the NRA) but thus far my search for information on the 270 Helldiver has been totally fruitless. Can you tell me who created it?

Your rifle is chambered for one of a trio of cartridges created during the late 1940s by L.R. (Bob) Wallack and Frank Hubbard. The other two cartridges are the 250 Helldiver and the 300 Helldiver. In addition to being a writer and gunsmith, Wallack was an avid benchrest shooter and often experimented with various rifling twist rates in his barrels. When shooting the 270 Helldiver in competition, the Sierra 110-gr. spitzer was his favorite bullet. I mention this because of the possibility that the rifling pitch in your barrel is slower than the standard 1:10 inches for other 270 caliber cartridges. If you decided to shoot bullets heavier than 130 grains in your rifle and find them to be less than accurate, there is your answer.

Even though the 270 Helldiver and 270-257 Ackley Improved differ slightly in certain dimensions, they are close enough in case capacity to share the same load data. And since you obviously already have a copy of *Ackley's Handbook For Shooters & Reloaders,* you will find the data on pages 378 and 379. I do, however, strongly recommend that Ackley's powder charges be reduced by 10 percent for starting loads.

Ideal Custom Rifle and Cartridge for Pronghorn Antelope?

I have finally had my fill of cartridges that shoot bullets in rainbow trajectories so I plan to have a custom rifle built specifically for hunting pronghorn antelope. I want the fastest, flattest-shooting, most accurate rifle money can buy. If that were your project, how would its specifications read?

The first thing I would do is round up a Remington Model 700 action and have it blueprinted by a gunsmith who specializes in building super accurate rifles. I would also change out its trigger to one built by Arnold Jewell. The barrel would be a stainless steel Shilen of medium-heavy weight and measuring 26 inches in length. I would also specify a rifling twist rate of 1-10 inches. The synthetic stock would be the Griffin & Howe style from McMillan. The rifle would wear a top-quality variable-power scope with anywhere from 9X to 12X at the upper end of its magnification range. It would be in 257 Weatherby Magnum, a cartridge easily handloaded to 3300 feet per second with the Hornady 117-grain SST or the Nosler 115-grain Ballistic Tip bullets. I would sight in the rifle three inches high at 100 yards; that would put its bullet about three inches above line of sight at 200 yards, dead on at

300 yards and less than 10 inches low at 400 yards. I would then load up my perfect antelope rifle and head west.

Is 8mm-06 Rechambering Practical for a 1898 Mauser?

I would like to have a Model 1898 Mauser in 8x57mm rechambered to a wildcat formed by necking up the 30-06 case for 8mm bullets. Is the magazine box long enough for that cartridge when it is loaded with the heaviest bullets available? If not, how about a 8mm cartridge on the shorter 284 Winchester case?

The 8mm-284 Reamer won't completely clean out an 8x57mm chamber so that modification is less than practical. Your barrel can be rechambered to 8mm-06 and while the magazine box should be long enough to handle it with the lighter bullets it might be a bit short for the heavyweights. Why not simply have your rifle rechambered to 8x57mm Improved? That cartridge will equal the velocity of the 8mm-06 and even when loaded with the heaviest bullets available it is still plenty short for the '98 Mauser magazine.

What Is the Ideal 6.5mm Cartridge?

I want to build a rifle of 6.5mm caliber for long-range shooting and would appreciate your recommendations. I believe the 264 Winchester Magnum case is too big for the caliber while the 6.5 Swede and 260 Remington are too small. During my research I have uncovered several 6.5mm wildcats on the 30-06 case but all had sharp shoulder angles and very little body taper. Surely someone somewhere has simply necked down the 30-06 case for this caliber and come up with what I consider the ideal cartridge of its caliber. Who can rebarrel a Model 700 action for me?

Someone most certainly has and it is called the 6.5-06. It is basically a modern version of the old 256 Newton and mildly popular as wildcats go. The case is easily formed by necking up 25-06 brass or necking down the 30-06. Reloading dies are available from RCBS and Redding. As for load data, take a look at the reloading manuals published by Nosler, Sierra and Accurate Arms. Incidentally, the 6.5 Remington Magnum and the 6.5-06 are performance twins.

I am sure there are dozens of gunsmiths across the country who are quite capable of installing a barrel on your Model 700 action. For a really quick turn-around try Shilen Barrels, Inc.

Where Do I Get 45 ACP Shot Loads?

I live in a rural area where poisonous snakes are a problem. I have a pistol in 45 ACP and would like to know if anyone makes shot loads for it.

Speer sells a 45 ACP shot load under the Blazer banner. In addition to being quite effective out to 10 yards or so it will cycle through an autoloading pistol.

I took this buck with a Remington Model 700 in 220 Swift and the Speer 55-grain Trophy Bonded bullet.

The 223 on Deer?

As you probably know, opinions among hunters differ as to the suitability of the 223 Remington on deer. Although I mostly hunt deer with more powerful cartridges, my limited experience with the 223 leads me to believe it will work on deer. Do you agree?

When loaded with a bullet of controlled-expansion design, 22-caliber cartridges will work on deer if the range is not too great but only when they are used by someone who is capable of placing the bullet where it must go. As I write this, only Federal offers 22-caliber ammunition loaded with a bullet designed for use on game larger than varmints. As I have proven to my own satisfaction, Federal Premium 223, 22-250 and 220 Swift ammo loaded with the 55-gr. Bearclaw bullet works great on deer when broadside lung shots are taken but they are more limited in range than cartridges of larger calibers. I consider the 223 load to be a 100-yard deer cartridge at best while the 22-250 and 220 Swift loads begin to rapidly lose their effectiveness once range exceeds 200 yards or so.

Moose and Grizzly Load for 45-70?

I have just added a New Model Marlin 1895 to my hunting battery and plan to use it on a hunt in Alaska. What handload do you suggest for moose and grizzly?

Sometime back I compared the expansion characteristics of various 458-caliber expanding bullets and came to the conclusion that the 300-gr. Nosler Partition is the best all-around choice for use in the 45-70, regardless of whether the target is a 100-pound deer or a 1000-pound moose. Several handloading manuals contain loads capable of pushing that bullet from the barrel of your Marlin at 2000 to 2100 feet per second, making it plenty of medicine for any Alaskan game so long as the range does not greatly exceed 150 yards. Should you decide to use factory ammo on your hunt, Winchester offers a loading with that same bullet in its Supreme lineup, although it is called the 300-gr. Partition Gold there. Other 45-70 loads capable of handling anything Alaska has to offer are available from Cor-Bon and Garrett Cartridges.

Where Do I Get 358 Norma Magnum Cases?

I am having built a rifle in 358 Norma Magnum and need a supply of cases for handloading. Where can I get them?

The 358 Norma Magnum case is easily formed by necking up the 338 Winchester case and fireforming it in your new rifle. The necks of cases formed in that manner will be slightly shorter than 358 Norma factory cases but the minor difference will have no affect on performance.

Is the 307 Winchester Enough Cartridge for Elk?

I have a Winchester Model 94 in 307 Winchester. Is it enough cartridge to use on elk? I handload my own ammunition and would like your recommendation on a good bullet for this cartridge.

I wouldn't hesitate to hunt game as large as elk with your rifle but I would restrict my shots to 200 yards or less. Since your Model 94 has a tubular magazine, only flatnose bullets should be used in it. Most bullets of that type were designed to perform at 30-30 Winchester velocities and are too soft for use on game larger than deer when pushed to higher speeds by the 307 Winchester. This is why the 170-gr. Nosler Partition along with the 150- and 170-gr. XFN bullets from Barnes are the best choices available for that cartridge.

Can I Use 6.5 Swede Load Data for 6.5 American?

I would like to know all about a cartridge you developed called the 6.5x52mm American. I would also like to have a Savage Model 99 in 308 rebarreled for it. Where can I buy the reloading dies? Can loads listed in handloading manuals for the 6.5 Swede be used in the 6.5 American?

I introduced the 6.5x52mm American in the August 1994 issue of *Shooting Times* magazine. I developed the cartridge in response to readers who had requested a short-action cartridge capable of duplicating the performance of the 6.5x55mm Swedish. Since case capacities of the two are practically identical, starting loads published in various handloading manuals for the 6.5 Swede can be used for the same purpose in the 6.5 American. The 6.5 American is the 7mm-08 Remington case necked down and fireformed to minimum body taper and a 40-degree shoulder angle. It can also be formed by necking down the 308 Winchester case or necking up the 243 Winchester case. The 260 Remington can be fired in a rifle chambered for the 6.5 American and is an excellent way to fireform a supply of cases. Reloading dies are available from Redding.

Rifle in 6.8mm SPC Remington For Son?

My son is now old enough to hunt under my close supervision so I am shopping for his first deer rifle. I was on the verge of buying something in 243 Winchester and then I read your story on taking a caribou with a rifle in 6.8mm SPC Remington. It sounds like that is exactly what I am looking for. What factory load is best for deer? What rifle do you recommend?

As you may already know, the 6.8mm SPC Remington was originally designed as a military cartridge for use in the M16 rifle but as it turned out, deer hunters in search of a low-recoil cartridge are becoming quite fond of it as well. It uses a .277-inch bullet, same as the 270 Winchester, but lighter at 115 to 120 grains. If you plan to buy a bolt-action rifle for your son, take a look at the Remington Model Seven and the CZ 527. Both are light, compact and quite accurate. Another possibility is the G2 Contender rifle from Thompson/Center. It too is quite accurate and since it is a single-shot, it is a perfect first deer rifle for a youngster. Two of the best 6.8mm SPC factory loads available for use on deer are the 115-grain Core-Lokt Ultra from Remington and Hornady ammo loaded with a 120-grain bonded-core bullet. The Remington bullet also has a bonded core.

Can I Rechamber 243 Winchester to 240 Weatherby Magnum?

I have a new Remington Model 700 varmint rifle in 243 Winchester and would like to have it rechambered to 240 Weatherby Magnum. Is this possible?

While the 240 Magnum case is longer than the 243 Winchester case, its body diameter is actually a bit smaller. In addition, the Weatherby cartridge is a bit too long for the magazine box of the short-action Model 700. The best bet is to have your barrel rechambered for the 6mm-284 wildcat. Formed by necking down the 284 Winchester or 6.5-284 Norma cases, it is capable of duplicating the performance of the 240 Weatherby Magnum. The receiver rails of your rifle may have to be opened up slightly before the fatter case will reliably feed from the magazine, an extremely critical modification requiring the services of a gunsmith experienced in that type of work. The Hodgdon and Hornady handloading manuals have load data for the 6mm-284.

Live Happily Ever After with a 25-Caliber Cartridge?

The older I get the more sensitive I become to recoil and the more often I consider trading my 300 Magnum for a rifle that does not kick so hard. A friend of mine shoots a rifle in 257 Roberts and loves it, but he never hunts game larger than deer and pronghorn antelope. I mostly hunt game of that size but do occasionally head for the woods in pursuit of elk. I also plan to hunt moose in Alaska in the near future. So my question is, do you think I could swap my 300 for a 25-caliber rifle and live happily ever after?

The various 25-caliber cartridges are excellent choices for use on deer and while there are better elk cartridges, I would not hesitate to take on the biggest bull in the woods with a rifle in 257 Weatherby Magnum so long as it is loaded to maximum speed with a premium-grade bullet of controlled-expansion design such as the Nosler 120-gr. Partition, Swift 120-gr. A-Frame, Speer 115-gr. Trophy Bonded Bear Claw or Barnes 115-gr. XFB. Everything considered, the 257 Weatherby Magnum is one of the most useful big-game cartridges ever developed. But then, Roy Weatherby knew just that when he developed it back in the 1940s. The 257 Magnum eventually became his favorite cartridge and he used it on game all over America and Africa.

What Advantage Bonded-Core Bullets?

I notice that the ammunition companies are loading bonded-core bullets in many cartridges. What are the advantages of using that type of bullet on big game?

Since the lead core and the jacket of a bonded bullet do not separate during expansion it will retain a higher percentage of its original weight than a nonbonded bullet and this allows it to penetrate more deeply. Excellent examples of this type of bullet are the Swift Scirocco, Hornady InterBond, Nosler AccuBond, Remington Core-Lokt Ultra and Federal Fusion. The performance of a bonded bullet is actually a compromise between bullets of conventional construction and premium-grade bullets of tougher construction. Not long back I took a fantastic Utah elk with the Hornady 130-grain Interbond in the 270 Winchester then a few weeks later I took a mule deer in Wyoming with a rifle in 270 WSM handloaded with the same bullet. Its bonded construction enabled the bullet to work as well on a 1000-pound animal as on a 250-pound animal.

Is the 32 Special Enough Cartridge for Boar?

I have inherited a Winchester Model 94 in 32 Special from my grandfather who took numerous deer with it in Utah. What can you tell me about that cartridge? How does it compare to the 30-30 Winchester? Is the Federal 170-gr. factory load powerful enough to use on wild boar?

Winchester introduced its 32 Special in the Model 94 lever-action rifle in 1902. The very first whitetail buck I bagged as a youngster during the 1950s was with that combination. Even though the performance of the 32 Special on game is the same as that of the 30-30, it has never been as popular as that cartridge. In addition to the Federal 170-gr. Hi-Shok load you mentioned, you might also try Remington's 170-gr. Core-Lokt loading as well as the 170-gr. Silvertip load from Winchester. All are rated at a muzzle velocity of 2250 fps and they offer all the power needed for bagging wild boar out to 200 yards or so.

What Is the 240 PSP?

While at a gun show I examined a custom rifle built on the Remington Model 722 action. The owner was a collector of custom rifles and while he was not interested in selling it, he told me he had purchased it at an estate sale and it came with RCBS reloading dies. The rifle was chambered for the 240 PSP but that's all he could tell me about it. Are you familiar with the cartridge?

The 240 Page Super Pooper (or PSP for short) was a created during the 1950s by firearms writer Warren Page. It is the 244 Remington (or 6mm Remington) case with slightly less body taper than the factory version and a shoulder angle of 28 degrees. Another cartridge called the 240 Page was on the then-new T-65 military case and was quite similar to the 243 Winchester.

What Is Your Opinion Of The 325 WSM?

When it comes to introducing new cartridges Winchester has become as prolific as a rabbit. What do you think about the 325 WSM?

The 325 WSM uses bullets of the same diameter as the 8x57mm Mauser and 8mm Remington Magnum and since no cartridge of that caliber (including those two) have become very popular among American hunters, I have my doubts about the future of the Winchester cartridge. It is a nice little cartridge but the fact that it really won't do anything that cannot be done with the 300 WSM and 300 SAUM is not exactly in its favor so I doubt if it will make a very big splash among hunters.

Which Case for the 6mm-06?

I have several questions on the 6mm-06 wildcat. Which of the 30-06 family of cases is best to use in forming it? Can a rifle in 243 Winchester or 6mm Remington be rechambered without removing the barrel? Where can I find load data for the 6mm-06? How does it compare in velocity to the 6mm Remington Improved?

The 6mm-06 can be formed by necking down the case of any cartridge in the 30-06 family but the 25-06 is the best choice since necking it down does not require the use of a case-forming die, nor do the necks of formed cases have to be reamed or outside turned. Simply run 25-06 brass through a 6mm-06 full-length resizing die and the job is done. A rifle in 243 or 6mm Remington could be rechambered by hand without removing its barrel but since it would be impossible to keep the reamer properly aligned, the end result would likely

Can l Rechamber 243 Winchester to 6mm Remington?

The 6mm Remington is one of my favorite cartridges but it is not available in a standard-production factory rifle with a 26-inch barrel. If l buy a rifle in 243 Winchester can l have it rechambered to 6mm Remington?

A barrel in 243 Winchester can be rechambered to 6mm Remington but only if is it set deeper into the receiver by slightly shortening and then rethreading its shank. If this is not done the 6mm reamer won't completely clean up the 243 chamber. You will lose somewhere in the neighborhood of half an inch in barrel length with this conversion but even more important, the barrel will no longer fit closely in its channel in the stock.

The 243 Winchester to 6mm Remington switch?

be less than satisfactory. Starting loads published in the Barnes, Nosler and Hornady handloading manuals for the 240 Weatherby Magnum can be used for the same purpose in the 6mm-06. Everything including barrel length and the chamber pressure to which they are loaded being equal, the 6mm-06 is capable of about the same velocity levels as the 240 Weatherby Magnum. I once used a T/C Encore rifle with a 26-inch custom shop barrel in 6mm-06 to hunt pronghorn antelope in New Mexico and took a very nice buck with the 90-gr. Swift Scirocco loaded to 3450 fps. It is a great little cartridge.

How Many Cartridges On the 284 Winchester Case?

A friend of mine considers his heavy-barrel rifle in 6mm-284 the best long-range varmint poison he has ever tried. His favorite handloads push the Hornady 58- and 65-grain V-Max bullets along at respective velocities of 3800 and 3600 fps. When either bullet is zeroed two inches high at 100 yards it is dead on the money at 300 yards. That's flat-shooting in anybody's book. My friend's rifle has a Shilen barrel and it will keep five shots inside 1-1/2 inches 300 yards. He forms cases for his rifle by necking down 284 Winchester brass. What other calibers been developed on that case? Which are the most popular?

Very few cartridges escape wildcatters and the 284 Winchester is certainly no exception. In this case, two offspring have become more popular than the parent. According to the guys at Redding, about twice as many sets of reloading dies in 6mm-284 are sold each year than in 284 Winchester. The 6.5-284 is even more popular as it outsells the 284 by a four to one margin. Other less popular cartridges on the same case are the 25-284, 270-284, 30-284, 8mm-284, 338-284, 358-284 and 375-285.

I own rifles in 6mm-284, 25-284 and 6.5-284 Norma and like all of them. Powder capacity of the 6mm-284 is about the same as for the 240 Weatherby Magnum so the performance of those two is the same. The same comparison can be made of the 25-284 and the 25-06 and the 6.5-284 and the 6.5 Remington Magnum. Quite a few riflemen who shoot super-accurate rifles in 1000-yard competition use the 6.5-284 and this is mainly why it is more popular than its two siblings. It is also an excellent big-game cartridge. I have a beautiful English walnut-stocked Cooper Model 22 in this caliber and just as its factory guarantee promises, it will keep three bullets inside half an inch at 100 yards all day long, or as long as I can hold the rifle that close. I took my best pronghorn antelope to date with that rifle.

Why No 150-gr. Bullet in the 7.62x39mm Russian?

Why is there not a greater variety of bullet weights available in 7.62x39mm factory ammunition? Winchester, Remington, Federal and PMC offer factory ammo with 123- and 125-gr. softnose bullets but I would like to see someone load the cartridge with 150- or 165-gr. Nosler Ballistic Tips. In my opinion, that would make it a better deer cartridge for the thousands of SKS rifles owned by American hunters and shooters.

Traditional bullet weights for the 30 Russian are 122 and 125 grains and the ammunition manufacturers stay within that weight range in order to load the cartridge to its original velocity specifications. Heavier bullets can be loaded in the cartridge but velocity is quite low. As an example, a maximum charge of AA-1680 pushes the Sierra 150-gr. roundnose bullet to only about 2100 fps in my Ruger Mini Thirty whereas most loads with 123- and 125-gr. bullets are at least 300 fps faster. Also, bullets of pointed or spitzer form that exceed 130 grains in weight are too long to be loaded to an overall length that will work in the magazine of the Ruger, BRNO and SKS rifles.

What Bullets for the 7.62x54mm Russian?

I have a bolt action rifle chambered for the 7.62x54mm Russian cartridge and had long assumed .311 inch to be the correct bullet diameter for it. Then I bought a new set of reloading dies and discovered the expander button in the full-length resizer is for .308-inch bullets. Which bullet diameter am I supposed to use?

Correct bullet diameter for the 7.62x54mm Russian is actually .310 inch. The only readily available bullet of that diameter I am aware of is the 125-gr. spire point made by Hornady for the 7.62x39mm Russian. Through the years handloaders have discovered that some Mosin-Nagant rifles will produce acceptable accuracy with .308-inch bullets and this explains why it is not uncommon to see the expander button in a full-length resizing die sized for that bullet diameter. As a rule, 30-caliber bullets will work in a rifle with a barrel bored and rifled on the minimum side of the dimensional tolerance range. Depending on the neck wall thickness of a particular batch of cases, the expander button that came with your reloading dies may also work fine when bullets as large as .310 inch are used. If not, the manufacturer of the dies can furnish you with a slightly larger button.

I should also mention that some Mosin-Nagant rifles with slightly oversized bore and groove diameters will handle the .311-inch bullets made by Speer, Sierra and Hornady for the 303 British cartridge. To be on the safe side they should be used only if barrel groove diameter measures .310 inch or larger. You can determine the interior dimensions of your barrel with a Cerrosafe casting (available from Brownells).

How Do Weatherby's 30-378 and 33-378 Magnums Compare?

How do the 30-378 Weatherby Magnum and 33-378 Weatherby compare in downrange energy?

Respective muzzle velocity ratings for the 30-378 Magnum loaded with a 180-gr. bullet and the 338-378 Magnum with a 250-gr. bullet are 3450 and 3060 fps. Based on those initial velocities the 30-378 delivers 4204, 3709, 3264, 2865 and 2506 foot-pounds of energy at 100, 200, 300, 400 and 500 yards while the 338-378 delivers 4528, 3933, 3401, 2927 and 2507 ft-lbs at those same distances.

Best Big-Game Factory Loads for the 45-70?

While serving in the U.S. Army during the 1970s I bought a New Model Marlin 1895 in 45-70 and through the years while I have found its performance on big game to be satisfactory I am not exactly up to date on the latest in factory load development. What are the best 45-70 factory loads now available for deer as well as larger game?

You won't go wrong with either of the 300-gr. factory loads from Federal, Winchester and Remington as the bullets in all three loads are constructed for optimum performance on deer-size game. Out to 100 yards or so the old 400-gr. factory load (still available from Remington) is as effective now as it has ever been but when hunting deer I prefer the greater shocking power of the faster 300-gr. loads. As for larger game, Winchester's Supreme loading with the 300-gr. Partition Gold and the Cor-Bon load with a 350-gr. bonded core bullet should get the job done on not only deer but elk and moose. Either of those loads would also be good choices for huge black bear like those I recently hunted on Vancouver Island. Fact of the matter is, there is no animal in North America I wouldn't hunt with the Winchester and Cor-Bon loads. Hornady Light Magnum ammo loaded with a 265-gr. bullet is also a good choice.

What Can You Tell Me about the 7mm STE?

Your 7mm Shooting Times Easterner sounds like a great cartridge for deer hunters. What can you tell me about it?

A wildcat cartridge, the 7mm STE is the 307 Winchester case necked down and fireformed to minimum body taper and a sharper shoulder angle. Marlin 336 and Winchester 94 rifles chambered for the 307 Winchester, 356 Winchester and 444 Marlin can be converted simply by rebarreling. Maximum muzzle velocities for the Nosler 120-gr. and Hornady 130-gr. flatnose bullets in the 22-inch barrel of my Marlin 336 are 2900 and 2700 fps, respectively. My favorite powders for the cartridge are H414, W760 and RL-19 and Hodgdon's Nos. 26 and 27 Data Manuals contain load data for the Nosler and Hornady bullets. Reloading dies are available from Redding and RCBS. The gunsmith and barrelmaker who converted my rifle is Harry McGowen of McGowen Rifle barrels, Dept. ST, 5961 Spruce Lane, St. Anne, IL 60964.

What Happened to the 9x23mm Winchester?

Pushing a 125-gr. bullet to 1450 fps, the 9x23 Winchester duplicates the performance of the 357 SIG and is more powerful than standard factory loadings of the 38 Super. Considering this, how do you explain the fact that it is a dying cartridge?

Unlike the 357 SIG, which is short enough to work in the dozens upon dozens of autoloaders originally designed for the 9mm Luger cartridge, the 9x23 Winchester needs the extra magazine length of the 1911 style pistol. Add to this the fact that about 99.9 percent of those who buy 1911 pistols prefer the 45 ACP and it becomes easy to see why the 9x23 is dying at such a young age. What you have just read also applies to the 10mm Auto versus 40 S&W saga.

What Is the 40 Super?

I keep hearing about the 40 Super but nobody in my neck of the woods seems to know anything about it. Can you cast any light on the subject?

The 40 Super was developed by Triton Cartridge Corp (Dept ST, P.O. Box 50, Wappingers Falls, NY 12590). Cases were originally formed by shortening 45 Winchester Magnum brass to the same length as the 10mm Auto case and necking it down for 10mm (40 caliber) bullets. This gives the new round greater capacity and higher velocity than any other 40 caliber cartridge short enough to work in the 1911 pistol and this includes the 400 Cor-Bon. Triton currently offers three factory loadings: 135-gr. JHP at 1800 fps, 165-gr. JHP at 1500 fps and 200-gr. JHP at 1300 fps, all in a five-inch barrel. As I write this the only handgun available in this caliber is the 1911-style Trojan from STI International, Dept ST, 114 Halmar Cove, Georgetown, TX 78628.

What Is the 8mm Special?

While recently attending a gun show I saw a box of Remington cartridges identified as "8mm Special" in a cartridge collection. The ammo was loaded with 170-gr. bullets and the cartridges looked to be identical to the 8x57mm Mauser. I have enjoyed hunting with rifles in 8x57mm Mauser for many years but have never heard of a 8mm Special. Can you clarify this?

The box of cartridges you saw was loaded by Remington during the 1920s and was that company's way of offering 8x57mm Mauser hunting ammo suitable for use in rifles with a .318-inch groove diameter (commonly referred to as the 8x57J) and those with the more common .323-inch (8x57JS) barrels. The special soft-nosed bullet was large enough in diameter to be accurate when fired through the larger-diameter barrels and yet its extremely soft construction enabled it to squeeze through the smaller-diameter barrels without causing excessive chamber pressures. The same type of bullet was also once offered in 8x57mm Mauser ammo loaded by Peters and Winchester.

Is the 454 Enough Cartridge for Alaska Moose?

I enjoy hunting with handguns but have never taken any game larger than deer and wild hogs. I plan to book a hunt in Alaska for moose and am tempted to use a Freedom Arms revolver in 454 caliber. Is that enough gun for the job? If yes, what scope and ammo should I use?

I have yet to hunt moose with the 454 but not long back I took a very nice bull in Alaska with a revolver in 44 Magnum. After taking my first shot to the lungs from about 65 yards, the big animal slowly walked about half dozen steps and then fell

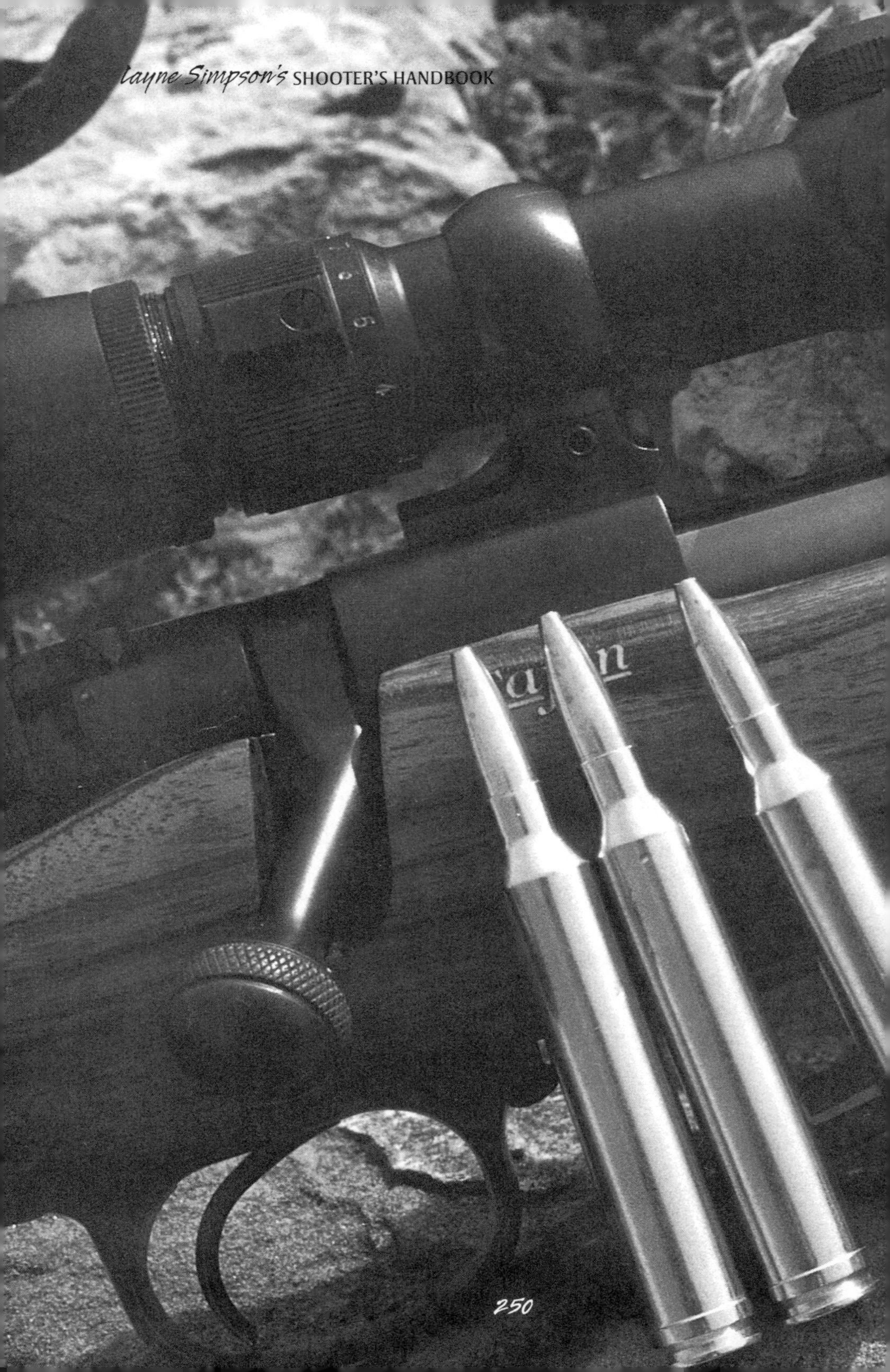

What Rifling Twist Rate for 7mm STW?

I plan to build a rifle in 7mm STW around a Sako action and will use a 27-inch barrel. What rifling twist rate is best for 160-gr. bullets?

I prefer a 1:9 rifling twist rate for the 7mm STW. It is fast enough to stabilize spitzers as heavy as 175 grains and yet accuracy is still quite good with bullets weighing 140 grains and less.

Choose your rifling twist rate carefully when building a rifle in 7mm STW.

on its nose. Since the 454 delivers a considerably heavier blow than the 44 Magnum I have to believe it is plenty of cartridge for Alaska moose–assuming the right load is used. As for my comments on ammo, while recently hunting with a 454-caliber Freedom Arms revolver I dropped a Texas nilgai in its tracks with a single round of Winchester's recipe with the 260-gr. Partition Gold bullet, and considering how well it worked on that hunt I see no reason why it would not be good moose medicine. Several of the 454 loads offered by Cor-Bon should also work quite well on moose. When hunting big game with a revolver I like a variable-power scope with 1X to 2X at the lower end of its magnification range and no more than 6X or 7X up top.

What Happened to the 375 Winchester?

Three years ago I bought a used Winchester 94 in 375 Winchester and have been impressed by its performance on deer and wild hogs. Why has this cartridge not become more popular?

My guess is the 375 Winchester failed to win the hearts of deer hunters for a couple of reasons, one being its poor timing; the 375 was introduced long after the dominance of pure woods rifles like the 94 Winchester had ended among America's deer hunters and those who continue to buy that type of rifle seem to prefer a more traditional cartridge such as the 30-30 Winchester. Secondly and probably equally important, the 375 is capable of doing nothing that can't be done just as well with the 35 Remington, a cartridge that has been on the hunting scene since 1906.

7mm-08 Remington vs. 7x57mm Mauser

I recently bought a Remington Model 700 Classic in 7x57mm Mauser and would like your opinion of the cartridge. What velocites is it capable of in a modern rifle like my Remington?

The 7x57mm Mauser is an excellent cartridge, one capable of doing anything that can be done with the more modern 7mm-08 Remington. Both of those cartridges tread closely on the heels of the 270 Winchester and 280 Remington in performance and that makes them suitable for use on all North American big game excepting really big bears such as the Polar and Alaska brown. When loaded to maximum but safe chamber pressures for the 22-inch barrels of modern rifles such as the Remington Model 700, Winchester 70, Ruger 77 and Ruger No. 1, the 7x57mm will approach 2900 feet per second with the 140-gr. bullet, making it one of the really great big-game cartridges of all time. As a bonus, it also generates less recoil than more powerful cartridges of its caliber.

Is the 7mm-08 Remington Only a 200-Yard Cartridge?

I hunted deer for many years with the 270 Winchester and recently switched to a bolt action carbine with a 20-inch barrel in 7mm-08 Remington. I like the outfit but keep hearing the 7mm-08 is a 200-yard cartridge at best. This puzzles me greatly since the box of 139-gr. Hornady Light Magnum ammo I recently bought is rated at 3000 fps. According to Hornady's ballistic chart, the load delivers close to 1800 foot-pounds of energy at 300 yards and when zeroed three inches high at 100 yards the bullet is down less than three inches at 300. Am I missing something here?

It is quite common to hear someone praise their favorite cartridge at the expense of one they have absolutely no experience with and it sounds like you have fallen victim to that type of biased opinion. When the Hornady Light Magnum load is fired in the short barrel of your rifle, muzzle velocity will probably be closer to 2800 fps than 3000 fps but that's still as fast as some 130-gr. 270 Winchester factory loads I've chronographed. Few people who have experience with the 270 would classify it as a 200-yard cartridge at best.

A 303 British Fan

I recently celebrated my 79th birthday and the 303 British is still one of my favorite cartridges. For several generations it was the standard moose and bear cartridge in Canada and some hunters continue to use it. CIL, the Canadian ammunition manufacturer, once offered six different loadings which indicates just how popular it was back in the good old days.

The 303 British is still an excellent cartridge and not too far behind the 308 Winchester in performance. Back when I was a youngster it was quite popular among deer and bear hunters in my neck of the woods, mainly due to the low cost of Enfield rifles in those days. The fact that the 303 is now overshadowed by more modern cartridges doesn't prevent sentimental shooters like you and me from enjoying an occasional range session or deer hunt with it for old times' sake.

Is Winchester 357 Magnum Ammo Safe to Use in a Lever Action?

During the past year I purchased Winchester Model 94 and Marlin 1894 lever action rifles in 357 Magnum. Since certain bullet shapes are not supposed to be used in rifles with tubular magazines I am careful about what I feed my two. Can I safely use Winchester Supreme ammo loaded with the 180-gr. Partition Gold bullet in my rifles?

The exact same thing crossed my mind back when I received my first box of 44 Magnum Supreme ammo loaded with the 250-gr. Partition Gold bullet. So I asked the question of two Winchester officials and was told the Supreme loadings of the 357 Magnum and 44 Magnum can be safely used in rifles with tubular magazines.

Info on 40-82 Winchester?

I own a Winchester Model 1886 in 40-82 and would like to know what the cartridge was developed for.

Winchester introduced the 40-82 in 1885 in its Model '85 single shot rifle and

The 45 ACP is an excellent choice for competition, but it is no bear cartridge.

Is the 45 ACP Enough Cartridge for Bear?

I am trying to decide on a trail gun to carry in the outdoors while camping in a western state. I need one powerful enough for possible defensive use against not only two-legged varmints but also those with two more legs such as mountain lion and black bear. Whatever gun I decide on needs to be light and compact enough to be carried all day in a shoulder holster. I still have a Colt Combat Elite in 45 ACP from my law enforcement days and know it will get the job done on everything except possibly black bear. If my old 1911 isn't enough gun for that what do you recommend?

Even though the 45 ACP is one of my favorite cartridges for personal defense I'll have to say it is underpowered for black bear. Assuming you prefer to stick with the 1911 pistol, my advice is to purchase a drop-in barrel and conversion kit in 45 Super. In a five-inch barrel the 45 Super is capable of pushing a 230-gr. bullet along at close to 1200 feet per second and that should be enough power to discourage any black bear in a close-range confrontation. Another more powerful option for your Colt is to buy a 460 Rowland conversion from Clark Custom Guns (Dept. ST, 336 Shootout Lane, Princeton, LA 71067).

Also available in a drop-in kit, that cartridge is capable of exceeding 1300 fps with a 230-gr. bullet, putting it in almost the same power class as the 44 Remington Magnum. One of the nice things about the 45 Super and 460 Rowland conversions is a 1911 so converted is easily switched back to shooting the 45 ACP by simply changing barrels and recoil springs.

This Springfield 1911 race gun is accurate with factory ammo.

SPRINGFIELD
Custom

Favorite 38 Super Factory Load?

Sometime back you described a Springfield Armory 1911-A1 in 38 Super as one of your favorites for personal defense use. Soon after reading your article my husband presented me with an identical gun. The light recoil of a 1911-style pistol in 38 Super enables me to shoot it more accurately than any other handgun I have tried to date. What factory load do you prefer?

My favorite 38 Super factory load is available from Cor-Bon, Dept. ST, 1311 Industry Rd, Sturgis, SD 57785. Rated as a +P load with a 125-gr. hollowpoint bullet, it averages 1365 feet per second in the five-inch barrel of my Springfield and is extremely accurate. Cor-Bon also offers a 115-gr. +P load rated at 1450 fps.

later offered it as one of many chambering options in the Model 1886 lever action. Originally loaded with a 260-gr. lead bullet at a muzzle velocity of 1490 feet per second, the 40-82 was developed as a big-game cartridge and enjoyed at least mild popularity among hunters who took to the hills for larger game such as elk and moose.

Can 45 Colt Equal 44 Magnum?

It appears to me that when the modern 45 Colt case is handloaded to maximum but safe chamber pressure for a modern handgun it will do about anything the 44 Magnum can do. Am I correct in assuming this?

The new No. 27 Data Manual from Hodgdon Powder agrees rather closely with your assumption. According to Hodgdon, when maximum 45 Colt loads are put up in Winchester cases and fired in the Ruger Blackhawk and the Casull single-action revolvers, maximum velocities with 240- and 300-gr. jacketed bullets are 1532 and 1202 feet per second, respectively. That same source shows maximum velocities for the 44 Magnum with those same bullet weights to be 1522 and 1325 fps. Barrel lengths used in the development of the data were 8.30 inches for the 44 Magnum and 7.25 inches for the 45 Colt. Squeezing those levels of performance from the old cartridge is recommended only for Ruger, Freedom Arms and Thompson/Center firearms chambered for the 45 Colt or firearms chambered for the 454 Casull.

How Good Is The 30-30 Winchester?

I'm thinking a milder cartridge such as the 30-30 Winchester is all the average deer hunter needs. What is your opinion of the ancient old "Dirty Thirty"?

I also enjoy hunting with old timers such as the 30-30 Winchester, 35 Remington, 300 Savage and 348 Winchester. In the hands of a good rifleman who knows where a bullet must be placed, the 30-30 is plenty of cartridge for deer out to 200 yards or so. Handloading it with pointed bullets for rifles such as the Savage 99, Winchester 54, Remington 788, Thompson/Center G2 Contender and New England Handi-Rifle extends its reach out to and easy 300 yards. I recently took a 160-class buck in Kansas with the G2 Contender rifle and the 30-30 loaded to 2500 fps with the Hornady 150-grain SST bullet. One shot across a winter wheat field ended my hunt. Of course, pointed bullets should never be used in rifles with tubular magazines.

One 44 Magnum Load for Several Guns?

I enjoy shooting the 44 Magnum cartridge as it suits my needs perfectly for woods hunting and casual target shooting. My collection now contains four guns in this caliber, a Marlin 1894, two of the old Ruger autoloading carbines and a Ruger Super Blackhawk with a 7-1/2 inch barrel. I want to get into handloading and hope you will help me decide between a progressive or single-stage reloader. I also want to keep life simple by stocking up on as few different reloading components as possible. What single load can I use on all my guns?

Only you can decide on the type of reloader you need simply because only you know how many rounds you shoot annually and how much time you are able to devote to reloading ammo. Either type of machine can turn out top-quality ammunition but the production rate of a progressive is considerably higher. Unless you really want to shoot full-power loads all the time you'll probably be much happier to settle on two loads rather than one and this would require only that you stock one additional powder. I'd stick with a good jacketed bullet in the 240- to 250-gr. weight range and use either H110 or W296 when putting together full-power loads. Using that same bullet I would also back off on the throttle to the 800 to 900 feet per second range and that would be my combination plinking and practice load. Unique would be an excellent second powder candidate for that application, as would Green Dot and HS6. A good magnum primer such as the CCI 350 is required for good ignition of slow powders such as H110 and W296 and you could also use it when switching to faster burning propellants for the reduced velocity load.

22 WRF in 22 WMR?

I have a Marlin bolt action rifle in 22 WMR. I also have some Winchester 22 WRF ammo of recent production and it shoots quite accurately in my rifle as well as my son's rifle in 22 WMR. Will shooting the short ammo in the long chamber cause any problems with our rifles?

As popular theory has it, if you fire many thousands of rounds of 22 WRF ammo in a rifle chambered for the 22 WMR the chamber might eventually erode to the point where smooth extraction of the longer case might become a problem. Even so, I doubt if you, I or anyone else would ever shoot enough 22 WRF ammo to experience such a problem.

Why Don't Writers Always Hit the Bullseye?

On a number of occasions I've seen photos of nice groups included in various articles written by you and other writers and while group size is often impressive, it is common to see many shots miss the bullseye. Why can't you writers always hit the bullseye like we readers do?

The universally accepted method for measuring the accuracy of a rifle is to see how closely together it can place its shots on a target, and whether the bullets land inside a bullseye or adjacent to it is immaterial. When shooting in registered competition, benchrest shooters always zero their rifles to place the group outside the bullseye or square simply because they don't want to see bullet holes cut their aiming point into an irregular shape. The same holds true when I accuracy-test an extremely accurate rifle equipped with a high-magnification scope. There are also the matters of convenience and economics. It is not at all unusual for me to spend an entire day at the range testing several rifles and it is simply not practical for me to make sure each and every group I fire is perfectly centered in a bullseye. If on a given day I test, say, five rifles by firing five, 5-shot groups with 10 different loads with each of

The 30-06 is plenty of cartridge for moose.

The 30-06 for Moose?

A friend and I are planning a hunting trip to Alaska for moose. I have been told that my rifle in 30-06 is not adequate for such a large animal and suspect this is true. What cartridge and bullet weight should I switch to?

Anything from the 270 Winchester on up is all the cartridge needed for Alaska moose and this includes the 30-06 Springfield. I have taken moose with a number of cartridges, including the 44 Remington Magnum in a revolver, and as rifle cartridges go I wouldn't hesitate to use the 257 STW or 257 Weatherby Magnum loaded with a premium-grade 120-gr. bullet such as the Nosler Partition and Barnes X-Spitzer. My advice is to stick with your rifle in 30-06 if you're happy with it and use ammunition with a 180-gr. premium grade bullet such as the A-Frame from Remington, Federal's Bear Claw and either the FailSafe or Nosler Partition Gold from Winchester.

them I will have fired 250 groups by day's end. In order to conserve targets I fire as many groups as possible on each one. It is common for the number of groups I fire on a target to outnumber the number of bullseyes it has in which case I often add additional aiming points in the form of pasters.

Which Nosler Partition for Elk?

I plan to hunt during a special cow elk season in Colorado and will use a Browning 1885 in 270 with the 150- or 160-gr. Nosler Partition. Which bullet do you recommend? Another question; one of my reloading manuals lists data for a 170-gr. bullet in the 270 Winchester but I am unable to locate any company offering that weight. Do you know who it might be?

While the 160-gr. Partition is capable of a bit deeper penetration than its 150-gr. mate, either is plenty of bullet for elk when loaded in the 270 Winchester. If it were my hunt I would choose whichever shoots the most accurately in my rifle.

The 170-gr. 270 bullet listed in your handloading manual is probably the old Speer roundnose which has not been available for some years now. Barnes still offers a .277-diameter 180-gr. roundnose in its Original line and data in that company's reloading manual has it exiting the 24-inch barrel of a rifle in 270 Winchester at a maximum of 2762 feet per second.

What Is 22 K-Hornet?

I recently learned about a cartridge called the 22 K-Hornet and understand it is faster than the standard 22 Hornet. What is your opinion of this cartridge? Could I have my NEF Handi-Rifle in 22 Hornet rechambered for it?

Often described as our first improved cartridge, the 22 K-Hornet was introduced many years ago and is nothing more than the standard 22 Hornet case fireformed to less body taper and a sharper shoulder angle. Through the years I have owned several rifles chambered for both cartridges and find the improved version, on average, to be about 100 fps faster than the factory cartridge. As a rule, 22 K-Hornet cases last a bit longer than standard cases but neither will last very long when fired in oversized chambers which seem to be so common among rifles of this caliber. Rechambering your Handi-Rifle to 22 K-Hornet is a rather simple job any good gunsmith should be capable of handling.

Load Data for 6mm Holmes?

I own a custom benchrest rifle in 6mm Holmes that my father once used in competition. I have RCBS reloading dies and plenty of cases but no load data. Can you recommend starting loads for this cartridge?

The best way to come up with starting loads for any wildcat is to measure its water capacity and compare what you get with other cartridges for which load data is available from a reliable source. If you find a 6mm cartridge with the same or close to the same capacity as the 6mm Holmes, starting loads will be quite similar for the two.

Rifle for 35 Winchester?

I am interested in the 35 Winchester. What rifle should I start with? Can the 35 Winchester case be formed from any other existing case? Where do I find reloading data?

One way to add a rifle in 35 Winchester to your battery is to buy an original Winchester Model 95 lever action already chambered for it. The Model 1895 reproduction presently available from Browning in 270 and 30-06 could be converted but having one rebarreled along with all the action modifications needed to make it work with the rimmed 35 Winchester cartridge could be quite costly. A less expensive route would be to have a single shot such as the Ruger No 1 or Browning 1885 rebarreled. An 1898 Krag rifle in 30-40 Krag could also be rebarreled and shouldn't require any other modifications. Cases can be formed by firing 30-40 Krag factory ammo in a rifle chambered for the 35 Winchester. The necks of formed cases will be about 1/8 inch shorter than those of original 35 Winchester cases but it won't have any affect on performance. Load data is not available from the regular sources so if it were my project I would reduce starting loads commonly used for the 35 Whelen by 20 percent and use that as my starting point for 35 Winchester load development.

What Rifling Twist Rate for 358 STA?

I am having a rifle in 358 Shooting Times Alaskan built around a Model 700 action and plan to use it on a once-in-a-lifetime hunt in Alaska. What rifling twist rate do you recommend for the 225- and 250-gr. Nosler Partition bullets and what is your preference in barrel length? What stock did you choose when building your rifle and what is its trigger pull weight? I'm considering a muzzle brake but am concerned about hearing loss. Does the 358 STA really require a brake?

I like a 24-inch barrel on a rifle in 358 STA but wouldn't object if it measured 26 inches mainly because it puts muzzle blast a bit farther away from the ears. The Lilja barrel on my rifle has a 1:14 inch twist but 1:16 is plenty quick for the 225- and 250-gr. bullets you intend to use. My rifle's fiberglass stock is by McMillan and the weight of its trigger pull is four pounds which is plenty light for a big-game rifle built to be used in cold weather. While I don't consider a muzzle brake an absolute necessity on a rifle in 358 STA I'll have to admit a good one does reduce recoil and it's something worth considering to someone who is not accustomed to shooting powerful rifles. You might take a look at the adjustable brake from Brockman Distributing, Inc., (P.O. Box 357, Dept. ST, Gooding, ID 83330); it can be turned "on" while you're practicing with ear protection and then turned "off" for hunting without affecting bullet point of impact.

5.6x52R Has American Connection?

Roe deer hunters here in Germany use rifles chambered for a cartridge called the 5.6x52R and it is also commonly used to take fox. I have heard the cartridge described as the 5.6x52 Savage and since Savage is an American company I have often wondered about the possibility of the cartridge having an American connection in some way. What can you tell me about it?

The cartridge described as the 5.6x52R or 5.6x52mm in your country is an American invention and is called the 22 Savage Hi-Power here in the United States. It was designed by bolt-action rifle designer and manufacturer Charles Newton and introduced commercially by Savage in its Model 99 lever action rifle around 1912. During its first few years of existence the 22 Hi-Power was promoted as a big-game cartridge and hunters used it to take everything from whitetail deer to grizzly bear. Among today's hunters it would be considered at its best when used on varmints although those who advocate the use of the 222 and 223 on deer might disagree. The case can be formed by necking down 30-30 brass in a series of form dies and the .227-inch, 70-gr. bullet offered by Hornady works great. Hornady's handloading manual also has 5.6x52R loading data.

22 Long Rifle at 400 Yards?

I recently read in another magazine an article on a super-accurate custom rifle in 22 rimfire built on the Ruger 10/22 action. The rifle wore a 6-24X scope with a mil-dot reticle. According to the author, he was able to connect on prairie dogs at 300 to 400 yards with that outfit. Is the 22 Long Rifle capable of such performance or was that guy simply hoping the gunsmith who built the rifle would give it to him after reading his write-up?

The key word there is "connect." While it is possible the author of that piece did occasionally hit a prairie dog at such ranges, I'm wondering how many he actually killed and how many were allowed to escape wounded, only to die a lingering death? The 22 Long Rifle cartridge simply doesn't deliver enough energy at long range to quickly kill an animal even as small as a prairie dog unless the bullet strikes its brain or spinal column and those are extremely small targets at 300 and 400 yards. Using any cartridge at ranges where it has lost most of its effectiveness is bad business and on top of that, anyone who assumes the responsibility of killing an animal owes it nothing less than a quick and humane death, regardless of whether we humans choose to classify it as game or varmint.

30-40 Krag on Elk?

I have a Krag rifle in 30-40 caliber and would like to use it on elk with a handloaded 220-gr. roundnose bullet. Will it get the job done? My rifle has a side-mounted scope and I am wondering it you are aware of any type of inherent problem with that system.

At close to medium ranges the 30-40 Krag is plenty of cartridge for elk if you put the right bullet in the right place. The 220-gr. roundnose you are considering would probably work okay but maximum velocity for that bullet weight in the old Krag is only a bit over 2000 feet per second (fps). If I were planning to use the 30-40 on elk I would load it in the neighborhood of 2300 to 2400 fps with a 165-gr. bullet, either the Barnes X-Bullet or Nosler Partition. The design of the Krag action requires the use of a side-mounted scope. An old custom varmint rifle in 22 Hornet I own was built by Griffin & Howe on the Krag action back in the 1930s and I have never experienced the first problem with its side-mounted scope.

The 22 Long Rifle does a great job on small game at close range but it was never meant to be a long-range cartridge.

What X-Bullet Weights?

Since the Barnes X-Bullet retains most of its weight during expansion, lighter weights in a given caliber will penetrate as deeply and sometimes more deeply on game than heavier bullets of conventional construction. My question is, how much lighter should I go when choosing X-Bullets for various game?

Sometime back I discussed this very subject with Randy Brooks, owner of Barnes Bullets, and he recommends either using the same weight X-Bullet as you would commonly use when choosing a conventional bullet or dropping back to the next lighter weight. As an example, when it comes to bullets of conventional design, I consider 180 grains to be about the optimum weight for elk when using a rifle chambered for one of the 30-caliber cartridges from the 30-06 on up. If I were to develop an elk load with an X-Bullet in one of those cartridges I would choose either the 180- or 165-gr. version. On the other hand, I prefer 150-gr. bullets in deer loads and would have the options of choosing either the 140- or 150-gr. X-Bullets for that application. As for even lighter game such as pronghorn antelope, I would take a long hard look at the 125-gr. X-Bullet which can be pushed to 3200 fps in the 30-06. Actually, all those decisions are already made for you in the new Barnes reloading manual since recommended uses are listed for each and every bullet made by Barnes.

44 Special, 44 Magnum, 444 Marlin in Same Gun?

As everyone knows, it is safe to fire 38 Special ammo in guns chambered for the 357 Magnum and the same goes for 44 Special ammo in 44 Magnum guns. Could the concept be taken a step further by using 44 Special, 44 Magnum and 444 Marlin ammo in a Marlin 336 or Winchester 94 chambered for the latter cartridge?

Since the 444 Marlin chamber is slightly larger in diameter than the 44 Special and 44 Magnum chambers, firing either of those two cartridges in it could result in ruptured cases and damage to both rifle and shooter. The best way to accomplish the three performance levels you're interested in with one rifle is with handloads; it should be easy to come up with reduced-power loads for the 444 that duplicate the velocities of the 44 Special and 44 Magnum cartridges.

The 45 ACP vs. Wild Boar

I agree with your comments on using handguns in 45 ACP on wild boar and consider it capable of getting the job done at close range. Back in the days of the Korean unpleasantness, we often took our rest and recreation on Cheju Do, a then-deserted little island which has since become a major international resort area. When hunting wild hogs with our 1911 pistols and government-issue 45 hardball ammo, my buddies and I found the combination to be quite effective. In fact, since the shooting was almost always close and the targets were moving fast through thick brush, we found the old 45 to be much better hog medicine than a rifle or carbine.

SECTION FOUR: *Cartridges & Shotshells*

It is always nice to hear from a fellow 45 ACP fan. I have used it to take wild hogs at close range but an sure you will agree when I say there are better cartridges for the job.

Loads For 338 BGS?

I am having a rifle built on the Remington Model Seven action and it will be chambered for a wildcat I came up with. Called the 338 BGS, it is basically John Lazzeroni's short, fat, beltless 6.5mm case necked up for 338 caliber bullets. As powder capacity goes, it is equal to the 338-06 but unlike that cartridge it is short enough to work in a short-action rifle such as the Remington Model Seven. I have ordered the chamber reamer from JGS, have reloading dies on their way from RCBS and all I need now is load data. Can you help? Also, any recommendations on powders and bullets would be greatly appreciated.

If the net powder capacity of your wildcat turns out to be the same as that of the 338-06, load data for that cartridge in *Nosler's Reloading Guide No. 4* and the *Accurate Loading Guide* can be used. One of my favorite powders for the 338-06 is IMR-4320 and it should work equally well in the 338 BGS. Other good choices are AA-2520, Reloder 15, VV-N150, H380 and IMR-4064. For all-around use on all game for which your cartridge will be suitable, the Nosler 210-gr. Partition as well as the Barnes 200-gr. X-Bullet will be tough to beat. For deer-size game only, the Barnes 160-, 175- and 185-gr. X-Bullets along with the Nosler 200-gr. Ballistic Tip, Sierra 215-gr. spitzer boattail and Hornady 200-gr. spire point should work quite well.

Which 243 Factory Load Is Fastest?

I plan to buy a Winchester Model 70 Featherweight in 243 and will use it when hunting deer. The maximum distance most shots are taken in the areas I hunt is around 200 yards. What 100-gr. factory ammo produces the highest velocity? I want to equip the rifle with a scope but don't want to spend more than $250 for it. What scope do you recommend?

I recently chronographed various 100-gr. factory loads in a Prairie Gun Works Model 15-T1 rifle with a 22-inch Gaillard barrel and the Norma load was fastest at an average of 3019 fps. Virtually tied for second place in speed were Remington's Pointed Core-Lokt and Federal's Premium spitzer boattail loadings at respective muzzle velocities of 2888 and 2872 feet per second (fps). At 2819 fps, the Winchester Supreme spitzer boattail was the only other 100-gr. load that exceeded 2800 fps at the muzzle. Velocities will vary among different manufacturing lots of the same load but the Norma load (which is manufactured in Sweden) is always fastest simply because it is loaded to higher chamber pressures than is the case for ammo loaded in the U.S.

By shopping around for the best street price, you should be able to find a satisfactory scope for your rifle for less than $250. Examples that come to mind are the Bushnell Trophy 3-9X, Simmons 44 Mag 3-10X, Weaver V9 3-9X and Millet Buck 3-9X.

Cases for 22-3000 Rifle?

I recently acquired an old single-shot rifle chambered for the 22-3000 and cannot find ammo for it. Can you help? What can you tell me about this cartridge?

Prior to the introduction of the 222 Remington cartridge, the 22-3000 was an extremely popular wildcat among varmint shooters. More commonly known as the 22-3000 Lovell, its developer, Harvey Lovell, unveiled it to the shooting world in the May, 1934 issue of *American Rifleman*. The 22-3000 was formed by necking down the old 25-20 Single Shot case (which is not the same as the 25-20 Repeater case). Since the 25-20 Single Shot cartridge has long been out of production, the ammo and cases now bring collector prices when they can be found.

Your best bet for keeping that old rifle active in the varmint fields is to have a good gunsmith determine its suitability for rechambering to 222 Remington or 223 Remington. The conversion would also require modification of the extractor to handle the rimless style of case. If you prefer to stay with a rimmed case, other rechambering options are the 219 Zipper, 219 Zipper Improved and 219 Donaldson Wasp, all easily formed from the 30-30 case.

What Does "Improved" Mean?

I recently purchased a custom rifle in 30-06 built on the 1903 Springfield action. It is quite accurate but after firing several rounds I noticed that the shoulders of ejected cases had taken on a much sharper angle and the diameter of the body of the case had increased a bit. The barrel is on my rifle is marked "30-06 Improved." What does that mean?

As the engraving on the barrel of your rifle indicates, it is chambered for an improved version of the 30-06 cartridge. Use of the word "improved" in cartridge nomenclature means that case shape is changed to less body taper and usually a sharper shoulder angle as well in order to slightly increase powder capacity over the standard 30-06 case. Firing standard 30-06 cartridges in an improved chamber is the most common way to form cases and there is no danger involved in doing so as long as the headspace in your rifle is not excessive. As a rule, when a standard 30-06 cartridge is fired in the improved chamber its velocity will be anywhere from 75 to 100 feet per second lower than when it is fired in a standard chamber. Should you choose to reload cases fired in your rifle you will need to obtain special dies from RCBS or Redding. Several versions of the 30-06 Improved do exist so you should send five cases fired in your rifle along with your order for the dies.

Which Cartridge for New Rifle?

I have a 1936 Oberndorf '98 Mauser action in excellent condition. I plan to install a 20-inch barrel on the action and stock it Mannlicher-style. What I'm after is a fast handling rifle to be used for hunting deer and black bear in the Adirondack mountains of New York state. I also anticipate eventually using the rifle on hunts for moose. As chamberings go, I have thought about the 338-06, 35 Whelen, and 9.3x62mm Mauser. Which should I choose?

You are considering an excellent trio of cartridges, any of which would serve your needs quite well. I first used a Sako rifle in 9.3x62mm Mauser several years ago while hunting moose in Finland and liked the outfit so well that I bought it and had it shipped home. Sako and RWS load the ammo, and bullets are available from Nosler, Speer and Barnes, but since you are not likely to find either on the shelves of many gun shops, the 9.3x62mm is far from a practical choice. I have also hunted with rifles in 338-06 and 35 Whelen and both have obvious advantages. The 35 Whelen is factory-loaded by Remington and Federal while a somewhat better selection of bullets might make the 338-06 more appealing to some handloaders. As for effectiveness on game, I have never been able to see more than two cents worth of difference between the three cartridges.

Is 257 Improved Enough Cartridge for Elk?

I have a Ruger Model 77 in 257 Ackley Improved with a 40-degree shoulder angle. Where can I find load data for this cartridge? Is if powerful enough to use on mule deer and elk?

The latest Nosler and Sierra reloading manuals have plenty of load data for the 40-degree 257 Improved. Although data shown for the 257 Improved in the Hornady manual is for the 28-degree cartridge, it too can be used in your rifle since powder capacity of the two cartridges is virtually identical. The 257 Improved is an excellent mule deer cartridge and while a good rifleman using the right bullet (such as the Nosler Partition or Barnes X-Bullet) would have no problem bagging larger game such as elk at reasonable ranges, a number of far better elk cartridges do exist.

22 Long Rifle in 22 WRF?

I have a Winchester Model 90 in 22 WRF in near mint condition. I'd like to shoot the gun but cannot find the ammo. Having it rechambered to 22 WMR is out of the question due to the higher chamber pressures to which that cartridge is loaded. How aout the 22 Long Rifle cartridge; can it be safely fired in my rifle?

Firing 22 Long Rifle ammo in a rifle chambered for the larger-diameter 22 WMR is likely to result in ruptured cases which can cause damage to both gun and shooter. Every couple years or so Winchester produces a run of 22 WMR ammo and its quality is excellent. A close look at the shelves of dealers in your area might turn up a few boxes.

Which 6mm Cartridge for Long-Range Varminting?

I plan to have a super-accurate 6mm caliber varmint rifle built around a short Remington Model 700 action. I'll use it for long range shooting of prairie dogs and rockchucks. Since only the very best parts and materials will be utilized in building the rifle, it is bound to be somewhat expensive so I want to make sure I choose the right cartridge. I'll probably stick with the Nosler 55-gr. Ballistic Tip and Sierra 60-gr. hollowpoint bullets and have boiled my choices down

The 7mm Remington Maximum is what I called the 7mm STW when I first developed it.

What Is the 7mm Remington Maximum?

I recall sometime back your mentioning a cartridge called the 7mm Remington Maximum. Was it a Remington experimental cartridge or a wildcat you cooked up?

Years ago, back when I first necked down Remington's then-new 8mm Magnum case to 7mm, I called it the 7mm Remington Maximum. But by the time I actually got around to ordering a chamber reamer and having a rifle chambered for the wildcat, I decided to dedicate it to the readers of *Shooting Times* magazine by renaming it the 7mm Shooting Times Westerner, or 7mm STW for short.

From left to right:
1. *6x45mm*
2. *6mm BR Remington*
3. *243 Winchester*
4. *6mm (or 244) Remington*

5. *243 WSSM*
6. *240 Weatherby Magnum*
7. *6mm-06*
8. *6mm-284*

to the 243 Winchester, 6mm Remington and improved versions of those two cartridges. Which would I most likely live happily ever after with?

Since you will be using your new rifle for shooting prairie dogs, an activity that requires a relatively large supply of cases, I believe you would be happier with the standard 243 and 6mm since they would not require fireforming. And besides, the improved versions are only about 100 feet per second faster. As for choosing between the two factory cartridges, it is a tough decision. I actually like the looks of the 6mm Remington better but believe the 243 Winchester might have a slight accuracy edge. Cases for the Winchester cartridge are also usually a bit easier to come by. Even with all that said I'll have to add that you can't go wrong with either cartridge.

Which 45-Caliber Bullet?

I enjoy hunting deer and elk with 45-caliber rifles. I often use a Marlin 1895 and a Browning 1885 in 45-70 and a Ruger No. 1 in 458 Winchester Magnum. I handload the Speer 400-gr. softnose to 1700 fps for the 45-70 and the same bullet at 2000 fps for the 458 Magnum. I have never had to shoot anything twice with those loads but my friends claim that the Speer bullet is too soft to use at those velocities and I should switch to the tougher Hornady 350-gr. softnose. Do you agree?

I consider the Speer 400-gr. bullet to be an excellent choice for use on deer-size game at velocities as high as 2000 fps. And as you have already discovered, it works equally well on game as large as elk so long as it is not pushed too fast. You should stick with that bullet when hunting either deer or elk with your rifles in 45-70 but since the Hornady 350-gr. roundnose was designed specifically for the higher impact velocities of the 450 Marlin and 458 Winchester Magnum, I suggest that you switch to it when using that cartridge on elk. I'm sure you could get by with the Speer bullet if only lung shots are taken on elk but the Hornady bullet is more likely to hold together and penetrate deeply with a shot to the shoulders, especially if it encounters heavy bone.

6.5 STW Faster than 264 Magnum?

I have a Remington Model 700 in 264 Winchester Magnum. I use handloads with the Nosler 120-gr. Ballistic Tip on deer and pronghorn antelope, and the Nosler 125-gr. Partition on elk. Through the years I have taken a great deal of game with this rifle and have been impressed with its performance but since its barrel is about shot out I plan to have it rebarreled. I want to stay with the same caliber but would like to switch to a bigger cartridge in order to reach the same velocity with the Nosler 140-gr. Partition as the 264 Winchester Magnum generates with 120- and 125-gr. bullets. Is the 6.5 STW capable of that level of performance? What barrel length and rifling twist rate do you recommend for that cartridge? How are cases formed? Where do I find load data? Which powders are best? Who can rebarrel my rifle?

You should have no problem reaching the same velocities with a 140-gr. bullet in the 6.5 STW as is possible with a 125-gr. bullet in the 264 Winchester Magnum. Your best bet is a 26-inch barrel with a rifling twist rate of 1:9 inches. Cases are easily formed by necking down 7mm STW brass in a 6.5 STW full-length resizing die. Cases can also be formed by necking down 8mm Remington Magnum cases but they will have to first be necked down in a 7mm STW full-length resizer before being necked on down to 6.5mm. Maximum loads shown in various handloading manuals for the 264 Winchester Magnum can be used as a starting point when developing loads for a rifle in 6.5 STW. For bullets up to 125 grains in weight, H1000, Reloder 22 and MRP are excellent powders in this cartridge but slower powders such as AA-8700, H50BMG, H5010, H870 and V-20N29 are best when loading heavier bullets. For rebarreling your Model 700 to 6.5 STW, contact Lex Webernick at Rifles, Inc.

How Good Is the 7mm-08?

I'd like your opinion on the Remington Model Seven in 7mm-08 Remington. I have heard many favorable comments on this combination but wonder if it is enough gun for elk?

The Remington Model Seven in 7mm-08 is no long-range elk rifle by any stretch of the imagination but out to 200 yards or so it is plenty of gun for the job. Its light weight and short overall length make the Model Seven an excellent timber rifle and when loaded with a good bullet of controlled-expansion design, the 7mm-08 is certainly adequate for the job. Your best bet in elk medicine is to load one of the following bullets to about 2600 fps: Nosler 150- or 160-gr. Partition, Speer 160-gr. Grand Slam, Swift 160-gr. A-Frame, Winchester 160-gr. Fail-Safe and the Barnes 160-gr. X. Powders such as W760, H414, RL-19 and V-N160 have the correct burn rate for loading behind heavy bullets in the 7mm-08 Remington.

Thoughts on the 6mm-06?

I'm intrigued by the 6mm-06 wildcat, but I'm wondering what you can tell me about forming cases. Also, is load data commonly available for this wildcat? If so, where can I find it? How does it compare in velocity to the 243 WSSM and the 240 Weatherby Magnum?

The 6mm-06 can be formed by necking down any of the 30-06 family of cases but the 25-06 is the best choice since necking it down does not require the use of a case-forming die, nor do case necks normally have to be reamed or turned. Simply run 25-06 brass through a 6mm-06 full-length resizing die and you're done. Starting loads published in the Hornady and Nosler handloading manuals for the 240 Weatherby Magnum can be used for the same purpose in the 6mm-06. Everything including barrel length and the chamber pressure to which they are loading being equal, the 6mm-06 is about 200 feet per second faster than the 243 WSSM and generates the same level of velocity as the 240 Weatherby Magnum.

Is There a 338-08?

Through the years I have read a number of articles written on the 308 Winchester and its various offspring in 224, 243, 6.5mm, 7mm and 358 calibers but have never seen anything published on the 338-08. Does such a wildcat exist? It should be an excellent chambering for a short-action bolt gun or perhaps a lever action such as the Savage Model 99. Where can I get load data? Which bullets would be best? Do you know of a gunsmith with a chamber reamer for this cartridge who can install a barrel for me?

The 338-08, or 33-08 as it is also called, does exist and you are correct: it is an excellent cartridge for short-action rifles. Reloading dies are available through your local Redding and RCBS dealers. You can begin load development for a rifle in 33-08 by reducing starting loads shown in various handloading manuals for the 358 Winchester by 10 percent. Your best choices in bullets for this cartridge are the 210-gr. Partition from Nosler, the Sierra 225-gr. spitzer boattail, the Swift 225-gr. A-Frame, the Hornady 200- and 225-gr. spire points, the 200-gr. spitzer and 225-gr. spitzer boattail from Speer, and the Barnes 200-gr. X-Bullet. For having an action rebarreled to 33-08, try Shilen Rifles, Inc. in Ennis, Tex.

Which 223 Factory Load for Deer?

I recently purchased a rifle in 223 Remington and intend to use it for hunting deer. Which factory load do you recommend for this?

Since you obviously are intent on using the 223 Remington on deer, I'll recommend the Federal 55-gr. Bear Claw load since it was designed for just that purpose. But I also want to make it perfectly clear that regardless of what bullet the 223 is loaded with, I do not consider it as good a choice for use on deer-size game as various cartridges of 6mm caliber. The 6x45mm (223 case necked up) is the absolute minimum cartridge that I will recommend for use on deer-size game and shots with it should be restricted to a maximum range of 200 yards or so. Even better are the 243 Winchester, 6mm Remington, 243 WSSM and best of all, the 240 Weatherby Magnum.

How Good Are Nosler Partition and Swift A-Frame?

I hunt big game with various 7mm cartridges and prefer bullets weighing 160 and 175 grains. What is your opinion of Nosler Partition and Swift A-Frame bullets in those weights?

The bullets you mentioned as well as Nosler Partitions and Swift A-Frames in other calibers and weights are excellent choices for use in cartridges of various velocity ranges. This is due to the fact that their design allows them to expand at extremely long range where velocity has dropped off, even when they are fired from relatively slow cartridges such as the 7mm-08 Remington and 308 Winchester. By the same token, that same construction enables those bullets to hold together and penetrate deeply when striking close-range game at the high impact velocities possible with belted magnums such as the 7mm STW and 30-378 Weatherby Magnum.

How Good Is the 30-338 Magnum?

What is your opinion of the 30-338 Magnum wildcat? Do you consider it superior in any way to factory-loaded 30 caliber magnum cartridges?

The 30-338 Magnum is a fine cartridge and it has an excellent track record among long-range target shooters. Because of its longer neck, I like its looks better than the 300 Winchester Magnum but as far as accuracy and downrange performance on game go, it would be impossible to detect any difference between the two. For the benefit of those who are not familiar with the 30-338, I will mention that its case is formed by necking down 338 Winchester Magnum brass.

240 Page Super Pooper Clarified

Sometime back you described the late Warren Page's 240 Page Super Pooper (PSP) as the T-65 case necked down. That cartridge is actually the 240 Page which was, as you mentioned, the forerunner of the 243 Winchester. The later 240 Super Pooper evolved when Page decided that Winchester's version could be improved by a longer neck and 28-degree shoulder angle. He and Fred Huntington of RCBS basically combined the body length, shoulder angle and neck length of the 244 Remington with the body taper of the 243 Winchester and came up with the 240 PSP. A rifle in 243 Winchester, 244 Remington or 6mm Remington can be rechambered to 240 PSP for an increase in velocity of

A Marlin lever-action in 444 Marlin worked great on this caribou hunt in the North-west Territories.

150 to 200 fps. After firing over 7000 rounds in two rifles and bagging over 250 coyotes along with quite a few whitetails with the cartridge, I can attest to the fact that it is indeed a Super Pooper.

I want to thank you for your clarifications on the 240 Page and the 240 Page Super Pooper. It was nice of you to have enough interest to write.

Is 444 Marlin a Good Choice?

I am seriously considering the addition of a lever action rifle to my hunting battery and have taken a close look at the Marlin Model 444 in that caliber. I have read that this cartridge/rifle combination is capable of bagging any North American game and on top of that a California friend swears by it for extremely large wild hogs weighing 400 pounds and more. What is your opinion of this cartridge?

The Marlin Model 444SS is an excellent woods rifle and capable of dropping any North American game at reasonable ranges. Remington offers a factory load with a 240-gr. softnose bullet at 2350 fps. I have used that load on whitetails and found its performance to be absolutely devastating out to 125 yards or so. Even better for use on larger game such as moose, elk and black bear are the Hornady 265-gr. Light Magnum load at 2325 fps and the Cor-Bon 280-gr. Bonded-Core load at 2200 fps.

As for handloading the 444 Marlin, any good 240-gr. bullet will work on small whitetails but for larger deer, the Hornady 265-gr. softnose is a better choice. The 250-gr. Nosler Partition HG and the Barnes 225-gr. XPB should be excellent performers in this cartridge but their hollow-cavity form with no soft lead exposed at the nose rules them out in my book for use in a rifle with a tubular magazine. Either could, however, be manually loaded directly into the chamber and the magazine then filled with rounds loaded with softnose bullets. The best bullet for all-around use on all game ranging in size from deer to elk and moose is the Swift 280-gr. A-Frame. For moose and elk only, the 300-gr. A-Frame should be an excellent choice.

The 338 GEF in the Model 94

In one of your columns a reader asked for advice on a wildcat cartridge for the Winchester Model 94 rifle. He was interested in the 356 Winchester case necked down (or the 307 Winchester necked up) for 338-inch bullets. When you recommended a minimum body taper and sharper shoulder angle for the case it rang a bell with me since I came up with just such a wildcat in 1992. The case of my cartridge has minimum body taper and a 40-degree shoulder angle. I designed it specifically for use in a T/C Contender and it should work equally well in the Winchester 94. The reloading dies are available from RCBS and the cartridge is identified by that company as the 338 GEF.

Thanks for the information on your wildcat cartridge. It sounds like a great candidate for the Model 94 Winchester, although the choices in flatnose bullets which would be required for its tubular magazine are rather slim. I'll also add that only those rifles that were originally chambered for the 307 Winchester and 356 Winchester cartridges should be rebarreled for it.

357 Magnum on Deer?

I would like to start hunting whitetail deer with a handgun and since I already own a S&W Model 686 in 357 Magnum, I'm wondering if it is powerful enough for that purpose. Most of my shots would be in the 50- to 75-yard ranges. Would I be better off using a jacketed bullet or will my 160-gr. cast bullet work just as well?

While there are those who would disagree, I don't consider the 357 Magnum an entirely suitable deer cartridge. Under ideal conditions and in the hands of an expert shot it will work most of the time but in the real world, conditions are not always ideal. I'm equally convinced that any shot beyond 50 yards is too far even when an experienced hunter is toting a handgun in that caliber. Most bullets that are cast of an alloy with sufficient hardness to prevent severe leading in the barrel when pushed to maximum 357 Magnum velocities are also too hard to expand when striking anything softer than a brick wall. For this reason, I strongly recommend that only jacketed handgun bullets be used on deer-size game. Truth of the matter is, I would really like to see you add a handgun in 41 Magnum or 44 Magnum to your battery before making that first deer hunt. Even when the latter cartridge is down-loaded to 44 Special velocity for a reduction in recoil it is still more effective on deer than the 357 Magnum. Of course, Elmer Keith discovered that long before most of us had popped our first cap.

Which Varmint Cartridge?

I plan to buy my first varmint rifle and cannot decide which caliber would be best. I'll be using the rifle on everything from crows to coyotes out to 300 yards or so. What do you recommend?

Had you not mentioned coyotes at 300 yards I would have recommended the 223 Remington but since you did, I believe you need the additional power of the 22-250 or 220 Swift. Either of those cartridges should suit your needs quite well.

Is Rifled Slug Load Good Enough?

Only shotguns with slugs are allowed where I hunt deer. According to everything I read, I should be using a shotgun with a rifled barrel and sabot slug loads but so far I have done okay with my old smoothbore gun and rifled slugs. Am I missing out on something?

About 70 percent of hunters who hunt deer with shotguns use the rifled slug load so it will be quite some time before the sabot load catches up in popularity (if it ever does). I recently compared the accuracy of Federal 12-gauge TruBall rifled slug load with the load it replaced by shooting five, 5-shot groups with each load. In a Winchester Model 1300 the score read 4.2 inches for the TruBall load and 3.3 inches for the new load. In a TCR 83 single-shot, it was 2.7 inches for TruBall and 4.6 inches for the old load. Such guns and loads are plenty accurate for shooting deer out to 100 long paces.

Why Is It Called 38 Special?

Why was the 38 Special given that name? I can understand why the 357 Magnum is called that since in addition to being more powerful than shorter cartridges of the same caliber, bullet diameter is .357-inch but I am puzzled by the 38 Special's handle.

How many of our cartridges came by their names will always remain a mystery but I suspect "38 Special" was settled on simply because it has a nice ring to it, one that most shooters find easy to remember. Same goes for other cartridges such as the 38 Super, 22 Hornet, 218 Bee, 221 Fire Ball and 220 Swift.

Needs 25 Souper Data

I recently bought a Ruger Model 77 International that has been rebarreled to 25 Souper. Can you furnish me with case-forming instructions and load data for that cartridge?

If your Ruger is chambered for the original 25 Souper, you can form cases by simply necking down 308 Winchester cases or necking up 243 Winchester cases. When ordering reloading dies from RCBS or Redding, specify a tapered expander button in the full-length resizing die. This will give you the options of necking down 308 cases or necking up 243 cases with one pass through that die. The A-Square handloading manual contains data for the 25 Souper with 87- and 117-gr. bullets. When developing your own handloads for the 25 Souper, you can also begin with starting loads shown in various handloading manuals for the 257 Roberts and cautiously work up to maximum in your rifle.

7mm-08 & 30-06 vs. 284 & 280

I am an avid whitetail hunter and own two rifles. One is a short-action Model 700 Mountain Rifle in 7mm-08 and the other is a Browning A-Bolt in 30-06. The more I read about various big-game cartridges the more I think I can do better by switching to the 284 Winchester in a short-action bolt gun and the 280 Remington in a long-action rifle. Am I on the right track?

The 284 Winchester and 280 Remington are ballistic twins and while both are excellent big-game cartridges, any advantage you would gain by using them rather than the two rifles you already own is so insignificant it would be all but impossible to detect in the field. I suggest that you stick with the Mountain Rifle in 7mm-08, and if you need more power than the 30-06, go with a magnum such as the 7mm Remington, 7mm WSM, 7mm STW, 300 Remington SAUM, 300 Winchester or 300 Weatherby.

243 Winchester Enough Cartridge?

Time has not permitted me to hunt big game a great deal through the years but I've decided to change that. In addition to hunting whitetails more often, I also plan to go after black bear. I own several rifles with my favorites being a Remington Model Seven and a Ruger Model 77RSI International, both in 243 Winchester. While I realize there are those who consider the 243 a bit light for anything bigger than woodchucks I really don't enjoy shooting more powerful cartridges. Do you consider the 243 enough cartridge for use on deer and bear at reasonable ranges? I'm a good shot and have enough self-control to hold my fire until I am sure I can put the bullet in the right spot. Since I don't handload I also need your recommendations on factory loads.

The 243 Winchester is plenty of cartridge for hunting deer in your part of the country and while there are better black bear cartridges, it will also do the job on that animal if the right bullet is placed in a vital area. Any good load with a 100-gr. bullet is a good choice for hunting whitetails but since a really big black bear requires more penetration than the typical whitetail, you should opt for a load with a premium bullet of extreme controlled-expansion design. The only 243 Winchester factory loads currently available with that type of bullet are Remington Premier with the 100-gr. Core-Lokt Ultra and Federal Premium with the Nosler Partition of the same weight. I have found both to be a fine performers.

Any cartridge of 6mm caliber from the 243 Winchester on up is an excellent choice for deer.

6.5 American vs. 260 Remington

In the August 1994 issue of Shooting Times *magazine you wrote an article on the 6.5mm family of cartridges. I was particularly interested in a wildcat you had developed called the 6.5x52mm American. I can't decide whether to have a rifle rebarreled for that cartridge or buy a factory rifle in 260 Remington. What are the advantages of one over the other besides the fact that the 260 Remington is a factory cartridge?*

I developed the 6.5x52mm American in response to readers who were requesting a cartridge that produced 6.5x55mm Swedish performance in short-action rifles such as the Remington Model Seven, Savage Model 99 and Browning BLR. Since powder capacities of the two cartridges are virtually identical, their velocity potential is the same when both are loaded to the

Remington Model Seven in 260 Remington.

same chamber pressure. This enables the owner of a rifle in 6.5 American to use load data published in various handloading manuals for the 6.5 Swedish. The case is formed by necking down the 7mm-08 Remington and fireforming it to the improved shape with minimum body taper and a sharp shoulder angle. It can also be formed from 243 Winchester and 308 Winchester brass. Reloading dies are available from Redding.

When both are loaded to the same chamber pressure and fired in barrels of the same length, the 6.5 American is about 100 fps faster than the 260 Remington with all bullet weights. Whether or not this is enough to justify the existence of the wildcat is open to debate. Remington's 260 factory ammo can be fired in a rifle chambered for the 6.5 American but velocity will be a bit lower in the improved chamber.

Why So Few Hollowpoint Big-Game Bullets For Rifle Cartridges?

Many hollowpoint bullets are available for varmint-shooting but very few of that type are available in calibers and weights suitable for use on big game. Why is this?

Jacketed hollowpoint bullets designed for varmint shooting have proven to be satisfactory because the desired performance for that type of bullet is explosive expansion when contact is made with the target. The typical hollowpoint varmint bullet does, however, have more of a tendency to ricochet when striking the ground at long range where impact velocity has dropped off than is the case for a softnosed bullet having its lead core exposed at the nose (the TNT line of varmint bullets from Speer are exceptions). Since the jacket of a big-game bullet has to be thicker in order to control expansion, it is extremely difficult for a manufacturer to come up with a hollowpoint design that will do that plus expand to a larger frontal area at reduced impact velocities. Make the jacket too thick and the hollow nose of the bullet will collapse inward, thereby preventing the bullet from expanding. Make it too thin and the bullet will expand too quickly, resulting in lack of penetration on game. This is why expanding bullets with part of the lead core exposed at the nose and bullets with some type of expansion-initiator protruding from the nose (as in the Nosler Ballistic Tip and Remington Bronze Point) have proven to be extremely successful styles in big-game bullets of expanding design. Nonjacketed hollowpoint bullets of partial or total monolithic construction, such as the Winchester Fail Safe and Barnes X-Bullet, are exceptions because the wall of their nose cavities can be made quite thin for low-velocity expansion without seriously compromising weight retention.

What Is the 38 Special Magnum?

I recently bought a couple of boxes of ammunition loaded by Norma. Upon examining the cartridges I found case length to be the same as that of the 38 Special but since the box is marked "38 Special Magnum" I cannot decide if the ammo should be fired in my 38 Special revolver. Should I or should I not?

The Norma ammunition you bought was manufactured during the 1980s and should be fired only in revolvers suitable for use with +P loadings of the 38 Special. The boxes you have obviously are from an early manufacturing lot since Norma began to stamp the +P designation on the heads of the cases a year or so after introducing 38 Special Magnum ammunition. The ammo is loaded with a 110-gr. jacketed hollowpoint bullet and was rated at a muzzle velocity of 1542 fps in a six-inch barrel.

Are 450 Marlin and 458 American Cartridges Interchangeable?

I have been hunting with a short-action Remington Model 700 chambered for the 458 American for about 25 years. I have not actually seen a 450 Marlin cartridge but based on what l have read, it appears to be identical to the 458 American. Can l fire 450 Marlin ammo in my rifle? Is it okay to use 450 Marlin load data when handloading the 458 American?

Frank Barnes' old 458 American and the New 450 Marlin are virtually identical with one exception: when measured from front to rear, the belt on the Marlin cartridge is considerably wider than the belt on the Barnes wildcat. This would prevent 450 Marlin ammo from entering the chamber of your rifle. Any good gunsmith could easily modify your rifle to handle the new Marlin cartridge by increasing the headspace depth of its chamber to handle the wider belt but if this is done you will no longer be able to safely fire 458 American ammo in it. Starting loads published by various sources of reloading components for the 450 Marlin can be used in the 458 American. Incidentally, Frank Barnes also developed a wildcat called the 458 Barnes. Both of his wildcats are formed by shortening the 458 Winchester case but whereas the 458 American case ends up at two inches in length, the 458 Barnes case is only 1-1/2 inches long.

Why Is 264 Magnum Cartridge Shorter Today?

l have been hunting big game almost exclusively with a Winchester Model 70 Westerner in 264 Magnum since the mid-1960s and find it to be ideal for game ranging in size from deer to elk. When handloading for that rifle, l seat the Nosler 140-gr. Partition to an overall cartridge length that positions it 0.020-inch short of making contact with the rifling when a round is chambered. l recently ran out of the old Nosler bullets l had bought decades ago and bought a couple boxes at a local gun shop. l was surprised to find that the new bullets differed enough in shape from the old ones to prevent me from coming anywhere close to seating them to the overall cartridge length l had used for years. What gives?

When Winchester introduced the 264 Magnum in 1958 it was loaded with a 140-gr. Power-Point bullet of two-diameter design. While the shank of the bullet measured 264 inch in diameter, it was reduced in diameter to 257 inch just forward of its shank. The shank of the bullet matched the groove diameter of the barrel while the forward section of the bearing surface matched its bore diameter. This allowed the bullet to be seated forward with all of its length out of the powder chamber of the cartridge. In addition, when developing the cartridge Winchester engineers found that the smaller full-diameter bearing surface area of the bullet allowed it to be fired at higher velocities than a bullet of conventional shape when both were loaded to the same chamber pressure. In those days Remington also loaded the 264 Winchester Magnum with a 140-gr. Core-Lokt bullet and it too was of two-diameter shape.

The original 140-gr. Partition introduced by Nosler for the 264 Magnum during the early 1960s was a two-diameter bullet but years later it was discontinued and replaced by a bullet of more conventional shape like those you recently bought. The lack of a 140-gr. two-diameter bullet is the primary reason why today's handloaders find it impossible to load the 264 Magnum to its original velocity of 3200 fps at acceptable chamber pressures. Winchester also stopped using a two-diameter bullet

How Many 22-Caliber Centerfire Cartridges?

My favorite varmint rifle is a Remington 40-X in 220 Swift. What other smokeless cartridges of the same caliber have been developed by American ammunition companies?

Starting back in the 1920s with the 22 Savage Hi-Power, we move forward in no special order to the 22 Hornet, 220 Swift, 218 Bee, 219 Zipper, 228 Weatherby Magnum, 222 Remington, 22 Remington Jet, 221 Remington Fire Ball, 222 Remington Magnum, 223 Remington, 224 Weatherby Magnum, 225 Winchester, 22-250 Remington, 223 WSSM, 22 BR Remington, 22 Remington Accelerator (on the 30-30, 308 and 30-06 cases) and the 22 PPC. Except for the 22 Savage Hi-Power and 228 Weatherby Magnum, all are loaded with bullets measuring .224-inch in diameter.

From left to right:
1. 22 Hornet
2. 218 Bee
3. 221 Fire Ball
4. 222 Remington
5. 223 Remington
6. 222 Remington Magnum
7. 224 Weatherby Magnum
8. 225 Winchester
9. 22-250 Remington
10. 220 Winchester Swift

years ago, which is why 264 Magnum ammunition loaded by that company today is both shorter in overall length and considerably slower than it was when the cartridge was brand-new.

Why the 32 Winchester Special?

I own two Winchester Model 94 rifles, one in 30-30, the other in 32 Special. Those two cartridges are so much alike in both appearance and performance I have yet to figure out why Winchester came up with the latter. Why did Winchester develop the 32 Special when the company had already introduced the 30-30 Winchester?

Winchester's 25-35 and 30-30 were the first American-developed sporting cartridges to be loaded with smokeless powder and they came along at a time when most who handloaded still used black powder. Apparently convinced that 30 caliber and the 1:12 inch rifling twist of the 30-30 were not the best combination to use with black powder, Winchester came up with a similar cartridge of slightly larger caliber and offered it in the Model 94 rifle with a slower rifling pitch of 1:16 inches. In doing so they killed two birds with one cartridge, so to speak; those who did not handload could buy Winchester 32 Special ammo loaded with smokeless powder and have a cartridge as modern in every way as the 30-30 Winchester; those who did handload could shoot 32 Special factory ammo and then recharge the fired cases with readily available black powder. Performance did, however, differ dramatically when the cartridge was loaded with the two types of powder. When introduced, the 32 Special was loaded with a 165-gr. bullet at a muzzle velocity of 2057 fps. When it was handloaded with "40 grains of black powder" (as recommended by Winchester) its velocity dropped to 1385 fps.

Can I Rely on Trajectory Charts Published by Ammo Manufacturers?

I have access to a private rifle range but the maximum distance I can shoot there is 100 yards. It is possible for me to shoot out to 400 yards on a friend's ranch but the long drive makes doing so rather inconvenient. I hunt with rifles of several different calibers and enjoy trying new factory loads as they are introduced. If I zero a rifle three inches high at 100 yards (as I prefer to do) can I get by on a hunt by assuming that bullet point of impact at the longer distances will be close enough to what the manufacturer of the ammo publishes to make actually checking trajectory at longer ranges unnecessary?

The trajectory charts published by ammunition manufactures are based on calculations rather than actually firing the loads out to various ranges. They are published for general information only and are not meant to replace actual shooting by those who buy the ammo. Sometimes they are very close. Not long back I checked out a popular 270 Winchester factory load by shooting it at 100, 200, 300 and 400 yards and actual trajectory was almost exactly what the manufacture indicated it should be. On the other hand, I more recently tried a

308 Winchester load from the same manufacturer and its bullet landed almost six inches lower at 300 yards than it was supposed to. Sorry, but there are no shortcuts here. The only way you can determine the trajectory of any factory load fired in your particular rifle and under your conditions is to actually shoot it on paper at various distances.

What About the 7x33mm Sako?

During a recent visit to Sweden I met a fellow who said he had hunted a lot with the "7-33." Upon returning home I tried to find such a cartridge in a book on cartridges but it wasn't there. What can you tell me about it?

The cartridge your Swedish friend mentioned is most likely the 7x33mm, a late-1940s development of Sako of Finland. After loading millions of rounds of 9x19mm Luger ammo for the war effort, Sako found itself with a lot of idle production machinery during the post-war period. So, after discovering that their equipment was capable of a producing a 9mm Luger case 33mm long (and you thought Winchester's much-later 9mm Magnum was new?), they decided to neck it down for a 7mm caliber bullet. The new cartridge was called the 7x33mm Sako and introduced in the equally new Sako L46 rifle. The 7x33mm was loaded with a 93-gr. bullet at 2200-2300 fps and was designed specifically for use on seals and large birds. It became especially popular among Scandinavian hunters who hunted seals for the fur market and those who hunted the capercaillie, a giant grouse which is only a bit smaller in size than our American wild turkey. The little cartridge is still loaded in Finland by Sako and possibly in Sweden by Norma.

Is 300 H&H Magnum Enough for Brown Bear?

I plan to hunt brown bear in Alaska and while I would like to use my Winchester Model 70 in 300 H&H Magnum, a friend who has hunted there several times is of the opinion that I need a cartridge of larger caliber. He recommends the 338 Winchester Magnum and your 358 Shooting Times Alaskan. I have taken a number of elk and mule deer with my old Model 70 and shoot it quite accurately but my friend has about convinced me that I need to shop for a more powerful rifle. Do you think my Model 70 is enough rifle for the job? If no, what rifle should I buy? If yes, what 300 H&H Magnum factory ammo do you recommend for brown bear?

When hunting a big-game animal as large and potentially dangerous as the Alaska brown bear I believe any hunter is wise to use the most powerful rifle he can shoot accurately but I'll have to disagree with your friend. When loaded to maximum velocity with a good premium-grade bullet the old 300 H&H Magnum in the hands of someone who knows where to place the bullet and is capable of placing it there is plenty of cartridge for brown bear under normal conditions. Considering this plus the fact that you shoot your Model 70 quite accurately, I recommend that you keep it and spend some of the money you will save by not buying a new rifle on practice ammunition. I wouldn't hesitate to hunt brown bear with either of two 300 H&H Magnum factory loads—Federal Premium Safari loaded with the 180-gr. Nosler Partition and Winchester Supreme loaded with the Fail Safe bullet of the same weight.

How Do 300 Ultra Mag and 300 Weatherby Mag Compare?

I have hunted big game almost exclusively with a Weatherby Mark V in 300 Magnum since buying it in 1968. I have used that rifle along with Weatherby factory ammunition to take at least one each of most North American game and have also used it quite successfully on two African safaris. Still, I am bitten by the custom rifle bug and have decided to have one built around one of the 300 magnums. Making the right decision is important since I shoot factory ammo exclusively. I am considering Remington's new 300 Ultra Mag and would like to know how its performance compares to that of my old favorite, the 300 Weatherby Magnum. Does anyone besides Remington offer 300 Ultra Mag ammo?

Very little difference in performance exists between your old favorite Weatherby cartridge and the new Remington cartridge. Remington rates its 300 Ultra Mag at 3300 fps with a 180-gr. bullet while Weatherby rates its 300 Magnum at 3250 fps with a bullet of the same weight. Federal's Premium High Energy loading of the 300 Weatherby Magnum is faster than either of those two as it is rated at 3330 fps with the 180-gr. Bear Claw bullet. To answer your other question, the Federal catalog lists in the company's Premium Safari line a 300 Remington Ultra Mag loading with the 180-gr. Bear Claw at 3250 fps.

What Are Top Speeds for 32 H&R Magnum?

I own a Ruger Single Six in 32 H&R Magnum. What loads have you tried in this cartridge that gave maximum velocities?

I must confess to having very little experience with the 32 H&R Magnum but in the Ruger Single Six I briefly worked with it produced top velocities of from 1000 to 1100 fps when loaded with the dozen or so powders I tried with several 90- and 100-gr. jacketed bullets. As for accuracy, that particular Ruger was quite fond of 10.0 gr. of H110, 6.8 gr. of AA-7, 8.8 gr. of V-N110, 4.3 gr. of Universal or Unique and 4.5 grains of Herco.

What Rifle Manufacturers Offer Your 358 STA Chambering?

I have three questions about your 358 Shooting Times Alaskan cartridge. Do any of the commercial rifle manufacturers offer that chambering? If you were having a custom rifle built in this caliber what gunsmith would build it? What barrel rifling twist rate do you recommend for this cartridge?

I am aware of two commercial rifle manufacturers who chamber rifles for my 358 STA cartridge. They are the Winchester Firearms Custom Shop and Ultra Light Arms. I prefer a 1:12 inch rifling twist rate for this cartridge. To answer your final question, Shilen Rifles, Inc., and Lex Webernick have plenty of experience in building rifles in 358 STA.

Difference in 7x61 S&H and Super 7x61 S&H?

I recently bought a Schultz & Larsen Model 68DL chambered for the 7x61 S&H cartridge. Several boxes of ammo came with the rifle, some marked Super 7x61 S&H and some marked just plain 7x61 S&H. What's the difference in those two cartridges? Is the case easily formed from any other brass? What do you know about this cartridge? Where do I find load data?

The 7x61 Sharpe & Hart cartridge was introduced in the U.S. in 1952 by the Swedish firm of Norma and rated at 3100 fps with a 160-gr. bullet. That put it in the same performance category as the 7mm Weatherby Magnum which was introduced about three years earlier and the 7mm Remington Magnum which did not come along until 1962.

Years later, in 1968, in an attempt to make the 7x61 more attractive to hunters who by that time were buying Model 700 rifles chambered for the 7mm Remington Magnum in record numbers, Norma countered by introducing the Super 7x61 loaded with a 160-gr. bullet at an advertised 3150 fps. External dimensions of the standard and Super versions of the 7x61 case are identical, but Norma created the Super version by thinning the web and wall of the standard 7x61 case on order to slightly increase powder capacity; the small gain in capacity enabled them to load the cartridge 50 fps faster at the same chamber pressure. Cartridges with either designation are suitable for use in your Schultz & Larsen rifle. The easiest way to form cases for your rifle is to full-length resize virgin 7mm Remington Magnum brass in a 7x61 S&H full-length resizing die and trim to a length of 2.384 inches. The Hornady reloading manual has the load data you are looking for.

How Do Remington's 6.5 and 350 Magnums Perform?

I recently bought a couple of Remington Model 600s in 6.5 and 350 Magnum calibers. Both have 18-1/2 inch barrels. How do those two cartridges compare in performance to others of the same or similar calibers? When were my carbines built? What did they cost? Have you hunted with the 6.5 and 350 Magnum cartridges?

Remington introduced the magnum versions of its Model 600 carbine in 1965 (350 Magnum) and 1966 (6.5 Magnum). Whereas the standard Model 600 in calibers such as 222, 308 and 35 Remington sold for $99.95, the magnum version with its laminated wood stock was priced at $144.95. All Model 600 variations were discontinued in 1967 and replaced by the Model 660 carbine in 1968. The Model 660 differs mainly by its slightly longer 20-inch barrel plus its barrel does not have the ventilated rib of the Model 600.

Remington's intent in designing the 6.5 Magnum was to duplicate 270 Winchester performance so it was loaded with 100- and 120-gr. bullets at respective muzzle velocities of 3450 and 3030 fps. Loaded with 200- and 250-gr. bullets at 2710 and 2410 fps, the 350 Magnum duplicated the performance of the 35 Whelen which was still a wildcat in those days. I once owned a Model 660 in 6.5 Remington Magnum and still own a Ruger No. 1 chambered for it. When used on deer-size game the 6.5 Magnum will do anything the 270 Winchester will do. I have also owned a Model 600 in 350 Magnum for many years and it works just as well on big game as the Remington Model 700 in 35 Whelen I also own.

Incidentally, the Remington Model 673 Guide Rifle is a distant copy of the old Model 600 Magnum on the Model Seven action. I took one in 6.5 Magnum on a hunt in Canada for caribou and black bear and it performed as nicely in the field as it had at the range. I have also shot the same rifle in 350 Magnum but have yet to hunt with it.

How Much Faster Is the 8mm-06 than the 8x57mm Mauser?

I own a mint-condition '98 Mauser in 8x57mm caliber and plan to use it for hunting deer. I'll attach a Williams peep sight to its receiver but otherwise the rifle will be left in its original condition. I am, however, thinking about having my Mauser rechambered to 8mm-06. How much faster is that cartridge than the 8mm Mauser? Considering the many thousands of 8mm rifles of this caliber in use today I'd dearly love to see you write an article on the cartridge.

American manufacturers load the 8mm Mauser to rather low chamber pressures and while this has led many to believe it belongs in the slow-poke class, nothing could be further from the truth. When handloaded to higher pressures for rifles in good serviceable condition the original Mauser cartridge is about as fast as the 8mm-06 with the lighter bullets, and data in the 13th edition of Speer's new reloading manual do a good job of illustrating just that.

According to the Speer manual, when the 8mm Mauser is loaded to a chamber pressure of 50,000 CUP in a 24-inch barrel, maximum velocities with 150- and 170-gr. bullets are 2915 and 2723 fps, respectively. When loaded to the same pressure level in the same length barrel, the 8mm-06 clocked 2981 and 2762 with those two bullet weights. This is hardly enough difference in velocity to have any influence whatsoever on the outcome of a hunt. With a top muzzle velocity of 2647 fps the 8mm-06 did, however, show a 178 fps advantage when loaded with the Speer 200-gr. bullet and while that's substantial it is important only if you decide to hunt game larger than deer and choose to use the heavier bullet. When loaded with bullets weighing from 150 to 180 grains, the standard 8mm Mauser will do anything in the deer woods the 8mm-06 and, for that matter, the 30-06 are capable of doing. To date, I have written two rather comprehensive articles on the 8x57mm Mauser, one published in *Shooting Times*, the other published in *Rifle Shooter*. In the latter article, I included the limited-edition Remington Model 700 Classic in that caliber.

Why No Sabot Loads in Centerfire Rifle Cartridges?

Numerous sabot-style slug loads with subcaliber bullets are available to shotgunners and the same type of projectile is available to those who shoot muzzleloaders. Why doesn't someone offer the same option to those of us who shoot centerfire rifles?

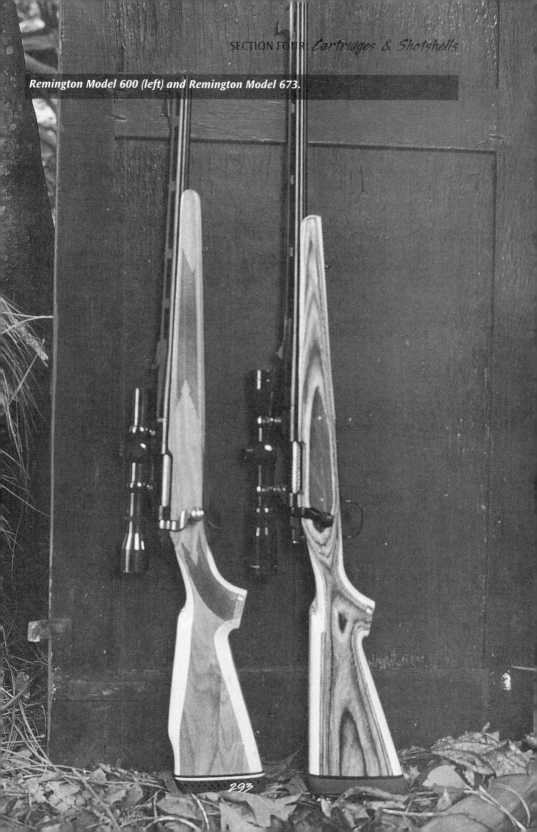

Remington Model 600 (left) and Remington Model 673.

Remington has long offered the type of ammunition you are looking for in its Accelerator loadings of the 30-30 Winchester and 30-06 Springfield. Both are loaded with sabot-enclosed 55-gr. softpoint bullets and rated at muzzle velocities of 3400 fps for the 30-30 and 4080 fps for the 30-06 Springfield. The 30-30 Accelerator load comes close to matching the 22-250 in velocity and trajectory while the 30-06 load is one of very few loads from Remington that exceed 4000 fps (another is the 17 Remington with its 25-gr. bullet at 4040 fps). I find that most rifles shoot the two Accelerator loads at about the same level of accuracy as they do with ammo loaded with the heavier conventional bullets.

How Fast Is the 22 BR Remington?

I recently bought a Remington 40X in 22 BR Remington and a varmint-shooting friend says it should be capable of the same velocity as the bigger 22-250 Remington. Is it really that good? Do you have a favorite load for this cartridge?

While the 22 BR is a very efficient cartridge and delivers extremely high velocity for its size, it is not quite as fast as the 22-250 when both are loaded with the same weight bullet and to the same chamber pressure. For example, when the two cartridges are loaded with 52-gr. bullets, maximum velocity for the 22 BR in a 24-inch barrel is usually around 3600 fps while the 22-250 is about 200 fps faster. The 22-250 must, however, burn about 15 percent more powder in order to beat 22 BR top speed by around five percent. Several years ago I had the craftsmen in Remington's custom shop build for me a Model 700 Classic in 22 BR, and its favorite varmint loads consists of the Hornaldy 50-gr. V-Max, Nosler 50-gr. Ballistic Tip or Speer 50-gr. TNT pushed to 3610 fps by 32.0 grains of H335. Other suitable powders for the 22 BR are VARGET, H4895, BL-C(2), W748, A-2460, A-2520, A-2230, RL-12, RL-15, IMR-4895 and IMR-4064.

SECTION FIVE
Reloading

Which Powders for the 243 Winchester?

I own a Ruger Model 77 in 243 Winchester and want to handload the cartridge to top velocities with the Barnes 95-gr. X-Bullet. What powders do you recommend? Should I use magnum primers?

When loading bullets weighing 80 grains and up in the 243 Winchester I prefer powders with relatively slow burn rates. To name but a few excellent candidates: H4350, IMR-4831, W760, RL-19, AA-3100, AA-4350, IMR-4831 and IMR-4350. If I had to pick just one among them it would be tough choosing between H4350 and RL-19. Standard-force primers work fine with many powders in the 243 under most conditions but I prefer to switch to magnum primers when loading Ball or spherical powders that will be used when hunting in temperatures below 30 degrees Fahrenheit.

How Did They Measure Velocity in the Old Days?

In firearms publications, a writer might state "this fine old cartridge was introduced in 1894 and it pushed a 200-gr. bullet along at 2000 feet per second." How did technicians of yesteryear put a handle on velocity numbers without the aid of modern electronics?

One of the first methods used to determine the velocity of a bullet was accomplished by firing it into the weighted end of a pendulum. Velocity was determined by how far the impact of the bullet made the pendulum swing. Later, when electricity came along, more accurate forms of chronographs were invented. One of the earliest was the La Boulenge', which was used by the larger ammunition manufacturers such as Winchester and Remington up until the 1920s. In those days it took several technicians and a room full of equipment to measure the speed of a bullet and the cost involved made doing so practical only for large companies. The introduction of modern chronographs by firms such as Oehler, PACT, Chrony and Competition Electronics made it economically possible for the individual shooter to measure velocity.

How Do Powders Get Their Names?

I have often wondered how the various powders used in loading rifle and handgun cartridges as well as shotshells got their names. Please shed some light on the subject.

Powders have received their names in a number of ways. Hodgdon's H380 was named by company founder Bruce Hodgdon after he discovered that 38.0 grains of the powder worked great behind bullets weighing from 50 to 55 grains in the 22-250 cartridge. H1000 powder is popular among target shooters who shoot at 1000 yards. IMR as in IMR-4320 and IMR-4350 is short for "Improved Military Rifle." Most powders were and still are given certain names to imply certain levels of performance. Good examples are Hodgdon's Benchmark which works great in cartridges used for benchrest competition and Varget which is popular among both

Bullets must be rotated quite rapidly for stability in flight.

varmint shooters and target shooters. Most other powders are given numbers or names that have no significance other than a way of identifying them from the rest.

How Fast Do Bullets Spin?

I realize that spinning a bullet rapidly in order to stabilize it in flight is necessary for accuracy. But just how fast do bullets actually rotate as they fly through the air?

The velocity or forward speed of the bullet and the rifling twist rate of the rifle barrel determine the rotational speed of the bullet. The quicker the twist and the higher the velocity, the faster the bullet will spin. A bullet which exits a barrel with a 1:10 inch rifling pitch at 2000 fps will be rotating faster than one that exits a barrel with a rifling pitch of 1:12 inches at the same velocity. By the same token, a bullet that exits a barrel with a 1:10 twist at 2000 fps will be rotating more slowly than one that exits a barrel with the same rifling twist rate but at a velocity of 2200 fps. The longer the bullet of a particular caliber, the quicker the rifling twist of the barrel must be in order to stabilize it in flight. For example, most 224-caliber bullets weighing up to 55 grains are stabilized by a 1:14 inch twist while a heavier (and therefore longer) bullet of the same caliber such as the Sierra 80-gr. MatchKing requires a much faster rifling twist rate of 1:8 inches. How fast a bullet is spinning in flight can be determined by multiplying its velocity in

How Do I Get Started Reloading?

I recently acquired a Marlin Model 336 in 30-30 and plan to start handloading for it. Since this is my first centerfire rifle, I have much to learn. How do I get started?

You should first buy a reloading manual. In fact, if you are really serious about handloading, you should buy at least two from different sources. Those published by Hodgdon, Nosler, Swift, Sierra, Hornady, Speer, Norma, Lyman, and others have entire sections devoted to instructions on how to reload ammo. Only after you thoroughly understand the basics should you start shopping for equipment. One of the better buys in single-stage reloaders is the Partner from RCBS. Lee also makes inexpensive reloading tools. In the beginning you can get by with a powder scale, reloader and dies, along with a few other inexpensive accessories such as a powder funnel, cartridge case block, shellholder, case trimmer and deburring tool. You may later decide to add other items such as a powder measure and case tumbler.

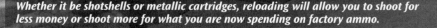

Whether it be shotshells or metallic cartridges, reloading will allow you to shoot for less money or shoot more for what you are now spending on factory ammo.

feet per second by 60 (constant), multiplying what you get by 12 (constant) and then dividing by the rifling twist rate of the barrel. For a muzzle velocity of 3000 fps and a rifling twist of 1:10 inches, bullet spin would be 216,000 rotations per minute or 3,600 rotations per second.

6.5 Swede Loads in 6.5 American?

I would like to have a Savage Model 99 rebarreled for your 6.5x52mm American. What can you tell me about the cartridge? Where can I buy the chamber reamer and reloading dies? Can loads listed in the various handloading manuals for the 6.5x55mm Swedish be used in the 6.5x52mm?

The 6.5x52mm American is the 7mm-08 Remington case necked down and fireformed to minimum body taper and a 40-degree shoulder angle. It can also be formed by necking down the 308 Winchester or necking up the 243 Winchester but since the necks of those cases are a bit shorter, the result would more correctly be called the 6.5x51mm. I introduced the 6.5 American in the August 1994 issue of *Shooting Times* and load data were included in that article. I developed the cartridge in response to readers who had requested a short-action cartridge that duplicates the 6.5mm Swede in performance. Since case capacities of the two are virtually identical, starting loads published in various manuals for the 6.5mm Swede can be used for the same purpose in the 6.5mm American. Clymer ground the first 6.5 American chamber reamer and Redding made the first handloading dies. Incidentally, the new 260 Remington works fine in my rifle and represents an excellent (albeit expensive) way to fireform cases. Firing the Remington factory load in the improved chamber does, however, reduce its velocity by about 75 fps.

What Happened to Western Tool & Copper Works?

I worked for the Denver & Rio Grande Railroad shortly after World War II. During that time I became acquainted with P.O. Ackley, Jerry Gebby, Paul Jaeger, Keith Stegall, Fred Barnes, R.B. Sisk, Rocky Gibbs and other famous rifle builders, bullet makers and wildcatters of yesteryear. This makes me a genuine graybeard and an early enthusiast of high-velocity cartridges such as Gebby's 22 Varminter and Ackley's improved version of the 257 Roberts. In those days the few reloading manuals we had often referred to bullets made by the Western Tool & Copper Works. Do you know what happened to that outfit?

In its heyday the Western Tool & Copper Works had a reputation for making some of the best big game bullets available. Most were of cavity point style and constructed with a soft lead core enclosed by an extremely thick copper jacket. The original Barnes bullets developed by Fred Barnes are similar in construction. Writers of yesteryear, Jack O'Connor and Elmer Keith in particular, often wrote about using W.T.C.W. bullets on various and sundry game. In fact, Keith's favorite bullets for two of his favorite cartridges, the 35 Whelen and 400 Whelen, were made by that company. I'm not sure when W.T.C.W. stopped producing bullets but it was probably during the late 1940s.

Needs 7mm STE Data

I recently obtained a Marlin Model 336 that had been rebarreled by Harry McGowen for the 7mm Shooting Times Easterner. Since you are the creator of the 7mm STE, I figured you would be my best shot at obtaining load data for it. Can you help?

I introduced the 7mm STE to the world in the June, 1989 issue of *Shooting Times* and included load data in that report. Load data have also been published in the Hodgdon reloading manual.

Needs Ballistic Gelatin

How do I go about mixing up the type of ballistic gelatin used by various firearms companies to test bullet expansion?

The ingredients for mixing Type 250A ballistics gelatin are available from Kind & Knox, Inc., P.O. Box 297, Sioux City, IA 51102. Instructions on mixing, molding and proper storage of the gel until it is used come with the package.

Handloads for the Ruger 96/44?

I recently bought a Ruger 96/44 in 44 Magnum and plan to hunt whitetail deer with it. I am hoping it will be accurate with ammo loaded with a hard cast bullet or ammo loaded with Nosler's new Partition bullet. Which is the better choice for deer?

Between the two I would choose the Nosler Partition bullet because it is more likely to expand on deer-size game. While some hunters have successfully used extremely hard cast bullets on heavier game where extremely deep penetration is needed, they are a poor choice for lung shots on smaller game. This is due to the fact that the bullet is likely to drill an extremely narrow wound channel through the animal, resulting in insufficient tissue damage for a quick kill. If you decide to use a hard cast bullet, your best bet is to forget the lung shot and place it through the shoulders of a deer.

Why Does the 338-06 Use More Powder than the 30-06?

I am puzzled by the fact that even though the cases of the 338-06 and 30-06 are virtually identical, the former uses heavier charges of various powders even when bullet weight is the same. Please explain why this is true. Which of those two cartridges do you consider best for use on game as large as elk?

When bullets loaded in the two cartridges weigh the same, the 338-06 uses a heavier powder charge because its expansion ratio is higher. Even though the two cases have the same capacity, the larger bore of the 338-06 requires a greater volume of propellant gas in order to reach a certain pressure, hence the need for more of the same powder. For example, *Nosler's Reloading Guide* lists 68.0 grains of Reloder 19 as maximum with a 200-gr. bullet in the 338-06 but shows only 56.0 grains of the same powder as maximum behind a bullet of the same weight in the 30-06. Moving on up to an even higher expansion ratio with the same case,

The case of the 8x57mm Mauser (center) is easily formed from the 30-06 case (right) but the 308 case on the left is obviously too short.

Nosler indicates the use of even heavier charges of various powders in the 35 Whelen than in the 338-06.

What Bullets for Bowling Pins?

I handload the 357 Magnum for a S&W Model 686 and plan to start using that combination in bowling pin competition. I also use the 38 Special in a Ruger Blackhawk and a Rossi lever-action rifle for cowboy action shooting. At present I am loading the 38 Special with a 158-gr. roundnose cast bullet seated atop 3.5 grains of Hodgdon's HP38. Would I be better off to switch to a bulkier powder such as H4227? What bullet should I use in the 357 Magnum for bowling pin shooting?

The HP38 load you are using in the 38 Special is an excellent choice for cowboy action shooting. Only recently I tried that exact same charge behind a 158-gr. cast bullet in two single-action revolvers and found accuracy to be quite good. If the accuracy of that load is satisfactory in your guns you would gain nothing by switching to a slower powder.

Any bullet weighing from 140 grains up and loaded to maximum velocity in the 357 Magnum will drive bowling pins off the table but most competitors prefer heavier bullets. The Sierra 170-gr. JHC and 180-gr. FPJ bullets will do the job. Same goes for a good cast bullet of the proper weight and shape. If you prefer to cast your own, the RCBS 180-gr. Silhouette and Lyman 358129 are the way to go. Depending on the alloy used, the latter will run from 165 to 170 grains in weight.

Can I Form 8x57mm Cases from 30-06 Brass?

I have a 1898 Mauser in 8x57mm and it is quite accurate. Good 8x57mm cases are scarce in my neck of the woods and I would like to form them from 30-06 brass. Would cases formed in this manner require fireforming? Would neck wall thickness of the formed cases be excessive and require reaming or outside turning?

The 8x57mm Mauser case is easily formed by first running a 30-06 case through a 8x57mm full-length resizing die with its expander/decap assembly removed. After the case is trimmed to an overall length of 2.235 inches and the inside of its mouth is chamfered, it is run back through the 8x57mm Mauser full-length resizing die with the expander/decap assembly installed. Neck reaming or outside neck turning will not be necessary and the new cases will not require fireforming. Only virgin 30-06 cases should be used when forming 8x57mm Mauser cases in this manner.

Low-Flash Powder for the 45 ACP?

Holding USPSA matches at night has become quite popular at the gun club I belong to. Some of the stages are set up to be shot while holding a flashlight, others are shot with the targets partially illuminated by the headlights of an automobile. Most of us use night sights with tritium inserts on our 45 ACP guns. Have you performed tests with various powders to determine which produce the least amount of muzzle flash during low light conditions?

I have not performed any such tests but my friend Bill Wilson of Wilson Combat recently did just that in preparation for filming his series of video tapes on self-defensive use of the handgun. According go Bill, Vihtavuori V-N320 produced the lowest level of muzzle flash of the powders he has tried in the 45 ACP.

Is 100-gr. Bullet Okay in the 7mm STW?

I recently discovered that the Barnes 100-gr. X-Bullet loaded to 3800 fps in the 7mm STW is quite accurate. It also shoots incredibly flat. When zeroed three inches high at 100 yards, it is three inches high at 300 yards, only three inches low at 400 and a mere 16 inches low at 500 yards. The bullet is still moving along at 2400 fps at 400 yards where it delivers almost 1200 foot-pounds of energy. I am tempted to use this load on a hunt for pronghorn antelope in Colorado. Do you think it would work okay?

Considering the relatively small size of a pronghorn buck, I see no reason why the 7mm STW load you have described would not work just fine. I have taken a number of antelope with various 100-gr. bullets in cartridges such as the 243 Winchester, 6mm Remington, 240 Weatherby Magnum and 257 Weatherby Magnum and they did an excellent job. Despite its extremely high initial velocity, the 100-gr. 7mm bullet does get blown a bit farther astray by wind than heavier bullets of the same caliber but the difference is not great. For example, with the 100-gr. X-bullet moving out at 3800 fps and the 140-gr. X-Bullet exiting the muzzle at 3400 fps, the lighter bullet is moved off course about 12 inches at 400 yards by a 10 mile-per-hour crosswind while the heavier bullet is blown about 10 inches astray.

Where Do I Get Bullets and Cases for 35 Winchester?

I have a Winchester Model 1895 in 35 Winchester and it is in excellent condition. Where can I find bullets and cases? Is the 35 Winchester powerful enough to use on moose?

Cases for your rifle are easily formed by running virgin 30-40 Krag brass through a 35 Winchester full-length resizing die with a tapered expander button. That die along with a bullet seater die is available from Redding and RCBS. Your choices in bullets are quite good since those of 358-inch diameter work in the 35 Winchester and the box magazine of the Model 1895 allows the use of pointed bullets. For moose or for all-around use on all game I would hunt with that cartridge, the Nosler 225-gr. Partition would be my first choice. For use on deer only, 200-gr. bullets available from Sierra and Hornady are worth a try, as is the 220-gr. flatnose from Speer. The 250-gr. bullets made by Speer and Hornady should work okay on larger game, but as I have already mentioned, I would stick with the 225-gr. Nosler for everything.

Does Linotype Wear Out Barrels?

When casting bullets for my Ruger Security-Six revolver, I have noticed that those cast of linotype are lighter than those cast of lead in the same mold. Can

Low-flash powder is best choice for defensive loads in the 45 ACP.

How Do I Reload a Muzzleloader Quickly?

During the past season I missed a shot at a nice buck with my inline muzzleloader and rather than the animal running off as I expected, it ignored my shot and hung around the doe it was courting. The mercury was hovering close to zero and by the time my near-frozen hands managed to reload my rifle, both deer had wandered off. The buck's antlers would now be hanging on my wall had I been able to reload a bit more quickly. What is the fastest way to reload an inline rifle with a saboted bullet?

The quickest, handiest and most fumble-free speed loader I have tried is the RMC Magnum EC-Loader from Cabela's. It has three rotating cylinders, each capable of holding any weight of conical bullet, saboted bullet or a patched ball and up to three 50-gr. Pyrodex or Triple-7 pellets or 150 grains of loose powder. Available for 45-, 50- and 54-caliber rifles, it is so fast, they should have named it the lightning loader. Place the unit on the muzzle of the gun, rotate one of the cylinders in alignment with the bore, shove powder charge and bullet partway home with the built-in starter, finish seating with the ramrod, cap the rifle, and you are ready to shoot. Loading the EC-Loader with a loose-fitting bullet such as the PowerBelt will make the process even faster. Should that bullet not deliver satisfaction in your rifle, the placement of a plastic sub-base from MMP between bullet and powder charge when loading the EC-Loader should improve accuracy considerably.

This speed loader from Cabela's is the quickest way to reload a muzzleloader.

307

How Good Is the Nosler Partition Bullet?

I hunt big game with various 7mm cartridges and prefer to handload bullets weighing 160 and 175 grains. What is your opinion of Nosler Partition bullets in those weights?

The bullets you mentioned as well as Nosler Partitions in other calibers and weights are excellent choices for use in cartridges of various velocity ranges. This is due to the fact that the design of the Partition bullet allows it to expand at extremely long range where impact velocity has dropped off, even when fired from relatively slow cartridges such as the 7mm-08 Remington and 308 Winchester. By the same token, that same construction enables the Partition to hold together and penetrate deeply when striking the target at close range where the impact velocities of magnum cartridges are extremely high.

Since its introduction in the 1940s, the Nosler Partition bullet has proven itself in the hands of hunters around the world.

NOSLER

50 PARTITION™

35 / 225
CAL.

SPITZER   800

Trim 44 Magnum cases to 44 Special length?

Should I Trim 44 Magnum Cases to 44 Special Length?

*I own a revolver in 44 Special and have on hand a large supply of 44
Magnum cases. If I trim and chamfer those cases back to 44 Special length,
can I use them for reduced-velocity handloads in my gun?*

Trimming 44 Magnum brass back to 44 Special length increases wall
thickness at the mouth of the case due to taper in the wall. This can
sometimes interfere with proper crimping but if you experience no such
problem then by all means have at it. Some 44 Magnum cases have a
thicker wall than some 44 Special cases and for this reason their capacity
will be slightly less when shortened. For this reason, when identical loads
are used, those fired in the shortened 44 Magnum cases will generate
slightly higher chamber pressure than those fired in 44 Special cases.
This is neither here nor there so long as you stick with reduced-velocity
loads but is something to be kept in mind should you decide to use the
shortened cases for full-power loads.

Is the 45 ACP a wild boar cartridge?

Do You Have a 45 ACP Load for Wild Boar?

I would like to hunt wild boar with my Springfield 1911-A1 in 45 ACP. The outfitter with whom I will be hunting uses hounds so the shooting will be at extremely close range. A friend tells me the 45 ACP is incapable of penetrating the shield of a mature boar and the minimum handgun cartridge I should use is the 454 Casull loaded with a 300-gr. bullet. Do you consider the 45 ACP enough cartridge for bagging a big wild boar? If so, what load do you recommend?

I am afraid your friend has been reading too many adventure magazines. I too have read about bullets from cartridges as powerful as the 44 Magnum bouncing off the gristle plate or shield of a boar but consider such tales pure nonsense. I have lived most of my life in country where there is no closed season on wild hogs on private land and have taken them with various handguns, rifles and muzzleloaders, as well as the bow and arrow. I took one of my largest with a 44-caliber cap & ball revolver at about 12 paces and its ball zipped through the animal like a hot knife though butter. Best bet for a hog load on your Springfield autoloader is a bullet that will penetrate deeply enough to make its way through the vitals of a boar. I have taken several with the 45 ACP and a handload consisting of the Speer 260-gr. JHP pushed to 850 fps by a maximum charge of Winchester 231 or Hodgdon's HS6. The Speer handloading manual contains that load.

heavier powder charges be safely used behind the lighter bullets? I have been told that since linotype is harder than lead, it will wear out a barrel faster; others have told me that linotype cannot be any rougher on a barrel than the use of jacketed bullets. Who's right?

While it might be safe to slightly increase the powder charge behind the lighter linotype bullet, the difference in weight between it a lead bullet cast in the same mold is seldom great enough to allow for a significant increase. Since a barrel suffers very little wear from bullets passing through its bore, the material a bullet is made of has almost no bearing on how long the barrel will last. The throat and rifling of a barrel are washed out by powders that produce flame temperatures higher than the melting temperature of most steels. The barrel doesn't melt because it is subjected to the high temperature for only a very short time, but its bore does become eroded.

Do Powders Become Too Old to Use?

I have a four-pound canister of Hercules Unique with an unbroken seal. I purchased the powder in 1968 and have kept it stored in a cool, dry room. I also have some DuPont No. 5 and No. 6 pistol powders which I bought in 1951. Are any of those powders safe to use?

The shelf life of a double-base propellant (which contains nitroglycerine) is indefinite so long as it is kept sealed in its original container and stored in a cool, dry environment. Since your canister of Unique meets those criteria, it may be safe to use. The only way to find out for certain is to contact a customer representative of Alliant Powder Company. A sample of your powder might be required for testing. The shelf life of single-base powders (no nitroglycerin content) is shorter than that of double-base powders. When stored under less than favorable conditions, the nitrocellulose can deteriorate and cause spontaneous combustion while the powder is sitting on the shelf. Your DuPont No. 5 powder is of single-base composition and was manufactured from 1933 until 1948. I believe DuPont No. 6 is a double-base propellant, but it too is an old-timer as it was manufactured from 1933 until 1948. Considering the age of those two, you would be wise to dispose of them by scattering them on your lawn as fertilizer.

What Bullet Weight for the 356 Winchester?

I am interested in buying a used Winchester Model 94 in 356 Winchester. How does it stack up against the 35 Remington? What is the lightest bullet that should be handloaded in the 356 for use on big game? Is it enough cartridge for moose and elk, or is it more of a deer cartridge?

The 356 Winchester is quite a bit more powerful than the 35 Remington and treads closely on the heels of the 358 Winchester in power. The lightest bullet I would load in it for use on deer is the Speer 180-gr. flatnose. When loaded with the 220-gr. Speer, the 356 should be an excellent choice for hunting elk and moose in wooded terrain, but it certainly is no open-country cartridge by any stretch of the imagination. As good as the 356 Winchester is, I am afraid it is a dying cartridge. U.S. Repeating Arms no longer offers it in the Model 94 rifle, and Winchester has dropped its 250-gr. moose and elk load. The 200-gr. factory load is still available but it is best suited for game no larger than deer and black bear. As much as I hate saying it, I won't be surprised to see the 356 Winchester disappear into history in the not too distant future.

Loads for 338-08?

I plan to have a rifle chambered for the 338-08 and will use it for hunting elk. Many good bullets are available for this wildcat and according to an article you wrote on it, it shoots a bit flatter than the 358 Winchester. Unfortunately, I have no chamber specifications for this cartridge and with the exception of the few loads you have published, I have no load data. Can you help?

Since the 338-08 is a wildcat its chamber dimensions have never been standardized. But, since it is nothing more than the 308 Winchester case with its neck expanded for use with 338-caliber bullets, any good gunsmith who has the chamber reamer can do the job for you. Loading dies for the 338-08 are available from RCBS and Redding. The full-length resizing die will have a tapered expander button for opening up the neck of a 308 case for a .338-inch bullet. The case can also be formed by necking down 358 Winchester brass with that same die. I know of no reloading manual that contains data for the 338-08 but most do have loads for the 358 Winchester. After deciding on the bullet weight you will load in the 338-08, reduce the starting load shown for the same bullet weight in the 358 Winchester by 10 percent and you are on your way. The Sierra manual, for example, shows for the 358 Winchester a starting load of 44.1 grains of IMR-4895 with a 200-gr. bullet. A safe starting load for that same bullet weight in the 338-08 is 40.0 grains of the same powder.

Why Are 45-70 Published Load Data So Confusing?

I am confused by load data published in various handloading manuals for the 45-70 Government cartridge. The Hornady manual lists loads for the Marlin New Model 1895SS up to 40,000 copper units of pressure (cup), while the Speer manual stops at 28,000 cup for the same rifle. To make matters even worse, the author of an article I recently read described the Marlin as one of the strongest rifles available in 45-70 and then went on to describe it as only moderately strong. Why the confusion?

Rifles in 45-70 generally fall into three categories: relatively weak, moderately strong, and extremely strong. The old Trapdoor Springfield and other rifles of its strength and vintage belong in the first category. Category two would include Marlin, Winchester and Browning lever-action rifles in excellent condition. Modern single shots such as the Ruger No. 1 and Browning 1885, along with conversions on the Siamese Mauser action make up the third category. If in doubt about which category a rifle I have not mentioned belongs in, consult its manufacturer.

The Marlin Model 336 Cowboy in 38-55 and my handload with the Barnes 255-grain bullet worked great on this black bear.

Loads for 38-55 Winchester?

I have a Winchester Model 94 in 38-55 caliber and find load data for this cartridge quite scarce. Can you suggest a starting load for the Hornady 220-gr. jacketed bullet? Do you have a favorite big-game load for the 38-55 Winchester?

Starting loads listed for the 38-55 Winchester in Hodgdon's data manual for a 255-gr. lead bullet are: 36.0 grains of BL-C(2) for a muzzle velocity of 1551 fps, 35.0 grains of H335 for 1564 fps, 30.0 grains of H4895 for 1519 fps and 29.0 grains of H322 for 1479 fps. Those powder charges should produce about 50 fps higher velocities with the lighter Hornady bullet. The Hornady reloading manual also has plenty of data for the 38-55 Winchester. My favorite big-game load for the 38-55 and one I recently used to take a very nice black bear on Vancouver Island consists of the Winchester case, Winchester WLR primer, 30.0 grains of Reloder 7 powder and the Barnes 255-gr. Original bullet. In the 24-inch barrel of the Marlin Model 336 Cowboy which I used to take the bear, that load averaged just over 1800 fps. Most groups fired on paper at 100 yards measured less than two inches which is not bad considering that the rifle wore a Marble's tang sight when I hunted with it. That load should be used only in rifles in good shape and those originally built for smokeless powder.

As you say, opinions on the strength of the current Marlin New Model 1895 seem to differ, so the best I can do is add mine to your list. The same Marlin rifle (which is actually the Model 336 with a different name) is also available in 444 Marlin and it is commonly loaded to a maximum chamber pressure of 44,000 CUP. For a short time the Model 336 was also available in 307 Winchester and SAAMI maximum for that one is even higher at 50,000 CUP. Given all of this, it might seem logical that the Marlin is a Category Three rifle but we must not overlook the fact that the 45-70 with its huge head surface area transmits far more backthrust against the locking mechanism of a rifle than a cartridge of smaller diameter. This is why the 223 Remington can be loaded to 50,000 CUP or so and safely used in the T/C Contender while 45-70 loads for that same gun must be kept below 30,000 cup. And we must not overlook how much thinner the chamber wall of a barrel reamed out for the 45-70 when compared to the same barrel chambered for a cartridge of smaller diameter. Bottom line? While I am sure any of the 45-70 data listed in various handloading manuals for the Marlin rifle are safe to use, I prefer to keep strain and stress on my Marlin rifles in the 30,000 psi range. And besides, if you can't bump off what your are shooting at with a 45-caliber bullet pushed along by that pressure level, a bit more isn't likely to have any bearing on the outcome of your hunt.

Where Do I Find a Load for the 300 STW?

I recently bought a rifle in 300 STW. Where do I find load data for it?

Case capacities of the 300 STW and 300 Weatherby Magnum are virtually identical, so you can begin load development for your rifle by reducing starting loads listed in various handloading manuals for the Weatherby cartridge by five percent. A reduction in powder charge is necessary because much of the data published for the 300 Weatherby Magnum was developed in rifles with freebored chambers while the chambers of rifles in 300 STW are usually reamed with a throat of standard length.

Can I Handload the 7.65mm Mauser?

I own a Model 1909 Argentine Mauser in 7.65mm. I find it to be a great deer rifle, but Norma ammunition is expensive and difficult to find in my area. Can I handload this cartridge?

The 7.65mm Mauser is an excellent cartridge with ballistics quite similar to those of the 308 Winchester. Back in the 1920s and 1930s, factory loads were available from Winchester and Remington. Winchester Model 54 and Model 70 rifles as well as the Remington Model 30 were available in that chambering. It is quite feasible to reload the 7.65mm. Your Norma cases can be reloaded with dies available from Redding and RCBS, or you can form cases by running 30-06 cases through the 7.65mm full-length resizing die and then trimming them back to a length of 2.10 inches. Bullets of nominal .311 to .312 inch in diameter (same as for the 303 British and 7.7mm Japanese cartridges) are available from Speer, Hornady and Sierra. The

Load data for the 300 STW?

Sierra reloading manual shows 150- and 180-gr. spitzers leaving a 29-1/2 inch barrel at respective muzzle velocities of 2700 fps and 2500 fps.

What Powders and Bullets Do l Use in the 5.7mm Spitfire?

I have a M-1 Carbine in 5.7mm Spitfire. It was manufactured by Iver Johnson. I also have reloading dies and case-forming dies but cannot locate load data. What powders and bullets work best in this cartridge? Do you have any history on the 5.7mm Spitfire?

The 5.7mm Spitfire was introduced during the early 1960s by Melvin Johnson, the owner of Johnson Guns, Inc. It is the 30 Carbine case necked down for use with 224-caliber bullets. Johnson advertised the velocity of his wildcat as 3000 fps with a 40-gr. bullet. Powder capacity of the 5.7mm Spitfire is quite close to that of the 218 Bee. A safe bet is to reduce starting loads shown in various reloading manuals for the Bee by 10 percent for starting loads in the 5.7mm Spitfire. From that point you could carefully increase the charge in half-grain increments until you have determined a maximum but safe load for your rifle. As for bullets, I would stick with those weighing 40 and 45 grains from Nosler, Speer, Sierra and Hornady.

Rifle Loads for 221 Remington Fire Ball?

I recently purchased a Kimber Model 84 in 221 Remington Fire Ball and plan to handload for it. I would like to use H322 powder behind the Nosler 50-gr. Ballistic Tip, but the Hodgdon handloading manual lists 221 Fire Ball loads only for the Remington XP-100 pistol. Can you come up with a good load for this cartridge that would work in my rifle? How fast is the 221 in a rifle?

Load data published in various handloading manuals for the 221 Fire Ball in handguns can be used in the Kimber Model 84 rifle. I have two rifles in that caliber, a Kimber Model 84 and a heavy-barrel varmint rig built around the XP-100 action. H322 does a good job in both of those rifles, but RL-7 has a slight edge in accuracy. Other propellants worthy of consideration in this cartridge are H4198 and IMR-4198. From a 22-inch barrel, the 221 Fire Ball will push a 50-gr. bullet along at 2900 to 3000 fps.

How Do l Form 8X60mm Mauser Cases?

My Mannlicher-Schoenauer rifle was built prior to World War II and is chambered for the 8x60mm Mauser cartridge. Factory ammo is quite scarce and while I have made the decision to start handloading, unprimed cases are just as difficult to find. I have been told that the 8x60mm case can be formed from 30-06 brass. How do I go about doing so? Where can I find load data?

The 8x60mm case is easily formed by trimming the 30-06 case to a length of 2.35 inches and then running it through an 8x60mm full-length resizing die. When placing an order for 8x60mm reloading dies from RCBS or Redding, be sure to specify the bullet diameter you are using and specify a tapered expander button in the full-length resizer. Starting loads shown in various handloading manuals for the 8x57mm Mauser can be used for the same purpose in the 8x60mm Mauser.

Reloder 7 in the 243 Winchester?

My target load for a Model 70 in 243 Winchester contains Reloder 7 powder and the Sierra 75-gr. hollowpoint. I have been told that RL-7 is not a good choice for the 243, but I have used if for several years in the 45-70 and 30-30 with no problems. What are your thoughts on using RL-7 in the 243 Winchester?

Reloder 7 is a relatively fast-burning powder best suited for use in cartridges of high expansion ratio. Good examples are the 222 Remington, 25-35, 30-30, 32 Special, 35 Remington, 375 Winchester, 444 Marlin, and 45-70 Government. Except for loading with extremely light charges for reduced velocities, RL-7 has limited application in a low expansion ratio cartridge such as the 243 Winchester. If top velocities in a target load are your goal, propellants of slower burn rates will generate higher velocities when loaded to the pressures generated when RL-7 is used in light target loads.

Favorite Deer Load for the 6.5x55mm Swedish?

I own a Winchester Model 70 Featherweight in 6.5x55mm Swedish, and it shoots beautifully. I recently shot a whitetail buck at about 100 yards with the Norma 139-gr. factory load, and it dropped after running for only about 20 yards. I also want to start handloading this cartridge. Do you have a favorite deer load for it?

My favorite deer load for the 6.5 Swede is the Nosler 125-gr. Partition bullet pushed to 2950 fps or so by a maximum charge of H4350. For long-range shooting in open country, I also like the Speer 120-gr. spitzer and the Nosler 120-gr. Ballistic Tip in this cartridge, but the Partition is the best choice for all-around use.

What Load Should I Use in My New Remington Model 7400?

I received a Remington Model 7400 autoloader in 30-06 as a gift and intend to hunt deer with it. What load should I use when hunting whitetails? Does my rifle shoot flat enough for hunting in open country?

I prefer the 150-gr. bullet when hunting deer-size game with the 30-06. The 30-06 most certainly shoots flat enough for use in open country. When a 150-gr. spitzer exits the muzzle at 2900 to 3000 fps and is zeroed three inches high at 100 yards, it strikes about three inches above line of sight at 200 yards and is only two inches low at 300 yards.

Why Is My Marlin 45-70 Inaccurate with Cast Bullets?

I have a Marlin Model 1895SS in 45 Government. Despite the best of my efforts, it refuses to shoot accurately with cast bullets.

H4831 powder is one of the best for handloading the 270 Winchester.

Best Powder for 270 Winchester?

I am the proud owner of a Dakota Model 10 rifle in 270 Winchester and plan to reload my own ammo for it. What powder do you consider best in this cartridge?

H4831 is the traditional powder for 270 Winchester handloads and it is the powder that Jack O'Connor favored. Other powders will do just as well in this cartridge and some are even better when the Nosler 160-gr. Partition is used, but none are better than H4831 with 130- and 150-gr. bullets.

Marlin rifles in 45-70 with their Micro-Groove barrels usually deliver acceptable accuracy when bullet speed is kept on the middle to lower end of the velocity scale, and when bullet diameter is about .001 inch larger than bore diameter. My Model 1895SS shoots most accurately with the old Lyman No. 457193 bullet cast fairly soft and sized to .459-inch. If you prefer a bullet with a gascheck, try RCBS mold No. 45-405-FN sized to that same diameter. When handloading cast bullets for my Marlin, I have yet to find a better powder than SR4759. I use standard-force primers during warm weather, but when the temperature drops below 40 degrees or so, I switch to a magnum primer such as the Remington 9-1/2M, Federal 215, or Winchester WLRM.

A Varmint Load for My 243 Winchester?

I use my Remington Model 700 in 243 Winchester for varmint shooting and have enjoyed excellent accuracy with various 70- and 75-gr. bullets seated atop IMR-4831 and W760 powders. I would like to try the Sierra 60-gr. hollowpoint and the Sierra 85-gr. spitzer but have not had any luck working up an accurate load with either bullet. Should I try other powders?

In my experience, 70 and 75 grains are the optimum bullet weights for varmint loads in the 243 Winchester, and you don't gain anything in the way of performance when using lighter or heavier bullets. Considering the accuracy you are getting with those two bullet weights, I believe you should stick with them.

Can I Convert 30-30 Rifle to 38-55 Winchester?

I have a Winchester Model 94 Canadian Centennial rifle with a 26-inch barrel in 30-30. Other than a severely pitted bore, the rifle is in excellent condition. Is it possible to have the barrel rebored and rechambered to 38-55 Winchester? I like the 38-55 cartridge because of its accuracy potential with cast bullets, and the rebore job would certainly be a tempting alternative to having a new 30-30 barrel installed on my rifle. What do you think?

Assuming the pits in its bore are not too deep, your rifle can be rebored and rechambered to 38-55 Winchester. In its heyday, the 38-55 was considered by many hunters to be one of the best cartridges available for hunting everything from deer and black bear to moose and elk in wooded country. If you go with the 38-55 conversion, the 375 caliber Sierra 200-gr. and Hornady 220-gr. bullets are excellent choices for deer since they are constructed to expand at relatively low impact velocities. Same goes for the 255-gr. bullet Winchester loads in factory ammo of that caliber. For larger game such as black bear, moose and elk, the Barnes 255-gr. Original is a better choice. My favorite cast bullet for the 38-55 is the old Lyman 375248. Depending on the alloy used, it will pop from the mold weighing somewhere in the neighborhood of 240 to 250 grains.

Do You Have a Favorite Elk Load for the 270 Winchester?

I have used a Winchester Model 70 in 270 Winchester quite successfully on deer and would like to hunt elk with the same rifle. What is your favorite recipe for an elk load in this cartridge?

The single best elk load for the 270 Winchester is probably the Nosler 160-gr. Partition pushed along at 2900 fps by Reloder 22. The Nosler reloading manual shows 56.0 grains of the Alliant powder doing just that in a 24-inch barrel. If your Model 70 has a 22-inch barrel, the load will likely be 60 to 80 fps slower in it. For a starting load with the Nosler bullet in your rifle, you should drop back to 50.0 grains of RL-22. Nosler's 160-gr. bullet has been quite accurate in most rifles in which I have tried it but if, by chance, your rifle does not like it, try the 150-gr. Nosler Partition or 150-gr. Swift A-Frame. H4831, RL-19 and RL-22 are the powders to try with those bullets.

Why Do Overall Cartridge Lengths Differ?

Handloading manuals that illustrate rifle cartridge dimensions often show a shorter overall length for a particular cartridge loaded with a hollowpoint bullet than when it loaded with a softpoint. Why is this? When handloading for a rifle in 220 Swift, I seat bullets out to just shy of touching the rifling in the barrel when a cartridge is chambered. I seem to get better accuracy by doing so. Why is this?

Given two bullets of the same shape but of softnose and hollowpoint styles, overall cartridge length with the softnose bullet will be greater because the lead core protruding from its nose adds to its length. It follows that when both styles of bullets are seated out of the case for the same ogive-to-rifling relationship, the overall length of the cartridge loaded with the softnose bullet will be greater. As you have discovered while working with your rifle in 220 Swift, some rifles shoot most accurately when fired with ammunition with bullets seated out so they either touch or almost touch the rifling when a round is chambered. Of course, some rifles will prove to be exceptions to this rule. Weatherby rifles with freebored chambers are excellent examples.

Where Do I Find 7mm STE Data?

I recently bought a Marlin Model 336 that had been rebarreled to 7mm Shooting Times Easterner. Since you are the creator of that cartridge I am sure you can tell me where to find load data for it. What cases can the 7mm STE be formed from? What velocities can I expect from it?

I introduced the 7mm STE in the June 1989 issue of *Shooting Times* magazine and included load data in that report. The Hodgdon reloading manual contains data for the 120-gr. Nosler and 139-gr. Hornady flatnose bullets. Data listed by that source for the latter can also be used with the Speer 130-gr. flatnose bullet. Reloading dies are available from RCBS and Redding. You can form 7mm STE cases by necking down 307 Winchester cases and fireforming them in the chamber of your rifle. My favorite fireforming load is 37.0 grains of H4895 behind the 120-gr. Nosler bullet.

The case can be formed by necking down 356 Winchester brass to 30 caliber in a 307 Winchester full-length resizing die and then going on down to 7mm with the 7mm STE die. The 7mm STE case can also be formed from 444 Marlin brass but doing so requires the use of form dies available from Redding.

What About Those Unusual Bullets?

A friend recently gave me a five-gallon bucket full of lead bullets salvaged from the dirt backstop of his firing range. While melting down the bullets, I discovered that some are 38 caliber and appear to be made of aluminum. Weighing only 100 grains or so, those bullets are extremely light for their size and would probably weigh at least 180 grains if made of lead. Can you tell me anything about those unusual bullets?

In their pursuit of extremely high velocities from revolvers, a few handloaders have experimented with bullets made of various low-density alloys. One of the more popular has been zinc. That material has been used due to its relatively low melting point, extreme hardness, low density, and the fact it can be cast in molds made for casting lead bullets. Years ago, zinc bullets were also available from a couple of commercial sources. Without actually examining the unusual bullets you have, it is impossible for me to say for certain what they are made of, but my guess is zinc.

Where Do I Find 22-243 Middlested Load Data?

My Remington Model 700 has been rechambered from 22-250 to 22-243 Middlested. Where can I find load data for that cartridge?

The 22-243 Middlested and two other similar wildcats called the 22 CHeetah and the 220 Jaybird are formed by necking down the 243 Winchester case, and their powder capacities are virtually identical. Consequently, starting loads listed in the Hodgdon reloading manual for the 22 CHeetah can also be used to begin load development for either of the other two cartridges.

When Do We Get the 257 STW?

I am a great fan of your 7mm STW and have taken lots of game with it. When will you neck it down for 25-caliber bullets and give us the ideal cartridge for hunting big-game such as deer and antelope where shots can be long?

Back when I first squeezed down the neck of the 8mm Remington Magnum case and created the 7mm STW, I also came up with cartridges of 6mm, 25, 6.5mm, 270, 30, 338, 358, 375, 416 and 458 calibers. But it took awhile for me to get around to seriously working with any except the 7mm STW and 358 STA. After introducing those two I received numerous requests from readers for a 25-caliber cartridge on the same case and responded by introducing the 257 STW. It is the 7mm STW case necked down for 25-caliber bullets and exceeds the maximum velocities of the 257 Weatherby Magnum by about 200 fps with all bullet weights. I later introduced the 6.5 STW, which I consider a better cartridge for all-around use on game ranging in size from deer to elk.

What Do Shiny Circles on Case Heads Mean?

I recently bought 100 Winchester unprimed cases for my Remington Model 700 in 7mm Magnum. After spending many hours in front of the reloading bench and at the range I settled on a load consisting of the Federal 215 primer, a maximum charge of H4831 and the Nosler 160-gr. Partition bullet. During my first hunt in Africa, that load proved so effective on everything from impala to eland that I came home and stockpiled 1000 of the Federal primers, 10 pounds of H4831 and 1000 Nosler 160-gr. Partition bullets. More recently, I bought a new batch of unprimed cases of a different brand and filled them with what I have come to call my favorite mouse-to-moose load. After firing several of the cartridges in my Model 700, I noticed that a shiny circle had appeared on the head of each case. Oddly enough, that never happened with my old batch of cases. What is causing those shiny circles to appear?

The shiny circle you describe is a sure sign of an excessive load in your rifle. Chamber pressure is high enough to cause the brass to extrude from the head of a case and into the ejector tunnel of the face of the bolt. As you rotate the bolt to its unlocked position after firing a round, the sharp edge of the ejector tunnel shaves brass from the very top of the extruded area, giving it a shiny appearance.

Several factors can cause a load that has proven to be safe in one brand of cases to be excessive in another brand. For one, the capacity of cases made for the same cartridge by different manufacturers can vary slightly. It is possible that your first batch of cases were a bit more capacious than your second batch and using the same load in the second batch probably caused chamber pressure to increase. The level of chamber pressure a cartridge case can handle is also greatly influenced by its degree of hardness. It could be that the cases in your second batch are softer in the head area. Anytime you decide to change any component part of a maximum load, whether it be a different brand or a different manufacturing lot of the same brand, you should reduce the powder charge by 10 percent and carefully work back up (or down) while keeping a sharp eye peeled for signs of excessive pressure.

What Powders and Bullets for 45-70 Handloads?

I hunt black bear, elk, and blacktail deer with a Marlin Model 1895SS in 45-70. My favorite load is 55.0 grains of IMR-3031 and the Hornady 350-gr. roundnose. I am happy with the performance of that bullet, but it is quite expensive for practice shooting. I would like to try a more efficient powder than IMR-3031. What are my options?

By more efficient, I assume you mean a powder that will produce the same velocities as IMR-3031 with the 350-gr. bullet but with lighter charges. This can be accomplished with Reloder 7, H322, H4198 and IMR-4198. Maximum charges of those powders in the 45-70 usually run at least five grains lighter but velocity is about the same. You obviously don't shoot a lot of the Hornady bullets at game, so I suggest that you take a serious look at casting bullets for your Marlin. They can be used for practice shooting while the more expensive jacketed bullets are reserved for hunting.

ELECTRIC PRIMED RIFLE CARTRID

Remington

EG000514

BAUSCH LOMB

Remington's ExtonX rifle needs no special cartridge case.

Special Cases for Remington EtronX Rifle?

*My Remington EtronX in 22-250 is the most accurate varmint rifle I have
ever owned. Several five-shot groups I have fired at 100 yards with factory
ammunition measure less than half an inch. I will soon be reloading for that
rifle and have a supply of Winchester 22-250 cases that were once-fired
in another rifle. Can I use those cases in my EtronX rifle or does it take a
special case?*

The only thing unique about the 22-250 ammunition made by Remington
for the EtronX rifle is the primer. Everything else, including the case, is the
same as for conventional 22-250 ammo. You will have to use the EtronX
primer manufactured by Remington but standard 22-250 cases made by
that company as well as Winchester, Federal, Hornady, Norma and others
will work fine.

329

Where Do l Find 25 Souper Data?

l recently bought a Browning A-Bolt rifle that has been rebarreled for the 25 Souper. Where can l find case forming instructions and load data for it?

If your rifle is chambered for the original version of the 25 Souper, you can form cases by simply necking down the 308 Winchester or necking up the 243 Winchester case. Brass can also be formed from 260 Remington and 7mm-08 Remington cases but it will need to be trimmed to an overall length of 2.035 inches after forming. When developing handloads for the 25 Souper, begin with starting loads shown in various handloading manuals for the 257 Roberts and carefully work from there.

Where Do l Get a Large Primer Flipper?

l recently bought several thousand Federal rifle and pistol primers and discovered that the new packaging they come in is too large for my older primer flipper. Does anyone make one big enough to work with those extra-larger primer boxes?

Most manufacturers now ship primers in the new large-size containers and most reloading tool companies have responded by offering king-size flippers. Four that come to mind are Dillon, RCBS, Redding and Lyman.

Which Heavy Bullet for the 25-06?

l use a Sako rifle in 25-06 for hunting deer. Some 1940s vintage load data l have seen for this cartridge called for bullets weighing 130 and 135 grains which should be just the ticket for woods hunting. Where can l find bullets in those weights?

The heaviest readily available 25-caliber bullet I am aware of is the 125-gr. Barnes Original. Another option is to reduce the diameter of heavier 264-caliber bullets to .257 inch by pushing then through special drawing dies available from Corbin. If the rifling twist rate of your barrel is no quicker than 1:10 inches (which is pretty much standard for 25 caliber rifles), bullets heavier than 125 grains probably won't stabilize in it.

Why 30-378 Weatherby Magnum Load Data Discrepancies?

As a proud owner of a Weatherby Mark V Accumark rifle in 30-378 Weatherby Magnum, l am puzzled by the fact that the 2nd edition of the Barnes reloading manual shows higher velocities for some bullet weights in the 300 Dakota in a 24-inch barrel than for the 30-378 in a 26-inch barrel. Barnes also shows gross capacity of the 300 Dakota as 97.0 grains (three grains less than for the 300 Weatherby Magnum) compared to 139.8 grains for the 30-378 Weatherby Magnum. How is it possible for a cartridge with 44 percent less capacity to produce higher velocities?

When everything including barrel length and the chamber pressures to which any two cartridges are loaded being the same, the cartridge with greater capacity will generally produce higher velocities simply because it is capable of burning a heavier charge of powder. In any accurate comparison, the 300 Dakota will produce about the same velocity as the 300 Weatherby Magnum while the considerably larger 30-378 Weatherby Magnum will beat both by 200 fps or so with bullets weighing 180 grains and heavier. Considering this, it becomes obvious that something was not exactly apples-to-apples when Barnes technicians developed data for those cartridges.

More on Barnes 30-378 Magnum Load Data

I read your comments on the 30-378 Weatherby Magnum load data we published in our reloading manual No. 2 and thought the following information might be of interest. When we began developing data for that cartridge we were quite disappointed by the velocities we were obtaining. I personally had built four custom rifles for customers in 30-378 Magnum by rebarreling Sakos in 338 Lapua and got velocities of around 3550 fps with 180-gr. bullets from those rifles. So you can imagine what we were thinking when the factory rifle we were using yielded velocities in the 300 Weatherby Magnum range using substantially more powder! However, we decided to go ahead and reluctantly print the results in our manual, knowing full well we would have many inquiries. We have since determined that the rifle we used for load development has an extremely slow barrel as we have now tested other factory rifles and experienced an increase in velocities at the same chamber pressure levels. We are currently developing data for our No. 3 manual and anticipate that velocities published in it will better show the true potential of the 30-378 Weatherby Magnum.

> *Jessica S. Harrison*
> *Public Relations Manager*
> *Barnes Bullets*

Thanks very much for the response to my comments about the 30-378 Magnum load data in your loading manual.

Minimum Amount Of Reloading Equipment?

I want to get into handloading but not in a big way. What is the minimum amount of equipment I can get by with?

In addition to a single-stage reloader, a powder measure and dies and shellholders for the cartridges you will be reloading, you will need a combination instruction/data manual from Hornady, Nosler, Hodgdon Sierra or one of the other components manufacturers. Other less expensive items include powder funnel, chamfer/deburr tool, case neck brush, case lube, loading block and case resizing lube. You will need a caliper for measuring cartridge overall length. Bottleneck cases occasionally require neck-trimming and if you do not plan to load more than a couple of different calibers you can get by with trim dies for them. More calibers than that calls for a trimmer. Some reloading machines will seat primers but if the one you decide to buy does not, you will need a priming tool. Some companies offer everything you will need in kit form, usually at lower cost than buying each item individually. As time goes on you will probably want to add a powder measure and a few other items.

Will Coated Bullets Harm the Bore of My Rifle Barrel?

I am confused as to whether coated bullets will harm the barrel of my rifle in 300 Winchester Magnum. Neither the maker of my barrel nor the gunsmith who installed it recommends the use of moly-coated bullets and that puts me in somewhat of a dilemma. I do all of my hunting with factory loads and prefer to shoot ammunition loaded with Nosler bullets. The Winchester ammo I prefer to use is loaded with the moly-coated Partition Gold and Lubalox-coated Ballistic Silvertip bullets. Will firing that ammo in my rifle harm its barrel? How do I remove any residue left in my barrel by those two coatings?

First of all, Winchester's Lubalox coating does not build up in the bore the way some moly coatings are prone to do so you can forget about any harmful effect it might have on your barrel. Secondly, the problem you have heard about is not with moly coating but with shooters who believe the use of moly coated bullets eliminates the need to properly clean a barrel at regular intervals. If you thoroughly clean your barrel every 50 rounds or so you should never experience a problem with moly build-up. Regular scrubbings with a bronze brush and a cleaner made of a 50-50 mix of Kroil and Shooters Choice, along with cleaning with J.B. Nonimbedding Bore Cleaner will keep the bore of your barrel free of moly build-up. All of those products are available from Brownells.

How Can I Salvage 40 S&W Cases?

I recently bought a huge supply of once-fired 40 S&W cases and considered them a bargain at $25 per thousand. After loading a few hundred on my progressive reloader I discovered neither of my two STI International guns would chamber a single round. Can all that beautiful brass I bought be salvaged or is it destined for the scrap yard?

Most of the once-fired 40 S&W cases on the market today come from the practice ranges of various law enforcement agencies around the country. The barrels of some of the handguns in which the ammo is fired allow a cartridge case to expand excessively, all the way back to its extractor groove. The shellplates of most progressive reloaders do not allow a full-length resizing die to squeeze the case back to its original dimension in that area. The solution is to run each case through a full-length resizing die in a single-stage press before reloading it on your progressive machine. The use of a die with a tungsten carbide insert will speed up the job by eliminating the need to apply lubricant to the cases and then removing it after they have been resized. Use of the single-stage press will have to be done only one time because once the cases have been fired in your guns the resizing die of the progressive loader will handle the job from that point on.

Is H1000 Powder a Good Choice for the 30-378 Weatherby Magnum?

I recently bought a Weatherby Mark V in 30-378 Magnum and intend to handload for it. I have two rifles in 7mm STW and since I use H1000 in handloads for both of them, I have a good supply on hand. Will that powder work as well in the bigger Weatherby cartridge?

H1000 is an excellent choice for the 30-378 Weatherby Magnum simply because it has the correct burn rate to squeeze top velocities from that cartridge. I just received a copy of Hodgdon's latest *Annual Manual* and it shows an average muzzle velocity of 3412 fps when a maximum charge of H1000 is burned behind a 180-gr. bullet. According to that source, only Retumbo powder delivers slightly higher velocities. Published annually, the *Annual Manual* contains thousands of loads for most of the popular rifle, pistol and shotgun cartridges. You can purchase a copy at your local Hodgdon dealer or order it by mail directly from Hodgdon Powder Co.

Why No W748 Data for the 30 Russian?

I use a rifle in 7.62x39mm for hunting wild hogs here in Florida and am having no luck finding load data for W748 powder in that cartridge. Even Winchester doesn't have data, which is a surprise to me considering how well it works in the 308 Winchester. Do you have such a recipe?

As you have already discovered, W748 is an excellent choice for the 308 Winchester but you obviously are not aware of the fact that its burn rate is far too slow for use in the much smaller 30 Russian. This is why the load data you are looking for does not exist. Of the powders readily available on the U.S. market, those best suited for loading in the 7.62x39mm are W680, H4227, AA-1680, IMR-4227, Reloder 7 and Norma N200.

What Load for Winchester 1886 and Marlin 1895?

I have an original Winchester Model 1886 in 45-90 and a Marlin Model 95 of current production in 45-70 Government. I would like to hunt bear, moose and elk with those rifles. Can you recommend a bullet and load for each of them?

Assuming that your Winchester 86 is in good, sound condition and its action is tight, the 300-gr. Lyman #457122 cast bullet of Gould design at 1600 to 1800 fps would be my choice in close to medium-range bear, moose and elk medicine for it. You may also be able to use lead bullets as heavy as 400 grains in your rifle but Model 1886s in 45-90 were manufactured with at least a couple of different rifling twist rates and those with the slower twist sometimes don't shoot the heavier weights as accurately. If the twist rate in your rifle is 1:24 inches or quicker, it should handle bullets up to 400 grains, possibly even heavier. The second edition of the Accurate reloading manual has loads for A-5744 powder with 300- and 405-gr. lead bullets at respective maximum velocities of 1780 and 1535 fps.

One Powder for All Shotshells?

I am shotgun poor and own far more than I will ever shoot in 410, 20, 28, 16 and 12 gauge. I am new to the reloading game and would like to simplify life as much as possible by using one powder to load all the various gauges. Is this possible?

I am afraid you are asking for the impossible simply because optimum propellant burn rates are different for the various bore sizes. Looking at the two extremes, the 410 requires the use of slow-burning powders such as H110, W296 and Lil'Gun while the 12 gauge calls for relatively fast burners such as Clays from Hodgdon and Red Dot from Alliant. At the very least, you could get by with H110 in the 410 and Hodgdon's Universal in the 28, 20, 16 and 12 gauges but you would not enjoy very much latitude in load flexibility. My favorite Hodgdon combinations and the ones I use most often are H110 in the three-inch 410, Lil'Gun in the 2-1/2 inch 410, Universal in the 28 gauge, International in the 20 gauge and Clays in the 12 gauge.

No single powder will work satisfactorily in all shotshells ranging from the 410 to the 12 gauge.

For your Marlin New Model 1895 in 45-70, I recommend handloading the Nosler 300-gr. Partition in the 1800 to 2000 fps range. You can use data shown in various handloading manuals for that bullet weight or you can obtain data by writing directly to Nosler Bullets at P.O. Box 671, Bend, OR 97709.

Which Reloading Manual Has Fast Loads for 7mm STW?

I recently bought a new rifle in 7mm STW and am disappointed by the relatively low velocities shown for it in the current Nosler reloading manual. Do other manuals contain faster loads for your cartridge?

Just as individual shooters with their individual rifles and individual chronographs often come up with variations in maximum velocities for the same cartridge, so it also goes among technicians who develop data for handloading manuals. Contrary to what you see listed in the Nosler manual, data in the Sierra manual has the 7mm STW stepping along right smartly at respective muzzle velocities of 3500, 3400, 3300 and 3100 fps with bullets weighing 140, 150, 160 and 175 grains. Data included in the current Barnes manual reads about the same as it lists those same bullet weights at maximum velocities of 3473, 3359, 3287 and 3127 fps, respectively.

Why Do My 222 Cases Fit Too Tightly?

I recently formed a batch of 222 Remington cases from 223 Remington brass. When the cases are trimmed to an overall length of 1.690 inches as recommended by various reloading manuals, they are too long for the chamber of my rifle and the bolt will hardly close on a chambered case. Trimming a case on back to 1.670 inches allows the bolt to close with no resistance. What gives?

Maximum overall length of the 222 Remington case is 1.700 inches and any rifle with its chamber correctly reamed to SAAMI dimensional specifications will accept a case that long. Since the neck area of the chamber in your rifle is obviously a bit short your alternatives are to have a gunsmith lengthen it with a reamer or continue trimming cases a bit on the short side. The cases of some 222 factory ammo I have checked ran as much as 1.698 inches long so to avoid the possibility of some future owner of your rifle experiencing excessive chamber pressures when firing factory ammo in it, your safest bet is to have the chamber problem corrected by a gunsmith.

Where Can I Buy a 410 Progressive Reloader That Works?

A friend and I own several 410 shotguns and since we shoot them a lot we have progressive reloaders of two different brands. We have owned the machines for close to a year now and despite the efforts of ourselves and customer service representatives with both companies, neither of them has ever worked satisfactorily. Where can I buy a 410 progressive reloader that works?

Building a progressive reloader that works 100 percent satisfactorily with the tiny 410 shotshell is a challenge no company has yet to master as far as I know. I seldom experience a major problem when reloading thousands of rounds of 28, 20, 16 and 12 gauge shells each year on various brands of progressive reloaders but after trying a couple in 410 and finding that I was spending less time shooting and more time clearing jams in the machine and breaking down ammo in which the powder charge or shot charge was missing, I finally threw in the towel and started using a single-stage machine. The Ponsness/Warren Du-O-Matic 375C and Mec 600 JR machines I use are capable of reloading 2-1/2 and 3-inch 410 shells and while my production rate is only about 125 rounds per hour, my time is spent loading ammo I can shoot rather than loading ammo that won't shoot.

Who Makes Bullets for the 9.3x62mm?

I recently bought a Sako rifle in 9.3x62mm Mauser and it is quite accurate with the Sako ammo that came with it. I want to start handloading for the rifle but before buying the dies I thought it might be best to ask you who makes bullets for it. I have only one box of fired cases; can the case be formed from any readily available case? How does the 9.3x62mm compare in performance with other cartridges?

Capable of pushing a 250-gr. bullet along at 2500 feet per second, the 9.3x62mm Mauser is quite similar in performance to the 35 Whelen and the case is easily formed by necking up 30-06 brass for .366-inch bullets. Nosler has long offered a 9.3mm 286-gr. Partition and will be introducing a new 250-gr. Ballistic Tip sometime during 2000. The Barnes 250-gr. XFB and Speer 270-gr. softnose are also excellent choices for this fine old cartridge.

Can 7mm STE Cases Be Formed from 308 Brass?

I have been interested in your 7mm STE cartridge ever since you first wrote about taking all those deer with a Marlin 336 in that caliber years ago. My question is, could basically the same cartridge be built around more readily available 308 Winchester brass rather than 307 Winchester brass? My plan would be to handload the same flatnose bullets from Hornady and Nosler as you use in the 7mm STE. Would it work?

I developed the wildcat you are interested in back in the 1970s. Called the 7mm SGLC, it is the 308 Winchester case necked down for .284-inch bullets and fireformed to minimum body taper and a sharper shoulder angle. I later came up with the 7mm STE by necking down and fireforming the 307 Winchester case in the same manner, making it nothing more or less than the original 7mm SGLC case with a rim added. Other than that, the only difference between the two is the chamber pressure levels to which they are loaded. Since the Marlin lever action is not designed to withstand chamber pressures as high as modern bolt actions, the 7mm STE is loaded to lower pressures than the 7mm SGLC. I see no problem with rebarreling a Marlin for the 7mm SGLC so long as 7mm STE load data is used and you stick with flat-nosed bullets. Your best bet would be to rebarrel a Model 336 in 35 Remington as its bolt face should not have to be modified for the 308 case. In addition to the Nosler 120-gr. and Hornady 139-gr. flatnose bullets you might also try the new 130-gr. flatnose from Speer.

Which Nosler 50-Caliber Saboted Bullet Should l Use on Moose?

l have a 50-caliber Thompson/Center Encore inline muzzleloader and it is extremely accurate when loaded with Pyrodex and either of the 250-gr. saboted bullets available from Nosler. Both bullets ride in the same type of 50-caliber sabot but one is Nosler's regular 45-caliber 250-gr. JHP and the other is the 44-caliber Partition HG. l'll be hunting moose and black bear in Alaska with my Encore and can't decide which bullet to use. Which one would you take hunting?

As a rule, 45-caliber saboted bullets are more accurate in 50-caliber inline rifles than 44-caliber saboted bullets but since your rifle is delivering equal accuracy with the two Nosler bullets, I would choose the latter. An Alaskan bull moose is a huge animal so if it were my hunt I would choose the bullet most likely to smash through heavy bone and do lots of damage inside where the animal lives. Between the two 250-gr. Nosler bullets you mentioned, I would head north with the 44-caliber simply because its higher sectional density and Partition HG construction will enable it to penetrate deeper than the 45-caliber JHP.

Which Bullet Type for Cape Buffalo?

A Remington Model 700 in 416 Magnum l just purchased will be used on an upcoming hunt in Africa for Cape buffalo but l can't decide whether l should handload solid or softnose bullets. Which do you recommend? If l opt for solids will they also work okay on antelope such as greater kudu and impala? There is the option of taking ammo loaded with both types of bullets but l am concerned about the possibility of a difference in their points of impact. Should this be a concern? What are your favorite 416 caliber bullets?

After bagging a number of Cape buffalo with cartridges of various calibers, including the various 416s, I am convinced beyond argument that the very best battle plan is to start the show with a softnose load in the chamber of a bolt action rifle and its magazine filled with solids. The first shot to the lungs with an expanding bullet capable of penetrating deeply will usually knock most of the fight out of the animal but as a rule, Cape buffalo take awhile to discover they are dead, so the solids come into play for follow-up shots through the shoulders or into whatever end of the animal happens to be pointed in your direction after that first shot is taken. To answer another of your questions, only softnose bullets should be used on antelope.

As for your concern about using two types of bullets, if they are the same weight they will usually shoot close enough to the same point of impact out to 100 paces or so, which is about 50 paces farther away than your professional hunter should allow you to shoot a buffalo anyhow. Three of the very best 416 caliber expanding bullets

Expanded Speer African Grand Slam softnose bullet fired from a 416 Remington Magnum at less than 40 yards and later recovered from the buffalo it killed.

available, all capable of doing an outstanding job on buffalo, are the Speer African Grand Slam, Barnes XFB and Nosler Partition, all weighing 400 grains. As for solids of the same weight, I especially like those from Speer, Barnes and Hornady.

Where Do l Find Load Data for the 6.5x65mm Brenneke?

Here in Argentina, l hunt European red deer and want to develop loads with the Nosler 140-gr. Partition and Barnes 130-gr. X-Bullet for a rifle in 6.5x65mm Brenneke. Do you think it possible for me to duplicate 270 Winchester performance with this cartridge? Where can l find load data?

Case capacities of the 6.5x65mm Brenneke and an old American wildcat called the 6.5-06 are virtually identical so you can safely use starting loads listed for the latter cartridge in Nosler's latest reloading manual. Nosler shows maximum velocities of 3120 and 2860 feet per second with 125- and 140-gr. bullets so you should be able to nip rather closely at the heels of the 270 Winchester. If your rifle is chambered for the rimmed version of the Brenneke cartridge (6.5x65mmR), I suggest that you reduce Nosler's starting loads by a couple of grains before carefully working up for your particular rifle.

Load Data for 7x57mm Mauser Improved?

I have a rifle chambered for the 7x57mm Mauser Improved. l also have

*Redding reloading dies but none of the handloading manuals I have includes that
cartridge. Can you supply me data for it? How fast is it?*

The best way to develop loads for any improved cartridge, and this includes the
7x57mm Mauser Improved, is to begin with starting loads shown in various manuals
for the standard cartridge and then carefully work toward maximum for your
particular rifle. For example, the latest Speer manual shows 46.0 grains of H-414 as
a recommended starting load with the 130-gr. bullet and 50.0 grains as maximum
for a velocity of 2960 feet per second (fps) in a 22-inch barrel. Increasing the powder
capacity of a cartridge by fireforming it to the improved configuration allows the use
of a slightly heavier powder charge but in my experience the amount of additional
powder that can be used seldom exceeds four to five grains in a cartridge the size
of the 7x57mm Improved. As a rule, an improved cartridge is usually about 100 fps
faster than its parent when both are loaded with the same bullet weight and to the
same chamber pressure, so in the case of the 7x57mm Improved you should be able
to safely reach 3000 to 3050 fps with the 130-gr. bullet in your rifle.

What Primers, Cases and Bullets for 45-70 Loads?

*Sometime back I read your article on loading pointed bullets in the 45-70 for
bolt-action and single shot rifles. Do you have a preference in primers and cases
for high-velocity loadings of this cartridge? When loading the Barnes 300- and
400-gr. pointed bullets to maximum velocities, what are the top velocities I can
expect from a 22-inch barrel? How much flatter do the pointed bullets shoot than
those of flatnose form and how much harder do they hit downrange?*

I have no preference in 45-70 cases and consider those made by Federal, Remington
and Winchester equal in quality. Same goes for primers. Maximum velocities of 300-
and 400-gr. bullets in the 22-inch barrel of a rifle such as the Ruger No. 1 are in the
neighborhood of 2300 and 2000 fps, respectively. As for a downrange performance
comparison, when the Barnes XFB 300-gr. pointed bullet exits the muzzle at 2300 fps
and is zeroed three inches high at 100 yards, it lands about an inch below point of aim
at 200 yards where it delivers just over 2100 ft-lbs of energy. Starting at the same initial
velocity and zeroed the same, the Barnes 300-gr. flatnose bullet is about two inches
low at 200 yards and is packing less than 1800 ft-lbs at that range. As you can see,
while loading the old 45-70 with a pointed bullet does very little to flatten its trajectory
at medium ranges its 200-yard energy delivery is increased by close to 20 percent. That
style of bullet should never be used in a rifle with a tubular magazine.

What Loads for the 348 Winchester?

*I recently bought one of Browning's Japanese reproductions of the Winchester
Model 71 in 348 Winchester caliber. How effective is that combination on
game ranging in size from whitetail deer to moose? What factory load do you
recommend? I handload several other cartridges and will probably start doing the
same for the 348 Winchester. Any suggestions on powders and bullets?*

I once owned a Winchester Model 71 carbine with a 20-inch barrel and found it to be a far more effective deer cartridge than the 30-30 Winchester and 35 Remington, both of which I also used a lot on those days. I still own a Model 71 rifle with the more common 24-inch barrel and with the right load in its chamber I wouldn't hesitate to use it for hunting any game animal on the North American continent. At present, only Winchester offers a 348 factory load and while its 200-gr. Silvertip bullet is an excellent choice for use on deer and black bear, the discontinued 250-gr. Silvertip loading was reputed to be a better choice for larger game such as elk and moose. Should you decide to start handloading the 348, the Barnes 220-gr. Original and Hornady 200-gr. flatnose bullets are good choices for deer. For larger game or for all-around use on all game ranging in size from whitetails to moose, the 200-gr. XFN, 220-gr. XFN and 250-gr. Original offered by Barnes are the best choices. A favorite load for my rifle consists of the Winchester case, Federal 210M primer, and the Barnes 220-gr. XFN seated atop 49.0 grains of H4895. Muzzle velocity averages just over 2300 fps in a 24-inch barrel and iron sight accuracy is right around four inches at 100 yards. Another equally accurate recipe my old Winchester lever gun appreciates is 50.0 grains of H380 for just over 2200 fps with the Barnes 250-gr. Original.

Which Bullets For Hornet, Bee and 223?

I am in the market for a centerfire rifle capable of taking fox and coyote at ranges out to a maximum of 150 yards. Since I'll be hunting in a settled area, noise is a factor so I have pretty much boiled down my options to a Browning 1885 Low Wall in 22 Hornet or a Ruger No. 1 in 218 Bee. A more remote possibility is the Winchester Model 70 in 223 Remington, although its greater noise level might rule it out. What are your thoughts on those three cartridges for my use? Regardless of which I choose, I will handload the ammunition; what bullets do you recommend?

I own several rifles in 22 Hornet and 218 Bee and my heart has a soft spot for both but I'll have to steer you toward the more powerful 223 Remington for shooting a live target as large as coyote. No doubt, with proper bullet placement the two smaller cartridges would work out to 100 yards or so and if you are willing to turn down longer shots then by all means go with one or the other. The 223 would allow you to use a reduced-velocity handload that approximates the velocity and noise level of the two smaller cartridges but it would also allow you to load to its full potential for more downrange energy delivery anytime you think you might need it. When handloading the Hornet and Bee, I like the Nosler 40-gr. Ballistic Tip and the Hornady V-Max of the same weight. The 40- and 45-gr. bullets designed by Speer, Sierra and Hornady to expand at the relatively low impact velocities are also excellent choices for those cartridges. As for the 223, my picks of the bunch are the Speer TNT, Nosler Ballistic Tip, Hornady V-Max and Sierra Blitz, all weighing 50 grains.

Load Data for 7mm SGLC?

Can you furnish me with load data and case-forming instructions for your 7mm SGLC (Simpson's Good Little Cartridge)? When did you develop that cartridge?

Performance of the 450 Marlin can be duplicated with 45-70 handloads.

How Do I Duplicate 450 Marlin Velocity with the 45-70?

I just learned about the new 450 chambering that Marlin is offering in its Model 1895 Guide Gun and understand it is rated at a muzzle velocity of 2100 fps with a 350-gr. bullet. I recently purchased a Marlin 1895 in 45-70 and have been told that handloading can boost the old cartridge to the same velocity level as that of the new 450 Marlin. How do I go about doing that?

For quite sometime now handloaders have been pushing the 45-70 to higher than normal velocities but this should only be attempted with modern cases and modern rifles such as the Browning 1895, Ruger No. 1 and the New Model Marlin 1895 which is actually built on the Marlin Model 336 action and should not be confused with the original Marlin Model 1895. Loads published for the 45-70 in the latest Hodgdon Data Manual push 300- and 350-gr. bullets to respective muzzle velocities of 2500 and 2200 fps. Other reloading manuals from Barnes, Speer, Accurate, Sierra and Hornady also contain high velocity loads for the old cartridge.

Back in the 1970s when I first came up with the wildcat you're interested in I formed cases by necking down 308 Winchester brass and fireforming it to minimum body taper and a 40 degree shoulder angle in the 7mm SGLC chamber. This is still a good way to form cases but nowadays I just as often come up with newly formed brass for my two rifles by firing 7mm-08 Remington factory ammo in them. As for load data, your best bet is to begin with starting loads shown in various handloading manuals for the 7mm-08 and work up from there in your particular rifle. When both are loaded with the same bullet weight and to the same chamber pressure, the 7mm SGLC is about 100 fps faster than the 7mm-08 Remington.

Can 224-Inch Bullets be Used in 223-inch Barrels?

I was told the groove diameter of the barrel of my Savage Model 340 in 22 Hornet is probably .223 inch while the Lyman reloading manual I have says it should be .224 inch. I am also told that factory ammo available today is loaded with the larger diameter bullet. First question: can .224-inch bullets be fired in a .223-inch barrel? Second question; can .223-inch bullets be fired in a .224-inch barrel?

You can determine the groove diameter of your barrel by slugging it with a kit available from Brownells and Midway. Modern 22 Hornet factory ammo is loaded with .224-inch bullets and it is safe to fire bullets of that diameter in a barrel with a .223-inch groove diameter if the neck of its chamber is large enough in diameter to allow the neck of the case to easily expand enough to release its hold on the bullet during firing. This can be determined by making a Cerrosafe casting of the chamber (available from Brownells). My experience has shown that .224-inch bullets often are not very accurate in .223-inch barrels and if you find that your barrel has the smaller groove diameter, Sierra offers its 40- and 45-gr. Hornet bullets in both diameters. To answer your second question, .223-inch bullets can be fired in a .224-inch barrel but seldom have I found the combination to produce acceptable accuracy.

Which Powder and Bullets for the 307 Winchester?

I recently purchased a Winchester Model 94 rifle in 307 Winchester and it will keep all its bullets inside four inches at 100 yards with iron sights when shooting the 180-gr. factory load. What powder do you recommend for handloads? Can the 307 case be formed from other brass? Can 180-gr. roundnose bullets be loaded in this cartridge? Bullets made for the 30-30 seem a bit too softly constructed for the considerably higher impact velocities this cartridge is capable of and I'm wondering if you have a favorite for it.

Winchester's 307 factory load contains W748 and that powder along with BL-C(2), IMR-4320 and AA-2520 are excellent choices for handloading the cartridge. The 307 case is easily formed by necking down 356 Winchester brass. Also, despite the fact that the 308 Winchester case is rimless I have found it to work fine in both of my 307-chambered Winchester 94s so I use 308 brass for practice loads and reserve my stock of 307 brass for hunting loads. Back when the 307 and 356 were introduced, Winchester recommended that only flat-nose bullets be loaded in them when they are used in rifles with tubular magazines and as far as I know that recommendation still stands. Three flatnose bullets that will hold up to the higher velocities of the 307 Winchester are the 170-gr. Nosler Partition along with the 150- and 165-gr. XFN bullets from Barnes.

Which Loads for 264 and 6.5 Magnums?

I have a Browning Safari grade rifle on the FN Mauser action in 264 Winchester Magnum. I also have a Remington Model 673 Guide Rifle in 6.5 Remington Magnum. The Browning has a 24-inch barrel and the Remington has a 22-1/2 inch barrel. I intend to use both rifles when hunting whitetail deer in areas where the range can reach out to 300 yards. What loads can I use to squeeze maximum performance from their relatively short barrels?

The Nosler 125-gr. partition and Barnes 120-gr. XFB would be my picks for developing long-range whitetail loads for your rifles. With either of those bullets you should be able to reach 3200 fps in the 24-inch barrel of your 264 Magnum and around 3000 fps in the 22-1/2 inch barrel of your 6.5 Magnum. Zero the 264 Magnum three inches high at 100 yards and it will be just about dead on at 300. Zeroed the same, the 6.5 Magnum will be down about three inches at 300 yards. Both cartridges also pack more than enough punch for deer-size game at that range.

30-30 Equivalent Loads for 303 British?

I want to develop a deer load with a 150-gr. jacketed bullet for the 303 British cartridge that duplicates 30-30 Winchester performance with that same bullet weight. Any suggestions?

Several reloading manuals have the 303 British data you are looking for. As an example, the Hornady manual shows 31.5 grains of AA-2495, 35.0 grains of Varget or 37.0 grains of Reloder 15 producing a muzzle velocity of 2300 feet per second (fps) with the 150-gr. bullet in a 25-inch barrel. Those are reduced-velocity loads and the maximum velocities listed in that manual for the 150-gr. bullet in the 303 British is 2700 fps.

Which Powders and Bullets for 260 Remington?

I recently had a 24-inch barrel in 260 Remington installed on a Model 70 action. I want to develop a handload to be used for open-country hunting of mule deer and pronghorn antelope and would like your recommendations on powders and bullets. The first hunt I'll use my new rifle on is for pronghorn antelope in Wyoming.

Everything including bullet sectional density, trajectory, case capacity and downrange energy considered, optimum bullet weight range for the 260 Remington when that cartridge is used on deer-size game is 120 to 130 grains. Readily available big-game bullets in that category include the Sierra 120-gr. spitzer, Nosler 120-gr. Ballistic Tip, Barnes 120-gr. XFB, Speer 120-gr. Spitzer, Nosler 125-gr. Partition, Hornady 129-gr. spire point and Barnes 130-gr. XFB. Any of those bullets should perform satisfactorily on game like southern whitetails and pronghorn antelope but for larger animals requiring more penetration, such as mule deer and northern whitetails, I would stick with either the Nosler 125-gr. Partition or the Barnes XFB bullets weighing 120 and 130 grains. As a rule, I find powders with medium-slow burn rates to work best in the 260 Remington with excellent candidates being H4350, H414, RL-19, W760, XMR-4350 and IMR-4350. Average maximum velocity for bullets weighing from 120 to 125 grains in the 24-inch barrel of my rifle is 2850 fps although a few loads do exceed 2900 fps.

When Should I Use a Magnum Rifle Primer?

The rifles I now use most for big-game hunting are a custom job in 257 STW and a Remington Model 700 in 270 Winchester. When handloading those cartridges I am never really sure whether I should use standard or magnum primers. Do you have a rule of thumb for this?

As a rule, I use magnum rifle primers for two applications. One is when handloading cartridges that burn heavy charges of slow-burning powders. The various magnums ranging in caliber and size from the 240 Weatherby on up through the 460 Weatherby are good examples, as would be the 257 STW. I also use magnum primers anytime I load powders with burn rates equal to or slower than H4831 in any cartridge. For example, H4831 is one of my favorite powders for the 270 Winchester and when loading it in the 270 I use a magnum primer. On the other hand, if I were to load a quicker burning powder such as H4895 in the 270 I would use a standard primer. I also switch to a magnum primer anytime I load slow-burning powders in hunting ammo that is likely to be subjected to temperatures lower than 30 degrees Fahrenheit and consider this especially important anytime ball powders are used.

Which Deer Bullet for M722 Remington?

I have a Remington Model 722 in 244 Remington and while it is extremely accurate with varmint bullets weighing up to 85 grains it shoots 100-gr. bullets made by Nosler, Speer, Sierra and Hornady all over the paper. This is quite frustrating since I want to use the rifle for hunting deer. Could its odd preference in bullets be caused by excessive bore erosion of the barrel?

It is doubtful that your rifle would be accurate with any bullet weight if its barrel were shot out. The reason for its preference for lightweight bullets is more likely due to the rifling twist of its barrel. Model 722 rifles in 244 Remington were built with two rifling twist rates. Earlier rifles have twist rates of 1:12 inches while those built during the last couple years of production have a 1:9 twist. Since your rifle is accurate only with the lighter (and therefore shorter) bullets, its barrel obviously has the slower rate of twist. While rifles with the quicker 1:9 twist will often handle bullets as long as the Speer 105-gr. roundnose, 85 grains is the heaviest pointed bullet that will usually stabilize in the 1:12 twist. This is exactly why Nosler offers a Partition bullet of that weight. I own a Remington Model 725 in 244 and its barrel has the 1:12 rifling twist rate. My favorite deer and pronghorn load for it consists of the 85-gr. Nosler Partition seated atop 49.0

grains of Reloder 19 for an average muzzle velocity of 3355 fps. The Barnes 85-gr. XBT should also work on deer and while my rifle doesn't shoot it accurately due to its greater length, it might be worth a try in your rifle.

Where Do I Find Modern Load Data for the 6.5 Swede?

I own a custom rifle with a Shilen barrel in 6.5x55mm Swedish. Load data in the reloading manuals I have were developed in Models 93 and 96 rifles. Where can I find loads developed for stronger rifles?

Industry standard chamber pressure for the 6.5 Swede is 45,000 CUP and some who have developed data for the cartridge stay within that limit while others publish stouter loads for modern rifles. The latest Barnes, Nosler and Speer manuals are examples of the latter. As a rule, anytime a source shows velocities approaching 3000 fps for 120-gr. bullets and 2800 fps for 140-gr. bullets, those loads are intended for modern rifles in good, serviceable condition.

Why Is Case Neck Turning Better than Reaming?

I recently read that case neck wall thinning is best done by outside turning rather than by reaming but no further explanation was given. Can you tell me why this is true?

Reaming the neck of a case will leave its wall thinner but it will not improve thickness uniformity. This is due to the fact that the reamer will follow the path of least resistance, and as it does so it removes the same amount of material from the thick side of the neck as from its thin side. This is not good since lack of uniformity in neck wall thickness can introduce axial misalignment between the bullet and the bore of the barrel. An outside-turning tool holds the neck wall of the case between a snug-fitting mandrel on the inside and a sharp cutter blade on the outside. In addition to thinning the neck of a case, it also improves the uniformity of neck wall thickness by removing more metal from the thick side than from the thin side. Two basic types of outside turners are available. The bench-type—as sold by RCBS, Forster and others—is usually favored by those who need to neck-turn large quantities of cases while most benchrest competitors opt for the handheld-type as available from Sinclair International.

Why Can't I Partially Neck-Size 6.5 STW Cases?

My favorite rifle is a custom job built on the Weatherby Mark V action and chambered for your 6.5 STW. I have used it to take most of the big-game animals available in North America (including a grand slam on sheep and several elk) as well as numerous African plains antelope as large as sable and greater kudu. I have Redding dies and I want to partially neck-size the cases by backing out the full-length resizer. When I try doing so the cases won't enter the chamber of my rifle. How can I partially neck-size cases with that die?

Attempting to partially neck-size cases with a full-length resizer seldom works satisfactorily because as a case is forced into the die, its body is squeezed down to a smaller diameter and this causes its head to shoulder dimension to lengthen, often to the point where the case will not enter the chamber of the rifle. A die made specifically for neck-sizing squeezes down the entire neck of a case without resizing its body. Your best bet is to acquire a neck-sizing die from your Redding dealer. I should mention that while neck-sizing cases is okay for practice and target loads, I believe the cases of all ammunition used for hunting big game should be full-length resized for trouble-free chambering in the field.

Best Bullets for 9.3x62mm Mauser?

I am stationed in Germany and have just bought a new Churchill rifle with a 22-inch barrel in 9.3x62mm Mauser. I have been reloading various cartridges for over 30 years but the 9.3x62mm is a new experience for me. What is your opinion of the cartridge? Which bullet should I choose for hunting elk and moose?

Several years ago I hunted moose in Sweden as a guest of Sako. I used a Sako rifle in 9.3x62mm Mauser and liked it so much I added it to my battery and there it remains. The 9.3mm Mauser is a grand old cartridge, one in the same class as the 338-06 and 35 Whelen. While I have not tried them, RWS makes several bullets of this caliber and they should be readily available to you there in Germany. As .366-inch bullets of American make go, the Nosler 286-gr. Partition, Barnes 250-gr. X and the Speer 270-gr. softnose are quite accurate in my rifle. I would not hesitate to use either on elk and moose. Barnes also offers two 286-gr. 9.3mm options and while the roundnose solid works great where maximum penetration is needed, the X-Bullet in this weight is a bit too long for the magazines of some rifles.

Favorite Load for 416 Weatherby Magnum?

Sometime back you picked the 416 Weatherby Magnum as your favorite bolt action rifle cartridge for potentially dangerous African game such as Cape buffalo. What is your favorite load for that cartridge? I would also be interested in knowing if you have used the load in extremely hot weather.

The 416 Weatherby Magnum load I have used most on African game consists of the Weatherby case, Federal 215 primer and the Barnes 350-gr. XFB seated atop 120.0 grains of Reloder 22. Average muzzle velocity in the 24-inch barrel of my Weatherby Mark V is around 2850 fps. With that load I have taken cape buffalo, lion, leopard, zebra and various antelope and its performance has been outstanding. In fact, the only buffalo I have ever instantly dropped stone dead in its tracks with one shot was with that load. I have used it at ambient temperatures as high as 120 degrees Fahrenheit with no pressure problems whatsoever.

Which Bullets for the 22 Jet?

I have a Harrington & Richardson Topper in 22 Remington Jet and want to start handloading for it. I found reloading data in an old manual but it was developed in a Smith & Wesson revolver. Where can I find rifle data for this cartridge? Even though the groove diameter of my barrel is .224 inch it has not stabilized any of the bullets I have tried to date. What do you recommend?

Reloading data developed by Hornady for the 22 Jet in the T/C Contender can be used in your rifle although its longer barrel will probably produce slightly higher velocities. Also, starting loads listed for the 22 Hornet in the Hornady manual and others can be used for the same purpose in the 22 Jet. You didn't mention the rifling twist rate of your barrel but considering the bullet instability problems you are experiencing it is probably 1:16 inches which was once standard for the 22 Hornet. Bullets weighing from 33 to 45 grains and made by Nosler, Speer, Sierra and Hornady for the 22 Hornet should stabilize in your barrel.

Bullet for 25-35 Winchester?

I have a Winchester Model 94 in 25-35 and also have a good supply of fired cases and factory ammo loaded with 117-gr. flatnose bullets. I want to handload the cases with a bullet of the same weight but cannot find one with a blunt nose which is needed for the tubular magazine of my rifle. Can you help?

You are in luck. The Hornady 117-gr. roundnose bullet is made specifically for use in the 25-35 Winchester and 25 Remington cartridges. It is designed to expand on game at relatively low impact velocities and its cannelure is exactly where it is supposed to be should you decided to crimp the mouths of cases when loading for your Winchester 94. Hornady's handloading manual has five loads for the bullet in the 25-35 with the two fastest rated at 2300 fps. The Hodgdon handloading manual also has data for the 117-gr. in the 25-35 Winchester.

Which Deer Loads for SKS Rifle?

I recently gave my 80-year-old father an SKS rifle to use when hunting eastern whitetail deer since he was being bothered by the recoil of his old rifle in 30-06 caliber. What ammunition should he use?

Your father's best bets in deer medicine for his new SKS rifle are the factory loads available from Remington, Federal and Winchester with 123 to 125-gr. softnose expanding bullets. Those loads will deliver around 1100 foot-pounds of energy at 100 yards, making them quite suitable for use on deer-size game at relatively close range.

Load Data for XP-100 in 260 Remington?

I just had my XP-100 rebarreled to 260 Remington and badly need load data for it. Where can I find it? Have you developed a favorite deer load for this cartridge in a short-barreled pistol?

My favorite load for this cartridge for a MOA Maximum single-shot pistol consists of the Barnes 120-gr. XLC X-Bullet pushed along by 52.0 grains of Reloder 19. This is a maximum load in my gun and it produces around 2700 fps in its 15-inch barrel.

Properly prepared reloads work fine in the Benelli R1 autoloader.

Reload Ammo for Benelli R1 Autoloader?

My Benelli R1 in 30-06 is quite accurate with factory loads but I would like to start reloading ammo for it. Are there any precautions I should be aware of before attempting to handload for an autoloading rifle?

For smooth and trouble-free chambering of loaded rounds in your Benelli, all cases should be full-length resized (in lieu of neck-sized only). When choosing powders, avoid those with extremely slow burn rates. Some good choices for your rifle are Reloder 15, IMR-4895, W748, AA-2520, BenchMark and Varget. These rules, by the way, apply not only to the Benelli R1, but to any gas-operated autoloader such the Remington Model 7400, Browning BAR and the Garand. For more on the subject of handloading for gas guns I refer you to the reloading manual published by Sierra Bullets.

In California varmint country with a Weatherby Super VarmintMaster rifle in 220 Swift.

X-Bullets Okay for Elk?

My father and I plan to hunt elk this fall with rifles in 280 Remington and 7mm Remington Magnum. We normally use standard bullets in the 139- to 145-gr. weight range for eastern whitetails but have decided to switch to premium bullets for elk. Do you consider the 140- and 150-gr. Barnes X-Bullets adequate for that purpose?

I consider the Barnes X-Bullets you're interested in more than adequate for elk, and I wouldn't hesitate to take on the biggest bull in the woods with either weight loaded in the 280 Remington or 7mm Remington Magnum. Fact of the matter is, a friend of mine recently took an outstanding bull with the 140-gr. X-Bullet loaded to 2700 fps in a Model 700 Mountain Rifle in 7mm-08 Remington.

Favorite 220 Swift Load?

While shooting my new Weatherby Super VarmintMaster in 220 Swift at the gun club I was absolutely amazed at how flat it shoots out to 400 yards and how quickly the bullet gets there. I was also greatly impressed by the fact that it consistently shot groups as small as two inches at 300 yards with Hornady Varmint Express ammo loaded with the 50-gr. V-Max bullet. How can I duplicate that load by handloading? What are some of the most accurate bullets you have tried in the 220 Swift?

Performance of the factory ammo you tried in your Weatherby rifle should be easy to duplicate by loading the Hornady 50-gr. V-Max bullet atop any of several different powders. I have probably burned more IMR-4064 in the 220 Swift than any other powder but it is not the only show in town as propellants such as Varget, Reloder 15, H380, XMR-4064, Norma 203 and V-N140 also do a fine job here. As you have already discovered, the Hornady 50-gr. V-Max is a great bullet for the 220 Swift, as are the 55-gr. V-Max, the 50- and 55-gr. Ballistic Tips from Nosler, the Sierra 55-gr. spitzer boattail.

Good 308 Load for Bear?

I plan to use my Remington Model Seven SS in 308 Winchester when hunting black bear during the upcoming spring season. I'll be hunting over bait as well as spotting and stalking. Do you think a handload that pushes the Nosler 165-gr. Partition from the 20-inch barrel of my carbine at 2677 feet per second is enough medicine for a big black bear?

Not long back I bagged a nice black bear in Alberta, Canada with a rifle much like yours but I used the Federal High Energy factory load with the 165-gr. Bear Claw bullet. Muzzle velocity of that load in my 20-inch barrel averaged 2718 feet per second which is not enough faster than your handload to make a meaningful difference in the field. Performance of the Federal load was excellent and I see no reason why your handload with the Nosler Partition bullet would not be equally effective on bear.

This T/C Encore rifle in 204 Ruger put four of five bullets inside an inch at 100 yards.

Favorite Load for 204 Ruger?

I have ordered a rifle in 204 Ruger and plan to handload ammunition for it. How accurate is this cartridge? Do you have any favorite loads for that cartridge?

As I write this, the 204 Ruger is too new for me to have come up with more than a few super-accurate loads for it but I will say that I am having to work mighty hard to beat the accuracy of the Hornady factory loads. The very first five-shot group I fired in a T/C Encore rifle with the 32-gr. factory load had four shots close to half an inch but while fighting the six-pound trigger pull of that rifle, I blew it by placing the fifth shot well away from its mates. The 204-caliber Savage Model 12 varmint rifle I am shooting is just as accurate with the Hornady Factory loads as the Encore and its excellent trigger makes it much easier to shoot accurately. The most accurate handloads I have tried in both rifles to date are the Hornady 32-gr. V-Max and 30.5 grains of BL-C(2), the Berger 35-gr. hollowpoint and 27.0 grains H335 and the Hornady 40-gr. V-Max and 26.5 grains H335. Average muzzle velocities in the 26-inch barrels of both rifles are 4017, 3879 and 3754 feet per second. Hornady cases and Federal 205M primers were used.

Where Do I Get 7mm STW Load Data?

I recently bought a Remington Model 700 in 7mm STW and the first three-shot group I fired with Remington's 140-gr. factory load measured 0.580 inch. My handload with the Remington case, H1000 powder, Federal's 215 primer and the Nosler 140-gr. Ballistic Tip clocked 3497 feet per second and averaged .495 inch. I want to buy a new reloading manual that contains the most load data on this cartridge. Which one is it?

With 63 different loads for bullets weighing 100, 120, 130, 140, 150, 160, 175 and 195 grains, the latest Barnes manual has more data on the 7mm STW than any other. The Nosler manual is in second place with 52 loads and Sierra ranks third with 40 loads. If your local dealer doesn't have those manuals he can order them from his distributor.

Deer Loads for M1 Garand?

I intend to buy an M1 Garand, outfit it with a scope, and use it for hunting deer. Should I follow any special procedures when handloading for that rifle?

When preparing cartridge cases for your M1 Garand it is important that they be full-length resized so they will enter the chamber freely. If the chamber of the rifle you buy was reamed on the minimum side of the dimensional tolerance range, you might have to use a small base-style resizing die, available through any RCBS dealer. Also keep in mind that the prolonged use of extremely slow burning powders in any gas-operated autoloading rifle can damage it due to excessive gas port pressure. Stick with powders of medium-fast burn rate such as H4895, A-2230, A-2460, IMR-4895, IMR-3031, IMR-4064, V-N140 and V-N150 and you'll be in good shape.

How Accurate Are Fail Safe Bullets?

I own a Remington Model 700 Synthetic Varmint in 308 Winchester that averages .50- to .75-inch groups with Nosler Ballistic Tip bullets and Winchester W748 powder. I would like to try the Winchester Fail Safe bullet in my rifle but am wondering if it will be as accurate as the Ballistic Tip.

As a rule, premium-grade bullets of controlled-expansion design are not as accurate as bullets of more conventional design. This is due to the fact that the more complicated the construction of a bullet becomes, the more difficult it is to maintain a high level of concentricity in its component parts. While bullets such as the Winchester Fail Safe and Nosler Partition are not likely to be as accurate as the Ballistic Tip, they are usually plenty accurate in most rifles for big-game hunting.

Short 22 Hornet Case Life?

I recently purchased a Sako Model 78 in 22 Hornet and found its accuracy to be quite poor with .224-inch bullets. After slugging its bore and coming up with a groove diameter of .2225-inch, I switched to the Sierra .223-inch bullet seated atop 10.0 grains of W296 and the rifle immediately started shooting groups of less than one inch. After getting the Model 78 to shoot so accurately I was dismayed to discover that cases begin to separate after only two firings. What is the problem?

The wall of the 22 Hornet case is quite thin and if its shoulder is pushed back excessively during the resizing operation it will separate in one a few firings. It is important to set the die to barely bump the shoulder of a case enough to allow the bolt of the rifle to lock up smoothly on a chambered cartridge. Another possibility has to do with rifle design. The bolt of the Sako Model 78 has a tendency to compress more than the bolt of a rifle with locking lugs located at its front. This holds especially true when maximum or near-maximum loads are used. Bolt compression in your rifle may be allowing the case to stretch excessively and as a result you are experiencing short case life. Backing off on the powder charge should allow you to get more firings per case.

Which Loads for Ruger 96/44?

I recently bought a Ruger Model 96/44 in 44 Magnum and plan to hunt whitetail deer with it. I'm hoping it will be accurate with Federal ammo loaded with hard cast bullets or Winchester ammo with Nosler's new Partition bullet. Which is the best choice for deer?

Between the two I would choose the Winchester load because it is more likely to expand on deer-size game. While some hunters have successfully used extremely hard cast bullets on heavier game where extremely deep penetration is needed, they are a poor choice for smaller game. This is due to the fact that the bullet is likely to drill an extremely narrow wound channel through the animal, resulting in insufficient tissue damage for a quick kill.

Make My Own Bullets?

Can you tell me where to buy the equipment and supplies required for making jacketed rifle bullets?

The largest manufacturer of jacketed bullet manufacturing equipment in the U.S. is Corbin, Inc. of White City, Oregon. In addition to offering affordable presses and dies for making jacketed rifle and handgun bullets in calibers ranging from .22 to .50, Corbin also has all necessary supplies such as lead wire and bullet jackets. Detailed instruction manuals on the art of bullet making are also available.

Eliminating 7mm TCU Misfires?

I have a T/C Contender in 7mm TCU and am constantly plagued by misfires. On the typical misfire, the primer is only lightly indented by the firing pin. I've tried the same barrel on two different Contender receivers with no change in the results. Any ideas on what the problem is?

My guess is you're setting the shoulders of cases back too far when full-length resizing them. Try backing out the sizing die until it lightly bumps the shoulder of a case back only enough too allow the gun to fully lock up when it is chambered.

Why Powder Ignition Problems in My 308?

I recently experienced a mysterious problem with my rifle in 308 Winchester. I was using Remington BR basic cases primed with the CCI No. 450 magnum primer and loaded with IMR-3031 behind the Sierra 168-gr. MatchKing bullet. When shooting my rifle at a temperature of about 30 degrees Fahrenheit, I experienced several hangfires and several rounds did not fire at all. Back home, I pulled the bullets from the rounds that misfired and partially burned powder came out of the cases; the remainder of each powder charge was a dirty yellow in color. Last year, during midsummer weather, I experienced only two hangfires and not a single misfire with that same load. What's going on?

To begin, the Remington BR basic case was not designed to be used in its original, full-length form. Remington's intent was to supply a 308 Winchester case with a small primer pocket and thin walls so the handloader could reform it to the much shorter 22 BR, 6mm BR and 7mm BR cartridges. When this is done, powder capacity is reduced to within the normal ignition range of Small Rifle primers. When the BR case is used full-length, the reliable ignition of its larger powder charge by a Small Rifle primer is borderline at best, even at relatively high ambient temperatures. Add to this the fact that as ambient temperature decreases, powder becomes increasingly more difficult to ignite, and it is easy to understand why you experienced hangfires and misfires when shooting at a temperature of 30 degrees.

A single-base propellant, IMR-3031 is composed primarily of nitrocellulose (which is white in color) and coated with a deterrent to control its burn rate. The powder in your misfires is yellow because the primer produced enough heat to burn away its deterrent coating, even though it was unable to ignite the charge. I have worked with a rifle chambered for a wildcat called the 22 CHeetah and it is on the full-length Remington BR case. When loaded with some powders it works fine at summer temperatures, but I did experience misfire problems with it on cold days.

Load Data for 338-06?

I am having no luck finding load data for the 338-06 wildcat. Have you worked with this cartridge?

You obviously have not heard that the 338-06 is no longer a wildcat. Weatherby introduced the chambering in its Mark V rifle in 2001 and is also offering factory ammunition. I have owned a custom rifle built on the '98 Mauser action in this caliber for many years but it is nowhere near as accurate as the Mark V Lightweight I recently added to my hunting battery. Most handloading manuals now have data for the 338-06. My favorite bullet for all-around use of this cartridge on everything from deer to elk and moose is the Nosler 210-gr. Partition. The classic powder is IMR-4320 and 52.0 grains of that propellant behind the Nosler bullet is good for a muzzle velocity of 2600 to 2700 fps in most 24-inch barrels. Other good options, also with the Nosler 210-gr. bullet, are 53.0 grains of Reloder 15, 58.0 grains of H380, and 49.0 grains of AA-2520. All of those loads are maximum and the powder charges should be reduced by 10 percent for starting loads in other rifles.

To Crimp or Not to Crimp?

According to one of my handloading manuals, a bullet should be crimped tightly into the case of a hard-kicking cartridge such as the 375 H&H Magnum to prevent it from being seated more deeply during recoil. My rifle in 338 Winchester Magnum kicks just as hard as my rifle in 375 H&H Magnum, and yet the 250-gr. bullets available from Speer and Sierra do not have cannelures for crimping. Same goes for several 375 caliber bullets, including the 300-gr. Sierra. Should bullets be crimped into the cases of those cartridges? If the answer is yes, why do some of the available bullets not have crimping cannelures. If the answer is no, why do some of the bullets come with cannelures?

Cannelures are applied to factory-made rifles bullets for two primary purposes. When loading for rifles with tubular magazines, especially those chambered for hard-kicking cartridges such as the 45-70 and 450 Marlin, crimping the mouth of the case into the cannelure of a bullet prevents the bullet from being driven deeper into the cases of cartridges loaded nose-to-head in the magazine when the rifle is fired. A heavy crimp applied to the bullet prevents the same thing from happening as a cartridge makes its rather violent journey from the magazine to the chamber of an autoloading rifle such as the Ruger Mini-14 and Colt AR15. Some bullet makers also feel that the application of a cannelure to a finished bullet helps the jacket to retain its lead core during expansion.

When handloading for various bolt-action rifles in 338 and 375 Magnum (or any other caliber for that matter), I have never found it necessary to crimp case necks so long at neck tension on the bullet is sufficient to resist movement of the bullet during recoil. If the expander plugs in your full-length resizing dies are at least .003 inch smaller than bullet diameter, you should have no problem with bullets moving in their cases during recoil.

Nosler Partition for Moose and Bear?

I plan to hunt moose and brown bear in Alaska and will use a Remington Model 760 in 30-06. It has been my favorite big-game rifle for several decades. What is your opinion of the Nosler 200-gr. Partition loaded in the 30-06 as a moose and bear load?

The Nosler 200-gr. Partition is an excellent choice for the 30-06 when it is used for hunting heavy game. It packs a lot of punch and holds together during expansion for deep penetration, which is what you will need on moose and brown bear. As for powders, try H4350, Reloder 19, H414, W760 and IMR-4350 for top velocities with that bullet in the 30-06.

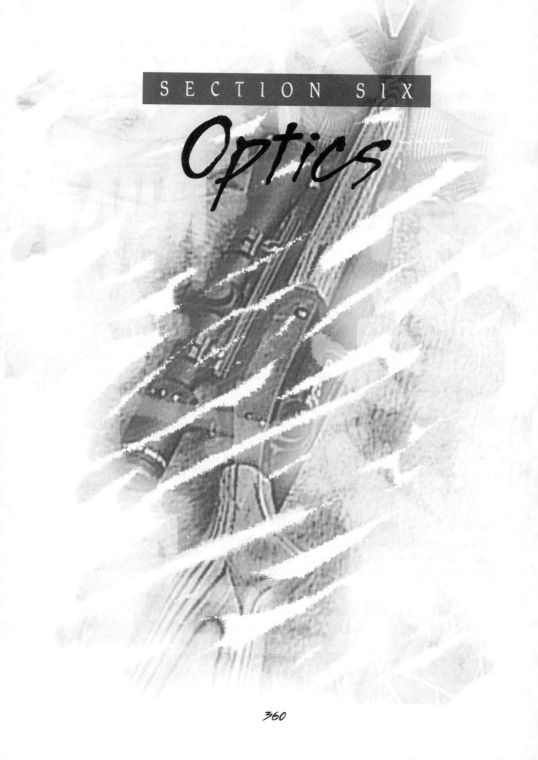

SECTION SIX

Optics

How Do I Find the Exact Mechanical Center of My Scope?

The rifle in 7mm Remington Magnum I have carried on several hunts wears a 3-12X Burris Black Diamond and it is absolutely the best and brightest scope I have ever used. I just had a custom rifle in 6.5 STW built and want to use that scope on it. How do I locate the mechanical dead center of its windage and elevation adjustments?

The mechanical center of any modern rifle scope is easily found by rotating the two adjustment knobs in one direction until they come to a stop. Then while counting the clicks or graduations, rotate them in the opposite until they stop. Divide the number of clicks you came up with by two, turn the knobs back in the opposite direction by that number of clicks and the windage and elevation adjustments are at their mechanical centers. An even quicker method and almost as accurate is to count the number of full turns the knobs make as you turn them from one stop the other and divide by two. In other words if a knob has to be turned 5-1/2 rotations in order to take it from one stop to the other, turning it 2-3/4 rotations from either of the stops will put the adjustment at its mechanical center. I agree, the Burris Black Diamond is an excellent scope. I recently tried the new 6-24X version on a varmint rifle and its optical quality took my breath away.

Who Can Install Dot Reticles in Rifle Scopes?

I recently bought an old Lyman varmint scope and the vertical crosshair of its reticle has a series of dots that are used for hold-over at long ranges. According to the previous owner of the scope the dots were installed by a fellow by the name of Steen (or perhaps Stein). Do you know if that fellow is still in business and if so, where he is located? I'd like to have dot reticles installed in a couple more of my scopes.

I don't believe T.W. Stein of Butte, Montana is still in business but T.K. Lee of Birmingham, Alabama and Premier Reticles of Winchester, Virginia can install dot reticles in scopes. You might also be interested in knowing that companies such as Burris, Kahles and Leupold offer a mil-dot reticle consisting of dots spaced along the horizontal and vertical crosshairs. The dots on the lower quadrant of the vertical crosshair are used for holdover at various distances while those on the horizontal crosshair are used for holding into the wind. Those companies and others also offer other types of reticles designed for holdover only. A good example is the Ballistic Mil-Dot from Burris with its short lines spaced down the lower quadrant of the vertical crosshair.

How Do I Prevent Weaver Rings from Scratching Scope Tube?

I recently bought six pairs of Weaver Tip-Off scope mounting rings from the bargain table of a gunshop only to discover that they scratch the tube of a scope when they are installed. Are the rings defective or am I installing them wrong? What is your opinion of the Weaver mount?

What Scope for Open-Country Hunting?

I recently booked a hunt for caribou in the Northwest Territories of Canada and the outfitter tells me to be prepared for shots at long range in open country. I plan to use a Remington Model 700 in 7mm SAUM but have not decided on the scope it will wear. What do you recommend?

You can get by with any good scope with a magnification of 6X or 7X on your hunt, but for long-range shooting in open country I prefer a variable with no less than 9X or 10X at the upper end of its magnification range. Just as important as the magnification of a scope to be used in caribou country is its resistance to fogging up internally when exposed to rainy day hunts. Top-quality scopes from companies such as Kahles, Nikon, Bushnell, Burris, Zeiss, Leupold and Pentax are built to survive under the worst conditions Mother Nature can dish out. Nowhere is the old saying "you get what you pay for" more true than in the world of telescopic sights.

A variable-power scope with 9X or 10X at the upper end of its magnification range is not a bad choice for hunting any big game in open country.

The Zeiss 10X binocular I used on a hunt for Dall sheep in Alaska was just about perfect for the job.

What Is the Best Binocular Magnification for Hunting?

I keep hearing conflicting opinions on which magnification I need in a full-size binocular for hunting. What do you use?

Many years ago I started out with a 7x35 binocular and then switched to 8x42 when Bausch & Lomb introduced the new Elite in that magnification. For several decades I carried that binocular on hunts all over the world and then discovered that various brands and models of binoculars of higher magnification had become as light as, and in some cases actually lighter in weight than, my faithful old Elite which weighs 29 ounces. Three binoculars I have since taken on hunts and liked a lot are the Kahles 10x42 (24 ounces), Bushnell Legend 10x42 (29 ounces) and a Zeiss 10x40 (27 ounces). I have also used the Bushnell Legend 12x50 on several hunts and despite its high magnification, it weighs only 33 ounces. I now use nothing less than 10X magnification on my hunts. While I have no problem using a 12X binocular in the field, some hunters experience difficulty in holding it steady so you should try the various magnifications before making a purchase. And do not simply try the various magnifications inside a store. Any good dealer who considers customer satisfaction a high priority will allow you to take several models outside the shop, perhaps in his parking lot where you will be able to make an accurate comparison.

And by the way, I want to thank you for correctly saying "binocular" rather than incorrectly saying "a pair of binoculars" as I so often see written and hear spoken. Each and every time I include the word "binocular" in an article I write for a certain hunting magazine, the editor never fails to change it to "glasses," "binoculars" or "pair of binoculars." Each time that happens I visualize some poor hunter struggling to the top of a mountain with two binoculars hanging around his neck.

Eye relief is the distance from the eye to the ocular lens of the scope when the scope is positioned so its entire field of view is seen.

What Is Eye Relief in a Scope?

I keep reading about eye relief in a scope but still do not exactly understand the meaning of the term. Please explain it to me.

Eye relief is the distance from the pupil of the eye to the ocular lens of a scope when the scope is positioned far enough away from the eye for the entire field of view to be seen. The amount of eye relief in a scope will vary from brand to brand and from model to model. The amount required depends on the level of recoil of a particular rifle. Varmint shooters and benchrest competitors who shoot heavy rifles chambered for light-recoil cartridges such as the 223 Remington and 6mm PPC can get by with as little as two inches of eye relief while hunters who shoot relatively light rifles chambered for big-game cartridges need all the eye relief they can get. I consider 3-1/2 inches the minimum for rifles chambered for cartridges up through the 338 Winchester Magnum and 340 Weatherby Magnum. For rifles chambered for even more powerful cartridges such as the 416 Remington Magnum, 458 Winchester Magnum and 460 Weatherby Magnum, four to five inches of eye relief is none too much in a scope.

The rings you bought are the old style; those made by Weaver today are sprung a bit more open at the factory and that allows them to slip easily over the tube of a scope without scratching its finish. Tightly wrapping a thin layer of paper around the scope tube prior to installing the top-half of the old-style ring will prevent damage to the finish. After the ring is on the scope, the paper is removed before it is attached to the bottom-half and tightened. I have always liked the Weaver mount for three primary reasons. One is its ability to return the scope to zero when it is removed and then reinstalled with as much precision as quick-detachable mounts costing considerably more. I rate the Weaver as one of the better designs because both the front and rear rings resist recoil. Also, the extremely large contact surface area between the rings and the scope tube do a better job of preventing scope slippage during recoil than some of the other mounting systems with more narrow rings.

What Can I Do about Reticle Runout?

I recently bought a used 4-12X scope and had planned to use it on my favorite long-range deer rifle, a Model 70 in 270 Winchester. After mounting the scope on the rifle, I checked it out with a collimator and found that reticle runout is considerable. Later when shooting the rifle at 100 yards I discovered group point of impact to be more than an inch higher than point of aim with the scope set on 12X than when it is on 4X. Since the manufacturer of the scope is no longer in business I can't send it back to the factory so my question is—what can I do to fix the problem?

Reticle runout is something scope manufacturers lose sleep over and writers like to write about but so long as it is no worse than in your scope, it amounts to less than a hill of beans on a scope used for targets as large as the vital areas of various big game animals. The solution is quite simple and won't cost you a dime. When using a scope with this affliction, the error between point of aim and point of bullet impact becomes greater as the range is increased and by the same token it becomes less as range is decreased. Since you should be using the scope on 12X only when shooting at long range, carefully zero the rifle while it is set at that magnification. Then when using the scope on a lower power for short-range shooting the aiming error shrinks to insignificance due to the closer proximity of the target.

What Is Best Reticle for Varmint Scope?

I recently ordered a Remington 40X-KS in 220 Swift from the Remington custom shop and plan to outfit it with a variable-power scope with 20X or higher magnification at its top end. What reticle do you recommend in that type of scope for long-range varminting?

I prefer the mil-dot reticle consisting of evenly spaced dots on both crosshairs. Various dots on the vertical crosshair are used for aiming at targets at various distances while those on the horizontal crosshair are used for holding into the wind. When used in conjunction with an extremely accurate rifle, a good laser rangefinder and a partner who is good at calling shots, a powerful scope with the mil-dot reticle can be used to make some incredibly long shots on varmints under windy conditions.

How Can a Right-Hander Shoot with His Left Eye?

A friend wants to get back into rifle shooting but he has a serious obstacle to overcome before doing so. A right-handed shooter, he lost his right eye in an accident. Can you recommend a rifle or scope modification that would enable him to aim with his left eye while shooting right-handed?

It is possible to build a rifle stock with enough bend or curve in its butt section to enable your right-handed friend to shoot with his left eye but it can be a very expensive alternative. An offset scope mount will accomplish the same thing and since anyone who knows how to weld can build one, it is not very expensive. This type of mount is made by joining the inner edges of two one-piece scope mounting bases with a steel extension plate. The plate should be of the same thickness as the two bases and the same length as their midsections. One-piece, dovetail-style steel bases of the type required are available from Burris, Leupold, Conetrol and Redfield. After the three parts are welded together one base is fastened to the receiver of the rifle in a normal fashion and the other base (which accepts the scope) is extended out to the left by the extension. The amount of offset required will differ a bit from shooter to shooter but somewhere around three inches between the centerlines of the two bases should work for most.

Why Not Shoot Left-Handed?

You recently described how to build an offset scope mount for use by a right-handed shooter who had lost the use of his right eye. For me, a more satisfactory alternative was learning how to shoot left handed. It is not as difficult as many seem to think. The biggest obstacle to overcome is learning how to mount the gun properly but once that was taken care of the rest came easy for me, including sighting with my left eye and pulling the trigger with my left hand. With practice I have learned to shoot just as well as a southpaw as I did right-handed.

While reading the letters I received in response to my special scope mount recommendation I am surprised by several things. One is the number of right-handed shooters out there who for various physical reasons can no longer shoot right-handed. Secondly are the number of those shooters who chose to learn to shoot left-handed rather than relying on mechanical aids such as custom offset scope mounts and offset stocks. Thirdly are the number of shooters like you who were kind enough to write and let me know how they have managed to overcome a problem that I'm sure has caused no small number of other shooters to hang up their rifles and shotguns. Perhaps your letter will inspire others to once again become active on the range and in the field.

Another Solution to Loss of Shooting Eye

One of your recent columns carried suggestions on how to overcome the loss of one's shooting eye. A right-handed shooter, I lost the sight of my right eye at age 60 and was unable to master shooting from the left shoulder. My solution was to use extra-high scope mounts on my Sako, Remington, Walther and CZ rifles

Best Variable Scope for Dangerous Game?

I just purchased a Sako Model 75 Deluxe in 375 H&H Magnum. I will be heading to Australia to hunt Asiatic buffalo and will use that rifle. I am now shopping for variable-power scope for it. What do you recommend?

You will need plenty of field of view and eye relief in a scope for the 375, and since most guides and professional hunters discourage their clients from taking shots much beyond 100 yards on potentially dangerous game such as Asiatic buffalo, you will not need a lot of magnification. On a recent hunt for buffalo in Australia with Bob Penfold, I used a Remington Model 700 in 416 Magnum. My rifle wore a 1.75-5X Signature Safari scope with 70-foot field of view at 100 yards and it proved to be perfect for the job. On a number of safaris to Africa for cape buffalo, lion and other game I have used a variety of rifles in calibers ranging from 375 to 458 and all wore variable scopes with anywhere from 1X to 2X at the lower end of their magnification range. In addition to the 1.75-5X Burris Signature Safari, others I highly recommend are the 1-4X from Kahles, the Leupold 1.5-5X Vari-X-III, and the Bushnell 1.5-6X Elite 4200.

The Burris 1.75-5X Signature Safari scope I used on my 416 Remington Magnum when hunting buffalo in Australia proved to be exactly what I needed.

For hunting in open country, nothing less than 30X magnification will do for a variable-power spotting scope and 40X is even better.

Which Spotting Scope Should I Buy?

I am in the market for a spotting scope to use on hunts for mountain sheep, goat, pronghorn antelope an other open-country game. What should I buy?

Since you will be carrying a spotting scope into the high country, the one you choose should first and foremost be light. A top-quality spotter weighing 20 to 30 ounces will give you all the optical quality you need and yet it is not too heavy to carry up a mountain in a backpack. For sheep hunting, nothing less than 30X will do and 40X is even better when conditions allow the use of that much magnification. Companies such as Bushnell, Burris and Leupold offer variable-power spotting scopes with 40X at the top end of their magnification range. It is also extremely important that you buy a good tripod that is durable, compact and lightweight. The one I use on my mountain hunts is available from Leupold and called, aptly enough, the Compact Tripod.

A small dot in an electronic sight is best for bullseye shooting.

along with relatively low scope magnifications that produce maximum exit pupil diameter. The additional scope height allows me to shoot a rifle from the right shoulder by canting my cheek across the comb of the stock far enough to allow me to peer into the scope with my left eye. It works for me, not only on shots at stationary targets but on moving game as well.

Thanks very much for offering a suggestion which I am sure will be of interest to other readers who have suffered the loss of their shooting eye. Since writing that column I have received so many letters like yours that I may compile all of them into one report in a future issue.

What Size Dot for Precision Shooting?

I am a long-time rifle and pistol shooter and hunt a lot as well. I compete in USPSA/IPSC matches in Limited class (open sights only) and am somewhat familiar with the electronic sights other competitors use on their Unlimited class race guns. I want to try that type of sight for bullseye shooting but the dots in the sights my fellow USPSA competitors are using seem too large. What size dot should I use? Also, what type of sight and dot size would work well on a 22-caliber small-game rifle and on a SKS rifle in 7.62x39mm Russian?

I have used electronic sights a great deal and personally prefer a 10- or 12-minute dot for USPSA/IPSC competition and when hunting big game with a magnum revolver. A four-minute dot is about right for precision bullseye shooting, for small-game hunting and for hunting turkey with a shotgun. Most brands of electronic sights are available with those or similar options in dot size. Although they are larger, weigh a bit more and are slightly more expensive, sights with variable-size dots are the most versatile for obvious reasons.

What Scope for 416 Weatherby Magnum?

I just bought a Weatherby Mark V in 416 Magnum for an upcoming hunt in Zambia. I'll reserve the 416 for Cape buffalo and use a Mark V in 7mm STW for everything else. My 7mm STW wears a Kahles 3-9X scope but I have yet to buy a scope for the 416 Magnum. You have mentioned taking a variety of African game such as buffalo, lion and leopard with your 416 caliber Mark V and I'd like to know what scope it wears. Also, what is your opinion of the scope I have chosen for my rifle in 7mm STW?

The 416 Weatherby Magnum churns up a bit of recoil so you had best put durability and sufficient eye relief at the top of your priority list when shopping for a scope. Four inches should be the minimum eye relief in a scope for this type of rifle and even more is better. Just as important in a scope to be used on a dangerous game rifle is an extremely wide field of view and I will have to make 60 feet the minimum here. My Weatherby Mark V in 416 Magnum wears a Leupold 1.5-5X Vari-X-III; it has five inches of eye relief and a 100-yard field of view of 66 feet. The Burris 1.5-6X Signature Safari scope on my Remington Model 700 in 416 Remington Magnum has four inches of eye relief and a 70-foot field of view. The

WARNIN
for use
ear pro
muzzle

AVER

CONETROL
SEGUIN TEXAS

WB022793

Lightest All-Steel Scope Mount?

I plan to buy a Tikka T3 Lite Stainless in 270 WSM and want to keep its weight as light as possible by equipping it with a Leupold 3-9X Compact scope which weighs only 11 ounces. I also want to use a lightweight mount and prefer steel over aluminum. What is the lightest all-steel scope mount available?

At 3.75 ounces, the two-piece Conetrol is the lightest all-steel mount I have found. Several of my rifles wear mounts from that company and I find them to be quite durable and totally trouble free. The Conetrol is also the most handsome scope mount available.

The two-piece Conetrol is the lightest all-steel scope mount available and the most handsome.

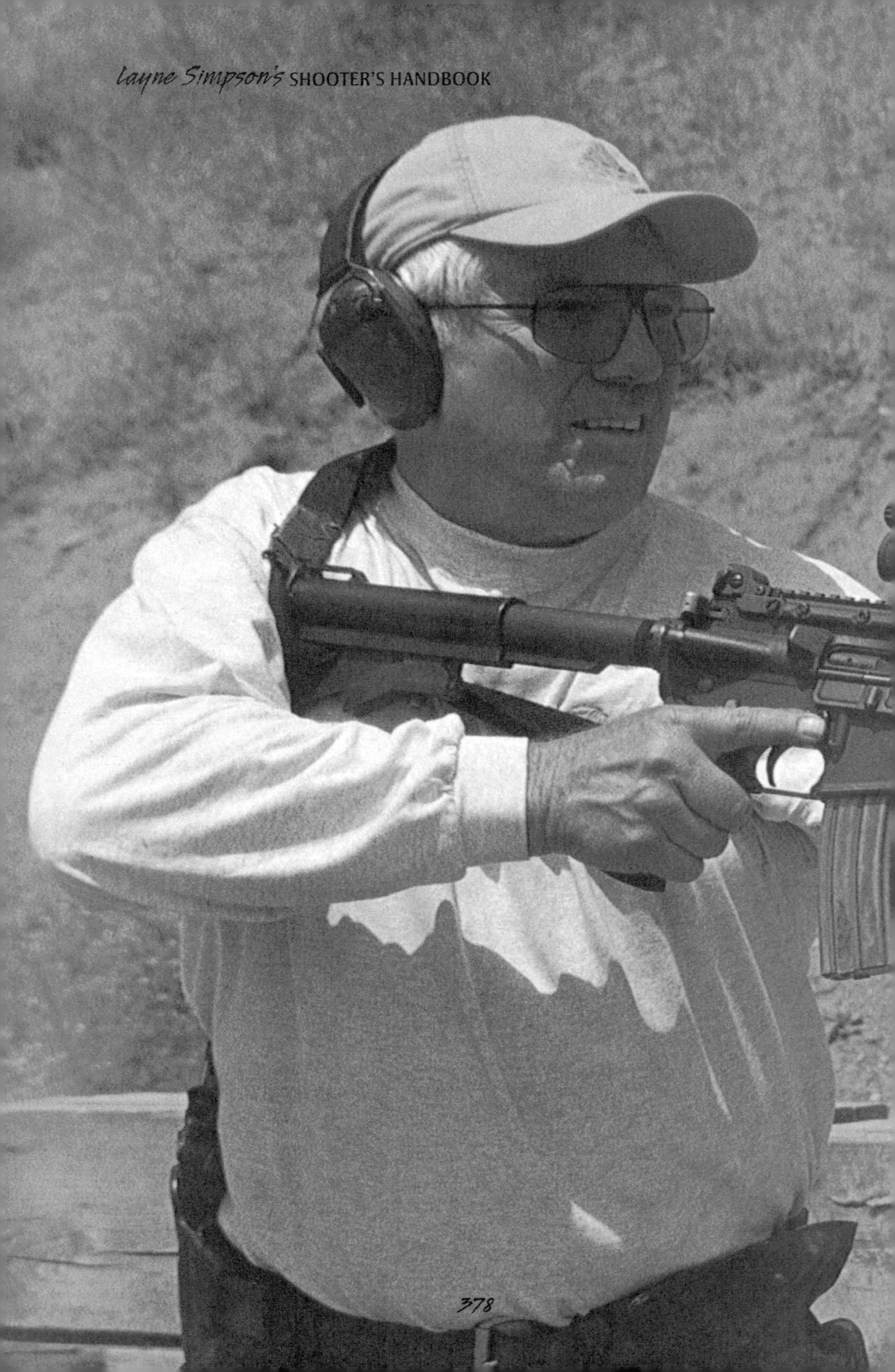

Which Type of Sight Is Quickest?

A friend of mine says open sights allow the shooter to get on target more quickly than any other type of sight. I say a low-magnification scope is quicker. Tell me my friend is wrong.

I hate to be the bearer of bad news but you both are wrong. The nonmagnifying electronic sight is the quickest of them all and those who shoot high-capacity handguns in USPSA unlimited-class competition prove it every weekend. It is also the fastest type of sight to use on rifles and shotguns. This is due to the fact that eye alignment is much quicker with the electronic sight than with the relatively small exit pupil of a telescopic sight. Open sights are slower because the eye is required to align the front and rear sights and then align the front sight with the target. With an electronic sight, you simply place the red dot where you want the bullet to go and pull the trigger.

Neither open sights nor telescopic sights are as quick to get on target as an electronic sight such as the one I am using here.

Kahles scope you have installed on your rifle in 7mm STW is an excellent choice for that application. I have used scopes from that manufacturer on several hunts and am quite impressed with their durability and optical performance.

Problems with Side-Mounted Scope?

My eyes are not what they once were so I want to install a scope on my M1 Garand. Since that rifle requires the use of a side-mounted scope my friends say I will find it difficult to sight in. They also say that if I am lucky enough to get the rifle zeroed at close range it will place its bullets off to the side of a target at longer range. Are they correct?

Even though the type of scope mount you describe attaches to the side of the receiver of a rifle, those I have used actually position the scope over or at least close to the center of the receiver. For this reason that type of mount works just as well as one that attaches to the top of the receiver. You did not mention which brand of mount you intend to use but even if the one you have decided on does not hold the scope in precise alignment with the axis of the barrel, your line of sight will still be close enough to the path of the bullet for long range shooting when the scope is properly zeroed.

Mount for Forward-Positioned Scope?

I would like to attach a long eye relief scope out on the barrel of my rifle. Does anyone offer that type of scope mount for the Remington Model 700?

Burris offers a one-piece scope mounting base designed to be mounted out on the barrel but attaching it takes a bit of work and requires tools most gun owners might not have on hand. Its bottom surface is contoured just short of a close fit with the Model 700 barrel and final fitting is required. The base is shaped that way at the factory so a gunsmith can final-fit it to barrels with various contours. And while the base utilizes the two rear sight holes on the Model 700 barrel for attachment it does require the drilling and tapping of an additional hole in the barrel.

Solving Scope Mount Problem?

I am having a problem mounting a Bushnell 4-16X scope on a Ruger No. 1V varmint rifle. When attaching the scope with the Ruger rings (which came with the rifle), interference between a ring and the scope prevents me from positioning it far enough to the rear. In other words, I must lean forward in an uncomfortable position in order to see into the scope. Can you suggest an easy fix?

I called a friend at Burris Scopes about your problem and believe he has come up with a solution. You didn't mention whether the interference is between one of the Ruger rings and the objective housing or windage and elevation turret housing of the scope but regardless of which be the case, Burris makes a reversible extension ring for the Ruger rifle that should solve your problem. The catalog number is 420549 and if your local gunshop owner doesn't have it in stock, he can order it from Burris Scopes.

In Which Direction Do I Shim a Scope?

My grandfather recently gave me my first 22 rimfire squirrel rifle. I have adjusted the scope as far as it will go and my rifle is still shooting too low. My grandfather once read that the one-piece base of a scope mount could be shimmed higher to compensate but he has not figured out in what direction to move which end of a scope in order to shift my aim in the direction I need. Please explain.

Simply remember that the rule for shifting the point of aim in relation to point of bullet impact by physically moving one end of the scope is the same as when adjusting the front and rear open sights on a rifle; move the rear end of the scope in the same direction in which you want point of bullet impact to change in relation to point of aim and move its front end in the opposite direction. Since your problem is with point of bullet impact being too far below point of aim, you would elevate the rear end of the scope by shimming up that end of the scope mount base. Conversely, if point of impact were too far above point of aim you would shim up the front end of the scope mount base.

Where Do I Find a Mount for a BALvar 8 Scope?

I have a Bausch & Lomb 2.5-8X scope. It has the standard one-inch tube, but oddly enough, it has no windage and elevation adjustment knobs. When was it made? How do I go about mounting it on my Remington Model 700?

Your scope is one of a series built by Bausch & Lomb during the 1960s. In addition the BALvar 8 like you have, there was a BALvar 4 (2.5-4X), BALvar 24 (6-24X), and three fixed-power scopes: BALtur (2.5X), BALfor (4X), and BALsix (6X). Your scope has no provisions for windage and elevation adjustment because the adjustments were built into special mounts designed for them. The old Weaver V8 was the same type of scope. You need mounting rings once made by Bausch & Lomb and a base made in those days by that company as well as Kuharsky Brothers of Erie, Pennsylvania. I don't believe Kuharsky is still in business, and B&L has not offered that type of mount in many years. The remaining inventory of windage- and elevation-adjustable mounts made for those scopes by Bausch & Lomb was purchased by H.E. Gibbs, 23 Dartmouth St., Amsterdam, NY 12010. If that doesn't work, you might find the mount you need for your scope and rifle in a couple of publications called *Shotgun News* and *Gun List*.

INDEX OF
Manufacturers

Accurate Powders
McEwen, TN
800-416-30-06

Aimtech Scope Mounts
Thomasville, GA
912-226-4313

Alliant Powder Company
Arlington, NJ
800-276-9337

Americase
Waxahachie, TX
800-880-3629

A-Square
Bedford, KY
502-255-7456

AyA Shotguns
Armes de Chasse
919-426-2245

Barnes Bullets
American Fork, UT
800-574-9200

Battenfield Technologies
Columbia, MO
877-509-9160

Benelli USA
Accokeek, MD
301-283-6981

Beretta USA
Accokeek, MD
301-283-2191

Bismuth Cartridge Co.
Dallas, TX
214-521-5880

Boyt Harness Co.
Osceola, IA
800-550-2698

Briley Manufacturing
Houston, TX
800-331-5718

Brownells, Inc.
Montezuma, IA
515-623-5401

Browning Arms Co.
Morgan, UT
801-876-2711

Burris Co.
Greeley, CO
970-356-1670

Bushnell Sports Optics
Overland Park, KS
800-423-3537

Cabela's
Sidney, NE
800-237-4444

Clark Custom Guns
Princeton, LA
318-949-9884

Competition Electronics
Rockford, IL
815-874-8001

Conetrol Scope Mounts
Seguin, TX
210-379-3030

Connecticut Shotgun Mfg.
Co.
New Britain, CT
860-225-6581

Cooper Arms
Stevensville, MT
406-777-5534

Corbin Mfg.
White City, OR
541-826-5211

Federal Cartridge Co.
Anoka, MN
612-323-2300

Franchi USA
Accokeek, MD
301-283-6981

Hodgdon Powder
Company
Shawnee Mission, KS
913-362-9455

Hornady Mfg. Inc.
Grand Island, NE
800-338-3220

Hunter's Specialties
Cedar Rapids, IA 52402
800-728-0321

IMR Powder Company
Plattsburg, NY
518-563-2253

Irish Setter Boots
Red Wing, MN 55066
888-472-0087
www.irishsetterboots.com

JGS Precision Tool
Coos Bay, OR
541-267-4331

Kahles North America
Cranston, RI
401-946-2220

Kimber Of America, Inc.
Yonkers, NY
800-880-2418

Lee Precision
Hartford, WI
414-673-3075

Lee, T.K.
Birmingham, AL
205-913-5222

Les Bauer Custom
Hillsdale, IL
309-658-2715

Leupold & Stevens, Inc.
Beaverton, OR
503-646-9171

Lyman Products
Middleton, CT
800-225-9626

Magnum Performance
Ballistics
(Poly-Wad)
Macon, GA 31209
800-998-0669

Marlin Firearms Co.
North Haven, CT
203-239-5621

MEC, Inc.
Mayville, WI
414-387-4500

M.O.A. Corporation
Eaton, OH
937-456-3669

McGowen Barrels
St. Anne, IL
815-937-9816

McMillan Fiberglass
Stocks
Phoenix, AZ
602-582-9635

Midway USA
Columbia, MO
800-243-3220

Muzzleload Magnum
Products (MMP)
Harrison, AR
870-751-5019

National Skeet Shooting
Association
San Antonia, TX
800-877-5338

Nosler Bullets
Bend, OR
800-285-3701

Oehler Research
Austin, TX
800-531-5125

Overly, Terry
(Pioneer Outfitters)
Tok, AK
907-734-0007

P.A.C.T., Inc.
Grand Prairie, TX
214-641-0049

Penfold, Bob
Shortland, Australia
011-61-2-4951-1198

Ponsness-Warren
Rathdrum, ID
208-687-2231

Premier Reticles
Winchester, VA
540-722-0601

RCBS
Oroville, CA
800-533-5000

Redding Reloading
Cortland, NY
607-753-3331

Remington Arms Co.
Madison, NC
800-243-9700

Shilen Rifle Barrels
Ennis, TX
972-875-5318

Sierra Bullets
Sedalia, MO
816-827-6300

Sinclair International
Fort Wayne, IN
260-493-1858

Snapp's Gun Shop
Clare, MI
517-386-9226

Speer Bullets
Lewiston, ID
208-746-2351

Sturm, Ruger
Southport, CT 06890
203-259-7843

Swift Bullet Company
Quinter, KS
913-754-3959

Thompson/Center Arms
Rochester, NH
603-332-2394

Turnbull Restorations
Bloomfield, NY
716-657-6338

VihtaVuori Powders
Bensenville, IL
708-350-1116

Volquartsen Custom
Carroll, IA
712-792-4238

Warne Scope Mounts
Clackamas, OR
503-657-5590

Weatherby, Inc.
Atascadero, CA
805-466-1767

Weaver Products
Onalaska, WI
800-648-9624

Webernick, Lex
Pleasanton, TX
830-569-2055

Wenig Custom Gun
Stocks
Lincoln, MO
816-547-3334

Wilson Combat
Berryville, AR
870-545-3618

Winchester Ammunition
East Alton, IL 62024
618-258-3566

Yale, David and Cathy
Yellow Jacket, CO
970-562-4225

Zeiss Sports Optics
Chester, VA
800-441-3005